Grow Your Own Family Tree

How to Make it in IT (2001), Virgin Books

Gathering the Clans: Tracing Scottish Ancestry on the Internet (2004), Phillimore

ALAN STEWART

Grow Your Own Family Tree

The Easy Guide to Researching Family History

ALLEN LANE

an imprint of

PENGUIN BOOKS

ALLEN LANE

Published by the Penguin Group
Penguin Books Ltd, 80 Strand, London WC2R ORL, England
Penguin Group (USA) Inc., 375 Hudson Street, New York, New York 10014, USA
Penguin Group (Canada), 90 Eglinton Avenue East, Suite 700, Toronto, Ontario, Canada M4P 2Y3
(a division of Pearson Penguin Canada Inc.)
Penguin Ireland, 25 St Stephen's Green, Dublin 2, Ireland (a division of Penguin Books Ltd)
Penguin Group (Australia), 250 Camberwell Road, Camberwell, Victoria 3124, Australia
(a division of Pearson Australia Group Pty Ltd)
Penguin Books India Pvt Ltd, 11 Community Centre, Panchsheel Park, New Delhi – 110 017, India
Penguin Group (NZ), 67 Apollo Drive, Rosedale, North Shore 0632, New Zealand
(a division of Pearson New Zealand Ltd)
Penguin Books (South Africa) (Pty) Ltd, 24 Sturdee Avenue, Rosebank, Johannesburg 2196. South Africa

Penguin Books Ltd, Registered Offices: 80 Strand, London WC2R ORL, England

www.penguin.com

First published 2008
1

Set in 10.5/14 pt Linotype Sabon
Typeset by Palimpsest Book Production Limited, Grangemouth, Stirlingshire
Printed in Great Britain by Clays Ltd, St Ives plc

A CIP catalogue record for this book is available from the British Library

ISBN: 978-0-140-51588-6

www.greenpenguin.co.uk

*For my wife Linda, whose 'missing' ancestors
are keeping us on the go.*

People will not look forward to posterity, who never look backward to their ancestors.

(Edmund Burke, 1729–97)

Contents

Scotland

Ireland

Isle of Man and Channel Islands

PART TWO

Extra Branches

Appendices

Introduction

Why do people trace their ancestors?

When I was a child, I was fascinated by our large family Bible. Every so often, I'd ask if we could get it out from under the bed – where it was kept, wrapped in thick brown paper to keep the dust off – so I could look at the names and dates that had been written on special pages at the back. I believe my maternal grandfather had inherited that Bible from his father, who had been a sergeant in the police force. The names were those of my great-aunts and -uncles, and the dates were those of their births (or more likely, of their baptisms). You can see them all, together with my great-grandparents (Donald MacKenzie and his wife, Mary Ann Ritchie),

Portrait of the MacKenzie family c. 1913.

in this photograph taken about 1913 (the baby in the picture is my mother).

I would have liked to have found out more about my ancestors then, but at that time record offices and archives wouldn't have let me in. I suspect that most of them still don't let children in today.

The birth of my son Roger twenty-five years ago made me decide to stop thinking about tracing my ancestors, and get on with it. Little did I know I would discover that my wider family included blacksmiths, shepherds, weavers, a gamekeeper, an innkeeper, a fisherman, a shoemaker, and several soldiers and sailors.

My 6× great-uncle Alexander Brodie (on my mother's side) went from being a blacksmith's apprentice in a remote village to buying an ironworks in Ironbridge Gorge in 1786, and setting up a woollen mill in Scotland in the same year. He also owned businesses in London and Manchester, as well as houses in Surrey and the south of Scotland. And he built the galley stove that you can see on board Nelson's flagship HMS *Victory*.

On my father's side, my ancestor William Godfrey was shipwrecked in 1766, and 'was 42 days in an unexplored country before I reached Calcutta nearly starved to death', as he put it later. William was only sixteen, and this was his first voyage in the merchant fleet of the East India Company. He later joined the company's army and fought in various campaigns in India.

Twenty years after his shipwreck, William fathered my 4× great-grandfather Samuel Godfrey by an Indian woman (whose name is not recorded), whom he treated like a real-life 'Madam Butterfly'. Shortly after Samuel was baptized in St Mary's Church, Fort St George, Madras (now Chennai), a ship arrived bearing William's bride-to-be, whom he'd met while on leave in England.

Tip: 'Black sheep' may be lurking in your past

You'll probably find that some of your ancestors were not quite as pure as you'd like them to have been. Perhaps they had an illegitimate child – or maybe three, like my great-great-great-aunt Mary. Your great-great-grandfather may

---

have spent some time in prison. The upside is that there may be a photograph of him somewhere, whereas if he'd never been in trouble, there wouldn't be.

It was the birth of my son that got me interested in tracing my ancestors, but other people have taken up family history for a wide variety of reasons, such as:

- **school projects** are often responsible for getting the whole family interested in finding out where they came from. Often there's some family legend that's worth checking out;
- **television series**, such as the BBC's *Who Do You Think You Are?*;
- **old photographs (or letters)**;
- **the death** of someone in your family. So many family historians have said, 'If only I'd talked to my parents while they were still here';
- **marriage**;
- **retirement**.

Once you're hooked on family history, you just want to keep going because it's fun to find new people and places in your family tree. It's a real-life detective story, with (it is hoped) few criminals, but lots of bodies.

Tip: Family legends are rarely completely true

There may be a story in your family about how you're descended from a famous person, such as William Shakespeare. While such family legends may turn out to be true, unfortunately, it's more often the case that they're just wishful thinking.

You may indeed have an ancestor who lived in Stratford (but maybe Stratford in East London), and someone jokingly suggested they might have been related to Shakespeare. Over time, 'possibly related to Shakespeare' becomes 'descended from Shakespeare'. Unfortunately, although William Shakespeare did have children, his line died out with his grandchildren. (Well, his *legitimate* line did.)

There is usually some truth in the stories, however. If the legend is that four children were born in a workhouse in Bristol, then the truth may be that two of them were born in a workhouse in Bath.

What records do you need to look at to trace your ancestors?

You may well be thinking: yes, it would be quite interesting to find out who my ancestors were, what sort of jobs they had, and what villages and towns they lived in, but how do I go about it? You may feel that, as your people were 'ordinary', there won't be anything written about them.

1. Civil registration

Since the nineteenth century every birth in England and Wales has had to be registered with the local registrar, as has every marriage and death. (A few people did get away with not registering these life events, but the vast majority did so.)

					CERTIFIED COPY Pursuant to the Births and	of an ENTRY Deaths Registration Act 1953		FC 846672	
				Registration District Chippenham					
1853.		Birth in the Sub-district of Castle Combe				In the County of Wiltshire			
Columns:- 1	2	3	4	5	6	7	8	9	10
No.	When and where born	Name, if any	Sex	Name, and surname of father	Name, surname and maiden surname of mother	Occupation of father	Signature, description, and residence of informant	When registered	Signature of registrar	Name entered after registration
31	Seventeenth May 1853 Nettleton	William	Boy	Thomas Freeth	Jane Freeth formerly Kingstone	Labourer	Jane Freeth Mother Nettleton	Eighteenth June 1853	Thomas Shearn Registrar	

The birth certificate of William Freeth, born in Nettleton, Wiltshire in 1853.

This process, known as 'civil registration' (as opposed to recording life events in a church register) began in England and Wales on 1 July 1837, in Scotland on 1 January 1855, and in Ireland on 1 January 1864 (but with civil registration of non-Catholic marriages from 1 April 1845). The local registrar had to send his registers (and also those of marriages in churches) to the relevant Registrar General in London, Edinburgh or Dublin.

2. Census returns

Beginning in 1801 in England, Scotland and Wales, and 1821 in Ireland, a census has been taken every ten years to find out the size and composition of the population. From the start in Ireland and from 1841 in England, Scotland and Wales, each individual person was listed in the census returns, and all the censuses up to and including 1901 (1911 in the Republic of Ireland) are open to the public. Census returns are not usually made public in Britain and Ireland until they're 100 years old, out of respect for people's privacy.

Unfortunately for those of us with Irish ancestors, very little remains of the 1821–71 censuses of Ireland, and nothing at all of the 1881 and 1891 censuses. Those from 1861–91 were officially destroyed, and the earlier censuses were lost when the Public Record Office of Ireland (PROI) in Dublin was burnt down in 1922. Because of this loss, in the Irish Republic, the 1911 census was opened to the public early.

3. Parish registers

Before 1837, registrations were carried out by the church. Instead of births and deaths, however, baptisms and burials were recorded (except during the period of the Commonwealth under Oliver Cromwell in the mid-seventeenth century, when births and deaths were recorded).

The Church of England had been instructed by Henry VIII in 1538 to keep a register of all baptisms, marriages and burials in each parish. Some English and Welsh parishes did, but others didn't until 1598 (or even later), when each parish was required to send a transcript of its register entries to the bishop in whose diocese the parish lay.

Similarly, parish registers were supposed to be kept in Scotland from 1553, but only one register (for the parish of Errol in Perthshire) actually begins in that year. Some Scottish parish registers start as late as the early nineteenth century, and over a third of the nearly 900 Scottish parishes have no burial registers at all.

Although the Church of Ireland, the established (Protestant) church in Ireland, was likewise instructed to keep parish records of baptisms, marriages and burials from 1643, most of its registers don't begin until the end of the eighteenth century.

The Church of Ireland was disestablished in 1869 and its registers were supposed to be handed over to the PROI. About 60 per cent were handed in, and then destroyed in the 1922 fire. As well as the 40 per cent that were still in the parish churches, many of the registers that had been passed to the PROI had first been transcribed, so that around half of the registers are still in existence.

Most of the population of Ireland (except in the six counties of Northern Ireland) were Roman Catholic, rather than Protestant. The register for Wexford, which was started in 1671, is the earliest surviving Catholic register. Most of the Catholic registers start a good deal later, with those for the north and west beginning in the mid-nineteenth century.

In 1901, in what is now Northern Ireland, over 50 per cent of the population of four of its six counties were Protestant, many of whom attended Presbyterian churches, rather than the (Anglican) Church of Ireland. Presbyterian registers began to be kept about 1700.

4. Wills and administrations

Wills are another source of information, and not just for the well-off. Over 2,000 of the wills and administrations (for those who didn't leave a will) that were proved in the Prerogative Court of Canterbury (PCC), the main church court covering the south of England and all of Wales, were made by or related to labourers.

In the same court, there are wills and administrations that had been made by or concerned 2,800 servants, 2,700 blacksmiths, 2,100 shopkeepers, 1,400 innkeepers, 1,300 shoemakers, 1,000 sailors, 800 soldiers, 500 fishermen, 300 shepherds, 100 apprentices, 50 game-keepers, and a pauper!

As well as the PCC, there were many other church courts that dealt with wills. In the north of England, there was the Prerogative Court of York (PCY), and there was also a court for each bishop's diocese within the jurisdiction of the two prerogative courts (and various other lower courts). In 1858, the church courts were super-seded by a civil probate registry.

Scotland has its own legal system, under which wills and admin-istrations were dealt with by commissary courts up to about 1823. At that time, responsibility for confirming wills and authorizing administrations was transferred to the existing sheriff courts, which deal with both civil and criminal cases.

In Ireland, the system of probate was similar to that in England and Wales, with the Prerogative Court of Armagh as the main church court, and a consistorial court in each diocese. In 1858, a system of civil probate was established. Unfortunately, all the Irish wills were destroyed in the 1922 fire, although indexes, transcripts, abstracts and extracts are still in existence.

5. Military records

If one of your ancestors was in the armed forces, then military records may be helpful in disclosing his year and place of birth and previous occupation, not just for officers, but also for privates and non-commissioned officers. Most military records are at The National Archives (TNA) in London, whether the serviceman or -woman was English, Scottish, Welsh or Irish.

How do you go about finding your forebears?

To trace your ancestors, you need to start with yourself and work backwards in time via your parents, grandparents, etc. You may want to trace only your direct ancestors in the male line (who prob-ably share your surname) plus their wives, or you can look for all your ancestors in all lines (your four grandparents, eight great-grandparents, sixteen great-great-grandparents, etc.). After all, without any one of your ancestors, you couldn't be here – whatever his or her surname was.

There's much more to family history than just collecting names, however. It helps if you can put your ancestors into the context of the events of their time, and, conversely, history is much more interesting if you know that your ancestor took part in the General Strike in 1926, came to Britain because of the Irish Potato Famine in the 1840s, fought at the Battle of Trafalgar in 1805, lived in London at the time of the Great Plague and Great Fire in the 1660s, or died of the Black Death in the fourteenth century.

Tip: Don't believe everything you read

The records that we use to trace our ancestors are often incorrect. Census returns, in particular, can contain various mistakes, ranging from a different spelling of the surname to an incorrect place of birth. From one census to another, people often aged less than the ten years that had elapsed.

A father named on a civil registration marriage certificate may be fictitious, if one of the people marrying was illegitimate. When a baptism took place in the mother's home parish, sometimes the parish clerk would put down her maiden, rather than her married name.

Even wills were not immune to errors, with someone being named as a daughter and grand-daughter in the same will.

---

1. Using birth, marriage and death records

You'll almost certainly have your own birth certificate already, and your parents will probably have theirs, together with their marriage certificate. If not, it's quite easy to order certificates from the appropriate General Register Office (in London, Edinburgh, Belfast or Dublin).

Let's assume you know nothing about either set of your grandparents. From the ages of your parents on their marriage certificate, you can tell in what years your father and mother were born, so that you can then order their birth certificates. These will give you the names of your grandparents (and, if they lived in Scotland, when and where they married).

You can then keep sending for birth and marriage certificates, working backwards to the beginning of civil registration in the various parts of the British Isles. Death records for England, Wales and Ireland are not terribly useful, but a Scottish death certificate will tell you the name and occupation of the deceased person's father and the maiden name of his or her mother.

If you have Scottish ancestors, you'll also be able to use the Internet to search for, view online and print off copies of birth, marriage and death records that are over a hundred, seventy-five and fifty years old respectively. You'll find them at the Scotland's People website (*www.scotlandspeople.gov.uk*).

A project to digitize and index all of the English and Welsh civil records is under way at present, with the older records expected to be online by about 2009, probably on a similar basis to the Scottish ones. Although the records themselves aren't yet online, the indexes are. You can find them at several websites described in Chapter 5. Having found in an index the appropriate reference number for the record you want, you can order it by post, telephone or online at the certificate-ordering service of the General Register Office (GRO) at *www.gro.gov.uk/gro/content/certificates*.

The civil registration in the Republic of Ireland has also been digitized, and should go online at some point in the future. It is hoped that the records for Northern Ireland will also become available online. Although the indexes are not yet online, you can order Northern Irish records online from the General Register Office of Northern Ireland (GRONI) at *www.groni.gov.uk*.

2. Using the census records

Once you get back to the beginning of the twentieth century, you can look at the census to see all of the people in the family in 1901, 1891, etc. back to 1841. That was the first year in which individual names were recorded in England, Scotland and Wales, although some enthusiastic enumerators had listed the inhabitants of their areas in even earlier censuses. The first two Irish censuses (in 1821 and 1831) did list individual names, but see Chapter 17 for the unfortunate story of the Irish census records.

To see the census records, you can either visit TNA in London, the General Register Office for Scotland (GROS) in Edinburgh, the Public Record Office of Northern Ireland (PRONI) in Belfast or the National Archives of Ireland (NAI) in Dublin. In addition, many public reference libraries, record offices and family history societies also hold copies of the censuses for their local areas on microfiche and microfilm.

If you have Internet access, however, you can view all of the 1841–1901 censuses for England, Scotland, Wales, the Isle of Man and the Channel Islands online in your own home. The censuses for England, Wales, the Isle of Man and the Channel Islands are all available at Ancestry.co.uk (*www.ancestry.co.uk*) and some are at the other websites described in Chapter 6. All of the Scottish censuses are at Scotland's People (*www.scotlandspeople.gov.uk*), as well as at Ancestry.co.uk.

The Irish censuses for 1901 and 1911 are being digitized and indexed by the NAI, in conjunction with Library and Archives Canada, and are scheduled to be online in their entirety by 2009. These two censuses will most probably be joined online by the 1926 census of the Irish Republic, but perhaps not for some time.

3. Using parish registers

For the 300 years before civil registration began and individual names were recorded in the census, the main sources of information about our ancestors were the parish registers. Most of the pre-1837 registers for England are kept in county record offices, although some of the old baptism and death registers are still in use in small rural parishes. Most of the original Welsh parish registers are held by the National Library of Wales (NLW) in Aberystwyth.

The Church of Jesus Christ of Latter-day Saints (LDS; also known as Mormons) has compiled an International Genealogical Index

(IGI) of baptisms and marriages from most English and Welsh parish registers. The IGI is available in microfiche form in most record offices, reference libraries and family history societies, and is also accessible online at the LDS Church's Family Search website *(www.familysearch.org)*.

In Scotland, all the parish registers up to 1854 (known as the Old Parish or Old Parochial Registers, OPRs) were called in by the GROS in Edinburgh, where they're publicly available. Virtually all of the Scottish baptisms and marriages are indexed in the IGI. An index to the baptisms and marriages is also accessible online at the Scotland's People website *(www.scotlandspeople.gov.uk)*, as are digitized pages from the registers themselves.

Copies of the surviving Church of Ireland parish registers for the whole of Ireland are held by the NAI and the Representative Church Body Library, both in Dublin. The Church of Ireland and Presbyterian registers for Northern Ireland are available at the PRONI. Roman Catholic registers up to 1880 for the whole of Ireland are at the NLI. Many Irish baptisms and burials are indexed in the IGI.

4. Using wills and administrations

The English and Welsh wills proved in the PCC (and letters of administration issued by it) are available at TNA and also online at TNA's Documents Online website *(www.nationalarchives.gov.uk/ documentsonline)*, while those proved in the PCY are at the Borthwick Institute in York. Many other English wills are held locally in county record offices. Welsh wills are at the NLW, Scottish wills are at the National Archives of Scotland (NAS) and an index of extracts, abstracts and transcripts of Irish wills is at the NAI.

Family history makes good TV

Almost 5 million people watched the first series of the BBC's family history TV show *Who Do You Think You Are?*, in 2004. Each programme showed a celebrity being helped to trace their ancestors. The show was such a success that a second series was commissioned. The celebrities in this series

---

became even more emotional than those in the first, and the number of viewers increased to 23 per cent of the TV audience. The programme's success prompted the BBC to move it from its minority channel, BBC2, to the main BBC1 channel for the third series, in autumn 2006.

Heavyweight political interviewer Jeremy Paxman was initially cynical about taking part in the programme, but was then visibly affected by discovering that his widowed great-grandmother Mary McKay in Glasgow had had her benefits withdrawn when she became pregnant again after her husband's death. In spite of this Mary had chosen to keep her family (eight of her eleven children) together in one room in a slum tenement with no heating, lighting or running water, rather than enter the poorhouse, the Scottish version of the workhouse.

What's in the book

Chapter 1 explains how to go about collecting personal recollections and memorabilia from your family before (and while) you get hold of the official records to compile your family tree. It also looks at family tree charts and how they show ancestors and descendants.

Chapter 2 is about the national and local record offices and libraries throughout the British Isles – such as The National Archives, the National Libraries of Scotland, Wales and Ireland, the English and Welsh county record offices and Scottish local archives – what they hold, how to use the Internet to find out as much as possible from a distance, and the family history centres set up by the LDS Church.

After a general introduction to the British and Irish in Chapter 3, Chapter 4 contains short histories of England and Wales, together with historical and genealogical timelines for the two countries.

Chapters 5–10 describe in detail the main family history records of England and Wales, with examples and illustrations. Chapter 5 covers the civil registration of births, marriages and deaths in England and Wales. As yet, no English and Welsh civil registration records are accessible online, although their indexes are, and this chapter looks at several websites where you can find them.

The story of you

Rather than just telling you about my own experiences and discoveries in tracing my ancestry, I asked a number of people to answer some questions about their family history. You'll find their responses throughout the book in boxes like this one, headed 'The story of you' followed by the person's name.

Chapter 6 looks at the censuses that were taken between 1841 and 1901, and what they can tell us. It also describes the various websites where you can find indexed census returns for England and Wales. (The separate censuses that were carried out in Scotland and Ireland are covered in Chapters 12 and 17 respectively.)

Page from the 1871 census returns for Garboldisham, Norfolk.

Chapter 7 covers the registers of baptisms, marriages and burials that were kept in England and Wales from 1538, and where you can find them. Few parish registers are available on the Internet so far, although there are a number of online indexes at various websites.

Chapter 8 looks at English and Welsh wills and administrations (when the deceased person didn't leave a will), which were proved in church courts until 1858, when responsibility for probate was transferred to a new civil registry in London. It also details the websites providing access to wills.

The will of Richard Tyrell of Didcot, Berkshire.

The story of you: Hilary Hull

What prompted Hilary to start finding out about her ancestors was the death of a previously unknown relative who had died without having made a will.

'We had to send in the birth, marriage and death certificates of our parents and grandparents (as well as our own birth and marriage certificates),' she says. 'We had to prove how we were related to the deceased's sister (my husband Richard's grandmother).'

The estate was to be divided between his grandmother's six children. They had all died, however, so each sixth had to be subdivided into portions for the grandchildren.

'One of her sons had four children, so his sixth was divided by four,' explains Hilary. 'Richard was one of two sons, so he received a twelfth. We bought a conservatory with the money.'

Legally and administratively, Wales has been united with England since the thirteenth century, and the family history records described in Chapters 5–8 cover Wales as well as England. Chapter 9, however, examines some records specific to Wales, and some websites (such as the one set up by the National Library of Wales) that provide access to them.

Chapter 10 looks at Cornwall as an example of an English county and its records – although some would say Cornwall is a separate country, like Wales and Scotland.

Chapters 11–15 deal with Scotland, beginning with a short history of the country in Chapter 11, including historical and genealogical timelines. The historic Scottish civil registration records and census returns from 1841–1901 (Chapter 12), parish register baptisms and marriages (Chapter 13) and wills and inventories from 1513–1901 (Chapter 14) are all accessible at the official Scotland's People website. Scottish records online are described in Chapter 15.

Although Ireland's nineteenth-century census returns, wills and around half of the Protestant parish registers have been destroyed, other records (such as the 1901 and 1911 censuses, Irish civil registration records and Roman Catholic parish registers) are still in existence. After a short history of Ireland in Chapter 16, including historical and genealogical timelines, Chapter 17 looks at Irish census records (including census-substitutes such as Griffith's land valuation) and births, marriages and deaths. Chapter 18 covers church registers and wills, including transcriptions and indexes accessible via the Internet.

Chapter 19 deals with the records of the Isle of Man and the Channel Islands (Jersey, Guernsey and its dependent islands), which are not parts of the United Kingdom, but Crown dependencies.

Chapter 20 examines immigration to Britain and Ireland over the centuries and the ethnic make-up of the population. Many records for tracing the arrival of ancestors from South Asia (India, Pakistan, Bangladesh and Sri Lanka) and the West Indies are in TNA and the British Library. There are a number of useful websites, such as Moving Here (*www.movinghere.org.uk*) and some databases relating to Jewish ancestry.

Chapter 21 covers tracing ancestors who emigrated from the British

Isles to the USA, Canada, Australia, New Zealand and South Africa. There are a good number of immigration records in those countries and emigration records in Britain and Ireland, many of which are available online.

You may have had ancestors who lived in India when the British were trading with the country through the East India Company. The Company's various civil and military records are detailed in Chapter 22, including some useful websites, such as Family History in India (*members.ozemail.com.au/~clday*).

Chapter 23 looks at the information about your ancestors that you can discover from Army, Navy, Marine and Air Force records, most of which are held by TNA. There are a number of websites where you can find information about ancestors who were in the armed forces, including those of TNA and the Commonwealth War Graves Commission (*www.cwgc.org*), and these are dealt with in Chapter 24.

Electoral registers and poll books are useful for finding ancestors who are otherwise hard to track down, particularly in the time before and after the publicly available censuses. These electoral resources are covered in Chapter 25, as is the extension of the franchise during the nineteenth and twentieth centuries.

Chapter 26 gives useful sources of background information, such as the Victoria County History of England and the Statistical Accounts of Scotland (compiled in the 1790s, 1830s and 1950s), and looks at eighteenth- and nineteenth-century trade directories, criminal records (such as those of trials at the Central Criminal Court at the Old Bailey) and the workhouse system of poor relief.

Online gateways to family history information are covered in Chapter 27. These include Family Records (*www.familyrecords.gov.uk*), the GENUKI (Genealogy UK and Ireland) 'virtual reference library' (*www.genuki.org.uk*), Cyndi's List of Genealogy Sites on the Internet (*www.cyndislist.com*), Census Finder (*www.censusfinder.com*) and the UK Gen Web site (*www.ukgenweb.com*), each of which contains a multitude of links to other websites. I also look at using general 'search engines' to find information not covered by the sites mentioned above.

In Chapter 28 you will find various online 'mailing lists', 'message boards' and family history contact websites, such as Genes Reunited *(www.genesreunited.co.uk)*, which you can use to get help from and provide help to other people who are also tracing their ancestry. You're likely to discover and meet up with fourth and fifth cousins whose existence you were previously unaware of.

Chapter 29 lists the benefits of joining family history societies, both in your own locality and in those parts of Britain or Ireland where your ancestors lived. Many of the larger societies have their own research centres, sometimes in a county record office or library, where you can view records on microfilm, microfiche and CD, and also buy the society's (and other) publications.

In the Conclusion there's a review of the changes that have taken place in tracing your ancestors over the last hundred years, and a preview of what the family history world of the future might be like, as well as a brief introduction to the genealogical use of DNA testing.

At the end of the book, you'll find appendices containing information on:

- free family history websites;
- charges for pay-per-view and subscription websites;
- a list of all the web addresses mentioned in the book (and a few more);
- contact details for family history societies;
- addresses of archives and major libraries;
- Family History Centres of the Church of Jesus Christ of Latter-day Saints;
- Irish Genealogical Research Centres.

There's also a select list of useful books.

Family history and the Internet

The arrival of the Internet has revolutionized family history, particularly in Britain and Ireland. First, indexes and then digitized images of the records have been made available online.

Scotland led the way by putting the historical parts of its birth, marriage and death indexes online in 1998. The 1891 census of Scotland was digitized and put on the Internet in 2001. These were the first British records to become available online, and thus easily accessible to people all over the world, who want to trace their ancestors.

In 2002, the 1901 census of England and Wales was put online. Unfortunately, the website had received a great deal of publicity, and crashed on its first day (2 January 2002) because too many people tried to access it. The site had been designed to cope with 1.2 million enquiries in a twenty-four-hour period, but actually received 1.2 million per hour.

Since then, images of almost all the published censuses (1841–1901) of England, Wales, Scotland, the Isle of Man and the Channel Islands have become available online, as have Scottish births, marriages and deaths; English, Welsh and Scottish wills; Scottish parish register baptism and marriage entries; and Griffith's land valuation of Ireland.

More and more records are being digitized and indexed every year, such as Army and Navy service records; ships' passenger lists; English and Welsh births, marriages and deaths; the Irish 1901 and 1911 censuses; and English and Welsh parish registers.

Transcriptions of Irish birth/baptism, marriage, death and grave-yard records are also being indexed and made available online.

Acknowledgements

Thanks to all those people who helped to bring this book into existence:

- my agent Andrew Lownie, who saw promise in the original idea;
- Georgina Laycock at Penguin, who took the book on, broadened its scope and knocked it into shape;
- Ellie Smith and all those at Penguin (including freelance copy-editor Bela Cunha), who have made the book look good;
- Dennis Craddock, Jane Ferguson, Hilary Hull, Judith Mooney, Pamela Ormerod, Anne Simmonds, Mary Wooldridge, and many others who kindly contributed their stories;
- Caroline Davis at ABM Publishing in the UK, who commissioned me to write regular articles for *Practical Family History* magazine, thus providing much of the material for the book;
- Halvor Moorshead at Moorshead Magazines in North America, who commissioned my articles for *Family Chronicle* and *Internet Genealogy* magazines, providing more material;
- and, of course, my wife Linda for all her help and advice.

The illustrations have been reproduced by courtesy of: Office for National Statistics, pp. 4, 70, 71, 72 and 121; National Archives/The Generations Network, Inc., pp. 13, 83, 124, 213; Wiltshire and Swindon Archives, p. 14; The Generations Network, Inc. (produced using *Family Tree Maker®*), pp. 25 and 27; Archer Software (*www. archersoftware.co.uk*, produced using their Surname Atlas CD), p. 29; Eneclann (produced using the CD *Grenham's Irish Surnames* by John Grenham), p. 30; Dr Tony Thwaites, School of English, Media Studies and Art History, University of Queensland, p. 47; Medway Archives and Local Studies Centre (by kind permission of the Director of Community Services, Medway Council, and the priest-in-charge and parochial church council of the Ecumenical Parish of St John (URC/Anglican), including the United Benefice and Parish of St Mary and St John), pp. 91 and 97; Essex Record Office, p. 113; General Register Office for Scotland, pp. 147, 148, 149, 150, 153 and 159; National Archives of Scotland, p. 166; General Register Office, Ireland, pp. 190 and 192; National Archives of Ireland, pp. 194 and 195; National Library of Ireland, p. 197; US National Archives and Records Administration/The Generations Network, Inc., p. 242; Library and Archives Canada (Page: Census of Canada, 1871; Ottawa, St George's Ward, Library and Archives Canada, RG 31, District 77, Sub-district c-2, p. 9, reel C-10014. Source: Library and Archives Canada's website, *www.collectionscanada.ca*), p. 247; National Archives of Australia (Source: B2455, Civil, R W), p. 253. © Crown copyright material is reproduced with the permission of the Controller of HMSO and Queen's Printer for Scotland.

I

Gathering it all together

Getting started

Before you start going to record offices and libraries, or looking for records of your family on the Internet, talk to your parents and see what information they can give you. Usually, it will save you a lot of time and trouble (and money), if you find out as much as you can about your family from your parents, aunts, uncles and cousins (and from your grandparents' generation, if they're still alive).

Get hold of the family's old photographs before someone decides that they're just so much old rubbish and throws them away. It really does happen. Find out who the people in the photographs are while there's still someone who knows, and write the names in pencil on the back of the photos.

Ask your parents if there's a family Bible with pages at the front or back where the family's baptisms and burials have been entered. Perhaps there are some old birth, marriage or death certificates in the attic (or in the garage). Maybe your great-grandfather was in the forces and had a discharge certificate giving his description and date (or at least, year) of birth.

If your great-uncle was a member of an organization (such as a trade union, a professional body or the Freemasons), then there will be membership records about him. Perhaps there are old newspaper cuttings about one of your aunts. If not, but you know she was mentioned in the paper, then you could try to find the report in the local studies library's collection of newspapers on microfilm.

Remember that there's no such thing as a 'gap' in a family tree. If you can't link the tree that you've compiled with that of a celebrity, then until you can, you don't have a gap, you have two separate trees. You may be able to link them once you have more information, however.

Tip: Ask your parents

When I was a teenager, my maternal grandmother told me how, as a girl, she used to meet the boys at the gates to the big house. Why didn't I ask her the names of the boys, or the name of the big house? Why didn't I get her to tell me about her own grandparents?

It's too late to ask my grandmother, but I do ask my mother (who is in her nineties now) about her childhood in Edinburgh. She told me about the General Strike in 1926, when she was fourteen. She hadn't long been at work, and to get there she usually took a bus up the hill called the Canongate in Edinburgh's Royal Mile.

The bus drivers were on strike, with the buses being driven by students. The strikers wanted people to boycott the buses, but my mother didn't want to walk up the hill, so she got on a bus, on which there was only one other passenger. As it was travelling up the hill, a flowerpot came crashing through a window. My mother hastily got off, and walked to work for the rest of the strike.

Talking to older relatives

When you've talked to older relatives, use their information as a guide, but don't take it as gospel. People often 'know' something because someone has told them, rather than because they've ever seen any written proof of it. Even something in writing may be incorrect: my 3× great-grandfather Alexander Stewart is described in one military discharge record as having brown hair, hazel eyes and a fresh complexion, and in another (two years later) as having black hair, grey eyes and a dark complexion.

Try not to ask your relatives leading questions, as they may not know the answer any more than you do and may simply tell you what they think you'd like to hear. You may find that you already know more about your great-great-grandfather than your great-aunt does.

Watch out for sensitive areas. Your grandfather would probably be embarrassed if you mentioned that his father was born in the workhouse, but he might be angry too, if he hadn't been aware of that fact. Bear in mind that your great-grandfather may be part of your *history*, but he's very much *family* to your grandfather.

Your great-aunt or -uncle may think *you'll* be embarrassed about ancestors who were illegitimate, or who spent time in prison. In most family trees, you'll find at least one person who was imprisoned, usually for what we would consider a petty offence nowadays.

The story of you: Judith Mooney

'I knew I'd find a skeleton in the cupboard some time,' says Judith. 'It seems my great-great-grandfather married his deceased wife's sister in the 1880s, rather secretively and a long way from home. This only became legal in England in 1907, and there was apparently quite a scandal.'

Memorabilia

Watching the television programme *Flog It!*, I regularly see people sending family heirlooms to be auctioned off, usually fetching a relatively small amount of money. When asked why they want to sell the plate, teapot, painting or even medals that belonged to their parent or grandparent, the participants in the show say that they don't like the look of it, or that it just sits in a cupboard or in the attic.

Don't do it! Keep the little (or not so little) things you've inherited: the silver spoons that were a wedding present to your grandparents, the crystal bowl that was your mother's, and the book that belonged to your father. Keep them because of their associations with your family, not because they're pretty or useful, although so much the better if they are. How would you like someone to throw out something you treasure, once you're gone?

And don't throw away things that belong to your children. When I was a boy, my uncle made me a wooden garage for my Dinky Toy cars and lorries, and my grandfather made a brass top specially for me. You couldn't buy those presents (and you can't now).

Where are they now? They were thrown away, just like the two (empty) First World War hand grenades that used to sit on a shelf as ornaments in my grandparents' flat!

Hints and tips for tracing your ancestors

- Start with yourself, and work backwards via your parents and grandparents;
- talk to your oldest relatives to find out what they know;
- be tactful and don't upset them;
- don't necessarily believe what you've been told;
- make copies of family photographs, old and new;
- ask to see your family's birth, marriage and death certificates;
- look for a family Bible with baptisms and marriages recorded in it;
- ask whether anyone in your family left a will;
- never make assumptions (easier said than done!).

Storing your information

If you file your birth, marriage and death certificates and other documents in clear plastic wallets, make sure the wallets are acid-free. If you use ordinary clear plastic wallets, the ink on the certificates or photocopies will be absorbed into the plastic after a few years.

To let other people see what ancestors you've traced, you'll no doubt want to display your research in the form of a tree. There are various ways of drawing your tree, depending on whether you want to show ancestors, descendants or both. A 'drop-line' tree shows the people who are descended from someone.

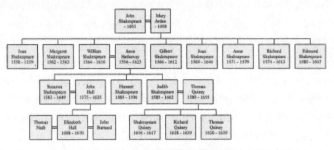

Drop-line tree of William Shakespeare.

A birth brief, on the other hand, shows your ancestry: your parents, four grandparents, eight great-grandparents and sixteen great-great-grandparents. To show more of your ancestors, you can simply continue the chart to include your 3× great-grandparents, or you can create up to sixteen more individual birth briefs with each of your sixteen great-grandparents in the position you occupied in the first chart. There are various other types of family tree chart, such as a 'circular' tree.

Family history software

Rather than drawing your family tree by hand, only to realize that it's out of date as soon as you find more ancestors to add to it, why not use computer software? In May 2006, the consumer-testing magazine *Computing Which?* published a review of the following family history programs:

1. Family Tree Maker;
2. Family Historian;
3. RootsMagic;
4. Family Tree Legends (Starter Edition);
5. Heredis;
6. Legacy Family Tree;
7. Genbox;
8. Kith and Kin Pro.

The American program Family Tree Maker was rated the 'best buy', with a score of 87 per cent, and Britain's Family Historian was felt to be 'worth considering', with an 82 per cent rating. RootsMagic also scored well (79 per cent), while Legacy Family Tree's score of 75 per cent was due to its basic charting facilities (which are supplemented by the additional program Legacy Charting Companion). Family Tree Legends (Starter Edition) scored 78 per cent and was very competitively priced, with Heredis (the only Apple Macintosh program on test) scoring 77 per cent. The other two programs on test received lower scores.

First you enter the details of your family members into the program. If you've already gathered a fair amount of information, you don't have to enter it all in one go.

With Family Tree Maker, you can print out various types of tree:

- a standard birth brief pedigree chart;
- three types of ancestor tree;
- two types of descendant tree;
- two hourglass trees (showing one person's ancestors and descendants);
- an all-in-one tree (showing all ancestors, descendants and their siblings).

In addition, Family Tree Maker can print:

- family group sheets (of a couple and their children);
- genealogy reports (of one person's descendants);
- kinship reports;
- a list of all marriages;
- age next birthday of all living people on the tree;
- other reports. (Genealogy reports are useful when trees become unmanageable, because of their size.)

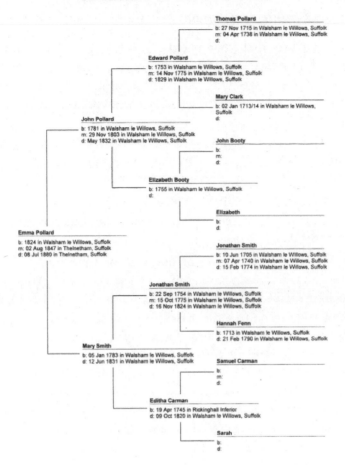

Thomas Pollard
b: 27 Nov 1715 in Walsham le Willows, Suffolk
m: 04 Apr 1738 in Walsham le Willows, Suffolk
d:

Edward Pollard
b: 1753 in Walsham le Willows, Suffolk
m: 14 Nov 1775 in Walsham le Willows, Suffolk
d: 1829 in Walsham le Willows, Suffolk

Mary Clark
b: 02 Jan 1713/14 in Walsham le Willows, Suffolk
d:

John Pollard
b: 1781 in Walsham le Willows, Suffolk
m: 29 Nov 1803 in Walsham le Willows, Suffolk
d: May 1832 in Walsham le Willows, Suffolk

John Booty
b:
m:
d:

Elizabeth Booty
b: 1755 in Walsham le Willows, Suffolk
d:

Elizabeth
b:
d:

Emma Pollard
b: 1824 in Walsham le Willows, Suffolk
m: 02 Aug 1847 in Thelnetham, Suffolk
d: 08 Jul 1880 in Thelnetham, Suffolk

Jonathan Smith
b: 10 Jun 1705 in Walsham le Willows, Suffolk
m: 07 Apr 1740 in Walsham le Willows, Suffolk
d: 15 Feb 1774 in Walsham le Willows, Suffolk

Jonathan Smith
b: 22 Sep 1754 in Walsham le Willows, Suffolk
m: 15 Oct 1775 in Walsham le Willows, Suffolk
d: 16 Nov 1824 in Walsham le Willows, Suffolk

Hannah Fenn
b: 1713 in Walsham le Willows, Suffolk
d: 21 Feb 1790 in Walsham le Willows, Suffolk

Mary Smith
b: 05 Jan 1783 in Walsham le Willows, Suffolk
d: 12 Jun 1831 in Walsham le Willows, Suffolk

Samuel Carman
b:
m:
d:

Editha Carman
b: 19 Apr 1745 in Rickinghall Inferior
d: 09 Oct 1820 in Walsham le Willows, Suffolk

Sarah
b:
d:

Birth brief chart.

Relationships

Great-grandparents, etc.

Just as your grandparents' parents are your great-grandparents and their parents are your great-great-grandparents, so you add another 'great' for every generation further back. To indicate your great-great-great-great-great-great-grandparents, however, rather than write 'great' six times, it's easier to refer to them as your 6× great-grandparents, or sixth great-grandparents.

Great-aunts and -uncles

In the same way that your parents' brothers and sisters are your uncles and aunts, your grandparents' brothers and sisters are your great-uncles and great-aunts, and your great-grandparents' brothers and sisters are your great-great-uncles and great-great-aunts, and so on.

In older books, you may see what we would call a 'great-aunt', referred to as a 'grand-aunt'. This made more sense, as a 'grand-aunt' is the same generation as your grandmother, and a 'great-grand-aunt' would be the sister of one of your great-grandparents.

Cousins

Your (first) cousin is the son or daughter of your aunt and uncle, and you and your cousin have grandparents in common. Your second cousin is the son or daughter of your mother's or father's cousin. You and your second cousin have great-grandparents in common. And so on. Your second, third, fourth, fifth cousins, etc. are all in the same generation as you, but with your common ancestor a generation further back with each increase from second to third, etc.

To work out what degree a cousin relationship is, you add one to the number of 'greats' in the common ancestor. So if my wife's 4× great-grandparents are also the 4× great-grandparents of Tim, then Tim is my wife's fifth cousin. My wife's sons are Tim's fifth cousins once removed (i.e. one generation further on), and her grandson is Tim's fifth cousin twice removed.

Surnames

Don't go jumping to conclusions about your family's connection with someone famous who had the same surname. Although my surname is 'Stewart', that doesn't necessarily mean I'm related to royalty: in the seventeenth century, King James I of England (and VI of Scotland) pointed out that not all Stewarts were 'sib' to the king.

You would expect it to be easier to research an uncommon surname, and it usually is. However, an unusual name nationally may turn out to be a common surname in a particular county (such as 'Kerridge' in Suffolk).

Don't despair if you have a common name like 'Smith' or 'Wood'. Once you've tracked down the home area, then a common name like that shouldn't give you any more trouble than any other surname. (My Smiths were from Aberdeenshire, and my wife's Woods were from the Herefordshire/Breconshire border area. She also has two Smith families from Suffolk.)

'Smith' and 'Wood' are the sort of names (one from an occupation, the other from a location) that you'll find all over what was the English-speaking part of Britain when surnames began to develop (i.e. England and the south of Scotland). So, are all Smiths related? They are, but only in the sense that everyone's related to everybody else, and not because of their shared surname.

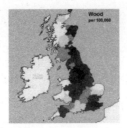

Distribution of the surname 'Wood/Woods' in Britain in 1881.

The *British 19th-Century Surname Atlas* CD (Archer Software, 2003) will show you where surnames were distributed throughout Britain according to the 1881 census. You can see the distribution of a surname (and its variants, if you wish) per 100,000 of the population, or based on actual numbers of people with the name.

Distribution of the surname 'MacKenzie/McKenzie' in Britain in 1881.

Distribution of the surname 'Williams' in Britain in 1881.

29

A similar CD covering Ireland is *Grenham's Irish Surnames*, compiled by John Grenham, an Irish professional genealogist. The CD shows the distribution of surnames throughout Ireland, according to Griffith's land valuation in the mid-nineteenth century.

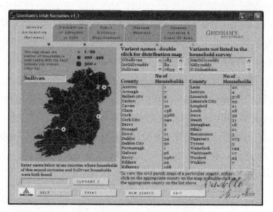

Distribution of the surname 'Sullivan' in Ireland in the mid-nineteenth century.

Patronymics and surnames

In Wales, unlike England, the south of Scotland and Ireland, the use of patronymics persisted in some areas until the early nineteenth century. This meant using the father's forename as the next generation's surname, so that, for example, Edward, the son of Richard Griffiths, would be known as Edward Richards, rather than Edward Griffiths. There was a similar situation in the Gaelic-speaking Highlands of Scotland until the mid-eighteenth century, and in Shetland until the mid-nineteenth.

Family surname histories

Beware if you receive a letter offering you the opportunity to buy a 'family book' that supposedly has a great deal of information on people with your surname. This is a scam. The perpetrators send out many letters that are identical apart from the surname. The writer of the letter usually claims to have come across a lot of information on the family while he has been carrying out other research. Very kindly, he's decided to put this information into a book. Should you send for the book, however, you're unlikely to receive anything useful. According to the Office of Fair Trading (OFT), the book will probably contain some basic advice on tracing your ancestors, a very general short history of your surname and a list of names taken from telephone directories. There won't be anything specific to your own immediate family.

The OFT also warns about similar family history and surname origin scrolls and plaques, which provide only a very general history of the surname. Their advice is to keep clear of any company suggesting that these mass-produced items have anything to do with your own family history.

Coats of arms

You also need to be wary of companies that offer to sell you what they claim is your family's coat of arms. The College of Arms in London, which is responsible for heraldry in England, Wales and Northern Ireland (and the Court of the Lord Lyon King of Arms in Edinburgh, which has a similar function in Scotland), will tell you that there is no such thing as a *family* coat of arms. The College of Arms points out that a coat of arms belongs to an individual, who must either have had the arms granted to him or her personally, or be descended in the legitimate male line from someone who did. People who share a surname may be entitled to use different coats of arms – or none at all!

Referring to the widespread misconception that a family or clan can have a coat of arms that its members are entitled to use, the Lord Lyon stresses that this is completely incorrect. A coat of arms can only be used by one person, and use by anyone else is a criminal offence in Scotland, punishable by a fine.

To get a coat of arms of your own, you need to apply for a grant of arms to the College of Arms, if you are from England, Wales, Northern Ireland, or anywhere else (except Scotland or Canada) where the Queen is head of state. If you are a US citizen with British ancestors, the College may grant you an honorary coat of arms.

Scots or those of Scottish descent need to apply to the Lord Lyon. The Chief Herald of Ireland is the person you apply to if you are Irish or of Irish descent, and the Canadian Heraldic Authority if you are a Canadian.

Clans and tartans

The Lord Lyon King of Arms states that, for Scottish clans, a coat of arms belongs to the clan chief only and not to all his or her clansmen and -women. What you may use, however, is the chief's crest encircled by a strap and buckle containing his or her motto. (The crest is the animal or bird that sits on top of the helmet above the shield.)

You *are* allowed to wear your clan's tartan, but not your mother's, unless you have taken on her surname. If you have no clan, you may wear a district tartan (such as Huntly, Lennox or Strathearn), provided you have an ancestor who lived in that area. If not, you may wear the Black Watch, Caledonia, Jacobite or Hunting Stewart tartan, but definitely not Royal Stewart, which is really 'Royal' rather than 'Stewart'.

Even flying a flag in Scotland is not without its problems. The Lord Lyon will let you fly the Scottish saltire (the St Andrew's cross) or the Union Flag (known to everyone as the 'Union Jack'), but not the lion rampant flag, which is reserved for royalty. I wonder if anyone has told the 'tartan army' of Scottish football fans!

So, when in Scotland, beware of being conned into using someone else's coat of arms, using anything more than the crest of your clan chief (if you have one), wearing an inappropriate tartan or flying a royal flag. Watch out, the tartan police are about!

2

Archives and libraries in Britain and Ireland

The main records and published information that you'll use to trace your British and Irish ancestors are held by several major archives and libraries in the United Kingdom and the Republic of Ireland. These are:

England

1. The National Archives (TNA) in Kew, London;
2. Family Records Centre (FRC) in central London;
3. Borthwick Institute for Archives (BIA) in York;
4. British Library (BL) in central London;

Scotland

5. General Register Office for Scotland (GROS) in Edinburgh;
6. National Archives of Scotland (NAS) in Edinburgh;
7. National Library of Scotland (NLS) in Edinburgh;

Wales

8. National Library of Wales (NLW) in Aberystwyth;

Northern Ireland

9. General Register Office (Northern Ireland) (GRONI) in Belfast;
10. Public Record Office of Northern Ireland (PRONI) in Belfast;

Republic of Ireland

11. General Register Office (Republic of Ireland) (GROI) in Roscommon and Dublin;
12. National Archives of Ireland (NAI) in Dublin;
13. National Library of Ireland (NLI) in Dublin;
14. Representative Church Body Library (RCBL) in Dublin.

You'll probably also want to see some of the records held by:

15. County record offices (CROs) throughout England and Wales;
16. Scottish local archives (Scotland has no county record offices as such).

Most of these repositories have information leaflets you can download from their websites and catalogues you can search online. In addition, the Access to Archives (A2A, *www.a2a.org.uk*), Scottish Archive Network (SCAN, *www.scan.org.uk/aboutus/indexonline.htm*) and Archives Network Wales (ANW, *www.archivesnetworkwales.info*) websites have online facilities that let you search the descriptions of collections in the catalogues of the county record offices and local archives.

You'll also find copies of many records in the:

17. Family History Centres of the LDS Church.

The following table shows where you can see the main family history records for the various parts of Britain and Ireland, or (for English, Welsh and Irish civil registration records) where you can order them.

Main family history records in archives in Britain and Ireland

Records	England	Wales	Scotland	Northern Ireland	Republic of Ireland
Civil registration (BMD)	FRC	FRC	GROS	GRONI[1]	GROI
Census enumeration returns	TNA, FRC and CROs	TNA, NLW and CROs	GROS	PRONI and NAI[2]	NAI[2]
Established church registers	BIA and CROs	NLW and CROs	GROS	PRONI[3]	RCBL and NAI[4]
Other church registers	TNA and CROs	TNA, NLW and CROs	NAS	PRONI[3]	NLI[5]
Wills and probate records	TNA, BIA and CROs[6]	TNA and NLW[7]	NAS	PRONI and NAI[8]	NAI[8]
Records of the armed forces	TNA	TNA	TNA	TNA	TNA

[1] Civil registration for Northern Ireland from 1 January 1922. Records for the whole of Ireland prior to that time are at the GROI.

[2] The 1901 is the earliest surviving complete census of Ireland. The NAI has the 1901 and 1911 censuses, and fragments of the 1821–51 censuses, for the whole of Ireland. The PRONI has the 1901 census, and fragments of the 1821, 1831 and 1851 censuses, for the counties of Northern Ireland.

[3] The PRONI holds originals and copies of (surviving) Church of Ireland, Presbyterian, Roman Catholic and some Nonconformist registers for Northern Ireland.

[4] In 1922, a fire at the Public Record Office of Ireland (PROI) in Dublin destroyed all the (Anglican) Church of Ireland registers held there (about 60 per cent). The remaining 40 per cent not held in the PROI, plus transcriptions of a sixth of those destroyed, are still in existence (i.e. around 50 per cent of the total number). The RCBL holds most surviving Church of Ireland registers for the Republic of Ireland, although some are in the NAI.

[5] The NLI holds microfilms of most Roman Catholic registers. You need written permission from the Archbishop of Cashel and Emly or the Bishop of Kerry, however, to view the microfilms of records of parishes in their respective dioceses.

[6] Wills proved at the PCC or PCY are held by TNA or the BIA respectively. Those proved in local church courts are held by the CROs.

[7] PCC-proved wills are held at TNA, while those receiving probate in Welsh church courts are held by the NLW.

8 The pre-1858 wills of Ireland and the centrally held post-1857 wills were all destroyed in 1922, although their indexes survived. Transcripts of the post-1857 wills that had been made by District Registries are still in existence at the NAI and the PRONI (for Northern Ireland).

1. The National Archives (TNA)
www.nationalarchives.gov.uk

The National Archives, at Kew in London, were formed in April 2003 by combining the Public Record Office with the Historical Manuscripts Commission. TNA is not only the main record office for England and Wales, but also holds many records relating to the United Kingdom as a whole. It has one of the largest archival collections in the world, spanning 1,000 years of British history, from the 'Domesday Book', compiled in 1086 and now accessible at TNA's Documents Online website (*www.nationalarchives.gov.uk/documents online*), to government documents only recently made public.

TNA holds many English and Welsh Nonconformist, Roman Catholic and foreign Protestant registers of baptisms, marriages and burials. These registers were called in by the government after the introduction of civil registration in England and Wales in 1837.

The National Archives also hold the birth registrations recorded in the Protestant Dissenters' Registry (Dr Williams' Library, established in 1742 for Baptists, Congregationalists and Presbyterians) and the Metropolitan Registry for Wesleyan Methodists (set up in 1818). The LDS British Isles Vital Records Index includes about 80 per cent of the births recorded in Dr Williams' Registry.

Births, marriages and deaths recorded by the Religious Society of Friends (Quakers) are also held by TNA; some of the records cover the Isle of Man and the Channel Islands. TNA also holds copies of the registers of clandestine marriages that took place in the Church of England in the London area in the seventeenth and eighteenth centuries.

Census returns for England, Wales, the Isle of Man and the Channel Islands from 1841–1901 are held by the National Archives, all of these now being available online (and free of charge in TNA reading rooms).

The National Archives, Kew.

Wills proved and administrations granted at the PCC from 1384–1858 are held by TNA. The wills, but not the administrations, are also accessible at Documents Online. TNA also has microfiche copies of the index to wills proved and administrations granted in the civil probate registry from 1858–1943.

The annual indexes to the Death Duty Registers (1796–1903) can help you find in which court a will was proved. Those from 1796–1811 are accessible at Documents Online.

In addition, The National Archives holds almost all the records of the British Army, Royal Navy, Royal Marines and Royal Air Force. The records cover servicemen and -women from England, Wales, Scotland and the whole of Ireland. Royal Navy service records (1873–1923) are available through Documents Online, while you can find brief information on soldiers who retired on pension from 1760–1854 by searching the TNA Catalogue (*www.nationalarchives. gov.uk/catalogue*).

2. Family Records Centre (FRC) *www.familyrecords. gov.uk/frc*

The Family Records Centre was set up jointly by the General Register Office (GRO, part of the Office of National Statistics, ONS) and the National Archives to provide a family history service in a building in central London.

The GRO part of the FRC (on the ground floor) provides access to the quarterly indexes to the civil registration birth, marriage and death certificates introduced on 1 July 1837 (and also to the overseas registration of British citizens' births, marriages and deaths). You aren't allowed to view the actual records, but you can order certificates for delivery to your home address or for collection at the FRC. The mother's maiden name is shown in the birth indexes from the September quarter of 1911, and the spouse's surname in the marriage indexes from the March quarter of 1912. From the March quarter of 1866 to the same quarter in 1969, the age at death is shown in the index, and thereafter, the date of birth.

Upstairs at the FRC is the part run by TNA, where you can view copies of various records held at Kew, including the 1841–1901 census returns, wills proved and administrations granted in the PCC from 1383–1858, Death Duty Registers (1796–1857) and Non-conformist and Roman Catholic church registers.

In 2006, TNA announced that it intended to withdraw from the partnership with the ONS, probably in late 2007, as many of its records were now online. The ONS has decided to move its physical indexes to Kew by April 2008, as not only are the indexes available online at several existing websites, but the ONS expects to launch its own online index in early 2009. The GRO already has its own website, from which you can place an online order for birth, marriage and death certificates.

3. Borthwick Institute for Archives (BIA) www.york. ac.uk/inst/bihr

The Borthwick Institute for Archives is part of the University of York, and is located on the university's Heslington campus. There you'll find the records of parishes in the present-day archdeaconry of York, as well as Bishops' Transcripts for most of Yorkshire (except the north-west of the county, which is held by West Yorkshire Archives in Leeds).

The institute also has marriage bonds and allegations (for marriage by licence, rather than by banns) issued by the Archbishop of York from 1660–1839 and by the Dean and Chapter of York from 1630–1839.

The BIA holds wills proved and administrations granted by the Exchequer and Prerogative Courts of York from 1267–1858, an index of which is in the course of being made available online at the British Origins website (*www.britishorigins.com*). You can already search an index of the smaller York 'peculiar' courts' probate records (1383–1883) at the same site.

4. British Library (BL) www.bl.uk

Among its huge collection of publications, the British Library holds UK electoral registers, with complete sets for England, Scotland, Wales and Northern Ireland from 1947 onwards, together with around 20,000 registers of electors from their introduction in 1832 up to 1931. The BL has records of the East India Company (1600–1858), including wills, pension, military and other records. The 'Ecclesiastical Returns' are copies of the baptismal, marriage and burial records from the registers of the Christian churches in India. The registers begin in 1698 for the Madras Presidency, in 1709 for Bombay and 1713 for Bengal.

In addition, at its Newspaper Reading Rooms in Colindale, north-west London, the British Library holds over 52,000 newspaper and periodical titles. The library is in the process of digitizing complete runs of certain newspapers between 1800 and 1900, and issues of London's *Daily News*, *News of the World* and *Weekly Despatch*, as well as the *Manchester Guardian* are accessible in a pilot system.

5. General Register Office for Scotland (GROS) www.gro-scotland.gov.uk

The General Register Office for Scotland in New Register House (NRH) in Edinburgh holds the records of the Scottish civil registration from its introduction on 1 January 1855 up to the present. These records are known as the statutory registers of births, marriages and deaths. Not only can you search the statutory indexes at NRH, you can view the actual records (right up to those of the present time) and make photocopies of them.

The GROS also holds the Scottish census records from 1841–1901, as well as the parish registers of the main Church of Scotland, which were called in up to 1854, when civil registration was introduced. Although parish registers were supposed to be kept from 1553 onwards, only those for one parish (Errol in Perthshire) begin in that year. The registers for Highland parishes (such as those on the Isle of Skye) can begin as late as the nineteenth century. As many as a third of the parishes have no burial registers.

The civil registration records, census returns and parish register baptisms and marriages have been digitized and can be viewed at the pay-per-view Scotland's People website (*www.scotlandspeople. gov.uk*). On privacy grounds, only births that took place over 100 years ago, marriages over seventy-five years ago, and deaths over fifty years ago can be viewed online, with an additional year's records becoming available each January.

New Register House, Edinburgh.

6. National Archives of Scotland (NAS)
www.nas.gov.uk

The National Archives of Scotland are also located in Edinburgh, in General Register House, next door to NRH. The Archives hold Scottish government records, together with those of the courts, churches, families, landed estates and businesses.

The baptismal, marriage and burial registers and other records of Presbyterian secession churches (which broke away from the Church of Scotland during the eighteenth and nineteenth centuries) are held by the NAS. In addition, the Archives hold those of Nonconformist, Episcopalian (Anglican) and Roman Catholic churches.

The NAS also holds wills and inventories, land records, criminal and civil court records, electoral and prison registers, militia lists and valuation rolls, as well as taxation, poor relief, apprenticeship, craft and trade records. In addition, some maps and plans are held.

You can search an index of wills and inventories confirmed in all the Scottish commissary and sheriff courts from 1513–1901 at the Scotland's People website (*www.scotlandspeople.gov.uk*) free of charge. On making an online payment, you can then view and download a digitized copy of a will or inventory.

The Scottish Archive Network (SCAN) is currently digitizing many of the church records held by the NAS in a major project that you can read more about at the Scottish Documents website (*www. scottishdocuments.com*). You can also see examples of the records being digitized.

7. National Library of Scotland (NLS) www.nls.uk

The National Library of Scotland on George IV Bridge in Edinburgh holds trade and professional directories, matriculation and graduation rolls from Scotland's older universities, emigrant lists, family histories and individual biographies, together with many local history publications, including the *Statistical Accounts of Scotland*.

The NLS Map Library is one of the ten largest in the world, with an extensive collection of maps and plans in its Causewayside Building (also in Edinburgh). You can view Scottish maps from 1560–1928 and Ordnance Survey town plans from 1847–95 online at the NLS Digital Library (*www.nls.uk/maps/index.html*).

In addition, the NLS is the main repository for Scottish newspapers, and receives a copy of every Scottish daily and weekly. It also holds many 'chapbooks' (small booklets) and single-page 'broadsides' from the mid-sixteenth to mid-nineteenth centuries. Over 2,000 broadsides have been digitized, and you can see these at the NLS's 'The Word on the Street' website (*www.nls.uk/broadsides/index.html*).

8. National Library of Wales (NLW) *www.llgc.org.uk*

You'll find the National Library of Wales in Aberystwyth, on a hill looking down on the town and the west coast of Wales. The NLW could well be named the 'National Archives and Library of Wales', as it holds many family history records that you'd find in an archive elsewhere.

The Library has microform copies of the 1841–1901 censuses for Wales, as well as some English border areas. The NLW also has microfiche copies of the GRO indexes of births, marriages and deaths in England and Wales from 1837–2000, and the 1988 edition of the IGI for the whole of Britain, Ireland and the Channel Islands.

The Library holds original registers of baptisms, marriages and

National Library of Wales, Aberystwyth.

burials for almost 500 of the *c.* 1,000 Welsh parishes and chapelries in existence in 1812, as well as microfilm copies of most of those held by county record offices. The NLW also has bishop's transcripts (BTs) of all the parishes in Wales that belonged to Welsh dioceses, mainly starting in the mid-sevententh century (Brecon and Llandaf from the beginning of the eighteenth). Most of the parish registers and BTs start from after 1660.

The Library has microfilm copies of Welsh pre-1837 Non-conformist registers, where the originals are at TNA. In addition, the NLW holds some original registers that didn't reach TNA when the Nonconformist registers were called in after the introduction of civil registration, and some later registers.

The Library holds marriage bonds and affidavits for marriages by licence, some starting as early as 1616, but mainly beginning in the late seventeeth–early eighteenth centuries. You can search an index of the marriage bonds not only at the NLW, but also online at *www.llgc.org.uk:81*.

You'll find the original wills proved and administrations granted by the Welsh ecclesiastical courts from the mid-sixteenth century (Bangor from the early seventeenth) at the NLW. The Library has a computer index of probate records, which you can use in the NLW building. Unfortunately, the index is not accessible online yet.

The NLW has copies of the wills from five of the post-1858 civil registries, covering all the Welsh counties except Montgomeryshire. In addition, it has a full set of the annual index listing all the wills proved and administrations granted in the whole of England and Wales from 1858–1972.

In addition you'll find various other records and publications that are useful for family history research, such as:

- Court of Great Sessions of Wales – criminal case records, which are indexed online at *www.llgc.org.uk/sesiwn_fawr/index_s.htm*;
- some education records;
- manorial records, which are indexed online at *www. nationalarchives.gov.uk/mdr*;
- estate records, schedules of which are searchable online at the NLW website;

- pedigree books of Welsh landed families;
- tithe maps;
- trade directories for North and South Wales, some counties and many towns and cities (particularly Cardiff, Swansea and Newport);
- newspapers and other periodicals;
- photographs and prints.

9. General Register Office (Northern Ireland) (GRONI) www.groni.gov.uk

The General Register Office (Northern Ireland) in Belfast holds civil registration birth and death records for Northern Ireland from their introduction on 1 January 1864, and marriage records from 1 January 1922 (the partition of Ireland between Northern Ireland and the Irish Free State, now the Republic of Ireland). Earlier civil registration marriages in Northern Ireland (from 1 April 1845 for non-Roman Catholic marriages, and from 1 January 1864 for all marriages) are held by the General Register Office in the Irish Republic and the twenty-six District Registrar Offices in Northern Ireland.

You can't view the actual records at the GRONI, but you can search the computerized indexes of births (from 1864), marriages (from 1845) and deaths (from 1864) in the public search room. Unfortunately, the indexes are not accessible online, although you can order and pay for certificates online through the GRONI website.

10. Public Record Office of Northern Ireland (PRONI) www.proni.gov.uk

The Public Record Office of Northern Ireland in Belfast holds the 1901 census for the six counties of Northern Ireland. This is the earliest complete surviving census of Ireland, as the 1821–51 censuses were almost all destroyed in a fire at the Public Record Office of Ireland (PROI) in Dublin, and the 1861–91 censuses were completely destroyed by government order. As well as the 1901 census, you can view fragments of the 1821, 1831 and 1851 censuses at the PRONI, which holds various census substitutes, including land records such as the Tithe Applotment Books (1824–38) and Griffith's Primary Valuation of Ireland (1848–64).

You'll find Church of Ireland, Presbyterian and Roman Catholic registers of baptisms, marriages and burials at the record office, together with Northern Ireland wills from 1900–1994. Although wills proved before 1900 were destroyed in the 1922 fire, the PRONI has copies of wills probated in local civil registries from 1858–1900. In addition, the record office has indexes to pre-1858 wills that were proved in church courts.

You'll also find valuation records dating back to the 1830s, school registers, poor relief records, trade directories, emigration records, militia and yeomanry lists, records of landed estates and Ordnance Survey (OS) maps and town plans. The PRONI is currently converting its catalogues to electronic form, and these will be available on its website in the future.

Already accessible online is a database of freeholders' records from the mid-eighteenth to early-nineteenth centuries, based on electoral registers and poll books. Another online database provides an index to the 500,000 signatories of the Ulster Covenant in 1912, complete with digitized images of the signatures. Future online records will include Northern Ireland wills from 1858–1900 and OS maps of Northern Ireland.

11. *General Register Office (Republic of Ireland) (GROI) www.groireland.ie*

Civil registration of non-Roman Catholic marriages began in Ireland on 1 April 1845, and of all marriages, as well as births and deaths, on 1 January 1864. The Irish Republic's General Register Office in Roscommon holds birth, marriage and death records for all of Ireland until 1922, when the island was divided into the Irish Free State and Northern Ireland. The GROI also holds the civil registration records of the Irish Free State, known as Eire from 1937 and the Republic of Ireland from 1949.

You can't view the actual birth, marriage and death records at the GROI, but you can carry out a chargeable search in the quarterly indexes at its research room in Dublin. Alternatively, you can download from the GROI's website application forms for birth, marriage and death certificates. You can then send the form to the GROI by post, either with a cheque in Euros drawn on an Irish bank, or with your credit card details entered on the form.

Although the GROI is registering births, marriages and deaths electronically, and digitizing the historic civil registration records, neither the recent nor the older records are available online yet, although this is planned for sometime in the future.

12. National Archives of Ireland (NAI) www.nationalarchives.ie

The National Archives of Ireland in Dublin are the successor organization to the Public Record Office of Ireland (PROI) and the State Paper Office. At the NAI, you can see the returns for the 1901 and 1911 censuses of the whole of Ireland, as well as fragments of the 1821–51 censuses, which were destroyed in 1922 in a fire at the PROI. The 1861–91 censuses were destroyed by government order, with nothing surviving. The 1911 census was made public in the Irish Republic in advance of the normal 100-year rule regarding privacy, owing to the loss of the nineteenth-century Irish censuses. Both the 1901 and 1911 censuses of Ireland are being digitized and made available online.

Because of the lack of nineteenth-century censuses, other records have taken on a greater significance than they would have otherwise. The most helpful of these is the Primary Valuation of Ireland carried out under the direction of Richard Griffith between 1848 and 1864, which lists all householders throughout Ireland. You can search Griffith's Valuation at the subscription-based Irish Origins website (www.irishorigins.com).

Similarly, the Tithe Applotment Books compiled from 1823–38 list occupiers of more than one acre of agricultural land, but don't cover urban areas or list farm workers.

The 1922 fire also destroyed virtually all of the (Anglican) Church of Ireland parish registers that had been stored in the PROI for safe-keeping. There still remained the registers that had not been handed in to the PROI (about 40 per cent of the total number), plus copies of some of those destroyed (around 10 per cent of the total). Some of the records still in existence are in the NAI.

Most Irish wills proved before 1900 (in church courts up to 1858, and in the civil registries afterwards) were destroyed in the 1922 fire. The NAI has created an index of pre-1858 wills, administrations and some marriage licences that survive in the form of summary transcripts (55 per cent), abstracts and extracts (28 per cent), original wills (10 per cent) and full copies (7 per cent). The index is accessible online at Irish Origins, and is also available on CD from Eneclann.

The NAI holds records of Irish prisoners transported to Australia. Although prisoners' petitions date back to 1788, the transportation registers cover the period 1836–57, as earlier registers were destroyed in 1922. You can search an index of the transportation records (1791–1853) online at *www.nationalarchives.ie/topics/transportation/search01.html*.

There are also many other family history-related documents in the NAI, such as education, poor law, electoral, landed estate and family records.

13. National Library of Ireland (NLI) www.nli.ie

At the National Library of Ireland in Dublin, you can view microfilm copies of Roman Catholic church registers. These begin in the

National Library of Ireland, Dublin.

mid-eighteenth century in some parishes of the cities of Dublin, Cork, Galway, Limerick and Waterford, although rural parishes in western counties tend to begin as late as the mid-nineteenth century. The cut-off point for the filming of the registers was 1880. You need to have the written permission of the Archbishop of Cashel and Emly or the Bishop of Kerry to view microfilms of the registers of parishes in their dioceses.

The NLI holds microfiche copies of Griffith's Valuation (1848–64) and microfilm copies of the Tithe Applotment Books (1823–38), as well as trade directories, newspapers, local and family histories, maps and estate papers.

14. Representative Church Body Library (RCBL) www.ireland.anglican.org/library

The Representative Church Body Library in Dublin is the (Anglican) Church of Ireland's reference library and main repository for its archives, where you can see registers from over 900 parishes in the Irish Republic. In addition, the RCBL is the home of the Irish Huguenot Archive. The library has published the registers of eight Irish parishes: three in Dublin, and one each in Cork, (London)Derry, Galway, Leixlip (County Kildare) and Lisnagarvey (County Antrim), as well as the vestry records of two Dublin parishes.

15. English and Welsh county record offices and local studies libraries

In England and Wales, many of the records that'll help you to trace your family history are held by county record offices, which tend to be based on the 1974–96 local government areas, including the former metropolitan counties. Some of the record offices have kept the name of the old administrative area, such as the Tyne and Wear Archives Service, while others have not. The former Greater London Record Office, for example, is now known as the London Metropolitan Archives.

Record offices and archives hold parish, Nonconformist and Roman Catholic church baptismal, marriage and burial registers, wills proved in local church courts, and many other useful records.

Although Welsh parish registers were supposed to be handed in to the National Library of Wales, the county record offices of Wales have some that didn't go to the NLW, as well as microfilms of those that did.

Tip: Some parish registers are still in the churches

Some baptismal and burial registers beginning in 1813 are still in use in rural parishes with small populations, so you'll have to visit the church to see them, if they haven't been microfilmed.

A couple of years ago, my wife and I stayed for a few days at a bed-and-breakfast farmhouse in the Golden Valley area of Herefordshire. On our way home, we visited the county record office in Hereford, and asked to see the baptisms and burials for the parish of St Margaret's. The archivist explained that the record office didn't have the post-1812 baptisms and burials for the parish, as they were still being used at St Margaret's church. 'You'll have to see one of the church-wardens,' he added, and looked in a directory to find their names. 'Oh, yes, here we are,' he said, and proceeded to give us the name of the person whose farm we'd left half an hour earlier.

As well as putting descriptions of their catalogues online through Access to Archives or Archives Network Wales, many of the record offices have also put their own more detailed catalogues online.

Gloucestershire (like several other counties) has combined its record office and its local studies library (which holds published material such as newspapers, trade directories, poll books, registers of electors, local and family histories, transcriptions of monumental inscriptions, and heralds' visitation records) in one location.

You can find information on what family history information is held by the public libraries of Britain, Ireland, the Isle of Man and the Channel Islands at the Museums, Libraries and Archives Council's Familia website (*www.familia.org.uk*).

Some English and Welsh local records online

Here is a selection of some of the various English and Welsh record offices that have made different parts of their collections available online:

- Bedfordshire and Luton Archives Service is putting the 35,000 entries in its gaol register from 1801–1901 online at *http://apps. bedfordshire.gov.uk/grd*;
- Bristol Record Office's website has a downloadable index of wills proved between 1793 and 1858 at *www.bristol-city.gov. uk/ccm/navigation/leisure-and-culture/libraries/archives*;
- Centre for Buckinghamshire Studies has made available online a database of prisoners entering Aylesbury gaol in the 1870s at *www.buckscc.gov.uk/bucks_prisoners/index.htm*. Many of the records contain a photograph of the prisoner;
- Cheshire Record Office has put its main catalogue and several other databases online at *www.cheshire.gov.uk/Recordoffice/ catalogues*. The databases include an index of 130,000 wills and administrations proved at Chester from 1492–1940, and an index of the staff of four railway companies, whose combined registers cover the period 1869–1950;
- Dorset History Centre (*www.dorsetforyou.com/index. jsp?articleid=2203*), which combines Dorset Archives and Local Studies, aims to create an online database of wills and administrations from 1554–1941, the first part of which is expected to be accessible in early 2008;
- Durham County Record Office (*www.durham.gov.uk/ recordoffice*) has set up an online database with information on Durham's Collieries (1850–1990). The record office's online catalogue includes 28,000 photographs of the Durham Light Infantry, plus 2,000 photographs of parts of County Durham;
- Glamorgan Record Office (*www.glamro.gov.uk*) has put online an index of 40,000 building regulations plans from 1857 to

the 1960s, under the title 'Cardiff: the building of a capital';

- Gloucestershire Archives has created an online Genealogical Database at *www.gloucestershire.gov.uk/index. cfm?ArticleID=1335*, which indexes wills proved in Gloucester from 1541–1858, prisoners in the county gaol register from 1815–79 and records of the Overseers of the Poor (responsible for poor relief before 1834). Nonconformist baptisms are being added to the database gradually;

- Isle of Wight Council has put online databases of people in receipt of poor relief in 1868 and 1875, and alehouse licences issued from 1766–1819 at *www.iwight.com/library/ record%5Foffice/Databases*;

- Lancashire Record Office has an online database of police officers who served in the Lancashire County Constabulary from 1840–1925, which you'll find at *www.lancashire.gov.uk/ education/record_office/records/police.asp*. The record office is currently indexing wills and marriage bonds;

- Lincolnshire Archives has set up a database of convicts transported to Australia, Bermuda and Gibraltar at *www.lincolnshire. gov.uk/archives/section.asp?docId=29249&catId=6722*;

- Powys County Council has created a Powys Heritage Online website (*http://history.powys.org.uk*), which consists of four sections on: a Powys Digital History Project for Schools (covering eighteen towns and their surrounding areas); Powys: A Day in the Life Project (accounts of life in 1891 and 2002); information on the Powys County Archives Office and its holdings; and Six Powys Communities Online;

- Warwickshire County Council (*www.warwickshire.gov.uk*) has a database of prisoners in the county's gaols in Birmingham, Coventry and Warwick between 1800 and 1900;

- Wiltshire County Council has put up a series of web pages with information (including photographs) on 261 communities throughout the county at *www.wiltshire.gov.uk/community*;

- Wiltshire and Swindon Record Office (*www.wiltshire.gov.uk/ archives.htm*) is currently digitizing and indexing its collection of 105,000 wills covering Wiltshire, Berkshire and parts of Devon and Dorset.

16. Scottish local archives

Although Scotland has no county records offices, it does have local archives in several towns and cities. In particular, the major cities of Aberdeen, Dundee, Edinburgh and Glasgow, as well as Inverness (the 'capital of the Highlands'), have significant holdings of local records. These include church, family, estate, business, trade union, criminal and administrative records. The local studies libraries in those towns and cities (such as the Edinburgh Room in the Edinburgh Central Library) hold newspapers, maps, town plans, photographs, prints and local histories. The Mitchell Library in Glasgow holds the city's archives.

The Scottish Jewish Archives Centre in Glasgow has a database with the names of 23,000 Jews who lived in Scotland before the Second World War, as well as an exhibition about the history of Jews in Scotland since the seventeenth century.

Some Scottish local records online

These are some of the Scottish archive records that are accessible online:

- The Friends of the Archives of Dumfries and Galloway have transcribed the 1851 census returns for Dumfriesshire, Kirkcudbrightshire and Wigtownshire. You can search them online at *www.dumgal.gov.uk/dumgal/MiniWeb.aspx?id=86& menuid=921&openid=921*, together with several other databases;
- The Friends of Dundee City Archives have indexed several collections: Methodist baptisms in Dundee (1785–1898); 80,000 burial records for the Howff, Dundee's cemetery; vehicle registrations for Perthshire (1909–11) and Kinross-shire (1904–52); Liff & Benvie Register of Poor (1854–65) and Dundee East Poorhouse Register (1856–78). These are all online at *www.fdca.org.uk/databases.htm*;
- Mitchell Library in Glasgow has set up a Virtual Mitchell website (*www.mitchelllibrary.org/virtualmitchell*) containing a large number of historic photographs and prints of the city;

- Scottish Archive Network's Virtual Vault (*www.scan.org.uk/ researchrtools/virtualvault.htm*) contains a number of useful records, such as the Lieutenancy Book of Roxburghshire (1797–1802) with militia lists of men from the county's thirty-one parishes.

17. LDS Family History Centres

The Church of Jesus Christ of Latter-day Saints has established Family History Centres around the world as branches of its Family History Library in Salt Lake City in the USA. There are over ninety-six centres in Britain, six in Ireland (three each in Northern Ireland and the Republic) and one on the Isle of Man. The Family History Centres are not restricted to members of the LDS Church, but are open to the general public. At any of the centres, you can order any microfilm from Salt Lake City for a small charge. This is very useful, as the LDS Church has made microfilm and microfiche records of a vast collection of records from around the world, including British and Irish parish registers.

PART ONE
Family Roots

Britain and Ireland

3

General historical introduction

What we thought we knew about the British and Irish people

Until quite recently, it was thought that Britain had been populated by Britons, a Celtic people, at the time that the Romans ruled over the island from AD 43–410. In Ireland lived another Celtic people, the Gaels, who spoke a language related to, but different from, that of the Britons. The British Celts had arrived sometime between about 2,000 and 700 BC, probably displacing the Gaels, who had prior to that time lived in both islands.

After the Roman army left in AD 410, the Angles, Saxons and Jutes (who lived in Denmark and North Germany) invaded, killing most of the Britons in what became England and driving the survivors into Wales, Cornwall and Cumbria.

In what is now Scotland, the Gaelic-speaking Scots invaded from Ireland in the sixth century and colonized Argyll. They later expanded into the whole area north of the Forth and Clyde and killed off the native Picts.

The Danish and Norwegian Vikings invaded in the ninth century. The Danes took over the east of England (the Danelaw), while the Norwegians colonized Orkney and Shetland (which remained Norwegian for about 600 years), completely replacing the original Pictish population. In addition, the Norwegians conquered the Hebrides, Scotland north of the Moray Firth, the Isle of Man, Cumbria and parts of Ireland (including Dublin).

What we *now* think we know about the British and Irish people

Instead of the English being descended from the Anglo-Saxons, the Welsh from the Britons, and the Scots and Irish from the Gaels, recent DNA research seems to show that the vast majority of the British and Irish people are descended from immigrants who had begun to settle in Britain and Ireland around 15,000 years ago after the last Ice Age. In his book *The Origins of the British* (Constable, 2006), Professor Stephen Oppenheimer of Oxford University re-analyses the results of several DNA-testing projects, finding that 88 per cent of the Irish, 81 per cent of the Welsh, 79 per cent of the Cornish, 70 per cent of the Scots and 68 per cent of the English are descended from these earliest immigrants. (See Conclusion for more information about DNA testing.)

Oppenheimer is not suggesting there was no Anglo-Saxon invasion, only that the numbers appear to have been much smaller than had previously been thought. He also suggests that the invasion may have been by the Angles alone, and that the Saxons may have arrived before the Roman occupation.

Over a ten-year period, a team under Bryan Sykes, Professor of Human Genetics at Oxford, collected the DNA of more than 10,000 volunteers across Britain. In his book *The Blood of the Isles* (Bantam Press, 2006), Sykes analyses his own data and that of a research team in Ireland. His analysis shows about 10 per cent of men now living in the south of England to be the patrilineal descendants of Saxons or Danes. The number rises to 15 per cent east of the Danelaw boundary (the River Lea and the A5 road) and 20 per cent in East Anglia. Initial results from Oxford University's *People of the British Isles* project appear to show, however, that the eastern regions of England are largely Anglo-Saxon in origin.

Sykes also estimates that around 40 per cent of men in Orkney and Shetland have Norse Viking ancestry, but he can detect no genetic difference between Picts and Scottish/Irish Gaels. As the Anglo-Saxons and the Danish Vikings (and even the ancestors of the Normans) came from the same area, it is difficult to tell their descendants apart on the basis of their DNA.

What the researches of Oppenheimer and Sykes show, however, is that the Britons were not wiped out in England. It seems likely that the Anglo-Saxons took over the running of Romano-British estates when they conquered England, but retained the existing British agricultural labourers (in the same way that the Normans did when they became the new leaders 600 years later).

The term 'Celtic' as a description of the pre-Anglo-Saxon inhabitants of Britain and Ireland and their languages has also been criticized (in particular by Professor John Collis of the University of Sheffield). The Britons and early Irish weren't described as 'Celts' until seventeenth-century language scholars linked the family of the Irish, Scottish Gaelic, Welsh, Breton, Manx and Cornish languages to the ancient Celts of central and western Europe.

Oppenheimer's analysis indicates that early settlement of western and northern Britain, as well as Ireland (between 15,000 and 7,500 years ago) was mainly along the Atlantic coast from the Iberian Peninsula, and also across Europe from the present Ukraine/Moldova. He suggests that the early Iberian settlers were related to the Celt-Iberi of what is now Spain. Oppenheimer also suggests that further settlement of Britain (and Ireland to a limited extent) in the New Stone Age (around 5,500 BC) was from the eastern Mediterranean area via the Atlantic, across Europe from the Balkans, and from the Ukraine via Russia and the Norwegian coast. Interestingly, his findings tie in quite well with the mythical settlers in Ireland described in the Irish sagas. Such people included the Fir Bolg (who were said to have come from Thrace in Greece), the Tuatha de Danann, the Formorii and the Milesians, descendants of Mile Easpain (soldier of Spain).

England and Wales

4

Historical introduction

England and Wales historical timeline

AD 43–410	Roman occupation of England and Wales
5th century	Angles, Saxons and Jutes invade England
789	Vikings (Danes and Norwegians) begin raiding England
865	Danes invade England
1066	Norman conquest of England
1284	English (Norman) conquest of Wales
1348–9	'Black Death' kills between a third and a half of the population
1381	Peasants' Revolt
1536	Union of England and Wales
16th century	English and Scottish plantations (settlements) in Ireland
1603	Union of English and Scottish crowns
17th century	Scottish and English plantations in Ulster and central Ireland
1649–60	Commonwealth (republic) established
1707	Union of English and Scottish parliaments
c. 1760	Beginning of the Industrial Revolution
1760–1820	Enclosure Acts appropriate common land as private property
1801	United Kingdom of Great Britain and Ireland created
1807	Abolition of the slave trade on British ships
1833	Abolition of slavery in British colonies
1914–18	First World War
1918–19	Influenza epidemic kills over 40 million people worldwide
1939–45	Second World War
1973	United Kingdom joins what is now the European Union

A short history of England

When the Romans invaded Britain in the first century AD, what later became England was home to fifteen tribes. Some of them had come to England from the continent, such as the Belgae (who give their name to Belgium) and the Parisi (whose namesakes – and possible cousins – in Gaul founded the city of Paris). After the official withdrawal of the Roman army in 410, the eastern coast of the future England was invaded by the Angles (from south Denmark/north Germany), Saxons (from north Germany) and Jutes (from Denmark). By 500, most of East Anglia and central England had been conquered. One hundred and fifty years later Cornwall, Devon, north Lancashire, Cumberland and Westmorland still remained in British control, but by 800, only Cornwall was not in Anglo-Saxon hands.

In 865, the Danes arrived in England and conquered east of Watling Street (the old Roman Road that is now the A5). The Danish (and, from 919, Norse) kingdom of York included Westmorland and part of Lancashire as well as Yorkshire itself. There were also many Norwegian settlements in Lancashire, Cumberland and Westmorland in the early tenth century.

In 1066, the Normans (descendants of Norwegians who had settled in northern France) conquered England. They didn't arrive in large numbers, but simply replaced the Anglo-Saxon aristocracy. The Angles, Saxons, Jutes, Danes and Norwegians did settle in considerable numbers, but without replacing the earlier inhabitants. Recent DNA testing has shown that the direct descendants of the ancient British peoples still make up over 60 per cent of the male population of England (and almost 80 per cent of the male population of Devon and Cornwall).

A short history of Wales

The Welsh are descended from four British tribes who lived there at the time of the Roman occupation of Britain: the Deceangli, the Demetae, the Ordovices and the Silures). After the Romans left, Irish settlements were established in south Wales by the Déisi from County Waterford and in north Wales by the Laigin from eastern Leinster. Some Norwegian Vikings settled in the early tenth century in Anglesey and in coastal areas of Flintshire, Cardiganshire, Carmarthenshire and Glamorgan. There was a settlement of Flemings in Pembrokeshire in the early twelfth century.

The descendants of the Britons had formed several independent kingdoms by the time of the Norman Conquest of England in 1066. King William appointed Norman earls to guard the English border areas, and these 'Marcher Lords' began the invasion of Wales. By 1284, Wales had been conquered, with the heir to the English throne becoming Prince of Wales. It was not until 1536, however, that the 'Principality of Wales' (most of the northern and western areas) and the Marcher lordships were combined to form a larger principality in the present borders of Wales.

England and Wales genealogical timeline

1538	Parish registers (recording baptisms, marriages and burials) are required to be kept in England and Wales
1598	Bishops' transcripts are required to be kept in England and Wales
1649–60	Commonwealth – first civil registration of births, marriages and deaths and civil probate of wills in England and Wales
1752	Changeover from Julian to Gregorian calendar with the 'loss' of eleven days (3–13 September)
1753	Hardwicke Marriage Act – with separate parish registers for marriages in England and Wales from March 1754
1784	Stamp Act – some English and Welsh parishes begin to use printed registers
1801	First official ten-yearly census of England and Wales
1812	Rose Act – baptisms and burials in England and Wales must be recorded separately in printed registers from 1 January 1813
1837	Civil registration of births, marriages and deaths begins in England and Wales on 1 July
1858	Civil probate of English and Welsh wills and administrations

The union with England left many Welsh-speaking people in the English counties of Shropshire (around Oswestry and Clun), Herefordshire (west of the River Wye) and Gloucestershire (on the edge of the Forest of Dean). If you look in the churchyards in Herefordshire's Golden Valley, for example, you'll see mainly Welsh surnames.

Many people have left Wales over the years. In 1865, emigrants founded a Welsh-speaking colony in Patagonia, in the south of Argentina; among the many Welsh emigrants to the USA were 5,000 of the 12,000 Welshmen and -women who converted to the LDS Church in the nineteenth century.

Many Welshmen left the country during the nineteenth century following the old cattle drove roads through Hereford, Kington and Ludlow towards London and the Midlands. Conversely, a large number of Englishmen (and some Scots and Irishmen) went to work in the coal mines of the South Wales valleys.

5

Births, marriages and deaths

Birth, marriage and death certificates are one of the basic resources for tracing your ancestors in England and Wales. On 1 July 1837 recording these life events in England and Wales became the responsibility of the newly set up General Register Office (GRO, *www.gro.gov.uk*) under control of the Registrar General for England and Wales. Before this 'civil registration' was introduced, baptisms, marriages and burials had been recorded by churches in their parish registers, some from as early as 1538.

In other parts of the British Isles, civil registration started later. In Ireland, non-Roman Catholic marriages were registered from 1 April 1845, with births, deaths and Catholic marriges following on 1 January 1864. Although civil registration of births, marriages and deaths didn't begin in Scotland until 1 January 1855, more information was collected on those vital events than in England and Wales.

Births

The English and Welsh birth certificate (with the entry in the original register copied on to a pink pre-printed form) contains information on the date and place of birth, the child's name and sex, the names of both parents (including the mother's maiden surname), the father's occupation, the signature, description and address of the person giving the information to the local registrar, and the date of registration. You won't always get all this information, however. If the parents hadn't agreed on a name for the child at the time that his or her birth was registered, then the certificate will simply state 'boy' or 'girl'. If the parents weren't married, then the father's name and occupation were not allowed to appear in the records. (Unfortunately, you won't get the date and place of the parents' marriage, as you do on a Scottish birth certificate.)

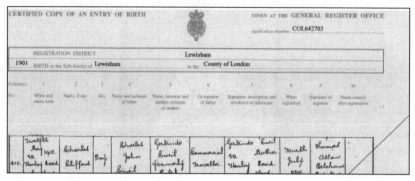

English birth certificate (1901 – Charles Clifford Civil).

Tip: Not everything on a birth certificate may be true

Although a child wasn't supposed to be registered in the father's surname if the parents weren't married, there doesn't seem to have always been a check for a marriage certificate. I know of the births of two brothers registered in the 1880s where the parents weren't married, although looking at the children's birth certificates, you'd think they must have been.

Marriages

The marriage certificate (on a green form) contains the date and place of marriage, the names of the bride and groom, their ages, marital status (such as widower or spinster), addresses and occupations. In addition, the certificate states the names and occupations of both fathers (but unfortunately gives no information on the mothers). It also gives the names of two witnesses, who may well be related to the couple who married.

English marriage certificate (1923 – Issac Anderton and Sarah Jones).

Tip: The name of a 'father' may have been invented

It's best not to rely too much on the name of the bride's or groom's father being correct, however. You can spend a long time looking for the 'father' of someone who was born illegitimate and may have invented the name purely for the marriage certificate.

To try to find the real name of that person's father, look at the marriage certificates of his or her brothers and sisters. You may well find several different name combinations given for the father, but with one name in common. If you're lucky, this will turn out to be the father's real surname.

Deaths

The death certificate (on a form pre-printed in black) lists the date and place of death, and the name, sex, age and occupation of the deceased, together with the cause of death and the signature, description and address of the informant. With the death certificate of a man with a common forename and surname (for example 'John Smith'), it can be hard to tell whether you've got the right document. At least with a married woman, the name of her husband and his job is given in the 'occupation' column.

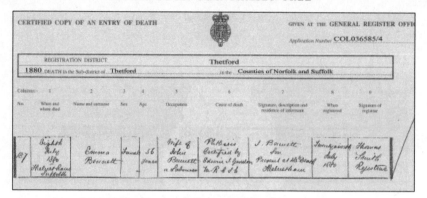

English death certificate (1880 – Emma Bennett).

Digitization of the records

The English and Welsh civil registration records have not yet been digitized, although their indexes have been. In August 2005, however, the Office of National Statistics (*www.statistics.gov.uk*), of which the GRO is a part, signed a contract for all the births, marriages and deaths from 1837 to the present day to be scanned, digitized and indexed. Unfortunately, the 250 million records are to be scanned from existing microfilms, rather than the original records. They will then be digitized and transmitted to India for indexing – by people unfamiliar with English and Welsh names. This is due to be completed by 2009, after which the older records are expected to be made available online.

Birth, marriage and death indexes on the Internet

FreeBMD

In 1998, when there seemed to be no likelihood that the GRO vital record indexes for England and Wales would ever be computerized – let alone digitizing the records themselves – a group of volunteers decided to build a computer index themselves under the name FreeBMD (*freebmd.rootsweb.com*). Over 100 million index records have been added to the FreeBMD database, covering mainly the period 1837 to 1910. The database is accessible free of charge, and its creation is an ongoing project.

The GRO references that you'll find by searching the database are in the form 'Chester 8a 445', which indicates that 'Chester' is the name of the registration district, and that the birth, marriage or death record is contained in volume '8a' on page 445. The results are shown by quarter (ending in March, June, September or December), as the original indexes were compiled on that basis. Once you've found the reference, you can then order from the GRO a paper certificate, which is sent to you by post.

Tip: Extra information is shown in the indexes from the dates below

Birth indexes
September quarter 1911 – mother's maiden surname

Marriage indexes
March quarter 1912 – spouse's surname

Death indexes
March quarter 1866 – age at death
June quarter 1969 – date of birth

The transcriptions of the indexes have not been added to the database in successive years, so that, unfortunately, many years are incomplete. This means that if your search is unsuccessful, you can't tell whether this is because the index entry you're looking for doesn't exist, or whether it simply hasn't been added to the database yet. There are charts on the site, however, that show what percentage of birth, marriage and death index entries are in the database for each year.

Digitized copies of the original paper indexes (used by the volunteers) are also accessible free of charge. If the event that you're looking for has been indexed, you can easily click through from the result of your search to the page in the original index. You can also go direct to the original index images, but this is rather a long-winded process. You select from drop-down menus the type of record (birth, marriage or death), the year (1837 to 1910), the quarter, and the fact that it's an A-Z search (although this is the only option you can choose). After each selection, you have to click on 'submit query'. As if this weren't enough rigmarole, you then have to guess which page the surname you're looking for will be on! At least it *is* free of charge.

Ancestry.co.uk

You can search the FreeBMD database at Ancestry.co.uk (*www.ancestry.co.uk*), the UK subsidiary of the American family company Ancestry.com, free of charge. There the database goes under the name 'England and Wales, Civil Registration Index 1837–1983', although there's not much in it after about 1910. Ancestry holds indexes for English and Welsh births and deaths (1984–2002) and marriages (1984–2000). In addition, Ancestry has the original index images, which you can search free of charge and much more easily than on FreeBMD.

Find My Past

This website had already made the images of the original paper indexes accessible at *www.findmypast.com* on a pay-per-view basis before they became available free of charge through FreeBMD and Ancestry. Although you have to pay, it's quite easy to search the images on this site, as you can search by surname (and forename, if it's a very common surname). The printed indexes cover the years 1837 up to 1983, and the indexes from 1984 onwards are held in a fully search-able database. In addition to the birth, marriage and death indexes, 1837online holds indexes of consular, high commission and armed forces vital records (some starting in 1761).

BMD Index.co.uk

Like 1837online, BMD Index (*www.bmdindex.co.uk*) is another pay-per-view site where you can view images of the original paper indexes from 1837–1983, as well as search a database of the indexes from 1984 up to the present.

Family Relatives

This pay-per-view website (*www.familyrelatives.org*) differs from the previous two sites in offering a complete database of the birth, marriage and death indexes covering the periods 1866–1920 and 1984–2003. For 1837–65 and 1921–83, the site provides images of the paper indexes.

How to order birth, marriage and death certificates

In England and Wales, births and deaths are recorded in local register offices, and the local registrars send copies of the entries to the Registrar General in London. Marriages can take place in churches, register offices or other designated places (such as hotels and country houses), with the records again held in the local register office and copies sent to London. If the marriage took place in a church, then it too will have a copy of the record.

You can order copies of the records either from the General Register Office (GRO) or the appropriate local register office. You can search the GRO's indexes either in the form of large printed registers or microfiche at the Family Records Centre in London, and on microfiche at libraries, record offices and family history societies elsewhere. The GRO Certificate Ordering Service is online at *www. gro.gov.uk/gro/content/certificates* – which contains a good deal of information about the indexes and certificates.

Alternatively, you can order certificates from the local office where the event was registered. Some of the local register offices have online indexes, which you can find through the UKBMD portal website at *www.ukbmd.org.uk*. Click on 'Local BMD' and you'll be taken to a list of birth, marriage and death (BMD) websites (twenty at the last count), which contain indexes to local registrations. These are continuing projects, however, and few of the indexes are complete. You need to be aware that the registration reference used by the local offices is different from the GRO reference, which applies only to the centrally held copies of the registrations.

You can order certificates by post or telephone from either the GRO or the appropriate local register office.

GRO registration districts 1837–51

Ref. No.	Registration District
I	London and Middlesex
II	London and Middlesex
III	London and Middlesex
IV	London and Surrey
V	Kent
VI	Bedfordshire, Berkshire, Buckinghamshire and Hertfordshire
VII	Hampshire and Sussex
VIII	Dorset, Hampshire and Wiltshire
IX	Cornwall and Devon
X	Devon and Somerset
XI	Gloucestershire, Somerset and Warwickshire
XII	Essex and Suffolk
XIII	Norfolk and Suffolk
XIV	Cambridgeshire, Huntingdonshire, Lincolnshire and Suffolk
XV	Leicestershire, Northamptonshire, Nottinghamshire and Rutland
XVI	Oxfordshire, Staffordshire and Warwickshire
XVII	Staffordshire
XVIII	Gloucestershire, Shropshire, Staffordshire, Warwickshire and Worcestershire
XIX	Cheshire, Derbyshire and Flintshire
XX	Lancashire
XXI	Lancashire and Yorkshire
XXII	Yorkshire
XXIII	Yorkshire
XXIV	County Durham and Yorkshire
XXV	Cumberland, Lancashire, Northumberland and Westmorland
XXVI	Breconshire, Carmarthenshire, Glamorgan, Herefordshire, Monmouthshire, Pembrokeshire, Radnorshire and Shropshire
XXVII	Anglesey, Caernarvonshire, Cardiganshire, Denbighshire, Flintshire, Merionethshire and Montgomeryshire

GRO registration districts 1852–1946

Ref. No.	Registration District
1a	London and Middlesex
1b	London and Middlesex
1c	London and Middlesex
1d	London, Kent and Surrey
2a	Kent and Surrey
2b	Hampshire and Sussex
2c	Berkshire and Hampshire
3a	Berkshire, Buckinghamshire, Hertfordshire, Middlesex and Oxfordshire
3b	Bedfordshire, Cambridgeshire, Huntingdonshire, Northamptonshire and Suffolk
4a	Essex and Suffolk
4b	Norfolk
5a	Dorset and Wiltshire
5b	Devon
5c	Cornwall and Somerset
6a	Gloucestershire, Herefordshire and Shropshire
6b	Staffordshire, Warwickshire and Worcestershire
6c	Warwickshire and Worcestershire
6d	Warwickshire
7a	Leicestershire, Lincolnshire and Rutland
7b	Derbyshire and Nottinghamshire
8a	Cheshire
8b	Lancashire
8c	Lancashire
8d	Lancashire
8e	Lancashire
9a	Yorkshire
9b	Yorkshire
9c	Yorkshire
9d	Yorkshire
10a	County Durham

10b	Cumberland, Northumberland and Westmorland
11a	Carmarthenshire, Glamorgan, Monmouthshire and Pembrokeshire
11b	Anglesey, Breconshire, Caernarvonshire, Cardiganshire, Denbighshire, Flintshire, Merionethshire, Montgomeryshire and Radnorshire

6

Census returns

Although censuses were taken in Babylonia, Egypt, China and the Roman Empire, in its modern form the census dates from the eighteenth century. The US Federal Census began in 1790, and the first census in the British Isles was carried out in 1801. This covered England, Scotland, Wales and the Channel Islands, with the Isle of Man following in 1811 and Ireland in 1821. Further censuses were taken every ten years apart from 1941, because of the Second World War.

Other than in Ireland, up to 1841 only general statistics were required, without individual names. Some of the early enumerators exceeded their instructions, however, and did record the names of those living in their areas.

After the creation of the General Register Office in 1837, the census was enumerated using the same registration districts as were used for births, marriages and deaths, but subdivided into several enumeration districts. Shortly before the census night, each enumerator gave all the households in his or her district a schedule to complete. The schedules were then collected and copied into enumeration books (the records you can see today), and the schedules destroyed.

Detailed census information is not made public in the UK until 100 years after the end of the year in which the census was taken, and so information on individual people is currently available from the 1841–1901 censuses. The release of the 1911 census had been expected on the first working day of 2012, but The National Archives (TNA) hope most of the English and Welsh census information will be available online nearly three years earlier.

Census dates and populations 1801–1901 plus 2001–02

Date of census	England and Wales	Scotland	Ireland
1801, 10 March	8,892,536	1,608,420	5,395,456
1811, 27 May	10,164,256	1,805,864	5,937,856
1821, 28 May	12,000,236	2,091,521	6,801,827
1831, 29 May	13,896,797	2,364,386	7,767,401
1841, 6 June	15,914,148	2,620,184	8,175,124
1851, 30 March	17,927,609	2,888,742	6,552,385
1861, 7 April	20,066,224	3,062,294	5,798,564
1871, 2 April	22,712,266	3,360,018	5,412,377
1881, 3 April	25,974,439	3,735,573	5,174,836
1891, 5 April	29,002,525	4,025,647	4,704,750
1901, 31 March	32,527,843	4,472,103	4,458,775
2001, 29 April (census held in UK)	52,041,916	5,062,011	1,685,267 (NI)
2002, 28 April (census held in RoI)			3,917,203 (RoI)

This change of plan has come about as a result of a family historian's successful request under the Freedom of Information (FOI) Act. TNA had initially refused to provide him with information from the 1911 census in response to a request made under the Act. The UK's Information Commissioner ruled, however, that TNA must supply the information. Because of this ruling, TNA has not only set up a chargeable FOI service to handle requests for information relating to specific addresses, but is also bringing the launch of the online service (minus certain sensitive information) forward to early 2009. FOI requests to see information contained in the 1921 census will be refused, however, as the 1920 Census Act prevents information being disclosed until 2021. (Scotland has its own differently worded FOI Act, and the Registrar General for Scotland doesn't expect to make the Scottish 1911 census available online until the spring of 2011.)

Despite rumours to the contrary, TNA says that the vast majority of the 1911 census volumes are in good condition and suitable for scanning. This census is twelve times as large as the 1901 census, because the documents that will be made available online are the householders' schedules, rather than the enumerators' returns. (In the Republic of Ireland, the 1911 census of the whole island has already been released. Although the 1911 Irish census returns publicly available in Dublin include Northern Ireland, the census is not yet open to view in Northern Ireland itself. US censuses are made available after seventy-two years, so American family historians are already able to view the 1930 Federal Census.)

The 1841–1901 census returns for England, Wales, the Isle of Man and the Channel Islands are available at the Family Records Centre (FRC) in London: the 1841–91 returns on microfilm and those for 1901 on microfiche. The returns have all been digitized and can be viewed on computers at the FRC, as well as online. Copies of the microfilm and -fiche census returns are also available at LDS Family History Centres, as well as at many libraries and record offices (although usually only for the local area).

The census returns for Scotland are covered in Chapter 12, for Ireland in Chapter 17, and for the Isle of Man and the Channel Islands in Chapter 19.

The 1851 census was the first to state a person's parish of birth and relationship to the head of the household. The information given on the census return is:

- name of street, and number or name of house;
- forename and surname of each person;
- relationship to head of family;
- marital status;
- age;
- sex;
- occupation;
- birthplace;
- certain disabilities.

If the birthplace was within England or Wales, the county and parish should be given, but if the birth took place elsewhere, then only 'Scotland', 'Ireland', or another country should be stated. Occasionally, the county and even parish in Scotland or Ireland was entered on a census return, so it's worth looking at all the different census years to see if this was the case. Middle names were rarely given, except in names like 'Mary Ann', although quite often one or even two middle initials were given.

In Wales (but not England) from 1891, whether a person spoke Welsh, English or both languages was stated. Similar information was given for Scotland regarding Scottish Gaelic (also from 1891), for Ireland re Irish Gaelic (in 1901 and 1911) and for the Isle of Man re Manx (from 1901).

The 1841 census, although listing individuals, is not as useful for family history as the later censuses. No relationships are given, and birthplace information is limited to whether born in the county or not (with place of birth outside England and Wales limited to 'S' (Scotland), 'I' (Ireland) and 'F' (foreign parts).

In addition, ages above fifteen were meant to be rounded down to the nearest multiple of five, although you'll often find exact ages given. Addresses are vaguer too, with street numbers usually omitted and country addresses limited to the name of a hamlet or village.

Census records online

1901 census for England and Wales

The 1901 census was put online for TNA in 2002 by the science and technology company QinetiQ. The census should have been online on the first working day of January, but because of problems with the implementation, it wasn't available until September. (The first digitized UK census returns to become available on the Internet were those for the 1891 Scottish census, which were put online in 2001.) You can now access the 1901 census (which covers not only England and Wales, but also the Isle of Man and the Channel Islands) at the pay-per-view website *www.1901census.national archives.gov.uk*. Searching on the site is free of charge, but there is a charge to view digitized census returns or transcriptions of them.

In a 'person search', you can search by surname, qualified by forename, gender, age (plus or minus up to ninety-nine years), place of birth, census district. Alternatively, you can search by forename without surname (in which case you need to specify gender, age and place of birth).

An 'advanced person search' adds 'other names', marital condition, occupation and relationship to head of family to the qualifying search items. You can tick boxes to include synonyms for the forename, as well as limiting the search to people on board ship. There is also an 'address search' facility.

In August 2005, the 1901 census website was bought by the school reunion site Friends Reunited (*www.friendsreunited.co.uk*), and is now run by its family history subsidiary Genes Reunited (*www. genesreunited.co.uk*). In December 2005, Friends Reunited was, in turn, acquired by ITV.

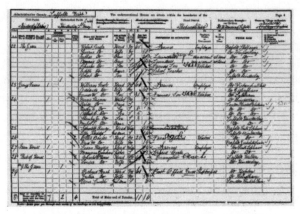

1901 census of England (Hinderclay, Suffolk).

Ancestry.co.uk

After the delay with the 1901 census going online, TNA licensed Ancestry.co.uk to make the 1841–1901 censuses available online. All of the censuses for those years for England, Wales, the Isle of Man and the Channel Islands are now accessible, complete with digitized images (plus Scottish censuses as transcriptions only).

As well as searching on surname, Ancestry lets you search on forename alone, without any other qualifying search items. If you specify a very common forename, however, you'll get an unmanageable number of results returned (such as 1,570,455 women and girls named 'Mary' in the 1901 census of England).

You can, if you wish, search for everyone in Gloucestershire (684,724 people) or in Sheffield (121,378), or all the females born in Swansea (4,973). (These figures are for the English 1901 census.) It's most helpful, though, if you combine these features to narrow down your search by specifying, for example, a forename, birth year (plus or minus two or five) and place of birth.

Tip: Widen your search

If you can't find (say) 'Margaret Ace' from Swansea in a census, and you know she should be there (because you have a later death certificate for Margaret, or you've found her in a later census), try widening your search to allow for mistranscriptions of her name.

In this case, if you search the English 1901 census for everyone with the surname 'Ace', and specify 'Swansea' as their birthplace, you'll find a 'Maggie Ace', born about 1876, who was a servant in Rickmansworth, Hertfordshire.

Family Search

The LDS Family Search site (*www.familysearch.org*) contains a transcription of the 1881 census for England, Wales, the Isle of Man and the Channel Islands, which is searchable free of charge. As well as the name of the person you're looking for, you can also specify the head of the household in your search, and you can qualify the search by the person's country and county of birth and by the country, county and district where he or she was at the time of the census.

(You can also search the 1880 US census and the 1881 census of Canada at Family Search.)

Family History Online

The 1881 census is also available free of charge at the Family History Online website set up by the Federation of Family History Societies at *www.familyhistoryonline.net*. In addition, parts of the 1841–71,

1891 and 1901 censuses are online at the site on a pay-per-view basis.

Find My Past

All of the 1841, 1861, 1871 and 1891 censuses are available online at the pay-per-view Find My Past website (*www.findmypast.com*). Searching the census databases and viewing the list of results is free of charge, although you have to pay to see the image of a census return. In an 'advanced search', you can specify a second person that you expect to be living in the same household at the time of the census. You can also carry out an 'address search'.

Tip: Errors in the census

You're likely to come across many errors in the census. There are mistakes in the indexing and transcription, which is often carried out by people overseas, who are unfamiliar with place-names in the British Isles. So don't forget to try searching by forename only or birthplace only. In institutions, forename and surname were sometimes transposed, or only initials used.

There are also errors in the census returns when the enumerator has most probably transferred information incorrectly from a household schedule, because he couldn't read the householder's writing (or his own, if the householder was illiterate).

You'll find that information varies from one census to another, such as place of birth. I suspect this depended on who was providing the information: the householder would know the birthplaces of his wife, his children and himself, but was perhaps not so clear about those of other relatives, friends staying with him on census night, or lodgers. And from one census to the next, ages on the returns often increase by less than ten years; many people lied about their age, particularly when their spouse was younger.

The Genealogist

S&N Genealogy has made census transcripts and indexes available for 1841–71, 1891 and 1901 for many counties, some with links to images. You can search and view them at its The Genealogist website (*www.thegenealogist.co.uk*) on either a subscription or pay-per-view basis.

S&N sells the censuses on CD on a county basis at its website *www.genealogysupplies.com*.

British Origins

At the subscription-based British Origins (*www.britishorigins.com*), you'll find indexed census images online for English and Welsh counties for the 1841, 1861 and 1871 censuses.

Stepping Stones

The 1841 census is available for many counties at the Stepping Stones website (*www.stepping-stones.co.uk*), with some counties online for 1851 and 1861 too. Stepping Stones provides only area and street indexes, rather than indexing each individual person in the census. The 1841–71 censuses are available on CD on a county basis.

FreeCEN

The Free Census Project (FreeCEN) was founded by volunteers in mid-1999 to provide free online access to indexed transcriptions of British censuses. This was two years before any census returns (or any other family history records) were accessible online in a digitized form. It was a further four years, however, before the first transcriptions (of the 1891 census) were available online through the FreeCEN website (*http://freecen.rootsweb.com*). The project is part of the FreeUKGEN initiative, which includes FreeBMD (see Chapter 5) and FreeREG (see Chapter 7).

The transcribers of the censuses of England and Wales began with the 1891 census and worked back through the census years (at first omitting the 1881 census, which already had a free transcription). Scottish transcribers, on the other hand, started with the 1841 census and worked forward. Many Scottish counties are complete for the earlier censuses, and several English and Welsh counties for the 1891 census.

Other census websites

You can find other local British and Irish census websites listed on the UKBMD (*www.ukbmd.org.uk*) site's 'Census' page or on the individual page for a county. The UK pages at the Census Finder (*www.censusfinder.com*) website contain links to many local census transcriptions, as well as many other population listings (such as trade directories, militia lists, poor relief applications and valuation rolls).

Tip: Missing census returns

Many census returns are missing. You can find out whether the area your ancestors are likely to have lived in is missing from any of the censuses by searching the TNA catalogue.

On the search page, enter the name of a place (for example 'Llanigon') in the 'Word or phrase' box and put 'RG9' (the code for the 1861 census) into the 'Department or series code' box. The results will tell you that Llanigon parish is missing from the 1861 census.

The codes for the various English and Welsh censuses are 'HO107' for 1841 and 1851, 'RG9' for 1861, 'RG10' for 1871, 'RG11' for 1881, 'RG12' for 1891 and 'RG13' for 1901. These codes enable you to identify which census a print-out refers to.

7

Parish and other church registers

A church parish is the area which provided payment to a priest in the form of 'tithes' (a tenth of each household's income or produce), which was made compulsory in England in the tenth century. In southern counties, parish boundaries were often the same as those of the much older administrative area known as the 'vill' or 'township'. In the south of England and Wales, parishes tended to consist of a single township or village, whereas those in the north could contain as many as a few dozen townships. For this reason, there tended to be many more parishes in southern counties than in the north. Norfolk, for example, contained nearly 700 ancient parishes, while Lancashire had just over 200, although its area was only slightly smaller.

Large parishes usually contained a number of chapels besides the parish church, to cut the distance people had to travel to a church service. These could be either 'chapels of ease' serving no particular district, or chapels to serve subdivisions of the parish, known as chapelries. The large parish of Clodock in Herefordshire, for example, consisted of the chapelries of Craswall, Llanveynoe, Longtown and Newton. Chapels were not necessarily licensed for baptisms or marriages, which took place at the mother church. Sometimes a chapel had no churchyard consecrated for burials, in which case you'll find your ancestors buried in the mother church's graveyard.

By the beginning of the fourteenth century there were around 9,000 ecclesiastical parishes in England, whose boundaries remained more or less static for the next 500 years. By the nineteenth century the growth of towns as a result of the Industrial Revolution led to the building of more churches and the creation of new parishes. Many of the chapels of ease became parish churches.

At the same time areas that had been considered 'extra-parochial liberties' were made into parishes. The inhabitants of the eastern and western extra-parochial areas of the Forest of Dean in Gloucestershire, for instance, could have baptisms, marriages and burials carried out at any of the small parishes that surrounded the forest. In the nineteenth century these extra-parochial areas became the parishes of East and West Dean.

Parish registers

In 1538, the ministers of the parish churches of England and Wales were instructed to keep a register of baptisms, marriages and burials. Many did not begin to do so until 1598, however, when a copy of the register was required to be sent to the local bishop or archdeacon. These copies are known as 'bishop's transcripts' (BTs).

Also from 1598, all registers were to be written on parchment, as this was more durable than the paper that most of the earlier registers had been written on. All the earlier entries were to be copied into the new registers, but particularly those entries made in the reign of Queen Elizabeth I. Since she had acceded to the throne in 1558, many parchment registers began from that year. The average year at which registers start in England is 1611, with around 10 per cent of parishes in an average county beginning in 1538. (The situation was similar in Scotland and Ireland, where registers were supposed to be kept from 1553 and 1634 respectively, but usually begin later. Much later, in some cases. Neither Scotland nor Ireland has bishops' transcripts. Parish registers in Scotland, Ireland, the Isle of Man and the Channel Islands are covered in later chapters.)

Early entries in the registers tend to give little information, making it difficult to know if you've found the right entry. Baptisms in the sixteenth century, for instance, give the name of the child and usually (but not always) the father's name. The mother's name is not stated in these early entries, unless the child is 'base-born' (illegitimate), and sometimes not even then.

Tip: Late baptisms

Sometimes baptisms took place months, or even years after the birth of the child. Occasionally, several children would be baptized together, over ten years after the birth of the oldest. Don't restrict your search to just a few years either side of the expected year of baptism.

Marriage entries simply give the names of the bride and groom. Early burials state only the name of the deceased, unless he or she was a child, in which case you're likely to find the father's (and sometimes the mother's) name too. By the seventeenth century you may also find the relationship of the deceased to another named person (such as son, daughter, wife or sister). Sometimes the parish clerk made a comment on a death, such as this one from the register of Walsham-le-Willows, Suffolk in 1655:

> John Orvis, died 25th January, buried 27th January, died at
> Stanton Cock, a very sad example to all pot companions.
> [John Orvis was 47 years old.]

Up to the mid-eighteenth century, baptisms, marriages and burials were usually recorded in the same register, but Lord Harwicke's Marriage Act of 1753 required separate registers for marriages. Here is a typical entry from the parish of Clifford, Herefordshire:

> William Cole and Lydia Wood, both of this parish, were
> married in this church by banns this 27th day of October
> 1778 by me
> > John Lloyd, curate.
> This marriage was solemnised between us: the mark of
> > William Cole
> > Lydia Wood
> In the presence of us:
> > Baldwin Higgins
> > Henry Jones

Tip: 'Of this parish' may not mean born there

'Of this parish' simply means that the person was a parish-
ioner of the church, i.e. he or she lived in the parish. In the
above case, for example, there are baptisms for neither
William Cole nor Lydia Wood in the registers of Clifford.

George Rose's Act of 1812 introduced separate printed baptism
and burial registers with headed columns. Some parishes had already

Page in a post-1812 register of baptisms (1851).

begun to use printed registers for baptisms and burials in 1784 after the imposition of Stamp Duty on register entries. For baptisms, the mother's maiden name and the date of the child's birth were entered in the register, while for burials, the age at death was given.

In baptism entries after 1812, all parishes were supposed to specify the address of the parents and the occupation of the father (although this wasn't always done), but were not required to give the mother's maiden name or the date of the child's birth. After 1812, the relationship of the deceased was no longer stated. For burials, all parishes had to specify the age.

In the period of the Commonwealth (under Oliver Cromwell), from about 1652–60, birth as well as baptismal dates were recorded, and similarly dates of death as well as burial. During this period, the marital status and parish of both parties began to be entered in the register. From 1837, church marriages were recorded using the same registers as civil marriages. Baptisms and burials continue to be recorded in church registers today, and in some parishes in country areas, the registers that were introduced in 1813 are still being used.

Monumental inscriptions

Because the information in a burial register entry can be minimal, the inscriptions on gravestones and on memorials inside churches can prove helpful in identifying relationships and supplying additional information about the people commemorated. A tablet on the north wall of the vestry at Walsham-le-Willows, for instance, gives useful information about the Nunn family:

> Mr. Martin Nunn, only son of Mr George Nunn and Margaret his wife (before Margaret Sparke spinster), 1 February 1770, aged 28.
>
> Margaret, widow of George Nunn, 15 May 1788, aged 84.
>
> Mr. John Warn, late of Rattlesden, who married Margaret, only daughter of George and Margaret Nunn, 15 May 1796, aged 50.
>
> Margaret, widow of John Warn, 15 July 1805, aged 61.

Similarly, this inscription from a gravestone in the churchyard at Huntley, Gloucestershire, is helpful in proving relationships:

> In memory of James Sanford of this parish
> who departed this life March 14th 1811, aged 73 years
> also of Ann, wife of the above,
> who departed this life January 12th 1823, aged 85 years
> also of James, son of the above,
> who departed this life April 30th 1847, aged 72 years
> and also of Sarah, his wife,
> who departed this life March 13th 1840, aged 61 years.

Most family history societies have a programme of transcribing inscriptions from the churchyards and cemeteries in their counties, and publishing them in booklet, microfiche or CD form.

Nonconformist registers

According to the religious census carried out in 1851, about a quarter of the population were 'Nonconformists' or 'dissenters', i.e. members of Christian religious groups outside the Church of England. These groups include Baptists (from 1611), Congregationalists or Independents (from 1831), Methodists (from 1740), Moravians (from 1738), Presbyterians (from the sixteenth century), Quakers (from the 1650s), Swedenborgians (from 1788) and Unitarians (formalized in 1825). In 1972, the Congregational Church and the Presbyterian Church combined as the United Reformed Church.

Roman Catholics are not, strictly speaking, Nonconformists, as Roman Catholicism was the religious denomination of the whole of the British Isles until England became officially Protestant in 1533 and Scotland in 1560. (If anything, it's the Anglicans and Presbyterians (in Scotland) who are not conforming.)

The Wesleyan Methodist Connexion was founded in 1740 by John and Charles Wesley, together with George Whitefield (until 1751). Methodism had various offshoots: the Countess of Huntingdon's Connexion (from 1779), Methodist New Connexion (1797), Primitive Methodists (1811), Bible Christians (1815), Protestant

Methodists (1827), Wesleyan Methodist Association (1836), Wesleyan Methodist Reformers (1849) and Wesleyan Reform Union (1859). The United Methodist Free Churches was formed in 1857 from the Wesleyan Methodist Association (which included the Protestant Methodists) and the majority of the Wesleyan Methodist Reformers. In 1907, the Methodist New Connexion, the United Methodist Free Churches and the Bible Christians joined together to become the United Methodist Church, which, in turn, combined with the Wesleyan Methodists and Primitive Methodists in 1932 to become today's Methodist Church.

Many Nonconformists kept registers of baptisms/births, marriages and burials/deaths, beginning in the sixteenth century. From 1754–1837, marriages of Nonconformists and Roman Catholics had to take place in an Anglican church, with only Quakers and Jews exempted from this restriction and allowed to keep their own marriage registers.

Location of parish registers

English parish registers have been deposited with the local county record office, although there are some pre-1837 registers still in use, not all of which have been copied by the county record office. Most of the registers from Welsh parishes have been deposited with the National Library of Wales, although some are held at the Welsh county record offices. Most parish registers have been microfilmed by the LDS Church, and you can view these at LDS Family History Centres around the world.

In 1837, Nonconformist and Roman Catholic baptismal, marriage and burial registers were called in by the Registrar General. The records are held by The National Archives (TNA) and you can view them on microfilm at the Family Records Centre (FRC) and at TNA. There are several thousand registers, mainly from the eighteenth and nineteenth centuries, most of which are included in the IGI. Many Nonconformist registers remained in their churches, and were later deposited with county record offices.

The FRC and TNA hold Church of England registers from the Greenwich Royal Hospital and Schools, Chelsea Royal Hospital, the

94

Foundling Hospital and the Holborn Lying-in Hospital. In addition, they hold 'Fleet Registers' of clandestine and irregular marriages and a few baptisms that took place in the area around the Fleet prison in London from 1667–1753, when they became illegal.

Although Roman Catholics were legally obliged to marry in the Church of England after Lord Hardwicke's Marriage Act of 1753 up to the introduction of civil registration in 1837, many still married according to Catholic rites. As a result, relatively few Catholic registers were handed in, as they contained evidence of these illegal marriages. Most of the seventy-seven registers handed in were of baptisms.

Between 1742 and 1837, nearly 50,000 births were recorded in a 'General register of births of Protestant dissenters' at Dr Williams' Library in London, set up by Baptists, Congregationalists and Presbyterians. A similar 'Wesleyan Methodist Metropolitan Registry' was established in 1818. The records of these two registeries are available at the FRC and TNA. They're not in the IGI, but many are included in the LDS 'British Isles Vital Record Index', which is available from the LDS Church on CD.

Many family history societies have compiled indexes of the baptisms, marriages and burials that took place in their county. Most of these indexes have been published in booklet, microfiche or CD form. You can view them at a society's research centre (if it has one) and/or the county record office.

The Society of Genealogists (SoG) has copies of a large number of parish registers at its library in London. These cover English, Scottish, Irish and Welsh counties, as well as the Isle of Man, Guernsey and many other countries.

Published Indexes of Parish Registers

The Society of Genealogists (SoG) has published a *National Index of Parish Registers* series of books containing details of the whereabouts and coverage of parish, Nonconformist and Roman Catholic baptismal, marriage and burial registers.

Another useful book is the *Atlas and Index of Parish Registers* (Phillimore, 3rd edition, 2003). This contains maps showing the parishes within each county, as well as nineteenth-century topographical maps, and an index listing the start and end dates of the registers and indexes for each parish.

Parish registers online

Online parish clerks (OPCs)

Few parish registers are available online. A number of counties in England have set up Online Parish Clerk (OPC) websites, however, where volunteers collect, collate and transcribe census returns, church registers, cemetery records and local histories for individual parishes. It was in Cornwall that three family historians (Paul Brewer, Michael McCormick and David Stick) came up with the idea which in January 2001 became the organization of Online Parish Clerks for Cornwall (*www.cornwall-opc.org*). Most of the county's parishes now have a clerk, many of whom have set up websites to provide access free of charge to the transcribed records. You can search a combined database of the baptisms, marriages and burials from all of the transcribed parish registers.

Several other counties (including Cumberland and Westmorland, Devon, Dorset, Kent, Lancashire, Sussex, Warwickshire and Wiltshire) have taken up the OPC idea. Nearly half the Devon parishes have an OPC, virtually all the Dorset parishes have some information online, a large number of parishes in Lancashire are covered (but few of those in Manchester) and around 30 per cent of Warwickshire parishes have an OPC, but only a small number of Kent, Sussex and Wiltshire parishes are covered by the scheme so far.

International Genealogical Index (IGI)

The Church of Jesus Christ of Latter-day Saints (LDS) has created an International Genealogical Index (IGI) of baptisms and marriages, which you can search online free of charge at the Family Search

BURIALS in the Parish of *Chatham* in the County of *Kent* in the Year 1813				
Name.	Abode.	When buried.	Age.	By whom the Ceremony was performed.
William Bowden No. 89.	Chatham	April 5th	21	A Rogers
Benjamin Henry Bennett Son of No. 90. Henry & Mary	Do	April 6th	one year 3 days	A Rogers
Catherine Corner Daughter of James & Mary No. 91.	Do	April 8th	2 years & Months	A Rogers
Mary Middleton No. 92.	Do	April 9th	23	A Rogers
James Sharples Son of James & Sarah No. 93.	Do	April 10th	2 years	A Rogers
John Turk Royal Marines Chatham No. 94.		April 10th	35 years	A Rogers
Douglass Henry Smith Son of Peter & No. 95. Eleanor	Gillingham	April 11th	ten Months	A Rogers
William Light Son of William & Mary No. 96.	Chatham	April 11	three years & three Months	A Rogers

Page in a post-1812 register of burials (1813).

website (*www.familysearch.org*). Most records indexed in the IGI are from the LDS Church's programme of 'controlled extraction' of entries from parish registers, while some have been submitted by church members. Most Nonconformist registers held by TNA are included in the IGI.

Not all parishes are indexed, and few of those that are in the IGI are covered from 1538 to 1837. You can find which periods are covered at the website of Hugh Wallis (*http://freepages.genealogy.*

rootsweb.com/~hughwallis), through which you can search individual parishes on the IGI.

Tip: Use the IGI with care

You can expand your family tree considerably using the IGI, which is an extremely useful resource. It is, however, an index, and you should take what you find 'with a pinch of salt', until you've checked it against the original records or other documents. Many parishes are either not covered by the IGI at all, or only to a limited extent, and the IGI can only index what exists in the parish register, so any gaps there will be gaps in the IGI too (unless a member of the LDS Church has added some information taken from a family Bible or elsewhere).

To illustrate: my great-great-grandparents John McKenzie and Christian Gow married in the parish of Kirkmichael, Perthshire in 1832, and their first son was born in the neighbouring parish of Moulin in the following year. I found a baptism on the IGI for a Christian Gow in Moulin in 1811, which seemed likely to be my ancestor. Later, however, I discovered (from her mother's 1855 death certificate) that 'my' Christian's family had moved to Kirkmichael from Blair Atholl twenty-nine years earlier. 'My' Christian appears not to be on the IGI at all, although Blair Atholl is covered for the relevant years.

Family History Online

The Federation of Family History Societies has set up the Family History Online website (*www.familyhistoryonline.net*). On a pay-per-view basis, you can search its databases of records (including baptisms, marriages and burials) transcribed by family history societies in England and Wales for most English and a few Welsh counties.

Phillimore's Marriages

At the pay-per-view Family Relatives site (*www.familyrelatives.org*), you can search for marriages in the twenty-six English counties included in the transcriptions of marriage registers published by Phillimore and Company in the late nineteenth and early twentieth centuries.

You can view digitized copies of Phillimore's marriage transcriptions for some parishes in Cornwall and Derbyshire free of charge at UK Genealogy Archives (*www.uk-genealogy.org.uk/Registers/index.html*).

FreeREG

The FreeREG website *http://freereg.rootsweb.com* contains a database of baptisms, marriages and burials from some counties in England, Scotland and Wales. This is a sister site to FreeBMD (see Chapter 5) and FreeCEN (see Chapter 6), and is still in the early stages of development.

Marriage indexes

Several marriage and marriage licence indexes are accessible online. The British Origins (*www.britishorigins.com*) website contains Boyd's Marriage Index, which includes over 7 million names and covers over 4,000 English and Welsh parishes (1538–1840), although none completely. In addition, the site holds a list of nearly 700,000 marriage licence allegations (applications) made between 1694 and 1850.

At Ancestry.co.uk (*www.ancestry.co.uk*) you can search the 200,000 entries in Pallot's Marriage Index (1780–1837), which focuses mainly on London and Middlesex, but includes index entries for marriages in thirty-eight other counties of England and Wales. Ancestry also has a number of databases containing parish and probate information for some English, Scottish, Irish and Welsh counties.

The National Library of Wales has put online an index of applications for marriage licences covering the period 1616–1837. You can search the index at *www.llgc.org.uk:81*. The applications cover the whole of Wales, as well as some Shropshire and Herefordshire border parishes that were included in Welsh dioceses at that time.

Annotated burials at Westbury-on-Severn

Chris Newall has set up a website of 'Annotated Burials at Westbury on Severn 1889–1895' (*www.rebus.demon.co.uk/wos_br.htm*). These are some of the burials in this riverside parish in Gloucestershire, where the vicar, the Revd Leonard Wilkinson, wrote notes in the margin of the register.

The burials include those of John Bellamy, aged eighty-five, reputed to have been the oldest showman in England, who had for many years travelled the country with architectural models made of cork. There was also Blanche Boseley, aged sixty-nine, who was living in the workhouse. According to the Revd Wilkinson, Blanche was the last representative of a family that had once occupied a proud position in Westbury. Her father had apparently rebuilt the Severn Mill, and moved it to the site that it occupied in the 1890s.

Revd Wilkinson comments that the winter of 1890–91 was long and hard, with the number of deaths 'much in excess of the average'. There were outbreaks of diphtheria, with five unrelated children under the age of eleven dying in 1897 and four in 1900. He may have been suspicious about some of the deaths, such as that of Maria Wood, aged sixty, who had only just received a legacy of several hundred pounds.

In a few cases, there is a good deal of information contained in the comment. Revd Wilkinson writes that Alice Hester Coleman, aged forty, was the wife of John Coleman, a builder, and had been missing since 28 January 1898. She was found drowned in the Severn at Gloucester three days later, and seemed to have fallen into the river at the city's Westgate Bridge at about 10.30 p.m. on the same day she went missing.

Other links to online parish records

You can find links to other websites holding parish records at the Census Finder (*www.censusfinder.com*), UKBMD (*www.ukbmd. org.uk*), GENUKI (*www.genuki.org.uk*), England Gen Web (*www. rootsweb.com/~engwgw*), Wales Gen Web (*www.walesgenweb.com*), Cyndi's List (*www.cyndislist.com*) and One-Place Studies Index (*www. wirksworth.org.uk/A43-OPS.htm*).

Digitization of parish registers

The LDS Church is in the process of digitizing the parish registers of many of the counties of England and Wales, which will then become available online at some point in the future. Genealogy Supplies is digitizing TNA's collections of non-parochial (i.e. Nonconformist, including Baptist, Methodist, Presbyterian and Quaker), foreign and maritime births, marriages and deaths, some of which had become available online by the end of 2007.

National Burial Index (NBI)

The Federation of Family History Societies (FFHS) has organized the publication on CD of a National Burial Index (NBI) of English and Welsh burial records from parish registers, bishop's transcripts, other existing transcripts and printed registers. The NBI does not contain any monumental inscriptions, however.

The first edition of the NBI was published in 2001 on two CDs, containing around 5.5 million burials from over 4,400 parish, Nonconformist and cemetery registers. These mainly covered the period 1813 to *c.* 1850. Coverage was patchy, ranging from very good (708,000 entries for the West Riding of Yorkshire, 616,000 for Lincolnshire and over 400,000 for Suffolk, Warwickshire and Worcestershire) to very low (fewer than 1,000 for Hampshire, Leicestershire, Monmouthshire and Montgomeryshire). Some counties were not included at all, because their family history societies chose not to participate, preferring to sell their transcriptions (in booklet, microfiche and CD form) direct to family historians.

Coverage improved considerably when the second edition of the

NBI was published in 2004 on four CDs. This time over 13.2 million burials were included, from over 8,000 registers. Whereas forty counties were included in the first edition (counting Yorkshire as three plus the City of York), the second contained nine more counties plus the Isle of Man. The West Riding of Yorkshire still had most entries, with 1.7 million burials, but some counties with few entries in the first edition were much better represented in the second. The number of entries for Dorset rose from 1,000 to 286,000, Essex from 48,000 to 508,000, Leicestershire from under 1,000 to 329,000, Nottinghamshire from none to 281,000, Somerset from 2,000 to 755,000, and Sussex from none to 315,000.

You can find details of the counties, places and time periods covered in the NBI at the FFHS website (*www.ffhs.org.uk/General/Projects/NBIcounties.htm*). Most counties' entries in the NBI are also available at the FFHS Family History Online (FHO) pay-per-view website (*www.familyhistoryonline.net*). In some cases, the online information contains details not in the NBI (such as the Worcestershire Burials Index on FHO, which includes abode, occupation and status).

Glossary

Anglican	Belonging to the Church of England
Archdeaconry	Subdivision of a diocese
Bishop's transcripts	Copies of parish registers sent to the bishop or archdeacon in whose diocese or archdeaconry the parish lay.
Boyd's Marriage Index	Index of over 7 million entries from 1538–1840
Chapelry	Subdivision of a large parish
Commonwealth	Form of government (effectively a republic) of Britain and Ireland from 1649–60

Deanery	Group of parishes forming a subdivision of an archdeaconry
Diocese	Area administered by a bishop
Dissenter	Member of a Christian religious group outside the Church of England, e.g. Methodist or Baptist
Extra-parochial area	Sparsely inhabited area not part of any parish
Hardwicke Marriage Act (1753)	Act of Parliament that required marriages in England and Wales to take place in an Anglican church, with Quaker and Jewish marriages the only exceptions. Marriages had to be recorded in separate registers from baptisms and burials
International Genealogical Index (IGI)	Computerized index of births/baptisms and marriages/banns compiled by the Church of Jesus Christ of Latter-day Saints
Monumental inscription	Inscription on a gravestone or a tablet inside or outside a church
National Burial Index (NBI)	Computerized index of burials in England and Wales
Nonconformist	Member of a Christian religious group outside the Church of England, e.g. Methodist or Baptist
Online parish clerk (OPC)	Volunteer who collects, collates and transcribes parish registers, census returns, cemetery records and local histories for an individual parish
Pallot's Marriage Index	Index of around 200,000 entries from 1780–1837
Parish	Area providing payment to a priest
Phillimore's marriages	Transcriptions of marriages in (not all) parishes in twenty-six English counties
Province	Group of dioceses administered by an

	archbishop. In England and Wales (until 1921), there were two: Canterbury and York
Rose Act (1812)	Act of Parliament that required baptisms and burials to be recorded in separate registers with headed columns
Township	Group of dwellings within a parish

8

Wills and administrations

Until 1858, English and Welsh wills were 'proved' (i.e. confirmed) and letters of administration granted (where the deceased person didn't leave a will) in church courts. The principal courts were those of the two provinces of the Church of England, Canterbury and York, each of which is headed by an archbishop. The Prerogative Court of Canterbury (PCC), which actually sat in London rather than Canterbury, had overall charge of probate in England south of Cheshire, Nottinghamshire and Yorkshire, as well as in virtually all of Wales. The Prerogative Court of York (PCY), in the City of York, had overall responsibility in the north of England (covering the counties of Cheshire, Cumberland, County Durham, Lancashire, Northumberland, Nottinghamshire, Westmorland and Yorkshire, as well as the Isle of Man).

Each province was divided into dioceses, in the charge of bishops, who each had his consistory court, and (except in Wales) dioceses were in turn divided into archdeaconries. Each archdeacon had his court too. As well as these ecclesiastical areas and their courts, there were areas known as 'peculiars'. A peculiar was a parish or group of parishes (not necessarily in the same county) exempt from the control of archdeacons (and sometimes bishops). There were over 300 ecclesiastical courts of all types in England and Wales.

When someone died, his will would usually be proved in the court of the archdeaconry or peculiar where he died. If the testator had possessions in more than one of these areas within the same diocese, then the will would be proved in the bishop's consistory court. If, however, his possessions were in more than one diocese, the archbishop's prerogative court would prove the will. If the testator had possessions in both provinces, then the will would be proved in the PCC, as the senior court, which also dealt with the estates of people who died overseas or at sea.

There was a property qualification of £5 for wills proved at the prerogative courts, but this was not adjusted to take account of inflation. By the 1830s, a third of English and Welsh wills were proved at the PCC, and many of the smaller courts were doing little business. This was partly because, from the early nineteenth century, the Bank of England would accept only grants of probate by the PCC in cases where government stock was involved.

In 1858, the ecclesiastical courts were closed and responsibility for probate was transferred to a new civil registry in London, something that had first been tried out from 1651–60, during the Commonwealth period. During that time, a Court for Proving of Wills and Granting of Administrations was set up to deal with all wills and administrations in England and Wales. This court took the place of the PCC in London, and its records were merged with the PCC's after the restoration of the monarchy.

Tip: Using death duties to find a will

Death duties had to be paid on a deceased person's estate (excluding freehold property before 1853) from 1796. The death duty registers (up to 1903) are held by TNA, and show:

- where and when the testator died;
- the value of his or her personal estate;
- information on the executors;
- details of the beneficiaries of the will, and their relationship to the deceased;
- any special arrangements;
- the amount of death duty paid.

You may find later additions to the record, showing the date of death of the deceased's spouse, death or marriage dates of the beneficiaries, birth dates of any posthumous children and grandchildren, and changes of address.

Location of wills and administrations before 1858

The National Archives/Family Records Centre

The National Archives (TNA) hold PCC wills from 1384–1857 and administrations from 1559–1858. Death duty records (1796–1858) indicate in which court a will was proved, as well as providing other useful information on the deceased person. You can view all of these records on microfilm at TNA and at the Family Records Centre (FRC).

Borthwick Institute

The Borthwick Institute at the University of York holds copies of the wills and administrations for the PCY and the local courts within the Diocese of York. You'll find the records of the Archdeaconry of Richmondshire (in the north-west of Yorkshire), however, which was transferred from the Diocese of York to the Diocese of Chester in 1541, at West Yorkshire Archive Service in Leeds.

Although Nottinghamshire was part of the Diocese of York up to 1837, Nottinghamshire wills proved in the Exchequer Court of York were transferred to Nottinghamshire Archives in Nottingham in 1972.

County record offices

You'll find wills proved and administrations granted in the English lower courts at the appropriate county and diocesan record office. As the boundaries of dioceses were not the same as county boundaries, you may well find that the ecclesiastical court records are not in the record office of the geographical county in which the testator died. Probate records for Derbyshire, for instance, are at Lichfield Record Office in Staffordshire.

National Library of Wales

Welsh wills and administrations are held at the National Library of Wales (NLW) in Aberystwyth, where there is a computerized index. This is not online, unfortunately. The courts covered are:

- Bangor (1635–1858);
- Brecon (1543–1858);
- Chester – Welsh wills only (1557–1858);
- Hawarden peculiar (1554–1858);
- Llandaf (1568–1857);
- St Asaph (1565–1857);
- St David's (1556–1858).

The NLW has copies of the civil will indexes for England and Wales, as well as copies of the wills (for all Welsh counties except Montgomeryshire) from 1858–1941.

Society of Genealogists

The Society of Genealogists (SoG) has copies of the PCC, PCY and most local will indexes, as well as those for death duty records. Some are in printed form, while others are on microfiche and microfilm. You can also view copies of many indexes at the LDS Church's Family History Centres.

Location of wills and administrations in the London area before 1858

London Metropolitan Archives

The London Metropolitan Archives (LMA) hold wills proved and administrations granted by:

- Consistory Court of London from the end of the fifteenth century to 1858 (as well as indexes from 1362–1559 for wills at the Guildhall Library), the superior court for the Diocese of London;
- Archdeaconry Court of Middlesex (Middlesex Division) from 1608–11 and 1662–1810, responsible for twenty-six parishes in Middlesex, around half in the West End of London and half in rural Middlesex;
- Commissary Court of the Bishop of Winchester in the Archdeaconry of Surrey (1662–1858), covering all of Surrey, except the peculiars;

- Archdeaconry Court of Surrey (1480–1858), also covering all of Surrey, except the peculiars.

Guildhall Library

At the Guildhall Library in the City of London, you'll find the records of:

- Commissary Court of London (1374–1857), responsible for about half the parishes in the City and Middlesex;
- Archdeaconry Court of London (1393–1807), covering around forty City parishes and three adjoining parishes in Middlesex;
- Peculiar Court of the Dean and Chapter of St Paul's Cathedral (1535–1840), whose jurisdiction covered four parishes in the City and five in Middlesex;
- Royal Peculiar of St Katharine by the Tower (1698–1793).

Lambeth Palace Library

Lambeth Palace in London is the home of the Archbishop of Canterbury. Its library holds records for:

- Peculiar Court of the Deanery of Croydon (1602 and 1614–1841), responsible for thirteen parishes in Surrey and two in Middlesex;
- Deanery of the Arches (1620–1780 and 1832), covering thirteen parishes in the City.

City of Westminster Archives Centre

The centre holds wills proved and administrations granted by the Royal Peculiar of the Dean and Chapter of Westminster (1504–1803), most of whose jurisdiction (three parishes in Middlesex and parts of two in the City) had passed by the eighteenth century to the Consistory Court of London or the Archdeaconry Court of Middlesex.

Corporation of London Records Office

The records of the Court of Husting (1258–1688) are held here. This was the court of the City corporation, with jurisdiction there and in the liberties (areas outside the City's jurisdiction).

Hampshire Record Office

The office holds the records of the Consistory Court of Winchester, whose jurisdiction covered Surrey and Hampshire, except the peculiars.

Centre for Kentish Studies

The centre holds the records of:

- Consistory Court of Canterbury (1396–1857), responsible for fifty-seven parishes in the Diocese of Canterbury;
- Archdeaconry Court of Canterbury (1449–1858), covering the remaining parishes in the Diocese of Canterbury;
- Consistory Court of Rochester (1440–1858), with jurisdiction over the whole of the Diocese of Rochester;
- Archdeaconry Court of Rochester (1635–1858), also covering the whole of the Diocese of Rochester.

Location of wills and administrations from 1858

Principal Probate Registry

Microfiche indexes of civil wills (1858–1943) are at the Principal Probate Registry in London, where you can order a copy of a will. From 1858–70, wills and administrations are indexed separately. You'll also find copies of the indexes at the FRC, TNA, SoG and many county record offices and family history societies. Commonwealth period wills are held with the PCC records.

Example of a will proved in the Consistory Court of Gloucester in 1847

In the name of God amen. I, James Sanford of the parish of Huntley in the County of Gloucester, blacksmith, being in perfect mind and memory – thanks be to God for it – calling unto mind the mortality of my body, and knowing that it is appointed for all men once to die, do make and ordain this my last will and testament, that is to say principally and first of all: I give and recommend my soul into the hand of almighty God that gave it and my body to the Earth to be buried in as plain a way as can be, and as touching my worldly estate, wherewith it has pleased God to bless me with in this life, I give, devise and dispose of the same in the following form and manner, that is to say . . .

[The above preamble is a standard form of words common to English and Welsh wills. After that come the bequests:]

*. . . first, I give, devise and bequeath to my daughter **Eliza Sanford** twenty pounds of lawful money of England, to be raised and levied out of my estate, together with my household goods now being in my present dwelling house in the parish aforesaid. Besides, I give to her, the said **Eliza Sanford**, her mother's gold ring, beside her share in the rest of my estate, ready money, securities for money, casks, hogsheads, harecloths, implements of husbandry, tools and all moveable effects that are on my land or in my outbuildings, and after my decease, I give, devise and bequeath all and every my said cottage, tenement or dwelling house, orchards, gardens and outbuildings, and all other my personal estate of what nature soever the same shall be unto my said sons and daughters, that is to say **James Sanford, Mary Ann Longney, Harriet Bright, William Sanford, Eliza Sanford and Henry Sanford**, that are severally living or his or her or their heirs and executors or administrators and assigns to be sold, and after my debts are paid, to be equally divided share and share alike between my above-named children,*

*but my son **James** being dead, my desire is that the share that would have come to him, that is, **James Sanford**, if he had been alive, to be put out to interest in trust, and his widow to have the interest till the youngest child is sixteen, and then they, that is, the children of my late son **James Sanford**, shall divide the proportion assigned for the aforesaid **James Sanford** deceased amongst themselves share and share alike, that is to say **Elizabeth, John, James, William, Henry, Sarah, Richard and Harriet Sanford** that are severally living or his or her or their heirs and executors or administrators and assigns.*

[It's quite normal to find children mentioned in a will. In this case, however, even some of the grandchildren are listed, because of the early death of their father (in 1840, he had drowned in the canal at the docks in Lydney, Gloucestershire at the age of forty-two).]

*And I do hereby nominate, constitute and appoint my son-in-law **James Bright** and my son **Henry Sanford** as trustees for the children of my late son **James Sanford** until the youngest living child shall have attained the age of sixteen years.*

*And I do hereby nominate, constitute and appoint my son-in-law **James Bright** and my son **Henry Sanford** executors of this my last will and testament, hereby revoking all former wills by me at any time heretofore made.*

In witness whereof, I have to this my last will and testament, contained in one sheet of paper, set my hand and seal, this ninth day of March in the year of our Lord one thousand eight hundred and fortyseven.

*Signed, sealed, published, pronounced and declared by the testator **James Sanford** as my last will and testament in the presence of us who, in his presence and presence of each other, have hereto subscribed our names.*

> *Witnessed this ninth day of March 1847 in presence of each other and by request of* **James Sanford:**
>
> **Stephen Hemsted Murley**, surgeon, Huntley, Gloucestershire
>
> **Harriet Murley**, Huntley
>
> **Anselm Bailey**, *wheelwright and machine maker, Huntley*

Wills online

Documents Online

Digitized images of the entire collection of over a million wills proved at the PCC between 1384 and 1858 are accessible on a pay-per-view basis at TNA's Documents Online website (*www.nationalarchives. gov.uk/documentsonline*). The administrations granted by the PCC (1559–1858) are not available online, however. You can search the database by surname, forename, place, occupation – there are 2,609 wills by labourers – or date, or any combination of these. The average length of a will is one page, although they can run to more than twenty pages. The database also contains 'sentences': judgments about disputed wills.

Documents Online provides access to nearly 70,000 records from the death duty registers (1796–1811). The records available online are those concerned with death duties on 'personal estates' (i.e. not freehold) where the probate was dealt with by the so-called 'country courts', i.e. those other than the PCC. Searching the databases is free of charge, but you do have to pay to download a document.

Will of John Mason, proved in Essex in 1713.

British Origins

At this subscription-based website (*www.britishorigins.com*), you can search the indexes of over 60,000 Bank of England will extracts (1717–1845). These are extracts of wills of those who died with investments in public funds, as well as abstracts of orders made for stockholders who went bankrupt or were declared lunatic. The original records are held by the Bank of England.

You can search an incomplete index of over 200,000 PCC wills held by TNA, covering the period 1750–1800. Hard copies of both the Bank of England will extracts and the PCC wills can be ordered online at extra cost, and these are then delivered by post.

British Origins has an index of over 5,000 wills proved at the Archdeaconry Court of London also from 1750–1800, the wills being held at the Guildhall Library in London. The court had jurisdiction over about half the parishes in the City of London and some nearby parishes in Middlesex (including Shoreditch and Clerkenwell). In addition, its jurisdiction covered St Botolph Aldgate, to which many seamen who died abroad were ascribed as resident.

Another index is that of 3,000 depositions made to the Consistory Court of London (1703–13), the main court dealing with separation and matrimonial disputes, among other things. The records are held by the London Metropolitan Archives.

All of the above databases have been created from indexes compiled by the Society of Genealogists (SoG). If you're a member of the society, you can carry out unlimited searches on all SoG databases free of charge for seventy-two hours once a quarter, and also get a 20 per cent discount on orders made via British Origins for hard copies provided by the society.

Other indexes at British Origins are those covering wills proved in the Prerogative and Exchequer Courts of York and the peculiar courts of the Province of York. The York Medieval Probate index covers over 10,000 wills proved in the Prerogative and Exchequer Courts of York between 1267 and 1500. British Origins is currently indexing the wills proved in those courts after 1500, beginning at 1858 and working backwards.

The York Peculiars Probate index includes over 25,000 wills proved in the fifty-four peculiar courts of the Province of York from 1383–1883. You can place an online order for copies of the wills, which are held at the Borthwick Institute, and they'll be delivered by post.

British Origins has an Inheritance Disputes Index (1574–1714) to over 26,000 lawsuits in the English Court of Chancery concerned with the inheritance of money or real estate. The records of these chancery cases, which typically involved several members of the same family, are held by TNA.

Bristol City Council

Bristol Record Office's website has a downloadable index of wills proved between 1793 and 1858 at *www.bristol-city.gov.uk/ccm/navigation/leisure-and-culture/libraries/archives.*

Cheshire County Council

Cheshire County Council's wills database (*www.cheshire.gov.uk/Recordoffice/Wills*) indexes 130,000 wills, administrations and inventories from 1492–1940. You can't view the actual wills online, but you can order a document by post, using the document reference from the search results.

Derbyshire wills database

Family historian Michael Spencer has created an index of Derbyshire wills and administrations, which you'll find on the website of John Palmer's one-place study of Wirksworth (*www.wirksworth.org.uk/WILLS.htm*). The index covers 35,000 wills from 1525–1928 and 1,800 administrations from 1858–73. The wills after 1858 are at the Derbyshire Record Office in Matlock, while those before that date are at Lichfield Record Office in Staffordshire.

Gloucestershire County Council

Gloucestershire County Council's Genealogical Database (*www.gloucestershire.gov.uk/index.cfm?ArticleID=1335*) lets you search an index of all wills proved in the local courts between 1541 and 1858.

You can order these by post, using the reference number from the index.

Kent Archaeological Society

Kent Archaeological Society has an index (and some transcripts) of over 2,000 Kentish wills transcribed by a lifetime member of the society, Leland Lewis Duncan (1862–1923). You'll find the transcriptions online at the society's website (*www.kentarchaeology.org. uk/Research/Libr/Wills/WillsIntro.htm*). The wills include those proved in Rochester Consistory Court from 1440–1561.

London Metropolitan Archives (LMA)

LMA's London Signatures (*www.cityoflondon.gov.uk/corporation/ wills*) is a pay-per-view website at which you can download digitized wills and administrations. The site contains 10,000 wills proved and administrations granted in the Archdeaconry Court of Middlesex between 1608 and 1810 (but mainly covering the periods 1608–11 and 1662–1780). The court's jurisdiction didn't cover all of Middlesex, but only two areas of the county: part of central London (from Kensington to St Clement Danes (just outside the City of London)), and what were at that time rural areas outside London (including parishes such as Twickenham and Staines).

Wills from other courts (the Consistory Court of London, and the Commissary and Archdeaconry Courts of Surrey) are to be added to the site later, as are marriage bonds and allegations, apprenticeship indentures and settlement certificates. Searching the database is free, but there is a charge to download an image.

Wiltshire County Council

The Wiltshire and Swindon Record Office is creating an online catalogue of its collection of 105,000 wills and administrations, which cover the whole of Wiltshire and Berkshire, parts of Dorset, and Uffculme in Devon.

The first part of the index became available online at *http://history. wiltshire.gov.uk/heritage* at the end of 2006, together with digitized images of some of the wills. More images are being added as they become available, although it may be some time before all the wills are online.

Other will abstracts online

The GENUKI website (*www.genuki.org.uk*) has links to various sites with calendars of wills, abstracts, etc. Click on 'Probate Records' on the pages for individual counties. Family History Online (*www.familyhistoryonline.net*) includes probate indexes for Northamptonshire and Rutland (87,000 entries), Shropshire and Montgomeryshire (31,000), Staffordshire (1,000) and Suffolk (11,000).

Glossary

Administration, letters of (abbreviated to admon.)	Authority to act as executor in the absence of a will
Commissary court	Bishop's court in one archdeaconry
Consistory court	Bishop's court in a diocese
Death duties	Tax on a deceased person's estate
PCC	Prerogative Court of Canterbury, the highest-level court of the Church of England
PCY	Prerogative Court of York, the highest court in the Province of York, but subsidiary to the PCC
Peculiar court	Church court exempt from the control of an archdeacon or bishop
Probate	Confirmation of the executor(s) of a will

9

More sources for Welsh ancestry

For family history, Wales is usually taken together with England, as the two have shared a government and legal system since the end of the thirteenth century. The forcible union of Wales with England was confirmed by King Henry VIII in 1536. In several ways, however, Wales is quite different from England.

The Welsh language

All road signs and public notices in Wales are written not only in English but also in Welsh, a Celtic language closely related to Breton and more distantly to Irish and Scottish Gaelic. The ancestor language of Welsh was probably spoken over the whole of Britain in Roman days.

According to the 2001 census, the Welsh language was spoken by 580,000 people living in Wales (21 per cent of the population over the age of three). Almost 70 per cent spoke the language in Gwynedd in the north-west, compared to just under 10 per cent in Monmouthshire in the south-east. A hundred years earlier, about half the population of Wales and Monmouthshire over three years old could speak Welsh, and 280,000 of those could speak only Welsh. Despite these figures, English had been the official language since 1536, and there was little use of Welsh in parish registers.

You may find Welsh inscriptions on gravestones, however, and John Ball's Welsh Family History Archive website (see below) can be helpful with its page of 'Welsh words and phrases on gravestones'. John has provided an English translation of a monumental inscription in Welsh, as well as sample phrases and a list of months of the year.

Surnames and patronymics

Until the middle of the eighteenth century, most Welsh people used patronymics rather than surnames, so that Evan, son of William Roberts, would have been known as Evan Williams rather than Evan Roberts. Evan's grandfather might have been Robert Richards. The upper classes had begun to use surnames about 200 years earlier, however.

Prior to sticking an 's' on the end of the father's name, the custom was to use 'ap' (son of), so that the Evan above would have been called Evan ap William ap Robert ap Richard. The 'p' of 'ap' (or in some cases a 'b') sometimes got attached to the patronymic to form surnames like Probert, Pritchard or Bevan.

Tip: Searching in the IGI for baptisms in Wales

The LDS Church has assumed in its International Genealogical Index (IGI) that for Wales (excluding Monmouthshire, which is treated as part of England) up to the end of 1812, in all baptisms the father's forename will become the child's surname, and that after 1812 the child will have the same surname as the father. This is not necessarily what actually happened, however. Many families had already switched from patronymics to a fixed surname by 1812, while some continued using patronymics until the middle of the nineteenth century.

My wife's 3× great-grandfather Richard Cole married Mary Prichard in 1808, and several of their children were born in Llanigon and Hay-on-Wye in Breconshire. There was no sign of Mary Prichard's own baptism in the IGI, but we did find a Mary Thomas, baptized in Llanigon in 1789, whose father was a Thomas Prichard.

The microfiche version of the IGI has both surname and given name (forename) indexes for Wales. Ideally, to search the online version of the IGI at the Family Search website

---

(*www.familysearch.org*) for Welsh baptisms before 1813, you would be able to specify the child's forename (e.g. 'Mary') and the father's surname (e.g. 'Prichard') in the search, and the results would list all matching children, irrespective of the surnames (such as 'Thomas') used for them in the IGI. Unfortunately, this doesn't happen. You *can* search the online IGI with the child's forename and father's surname (provided you don't specify a county), but you won't get the desired results. For the period before 1813, you'll get in your results only those entries in the IGI that have been submitted by members of the LDS Church, where the child's surname is the same as the father's.

To try to find a Welsh baptism before 1813 online, there are two main possibilities, neither of which is particularly quick. On the one hand, you can search the IGI for Wales using only the child's forename. To make the search manageable (and possible for the LDS computer), it's best to specify also a county and a particular year. For example, searching for 'Mary' in Brecon in 1789 will give you seventy-five results.

Alternatively, you can search the IGI using Hugh Wallis's website (*http://freepages.genealogy.rootsweb.com/~hugh wallis*) to enable you to target your search to a single parish. You're not able to specify a forename in your search, but only a surname, which you'll need to leave blank in this case. This will cause an entire batch of IGI entries to be listed, and you'll have to look through them all (and there may be a few thousands) for the forename you're searching for.

Local and national government in Wales

From 1536, Wales consisted of thirteen counties, including Monmouth-shire, which gradually came to be considered part of England. With the reorganization of local government in 1974, eleven of the Welsh counties were grouped together into four 'super-counties' (Gwynedd,

Clwyd, Powys and Dyfed), Glamorgan was divided into three parts and Monmouthshire was officially returned to Wales under its old name of Gwent.

In 1996, there was a further reorganization, under which twenty-two 'unitary authorities' were created. Clwyd and Dyfed were broken up again, Anglesey separated from Gwynedd, Glamorgan's three parts became seven, and Gwent was split into three small urban authorities and a rump, which was once again called Monmouthshire. Only Powys remained unchanged.

Wales has had its own devolved government with an elected Assembly since 1999. This is not able to pass its own laws or raise taxes (unlike the devolved Scottish Parliament), but this may well change if the UK moves to a federal structure with parliaments for England, Scotland, Wales and Northern Ireland.

Differences between the main Welsh and English records

While Welsh birth, marriage and death certificates are the same as English ones (but with the pre-printed text in Welsh as well as English), the 1891 and 1901 census returns have an additional column stating whether a person could speak English, Welsh or both.

Welsh birth certificate.

Although, as in England, Welsh parishes were instructed in 1538 to keep a register of baptisms, marriages and burials, you will find that only one of the 900 parishes and chapelries in Wales (Gwaenysgor in Flintshire) actually began its register entries in that year. Around six registers were started before 1560, and about seventy before 1600.

While almost all of the parishes in the diocese of St Asaph in the north-east of Wales began keeping registers before 1754, over half of those in the southern diocese of St Davids did not. There are no bishop's transcripts starting before 1662 for anywhere in Wales, virtually none for the eighteenth century for the archdeaconries of Cardigan and St Davids (Pembrokeshire), and very few for the diocese of Llandaff (Glamorgan and Monmouthshire) before 1723.

Welsh birth, marriage and death certificates

Since 1963, Welsh birth and death certificates contain general information and column headings in both English and Welsh, although the details on the person who was born or had died are in English only. This is because this information is usually photocopied from the original register entry. On the Welsh marriage certificate, even the column entries are in English alone, as these form part of the original entry. Modern copies of pre-1963 registrations are also printed on to the bilingual certificates, although the original certificates would have been in English only.

Welsh Nonconformists

Partly in reaction to English domination of Wales, Welshmen and -women deserted the Church of England for Methodist, Independent and Baptist chapels. According to the Religious Census of 1851, almost four-fifths of Welsh churchgoers were Nonconformists. From 1754 to 1837, however, Nonconformists (apart from Quakers and Jews) had to marry in the Church of England, and many were buried in parish church graveyards. In 1920, the Welsh part of the Church of England was disestablished and renamed the Church in Wales.

Welsh websites

English and Welsh sites

As Wales has been administered together with England for nearly 500 years, the websites that contain digitized versions, transcriptions and indexes of English family history records also contain information about those for Wales. The various census websites mentioned in Chapter 6, for instance, also cover Wales.

The Federation of Family History Societies' Family History Online website (*www.familyhistoryonline.net*) includes pay-per-view databases for the historic counties of Breconshire, Cardiganshire, Denbighshire, Glamorgan, Monmouthshire, Montgomeryshire and Radnorshire. The databases include entries in the National Burial Index as well as some census, marriage and monumental inscription records.

At the pay-per-view Documents Online website of the National Archives (TNA) (*www.nationalarchives.gov.uk/documentsonline*), Welshmen and -women are included in the wills and administrations (as Wales came under the jurisdiction of the Prerogative Court of Canterbury).

All thirteen historic Welsh counties are included in the LDS International Genealogical Index (IGI), online at its free Family Search website (*www.familysearch.org*). Be aware, however, that the LDS Church includes Monmouthshire with England.

There is a great deal of free information about Welsh family history in the GENUKI pages for Wales (*www.genuki.org.uk/big/wal*), including transcriptions of many interesting articles from the National Library of Wales (NLW) journal on topics ranging from 'Dress and dress materials for a serving maid c.1600' through 'Dissent in the counties of Glamorgan and Monmouth' to 'Welsh cattle drovers in the 19th century'. There are pages for each individual county and even for each parish, where you can find out where copies of the church registers are kept.

General Welsh websites

As well as all the sites mentioned above, there are various (mainly free) websites dedicated to Wales alone. You can discover a wide

variety of useful information about Wales on the Data Wales (*www.
data-wales.co.uk*) website. There are articles on Welsh surnames,
emigration to Patagonia, the Welsh flag, the Celts and the industri-
alization of the South Wales valleys during the nineteenth century.

Describing itself as 'the website for Welsh cultural history', Gathering the Jewels (*www.gtj.org.uk*) contains seventeen sections on
topics ranging from 'agriculture and food production' to 'working
lives'. This free website also includes articles on 'Discovering Your
Own History' and a Family History Quiz. It was set up by a group
of libraries, museums and archives, and contains more than 20,000
images of books, letters, aerial photographs, etc. The images include,
for example, a list of 328 'names of the poor of Brecon 1786',
showing where they lived and the number of children they had.

*Welsh census return 1901, with right-hand column
showing language(s) spoken.*

John Ball's free Welsh Family History Archive (*www.jlb2005.plus.
com/wales*) includes a glossary of Welsh placename elements, a gazetteer and coloured county maps (including those of the neighbouring
English counties Shropshire, Herefordshire and Gloucestershire) from
Tallis's Topographical Dictionary (published in the 1860s), and the
pronunciation of over 200 Welsh placenames. Also included on the
site are Welsh words and phrases on gravestones, and a Welsh
Ancestor List of surnames being researched by visitors to the site.
There are images of the 1873 Returns of Owners of Land for all the

Welsh counties (including Monmouthshire) on the free Online Genealogical Research Engine (OGRE) website at *www.cefnpennar.com*
(but bear in mind that few people actually *owned* land at that time).
The site also contains images of *Pigot's Directory of South Wales
1835* and a few parish registers, plus photographs of some war
memorials and monumental inscriptions.

The free Relative Links: Research in Wales website (*homepages.
rootsweb.com/~riggs/links/Wales.htm*), containing links to many
other family history-related websites for Wales, was originally created
for the Gwent Family History Society.

Regional Welsh websites

North Wales BMD (*www.northwalesbmd.org.uk*) is one of over
twenty websites (most of which are free) that are in the process of
putting the birth, marriage and death indexes of local registrars
online. (You can find the other sites through *www.ukbmd.org.uk*.)
The present-day unitary authorities participating in the scheme are
Conwy County Borough, Flintshire, Gwynedd, Powys and Wrexham
County Borough (which also has its own similar site at (*www.
wrexham.gov.uk/english/community/genealogy/MarriageIndex
SearchForm.cfm*).

Powys Heritage Online (*history.powys.org.uk*) is a free portal to
four websites relating to the large present-day county of Powys
(comprising the historic counties of Montgomeryshire, Radnorshire
and Breconshire). The sites are those of the 'Powys Digital History
Project' for schools, 'Powys: a Day in the Life' project on everyday
life in 1891 and 2002, information on the Powys County Archives
Office in Llandrindod Wells and 'Six Powys Communities Online'
(Machynlleth, Llanidloes, Rhayader, Presteigne, Hay and the Upper
Swansea Valley).

At the City and County of Swansea website, you can search a free
newspaper index (*www2.swansea.gov.uk/_info/cambrian*). Most of
the nearly 400,000 entries are from the *Cambrian*, the first newspaper
printed in Wales (from 1804–1930), but the index also includes
entries from the *South Wales Daily Post* and the *Western Mail*.

The 1841, 1871, 1881 and 1891 censuses for Pembrokeshire are accessible at the CenQuest pay-per-view website (*www.cenquest. co.uk/Home.htm*). CenQuest states that its Pembrokeshire censuses include the town of Cardigan, as well as neighbouring parts of Cardiganshire and Carmarthenshire. Searching is free of charge, and you can purchase transcriptions and digital images for a fee.

Family history society websites

At the website of the Association of Family History Societies of Wales (AFHSW) (*www.fhswales.info*), you can find links to the sites of the individual family history societies for Clwyd, Dyfed, Glamorgan, Gwent, Gwynedd and Powys. As well as being covered by the Powys FHS, Montgomeryshire has its own society.

Two societies that are not members of the AFHSW are the Cardiganshire FHS (*www.heaton.celtic.co.uk/cgnfhs*) and the Carmarthenshire FHS (*www.carmarthenshirefhs.co.uk*). There is also the Morgan Society (*freepages.genealogy.rootsweb.com/~morgan society/index.html*) for people with connections to that surname.

Occupational websites

Until the 1980s, coal mining was a major industry in the valleys of Glamorgan and Monmouthshire in South Wales. Created by former miner John Smith, the free Welsh Coal Mines site (*www.welshcoal mines.co.uk*) contains information about coal mines throughout Wales, together with photographs of them. In a section on mining disasters, you can find over 100 lists of the men who died, with ages and addresses for most of them.

At Bryan Richards's Cardiff Mariners (*www.cardiffmariners.org. uk*) and Swansea Mariners (*www.swanseamariners.org.uk*) websites, you can search for merchant seamen on ships registered in those two ports. There are around 2,000 records on the Cardiff site and nearly 40,000 on the Swansea site. Another useful site is Reg Davies's Welsh Mariners (*www.welshmariners.org.uk*), which contains an online index of 21,000 Welsh merchant masters, mates and engineers from 1800–1945.

National Library of Wales

You can find copies of the 1841 to 1901 censuses of Wales and the border regions of England not only in the Family Records Centre in London, but also in the National Library of Wales in Aberystwyth. The Library also holds copies of the registers of over 500 Welsh parishes, as well as many Nonconformist registers and also wills proved in the Welsh courts before 1858.

The website of the NLW (*www.llgc.org.uk*) provides access to several free databases that you can search online. An index of marriage bonds (required to obtain a marriage licence and avoid the need for banns) from 1661–1837 can be searched online at *www. llgc.org.uk:81*. The index includes some parishes in Shropshire (around Oswestry) and in Herefordshire (the hundred of Ewyas Lacy, which lay between the Golden Valley and the Black Mountains) that were still parts of Welsh dioceses at the period covered by the index.

You can also view online (at *www.llgc.org.uk/drych/Notitiae/nll_ s001.htm*) images of the St Asaph 'Notitiae'. These are lists of householders compiled in the 1680s in 108 of the parishes of the diocese of St Asaph in north-east Wales. The database includes Oswestry and neighbouring parishes in Shropshire, but unfortunately has no index of names.

A third online resource, at *www.llgc.org.uk/sesiwn_fawr/index_ s.htm* and entitled 'Crime and Punishment', contains information about crimes, criminals and punishments from the gaol files of the Court of Great Sessions in Wales from 1730 until it was abolished in 1830. You can search the index in various ways, such as by the name of the accused or the category of the offence.

Also at the NLW website (*www.llgc.org.uk/drych/drych_s071.htm*) are images of the Cardiganshire Constabulary register of criminals (1897–1933), complete with photographs. The criminals are not all local people, and come from as far away as Caithness in Scotland and Limerick in Ireland.

IO

Example English county: Cornwall

During the Middle Ages, Cornwall was considered to be one of the four main parts of Britain, like England, Scotland and Wales. At the time of the Roman occupation (AD 43–c. 410), its inhabitants and those of its neighbour Devon were a British people known as the Dumnonii. Their capital was Isca Dumnoniorum (Isca of the Dumnonians), now called Exeter, the county town of Devon. The Angles, Saxons and Jutes began invading what is now called England around 430, and over the succeeding centuries, Devon came under the control of the West Saxons. In 936, Cornwall acknowledged the overlordship of Wessex, and the River Tamar became its eastern border. The area was administered with England (but had special status, with laws referring to 'England and Cornwall'). Gradually, however, it came to be recognized as an English county. After the Norman Conquest, a number of Cornish manors were consolidated as an earldom. In 1337, this became a duchy, which provides an income to the English monarch's eldest son.

The majority of the 200+ ancient Cornish parishes (including five on the Scilly Isles) constituted the Archdeaconry of Cornwall within the Diocese of Exeter until 1876, when the Archdeaconry became the Diocese of Truro. Over the last 300 years, more than forty new parishes have been created, mainly in the nineteenth century. About a third of the ancient parishes have surviving registers from earlier than 1598, the first year in which transcripts had to be sent to the Bishop of Exeter. The Cornwall Family History Society estimates that around 50–60 per cent of Cornish parishes are covered by the LDS International Genealogical Index (IGI).

Cornish language

In Roman times, the entire population of Britain is thought to have spoken the Celtic Brythonic language. After the Anglo-Saxons had invaded and conquered large parts of southern Britain, the native Britons began speaking the language of the invaders (Old English). Cornwall (like Wales, Cumbria and south-west Scotland) still spoke Brythonic, however. After 577, the people of Cornwall and Wales were divided by the westward advance of the Saxons, and their language developed separately into Cornish (*Kernewek*) and Welsh. Although Welsh is still spoken by half a million people in Wales today, Cornish died out as the main language of the people of Cornwall in 1777. That was the year Dolly Pentreath of Mousehole died, who was reputed to have been the last person whose first language was Cornish. John Davey of Boswednack, who died in 1891, was reputedly the last person with traditional knowledge of Cornish.

In the twentieth century there was a movement to revive Cornish, which led to the founding of the Cornish Language Board in 1967. The Cornish language is now used on placename signs, and even in some branches of Asda. According to the Cornish Language Fellowship (founded by the Language Board in 1979), a few hundred people can speak the language fluently, with 5,000–10,000 able to understand basic phrases.

Cornish surnames

Most Cornish surnames are based on location names, such as Penhaligon (from *pen* head + *helygen* willow) and Trevelyan (*tre* homestead + *melin* mill). The surnames of speakers of other Celtic languages are mainly derived from patronymics (based on the father's forename), such as O'Neill (Irish), MacDonald (Scottish) and Williams (Welsh). Cornish patronymics include Pascoe and Clemmow (descendants of Pask and Clement respectively).

Emigration

Tin mining has been carried out in Cornwall for several thousand years: the 'Tin Islands' were written about by the Greeks before the

Roman conquest, and some writers believe the Phoenicians traded with Cornish mines as early as 1500 BC. Copper mining began in earnest in Cornwall at the end of the seventeenth century. About 150 years later, however, the mines were exhausted, and Cornish miners were forced to look for work overseas.

From 1841–1901 over 300,000 people (mostly miners, referred to as 'Cousin Jacks') emigrated from Cornwall to the United States, Australia, South Africa and Latin America. To put this into perspective, the present population of Cornwall is just over half a million, according to the 2001 census. A database of all emigrants from Cornwall is being compiled by the Cornish Global Migration Programme, whose work is being supported by the Institute of Cornish Studies at Exeter University.

Family history resources in Cornwall

These three types of resource (record office, local studies library and family history society) are typical for English and Welsh counties.

Cornwall Record Office

The Cornwall Record Office (*www.cornwall.gov.uk/indexcfm?articleid =307*) is the official archive for Cornwall, holding copies of most of the parish registers and all of the surviving bishop's transcripts, as well as Methodist, Quaker, Baptist and Congregational registers. Some Cornish census returns and tithe awards are also held. The website describes the Record Office's collections (including a gazetteer of Cornish manors, and correspondence from Matthew Boulton and James Watt to Thomas Wilson, their mining agent in Cornwall), its publications and projects (including the digitization of an 1840 tithe map).

Booking at least two weeks in advance is required, particularly in the summer, when the Record Office is busy. Alternatively, you can commission the staff to search the records for you on payment of a fee.

Cornwall Centre

Previously known as the Cornish Studies Library, the Cornwall Centre (*http://db.cornwall.gov.uk/librarydb/info/details.asp?Ibid=7*) is part of the Cornwall Library Service, and holds copies of the bishop's transcripts of most Cornish parish registers, as well as all of the 1841–1901 census returns for the county. The centre holds 21,000 books and 17,000 pamphlets about Cornwall, 5,000 volumes of periodicals, back copies of forty Cornish newspapers and large numbers of photographs and maps.

Cornwall Family History Society

The Cornwall Family History Society (*www.cornwallfhs.com*) has a research library in Truro, holding all the census returns for Cornwall for 1841–1901, many of which are indexed. The society has also indexed all Cornish marriages up to 1837 and is recording the monumental inscriptions in Cornish graveyards. In addition, it holds many parish register transcripts, family pedigrees, parish histories and much information on emigration, especially to the United States. The society is able to carry out some postal research for members.

Cornish family history information online

The Federation of Family History Societies' Family History Online website (*www.familyhistoryonline.net/database/index.shtml#CON*) provides access to indexes of more than a million Cornish baptisms (from over 300 parishes), about 250,000 marriages and the same number of burials (from over 200 parishes), and over 300,000 monumental inscriptions from gravestones and other monuments (from more than 400 churchyards – about 90 per cent of the total number).

According to the Cornwall Family History Society, the LDS Family Search site also includes baptisms and marriages from about 50–60 per cent of the Cornish parishes in its International Genealogical Index (IGI).

TNA's Documents Online site (*www.nationalarchives.gov.uk/*

documentsonline) includes over 7,000 wills and administrations for people who lived in Cornwall, while its Catalogue (*www.catalogue.nationalarchives.gov.uk*) contains details of more than 1,000 Cornish soldiers discharged to pension between 1760 and 1854.

The GENUKI 'virtual reference library' contains a good deal of information about Cornwall (with links to relevant websites) at *www.genuki.org.uk/big/eng/Cornwall*. Areas covered include church history, the whereabouts of church records, civil registration, court records, trade and other directories, emigration, land and property, maps, medical records, the merchant marine, military records, Cornish names, newspapers, occupations (in particular, mining), poor relief, the population of Cornwall from 1801 (188,269) to 2001 (501,267), wills and probate, and family and local history societies.

Online parish clerks

In 2000 three family historians (Paul Brewer, Michael McCormick and David Stick) came up with the idea which in January 2001 became the organization of Online Parish Clerks (OPCs) (*www.cornwall-opc.org*) for Cornwall. Each of the clerks collects, collates and transcribes local records for a specific parish in Cornwall. Most of the parishes now have clerks, many of whom have set up websites to provide access free of charge to records such as parish registers (baptisms, marriages and burials), census returns, monumental (gravestone) inscriptions and parish histories.

You can see what an online parish clerk can achieve at Sally Cann's website for Camborne parish (*freepages.genealogy.rootsweb.com/~camborneopc*). OPCs don't have to be local to Cornwall: Sally lives in New Zealand.

You can search in some of the baptism, marriage/banns and burial registers of over fifty Cornish churches (including some Non-conformist chapels) through the Cornish Parish Register Index database (*www.cornwalleng.com*), which has been developed in conjunction with the Cornish OPCs.

Since its beginnings in Cornwall, the OPC scheme has also been taken up by several other counties, including Cumberland and

Westmorland, Devon, Dorset, Kent, Lancashire, Sussex, Warwickshire and Wiltshire.

Census transcriptions

The Cornwall Online Census Project (COCP) is part of the UK-wide Free Census Project, and aims to make transcriptions of the 1841–91 censuses available online free of charge. The Cornish 1841, 1851, 1861 and 1891 transcriptions are complete or almost complete, while around half of the 1871 and a quarter of the 1881 returns have also been transcribed. All of these returns, together with a few unchecked 1901 returns are accessible at the COCP website (*http://freepages. genealogy.rootsweb.com/~kayhin/ukocp.html*). You can browse through the census transcriptions for all years, or search for a specific name, either through the Cornish Census Search pages (*http://free pages.genealogy.rootsweb.com/~kayhin/search.html*) or at the Free Census site (*http://freecen.rootsweb.com*).

Monumental inscriptions

A database of over 20,000 monumental inscriptions (MIs) from Cornish churchyards can be searched at the Cornish Cemeteries website (*http://freepages.genealogy.rootsweb.com/~chrisu/cemeteries. htm*) set up by Christine Uphill. The database is mainly composed of transcriptions made by Suezan Elliott between 1998 and 1999.

You can search a similar database of MIs at Michael Kiernan's Cornwall Inscriptions Project site (*www.cornwallinscriptions.co.uk/ index.html*), which contains transcriptions from burial grounds in ten other Cornish parishes plus five churchyards on the Isles of Scilly. The site also has transcriptions of Cornish gravestones in Mexico, Wales and New Zealand.

Cornish Mining

At the Cornish Mining Index website (*www.cornwall-online.co.uk/ genealogy.htm*) set up by Ian Richards, you can search an index of over 16,000 Cornish miners, and also view pictures of some Cornish churches.

The Cornish Mining site (*www.cornish-mining.org.uk*) was created to support a bid to have Cornwall's mining industry landscape recognized as a World Heritage Site by the United Nations Educational, Scientific and Cultural Organization (UNESCO). The bid was successful, and the Cornwall and West Devon Mining Landscape was added to the World Heritage List in 2006. The website contains information on the history of mining in Cornwall, engineers and inventors, working and living conditions, religion, emigration, descriptions of the various mining areas (with links to maps), the geology and wildlife of the mining district, a glossary of mining terms and an interactive map of Cornwall.

You can find out more about the emigration of Cornish miners at the BBC's Legacies website (*www.bbc.co.uk/legacies/immig_emig/ england/cornwall/index.shtml*) and also at *http://members.lycos.co. uk/troonexiles/the_cornish_in_west_cork.htm*, where you can read about 'The Cornish in West Cork' (in the Republic of Ireland) in an article first published in the Cornwall Family History Society's journal. In addition, at the Cornish in Latin America site (*www.projects.ex.ac. uk/cornishlatin/index.php*), you can search for an ancestor in a database containing information on 2,673 migrants.

Victoria County History of Cornwall

Volume I of the Victoria County History (VCH) of Cornwall was published in 1906 (covering general history), and two parts of Volume II in 1924 ('Romano-British Remains' and 'The Domesday Survey'). No further work was carried out until 1998, however, when funding through the Heritage Lottery Fund became possible. A steering group for Cornwall was set up in 2001, and studies covering 'Religious History' and 'Penwith Communities' (at Newlyn and Mousehole) are under way. You can read the draft text of the history of over thirty religious houses in Cornwall, together with information on the Penwith study schedule, at the VCH of Cornwall website (*www. cornwallpast.net*). For more information on the VCH, see Chapter 26.

Historic Cornwall

The Heritage and History pages at Cornwall County Council's website (*www.cornwall.gov.uk/index.cfm?articleid=270*) contain information on topics such as Cornish farming, the Cornish language, railways in Cornwall and a timeline of Cornish history.

Cornish surnames

Many surnames found in Cornwall are derived from words in the Cornish language, which is related to Welsh and Breton. At Jim Thompson's Cornish Surnames website (*http://freepages.history. rootsweb.com/~kernow/index.htm*), you'll find the origins of a large number of surnames, including those beginning with the Cornish-language prefixes Pen- (meaning 'head' or 'end'), Pol- ('pool') and Tre- ('homestead' or 'farm').

The Story of You: Jane Ferguson

Jane Ferguson started looking into her family history twenty-five years ago, when she developed an interest in who she was and what had contributed to 'making me me', as she puts it.

'I have a strong sense of history and an interest in genetics,' says Jane. 'I wondered how my father, who came from a Sheffield council estate, and whose parents were poor and uneducated, had managed to overcome his background. He was the first member of his family to go to university, and establish himself as a leader of education in the seventies. It seemed to me I'd find that answer somewhere in the past – and so it proved.'

When Jane first began tracing her family history, she found it a slow and painstaking process: visiting record offices, writing to people and then waiting for written answers. 'It was difficult to check information,' she says. 'There was a lot of pleasure in scrutinizing original registers and a "shock" in suddenly seeing your own family name appear. It took weeks for certificates to arrive from your visit to St Catherine's House [the forerunner of the Family Records Centre], and many weeks or months to gain information on two or three names.'

Jane was later able to purchase her own microfiche reader, but had to write to the local vicar for permission to get microfiche copies of parish registers. She also used records at the nearest LDS family history centre, which meant travelling there to order microfilms to view.

Pros and cons of using the Internet

'Now I'm able to access a lot of that information online: census returns and transcripts, for example,' she says. 'I use the Internet a lot to discover wills and the whereabouts of documents. In the space of a few hours, it's possible to trace many families back two or three generations, and order certificates online.'

Despite the wealth of information now available online, Jane never relies on material published on the Internet, unless it's a direct photocopy of an original source. 'Much of it is inaccurate and based on other people's wrongly put-together information,' she warns, and tells how she sent a copy of her family tree to a fellow researcher some years ago. 'This tree subsequently appeared on the Internet without my permission,' says Jane. 'I now know that much of my information was incomplete or inaccurate, but other people are still using this as a true family tree, and I've no control over it. I never send such information to anyone now, only excerpts with detailed notes explaining my thoughts.'

As well as getting information from other family members ('often misremembered and vague, or plain incorrect', according to Jane), record offices and libraries, she uses websites such as *Ancestry.co. uk, Documents Online, Access to Archives, Find My Past, British Origins* and *Family Search*. Jane is always cautious and verifies her findings against certificates or parish records. She has also used *Genes Reunited* and various Internet mailing lists. 'If you're lucky and make contact with a genuine researcher, the results can be very productive,' admits Jane. 'However, many of the people who place names on *Genes Reunited* aren't genuine researchers and, whilst they might add a name or two to your tree, aren't prepared to engage in solid research themselves. They want you to donate your years of research without being prepared to analyse the information and add to it themselves.'

Surprising and interesting ancestors

Jane's most recent ancestors lived in Sheffield, some having originated from Long Buckby in Northamptonshire where their families lived for 500 years. She also has ancestors from Chesterfield, and around Buckinghamshire, and has discovered distant cousins in New Zealand and Australia.

Jane particularly enjoyed finding out that her father's ancestors had come from an entrepreneurial family of wool merchants, who had become very wealthy in the eighteenth century. She's proud that one distant relative was Deputy Lord Lieutenant of Leicestershire. 'Through misfortune and being descended from younger sons, my branch of the family became quite poor,' says Jane. 'The drive that enabled my father to rise above his background was evident throughout, however. That led his great-grandfather to leave the shoe trade of Northamptonshire, which was declining, and move up to Sheffield to work in the steel industry.'

Jane's mother's family, who were farmers around Chesterfield, went on to own a steel foundry in Sheffield, as well as building several houses and owning parcels of land around Yorkshire. The ancestor she finds most interesting, however, is her great-great-grand-father Henry Warris, who died at the age of forty-seven.

'The death certificate stated that he hanged himself due to "lunacy",' says Jane. 'I found the 1857 newspaper report of his death, from which it appears he'd run away to America the previous year with "another man's wife". A year later he'd returned, and spent several weeks rampaging drunkenly around Sheffield. He'd had a violent argument with his wife who "had fled in fear of her life". After he'd searched for her for several hours, he was found hanging in Brightside Lane in Sheffield, with a newly sharpened kitchen knife plunged into the ground at his feet.'

Two of Jane's great-great-great-uncles were transported to Australia: one for gang rape, while the other had stolen woollen cloth and twice abandoned his wife.

'It's strange, but you do feel closer to some ancestors than others, almost as if they are calling to you,' says Jane. 'I always feel an affinity with Sarah Hanwell who got pregnant at the age of sixteen (probably whilst in service in Middleton Cheney), ended up living with the putative father in Northampton and had another child by him. In the next census they'd split up and Sarah was living with William Chamberlain as his wife, although I've never found a marriage certificate for her for either man. She went on to have several other children but died at the age of fifty-one from heart disease. Sarah was obviously still in touch with close family, as uncles and cousins appear with her in the census, and she and her son (my great-great-grandfather) were living with relatives later on. I often wonder about her and the hard life she must have had.'

Jane identifies with the Hanwell side of the family, who seemed supportive of each other. 'When my great-great-grandfather and his uncle went to Sheffield, they lived near each other,' she adds. 'They obviously helped each other out, appearing as "present at the death" in various certificates.'

Sensitive information

Jane is glad that her criminal ancestors were far enough away in time to be an interesting rather than a sensitive matter.

'My grandfather went to prison for fraud,' she says. 'This was already known, however, and he'd been cut off from his family because of it. I think you have to respect the feelings of the living regarding their immediate family, as illegitimacy was a great shame in those days, and you have no right to interfere with carefully constructed stories, even if you know the truth.'

Jane's parents delight in giving her snippets of 'unsavoury' information about their family. 'My father tells the story of how, during the war, his father Fred set up a hen coop. The eggs kept disappearing, so my grandfather Fred set up a vigil to find out what was happening to them. It turned out to be my great-grandfather, who was coming down at the dead of night to steal the eggs from his own son.'

What we owe to our families

Jane says researching her family history has made her realize how much we all owe to our families through the ages: the choices they made then, the good or bad circumstances they found themselves in, and the control they were able to take over their own lives, plus our genetic inheritance. 'We too will influence the life chances of our descendants by the way we raise our own children, the values we pass on and the opportunities we give them,' she adds. 'The past generations seem very close to me.'

Scotland

11

Historical introduction

	Scotland historical timeline
AD 78	Roman invasion of Scotland
6th century	Scots from Ireland colonize Argyll
6th century	Angles conquer Lothian and Berwickshire
794	Norwegian Vikings begin raiding Scotland
872–1468	Orkney under Norse rule (Shetland from 890–1469)
890–1266	Hebrides under Norse rule
987–1196	North of Scotland under Norse rule (Caithness from 890)
1349	'Black Death' kills between a third and a half of the population
16th century	English and Scottish plantations (settlements) in Ireland
1603	Union of English and Scottish crowns
17th century	Scottish and English plantations in Ulster and central Ireland
1649–60	Commonwealth (republic) established
1707	Union of English and Scottish parliaments
1715	Jacobite rebellion in support of James Stuart, pretender to the throne
1745	Further Jacobite rebellion, led by 'Bonnie Prince Charlie' (Charles Edward, son of James Stuart)
1746	Defeat of Bonnie Prince Charlie at Culloden, leading to the banning of tartan and the end of the clan system
c.1760	Beginning of the Industrial Revolution
1760–1820	Enclosure Acts appropriate common land as private property
1801	United Kingdom of Great Britain and Ireland created

1807	Abolition of the slave trade on British ships
1833	Abolition of slavery in British colonies
1914–18	First World War
1918–19	Influenza epidemic kills over 40 million people worldwide
1939–45	Second World War
1973	United Kingdom and Republic of Ireland join what is now the European Union

A short history of Scotland

At the time of the Roman occupation of Britain (AD 43–410), sixteen British tribes lived in what is now called Scotland. The tribes north of the Antonine Wall were known as the Picts, which may simply mean 'painted people'. There were two kingdoms, with their capitals at Inverness and Scone, where Scottish kings were later crowned on the 'Stone of Destiny'. This was brought to Scone by the Scots, a people who invaded from the north of Ireland in the sixth century and settled in Argyll. Around the same time, the Angles (from north Germany/south Denmark) conquered the British area of Lothian. About 250 years later Vikings from Norway started attacking Scotland, and the northern mainland and the islands gradually came under Norwegian rule over the next two centuries (from about 750–950).

For around 300 years (from about 950–1250), north Scotland and the Hebrides belonged to Norway, while the Orkney and Shetland Isles remained under Norse control for almost 600 years. Their people continued to speak the Norn language, a form of Old Norse, until the eighteenth century.

The tribes in the Highlands and the Western Isles broke up into smaller family groups or 'clans' (from the Gaelic word for children), such as the MacDonalds/McDonalds, Campbells, Stewarts, Robertsons, MacKenzies/McKenzies, Rosses and Munros.

In 1603, the Scottish King James VI inherited the English throne and moved south as James I of England. The two countries continued to have separate parliaments until 1707, however, apart from a time during the Commonwealth period when England, Wales, Scotland and Ireland were all under the rule of Oliver Cromwell.

Scotland genealogical timeline

1553	Parish registers are required to be kept in Scotland
1600	January 1 becomes New Year's Day in Scotland (instead of 25 March, Lady Day)
1752	Changeover from Julian to Gregorian calendar with the 'loss' of eleven days (3–13 September)
1801	First official ten-yearly census of Scotland
1824–36	Sheriff courts take over responsibility from commissary courts for confirmation of testaments in Scotland
1855	Civil registration of births, marriages and deaths in Scotland

I2

Births, marriages, deaths and census returns

The basic steps you need to take to trace your Scottish ancestors are the same as those you would take to find any English or Welsh forebears. Unlike the records for England and Wales, however, which are held in many different locations, all of the main Scottish records are in Edinburgh. They are in the process of being digitized (i.e. turned into computer images) and made available over the Internet to view and print out on your computer at home (or in a library, a record office or a family history society's research centre).

Civil registration (statutory registers)

The General Register Office for Scotland (GROS) in Edinburgh's New Register House holds the Scottish civil (as opposed to church) registration records. In Scotland, these are called the statutory registers of births, marriages and deaths. The GROS is also responsible for the censuses taken in Scotland and looks after the Church of Scotland registers (up to 1854) for the *c.* 900 Scottish parishes.

In Scotland, civil registration began on 1 January 1855, rather than 1 July 1837 as in England and Wales. Although later in starting, Scotland helpfully decided to put more information on birth, marriage and death certificates than England had. On a birth certificate, for example, you'll find the date and place of the parents' marriage, while the maiden name of the mother of each spouse can be found on a marriage certificate. An English (or Welsh) death certificate tells you very little, other than that the person died and of what. The Scottish equivalent, however, gives the name of the deceased person's spouse, as well as the father's name and occupation and the mother's maiden name (as long as the person reporting the death knew all of this information). The full details on the certificates are:

Birth certificate (from 1856)

- forenames and surname of the child;
- date and place of birth;
- the child's sex;
- the child's father's forenames, surname and occupation;
- the child's mother's forenames and maiden surname;
- date and place of parents' marriage (from 1861);
- signature, and relationship to child, of informant of the birth, and address (if not where birth took place);
- date and place birth registered, and registrar's signature.

Scottish statutory birth records (1878 – John Campbell, Jane Gillies and John McKenzie).

Marriage certificate (from 1856)

- date and place of marriage;
- signatures of the bride and groom;
- their occupations, whether single or widowed, and their relationship (if any);
- their ages;
- their usual addresses;

- each father's forename, surname and occupation;
- each mother's forename and maiden surname;
- signature of officiating minister and signatures of witnesses (if a regular marriage);
- date of 'conviction', Decree of Declarator or Sheriff's warrant (if an irregular marriage);
- date and place marriage registered, and registrar's signature.

Scottish statutory marriage records (1866 – George Thompson and Ann Henderson, William Begg and Sarah Ross).

Death certificate (from 1861)

- the deceased person's forename and surname;
- his or her occupation, and whether single, married or widowed;
- date and place of death;
- the deceased's sex;
- the deceased's age;
- the deceased person's father's forename, surname and occupation;
- the deceased person's mother's forename and maiden surname;
- cause of death, duration of disease, and by whom death certified;
- signature, and relationship to deceased person, of informant, and address (if not where death took place);
- date and place death registered, and registrar's signature.

From 1856–60, the following is also stated:

148

- last time the doctor saw the deceased (although it's quite common to see 'No medical attendant' specified);
- burial place of deceased, and undertaker or other person by whom burial certified.

Scottish statutory death records (1868 – Janet Young, Catherine Sutherland and (Female) Sutherland).

1855 certificates

In the system's first year of operation, Scottish certificates contained even more information, such as the ages and birthplaces of the parents (on a birth certificate), the dates and places of birth of the bride and groom (on a marriage certificate), and the forenames and ages of a deceased person's children (on a death certificate). Unfortunately, providing all this information was a bit too much of an effort for both the registrars and the informants, so it was dropped in 1856. The additional information was:

Birth certificate

- baptismal name of child (if different from registered name);
- parents' ages and places of birth;
- number and sex of child's brothers and sisters, both living and deceased.

Marriage certificate

- addresses of the bride and groom at present (if different to usual addresses);
- whether second or third marriage, if either bride or groom widowed;
- number of living and dead children of bride and groom by each former marriage;
- bride's and groom's birthplaces, and date and place their births registered.

Death certificate

- deceased person's spouse's name and occupation;
- forenames and ages of all deceased's children, in order of birth;
- year of death of any of deceased's children who have already died;
- length of time the deceased had lived in the area;
- deceased's place of birth.

Scottish statutory death records (1855 – Helen Gow, Grisel Fergusson and Grace Robertson).

Tip: Look in the Register of Corrected Entries

Look in the left-hand column of a birth, marriage or death certificate to see if a note has been made in the Register of Corrected Entries (RCE), held by the GROS. An entry might have been corrected when there was a mistake in the original entry, or when an enquiry was held into a suspicious death.

You can access births (over 100 years old), marriages (over seventy-five years old) and deaths (over fifty years old) on the Scotland's People website (*www.scotlandspeople.gov.uk*). Every January, another year's births, marriages and deaths are added to the online databases. For more recent records, you can either go in person or write to the GROS at New Register House, 3 West Register Street, Edinburgh EH1 3YT. The telephone number for the GROS's certificate-ordering service is +44 (0)131 314 4411.

Computer links to the GROS indexes and digitized records are available at the Strathclyde Area Genealogy Centre in Glasgow, as well as in the research centres of the Registrars of Births, Deaths and Marriages in Aberdeen, Dundee, Inverness and a number of other towns in Scotland.

Census records

As in England and Wales, the first official census was taken in Scotland in 1801 (with a census every ten years since, except in 1941) and the first four censuses required only total numbers of people in each enumeration district. While the English and Welsh censuses were under the supervision of the General Register Office in London from the 1841 census onwards, the GROS was not created until 1854 and so the first Scottish census it was responsible for was that of 1861. You can search the censuses for Scotland from 1841 to 1901 at New Register House and also online at the Scotland's People website.

Although, as in England and Wales, it was not required to record individual names until 1841, some of the school teachers responsible for the earlier censuses (and those of 1841 and 1851) recorded all the names anyway, and a few of these listings still survive, as well as other early censuses.

Tip: Early censuses and other population listings

As well as the official censuses, there are also other local population lists that exist for a few parishes in most counties. You'll find the majority of these lists at the NAS, although some are held by local archives.

There are, for example, censuses of the parish of Moulin (which includes the town of Pitlochry) taken in 1806–07 and 1820–21, the originals of which are at the NAS, with copies held by the North Perthshire Family History Group (*www. npfhg.org*). Both censuses list all the inhabitants of the parish, with ages given in 1820–21. The 1806 census also contains a list of farms with their size in acres, numbers of animals kept, quantity of crops grown, and rental.

Gradually, more and more questions were added to the census each time it was taken. The return for 1841 simply stated whether or not a person was born in the county he or she lived in. From 1851 on, the parish and county of birth were given, and from the 1891 return, you can tell whether your ancestors could speak Gaelic as well as (or instead of) English. Generally speaking, the information you'll find on the Scottish censuses is much the same as on those of England and Wales.

Gaelic and Scots

There are now fewer than 60,000 Gaelic-speakers left in Scotland, living in the Outer Hebrides, Skye and the west coast of the mainland. Two hundred years ago the language was spoken as far away from its present area as northern Perthshire and southern Caithness. Around 1700, Gaelic was spoken as far south as Fife.

Further south was the area where (broad) Scots was spoken. This was (and still is) a dialect of English, which some argue is a language in itself.

My grandfather John MacKenzie (whose own father had spoken Gaelic as well as English, according to the 1891 and 1901 censuses) spoke broad Scots. I don't remember him ever speaking anything else.

One day, he was walking his bulldog, Jock (both my grandfather and the dog were called Jock), by the Salisbury Craigs near Arthur's Seat in Edinburgh. He saw in the distance coming towards him two little girls, followed by a large man.

WHERE BORN.	Gaelic, or G. & E.	Whether 1. Deaf and Dumb. 2. Blind. 3. Lunatic, Imbecile, or Idiot.	Rooms with One or more Windows.
Caithnesshire, Latheron	G & E		3
Do. Reay			
Do. Latheron			
Do. Do.			
Do. D.			
Do. Do			
Do. Do.			
Do. Do.	G & E		
Do. Do.			
Sutherlandshire, Durnen			
Caithnesshire, Latheron	G & E		1
Do. Do.	G & E		
Do. Do.	G & E		
Do. Do.	G & E		1
Do. Do.	G & E		
Do. Do.	G & E		
Do. Do.	G & E		
Do. Do.	G & E		
Do. Do.	G & E		
Do. Do.	G & E		2
Do. Do.	G & E		
Do. Do.	G & E		
Do. Do.	G & E		
Do. Do.	G & E		2
Do. Do.	G & E		

Scottish 1891 census return showing languages spoken
(in third column from right).

Oh, no, he thought, it's the two princesses out for a walk from Holyrood Palace. I'll pretend I don't know who they are. So he continued to walk along, trying to ignore the two little girls. Unfortunately, Jock the dog had other ideas, and ambled over to see them.

'It's a' right, hen, he'll no touch ye,' said my grandfather, but Princess Elizabeth (who is well known to be fond of dogs) stroked Jock anyway, as the detective hurried to make sure his royal charges came to no harm.

When my grandfather returned home with the dog, he got the local children to pat Jock's head, as that was where a princess had stroked him.

Tip: Try all years for a birthplace outside the census country

Unfortunately, when someone was born outside Scotland, instead of giving his or her county and parish of birth in the census return, all that was required was to state 'England', 'Wales', 'Ireland' or whatever country the person came from. (In the censuses of England and Wales, only 'Scotland' or 'Ireland' were required.) Luckily, however, you'll sometimes find more information in one or other of the censuses.

In the 1871 census, for example, my 3× great-grandfather James Roxburgh is listed as being born in 'Ireland, County Londonderry', while in separate households, his son Henry's birthplace is given as 'Londonderry, Auchieduie' (presumably the parish of Aghadowey) and his daughter Priscilla's as 'Blackhill, Derry, Ireland' (which is within Aghadowey). In the other censuses, they're all listed simply as from 'Ireland'.

Missing census returns

For certain districts, the returns for some censuses have been lost (or never taken in the first place: St Kilda in 1841).

Scottish Family History Service (SFHS)

The SFHS is a new service, planned to be fully operational in 2008, which will be physically located in a new 'Scotland's People Centre' between New Register House (which houses the GROS and the Court of the Lord Lyon King of Arms, who is responsible for Scotland's heraldry) and General Register House (containing the NAS). The centre will have four search rooms to provide access to the physical and digitized records of the GROS, NAS and Lord Lyon.

13

Parish and other church registers

In 1553, the first register of church baptisms in Scotland was begun in the parish of Errol in southern Perthshire. Unfortunately, many parishes didn't start to keep records of baptisms, marriages (or proclamations of banns) and burials until much later. The earliest register on the Isle of Skye, for example, was that of the parish of Portree, whose earliest entry was recorded in 1800. In addition, around a third of Scottish parishes have no burial records whatsoever.

In England and Wales, copies of the registers were sent to the bishop responsible for the diocese in which the parish was located. The established Church of Scotland had no bishops for most of the time after it became Presbyterian in 1560, and there are no bishop's transcripts of the Scottish parish registers. Particularly during the eighteenth and nineteenth centuries, there were many breakaway dissenting Presbyterian churches, as well as a number of the Nonconformist churches (such as Baptists and Methodists) that were common in England and Wales. Because of the many congregations not worshipping at the established church, and as a result of a charge imposed briefly at the end of the eighteenth century, a very large number of baptisms, marriages and burials were not recorded in the parish registers. This was equally true of country areas such as, for example, the county of Sutherland as for the large cities of Glasgow and Edinburgh.

> **Tip: Why you may not be able to find your ancestors in the parish registers**
>
> For the *New Statistical Account of Scotland*, Dr James Cleland (co-author of the Glasgow entry in 1845) wrote to each of the city's seventy-five clergymen asking how many children they had baptized in 1830. He commented, 'It appeared that in the city and suburbs, there were 6397 children baptized, and of that number there were only 3225 inserted in the parochial registers, leaving unregistered 3172.'
>
> He described the situation in Edinburgh as similar: 'While the great importance of accurate Parochial registers is admitted by all, it is astonishing how little they have been attended to in this country. In Edinburgh, the metropolis of Scotland, a city distinguished for its erudition, and for its numerous and valuable institutions, the baptismal register is miserably defective. It appears from a printed report of a Committee of the Town Council of that city, of date 20th February, that in 1834, the baptismal register for the thirteen parishes contained only the names of 480 children.'

Church of Scotland registers

In 1855, the parish registers that had been compiled up to the end of 1854 were called in by the new GROS. These are known as the Old Parochial or Old Parish Registers (OPRs) and are held in New Register House. The OPR indexes are online at the pay-per-view Scotland's People website (*www.scotlandspeople.gov.uk*) and also on the LDS Church's free Family Search site (*www.familysearch.org*). Digitized copies of pages from the baptism and marriage/banns registers are also accessible at Scotland's People.

Unfortunately, the parish records contain less information than the Scottish civil registration (statutory) records. You do, however, usually find in a baptismal record:

- the child's name;
- both parents' names, including the mother's maiden name (sometimes, however, there's no mother's name given at all);
- the date of the baptism (and sometimes also the date of birth);
- the father's occupation (in urban areas);
- address of the parents (not too specific, usually);
- whether the child was illegitimate (in earlier records).

Here's an example of the record of a baptism in 1854 in the parish of Belhelvie, Aberdeenshire:

Name of child	sex	father	mother	date	place	date of baptism
James	male	James Smith	Catherine Ross	May 22	Menie	Aug. 21

From the parish of Dunnet in Caithness we have this record:

Allan, Janet, lawful daughter of George Allan and Margaret Shearer in Toftlyon, was baptized March 12th 1791 before these witnesses: William McBeath and Jean Coiston.

In a marriage record, you'll sometimes find the name of the bride's father, but not the groom's. Some records are of the proclamation of banns, rather than of the marriage itself, such as this one from the parish of Kirkmichael, Perthshire:

John McKenzie foxhunter in Glenshee of this parish and Christian Gow in Ground of Finegeand of this parish were proclaimed three times on sabbath the 19th August 1832 in order to be married.

Similarly to a marriage record, the burial record of a woman may give the name of her husband, or a child's the name of the father, but the record of the burial of a man may tell you very little.

Unlike in England and Wales after 1753 (for marriages) and 1784 or 1812 (for baptisms and deaths), in Scotland there was no standardization of the recording of these life events until the introduction of the statutory records in 1855. You'll find a lot of variation, therefore, in what the records of individual parishes contain.

Scottish parish register.

Scottish National Burial Index

The Scottish Association of Family History Societies (SAFHS) is coordinating the recording of burials by the various Scottish family history societies with a view to publishing a Scottish equivalent of the National Burial Index (NBI) already published for England and Wales. Unfortunately, a national CD on the lines of the English and Welsh NBI still seems to be a long way off. Individual societies have produced burial indexes for their own areas, however. The Fife Family History Society, for example, has published a Pre-1855 Fife Death Index on CD, which contains more than a quarter of a million names.

Tip: Scottish names

The Scottish naming pattern (first three boys named after paternal grandfather, maternal grandfather and father, and first three girls after maternal grandmother, paternal grandmother and mother) can help you find ancestors and relatives, although this was not always followed (e.g. in cases of illegitimacy).

Some forenames were interchangeable in Scotland (e.g. Jean and Janet, Daniel and Donald, Peter and Patrick), and watch

---

out for Gaelic versions of forenames in Highland areas (e.g. Hamish for James, Alistair for Alexander).

'Mac' and 'Mc' (meaning 'son of') are interchangeable as a prefix to a surname, and although 'Mc' (as opposed to 'Mac') is often thought of as Irish rather than Scottish, a survey by the GROS showed there are four times as many Mcs as Macs in Scotland.

Patronymics survived until the eighteenth century in the Highlands and the nineteenth century in Shetland. This meant that John, the son of William MacDonald, would be known as John MacWilliam, rather than John MacDonald.

Seceding churches and Nonconformist registers

The National Archives of Scotland (NAS) hold many church records, which are currently being digitized by the Scottish Archive Network (SCAN) in a major project expected to take five to seven years. You can read about the project and see examples of the digitized records at the Scottish Documents website (*www.scottishdocuments.com*).

In 1560 the Church of Scotland changed from Roman Catholic to Protestant and Presbyterian, organized on the basis of a number of courts. At the level of the parish, there's the kirk session, and at district level, the presbytery, while the General Assembly governs the church at national level. This is chaired by a Moderator who is elected for just one year. Presbyterianism is very democratic: there are no bishops or archbishops, and only God is recognized as head of the church. The pre-1855 Church of Scotland parish registers are held by the GROS, while kirk session records are held mainly by the NAS, although there are some kirk session entries in the parish registers.

Bishops were reintroduced into the Church of Scotland during the seventeenth century, but this was not accepted by many people who signed a National Covenant at Greyfriars Church in Edinburgh in 1638. These 'covenanters', who wanted to keep the church free from interfering monarchs, were persecuted. The Revolution Settlement, which followed the flight of Britain's last Roman Catholic king, James VII of Scotland (and II of England), in 1689, saw the return of Presbyterianism to the Church of Scotland. This, however, led to the founding of the Scottish Episcopal Church (which is a member of the Anglican family of churches). Some of the former covenanters, who were unhappy with the main Presbyterian church, formed the Reformed Presbyterian Church (also known as the 'Cameronians').

The various secessions

This was just the beginning of a series of secessions from the main Church of Scotland, followed by further splits among the seceders. Some of the seceding churches combined, and eventually nearly all had rejoined the Church of Scotland. With each union of seceding churches, however, there were always some members of the churches who went their own way.

In 1733, the Revd Ebenezer Erskine and others founded the Original Secession Church, because they disagreed with the right of landowners to appoint ministers to churches on their estates ('patronage'). There was then a division of this church in 1747 into 'Burghers' (the Associate Synod) and 'Anti-Burghers' (the General Associate Synod). This split occurred over the requirement of burgesses (city dignitaries) to take an oath acknowledging the 'true religion'.

Burghers and Anti-Burghers then divided into 'Auld Lichts' (Old Lights) and 'New Lichts' (New Lights), the Burghers in 1799 and the Anti-Burghers in 1806. Auld Lichts believed the church should be supported by the state (establishmentarianism), while the New Lichts believed church and state should be independent of one another (disestablishmentarianism or voluntaryism). Before the Auld and New Licht division took place, however, the Revd Thomas Gillespie had been expelled from the Church of Scotland, and in 1761, with two colleagues, had formed the Presbytery of Relief (the Relief Church). This second secession was also about patronage.

In 1843, the largest secession of all took place, when the Revd Thomas Chalmers and over 450 other ministers (one-third of the total number) left the Church of Scotland to form the Free Church of Scotland. Once again, patronage was the cause of the disagreement, particularly in Highland areas. This major breakaway was known as the 'Disruption', with nearly 900 Free Church congregations in existence by 1851.

Tip: Scottish places

Scottish county boundaries were tidied up in 1891, with some parishes coming under a different county (e.g. Culross changed from Perthshire to Fife, and Alva from Stirlingshire to Clackmannanshire). In 1890 the separate counties of Ross and Cromarty were amalgamated.

Some counties had two names: Zetland or Shetland, Elginshire or Moray, Forfarshire or Angus, Dumbartonshire or Dunbarton, Linlithgowshire or West Lothian, Edinburghshire or Midlothian, Haddingtonshire or East Lothian.

Reunions

The secessions are complicated enough, but then the seceding churches began to unite with each other, although there was usually the rump of one of the churches that refused to combine with the other.

Before the Disruption, 154 congregations of New Licht Burghers and 129 of New Licht Anti-Burghers merged as the United Secession Church in 1820. Nearly twenty years later, the Auld Licht Burghers rejoined the Church of Scotland, while the Auld Licht Anti-Burghers continued to exist as the Original Secession Church.

All of the United Secession Church congregations and 118 of the 136 congregations of the Relief Church combined in 1847 as the United Presbyterian Church. This had 465 congregations by 1851. The Original Secession Church joined the Free Church in 1852, and the Reformed Presbyterian Church in 1876, but with minorities in those churches remaining outside the union. Some members of the Free Church broke away in 1893 to form the Free Presbyterian Church.

The United Presbyterian and Free Churches combined as the United Free Church in 1900, although twenty-five Free Church ministers and sixty-three congregations did not join. The biggest change for over eighty years took place when the United Free Church rejoined the Church of Scotland in 1929. Once again, however, a minority in the United Free Church remained outside the reunion.

Even in recent years there have been more secessions. The Associated Presbyterian Church broke away from the Free Presbyterian Church in 1989, and the Free Church Continuing seceded from the Free Church in 2000.

Despite 400 years of Protestantism in what has (half) jokingly been called the most 'reformed' nation of the Reformation, the Roman Catholic Church is again strong in Scotland. This is largely due to immigration from Ireland in the nineteenth century.

Church records held by the NAS

Many of the registers of the seceding Presbyterian churches are held by the NAS. These include baptisms, marriages, burials and minutes of the kirk sessions. The NAS also holds records of some congregations of the Scottish Episcopal Church, as well as some Roman Catholic and Nonconformist records (such as Congregational and Quaker records). In addition, the NAS holds some Church of Scotland registers that completely or partly supplement the parish registers held by the GROS. The church records that are being digitized at present are those of kirk sessions, presbyteries, synods and the General Assembly of the Church of Scotland from the sixteenth century to 1901. You can view some examples of these at the Scottish Documents website (*www.scottishdocuments.com/ examples.asp*).

Glossary

Banns, proclamation of	Announcement of an intended marriage, made in the churches of the bride and groom on three consecutive Sundays
Kirk session	Local church court, composed of the minister and 'elders' of the church
OPRs	Old Parish or Parochial Registers. In 1854 the Church of Scotland registers were called in by the new General Register Office for Scotland.
Secession churches	Presbyterian churches that broke away from the Church of Scotland in the eighteenth and nineteenth centuries.

14

Wills and inventories

Testaments

At the National Archives of Scotland (NAS), previously known as
the Scottish Record Office until January 1999, you can find the
records of Scottish wills and inventories from 1514 up to ten years
ago. These can be viewed free of charge at the NAS, and those up
to 1901 are also accessible online. For information on Scottish wills
and inventories less than ten years old, you need to get in touch
with the Commissary Department, Edinburgh Sheriff Court, 27
Chambers Street, Edinburgh EH1 1LB.

The wills and inventories you can view at the NAS or over the
Internet are actually 'testaments' written by clerks of the Scottish
courts, which confirm or appoint executors. These are of two
types:

- testament testamentar (including a will);
- testament dative (with no will).

A testament testamentar is the equivalent of a 'grant of probate' in
England and Wales, where the deceased would have previously made
a 'testamentary writing' ('will' is not really a Scottish legal term)
such as a deed of settlement, naming executors. A testament dative
is similar to the English 'letters of administration' when someone
dies intestate (i.e. without having made a will). In the absence of a
will, the court would appoint an executor, either a relative or cred-
itor of the deceased.

An inventory would usually be drawn up for both kinds of

testament. This is an itemized list of the deceased person's movable possessions (i.e. everything but land and buildings). Under Scots law, the movable property was divided into three parts, with one-third going to the widow (the 'jus relictae'), one-third (or half, if their mother was already dead) divided between the children (the 'legitim' or 'bairns' pairt', with all children of either sex having equal rights), and the remainder (the 'deid's pairt') left to whoever the deceased wished.

Land and buildings were 'heritable property', which was inherited by the eldest son automatically and therefore not mentioned in wills. In the early nineteenth century, however, heritable property began to be included in wills and inventories, and was regularly contained in them once the Heritable Jurisdictions Act was passed in 1868.

Scottish land was still held under the feudal system until the end of 2004. Under this, all land was held by the Crown, with no land owned outright but held by 'feudal superiors' from whom land was

Scottish testament (1853).

held by a hierarchical structure of 'vassals'. One of the first acts of the new Scottish Parliament was the Abolition of Feudal Tenure Act 2000. Although this became law in Scotland on 9 June 2002, its provisions didn't all come into force until 28 November 2004.

All the Scottish testaments for the period 1514–1901 have been digitized by the Scottish Archive Network (SCAN) in a joint project between the NAS and the Genealogical Society of Utah (part of the LDS Church), with financial backing from the Heritage Lottery Fund. You can search the index of over 600,000 testaments free of charge at the Scotland's People website (*www.scotlandspeople.gov.uk*).

Downloading the digitized image of a testament will cost you the same amount (see Appendix B), irrespective of whether it's a testament testamentar (usually longer) or a testament dative. If you'd like to order a printed copy of a will from the NAS, then you can send an e-mail message to *enquiries@nas.gov.uk* to ask for an estimate.

Tip: Even poorer people can be listed in the index of wills and inventories

You may feel that there's no point in looking for wills in your family, as your ancestors may well have been poor agricultural labourers without anything to leave. It's certainly true that most wills were made by the upper classes and the gentry, but that doesn't mean that other people don't appear in the index. You'll find quite a few less well-off people in the records: there are wills or inventories for fifty-two carters in Glasgow (between 1817 and 1901), as well as twenty-three plasterers in Edinburgh (1844–1901), fifteen fishermen in Aberdeenshire (1824–1901), fifty-nine servants (both domestic and farm) in Angus (1832–1901) and 286 blacksmiths in the whole of Scotland (1750–1850). In the Glasgow Commissary Court alone, eighty labourers (many of them working on the land) or their widows appeared in the records between 1678 and 1823.

On the Scotland's People website (*www.scotlandspeople.gov.uk/content/help/index.aspx?r=551&636*), you'll find a map of the historic Scottish counties and information on the relevant courts. At the NAS website (*www.nas.gov.uk/guides/wills.asp*), you can view a guide to Wills and Testaments, which also includes information on the commissariot and sheriff court areas, as well as on the periods covered.

Extract from the Registered Trust Disposition and Deed of Settlement by Mrs Euphemia Dick or Ritchie – No. 68, 1859

1. Introductory clause

*At Perth, the 22nd day of September 1859 years, in presence of Edward Strathearn Gordon, Esquire, Advocate Commissary of the Commissariot of the County of Perth, compeared Andrew Davidson, solicitor in Perth, as procurator for the executor afternamed, and designed and gave in the Extract Registered Trust Disposition and Deed of Settlement by **Mrs. Euphemia Dick or Ritchie** residing at Hill of Ruthven by Perth, along with inventory of the personal estate of the said **Mrs. Euphemia Dick or Ritchie** (duly stamped with £30 sterling of duty) and oath thereon afterwritten, desiring the same to be recorded in the Commissary Court Books of Perthshire conform to act of Parliament, which desire the said Commissary finding reasonable, he ordained the same to be done accordingly, whereof the tenor follows, vizt.*

The above is the standard introductory part of a testament. To 'compear' is to 'present yourself before a court', while a 'procurator' is a person authorized to act on someone else's behalf. Euphemia Ritchie, whose maiden surname was Dick, was my 3× great-grandmother. Names of members of her family are shown in bold type.

2. The actual will

The will itself is the second part of a testament testamentar, but doesn't appear in a testament dative, which is the equivalent of an administration in England and Wales.

*I, **Mrs. Euphemia Dick or Ritchie** residing at Hill of Ruthven by Perth, relict of the late **George Ritchie**, Esquire of Hill of Ruthven, being desirous of settling my affairs with reference to my decease, do hereby give, grant, assign and dispone ['assign'] to and in favor of the **Reverend Doctor Alexander Ogilvie Beattie**, minister of the gospel in Glasgow, my brother-in-law, **George Cunningham**, Esquire, civil engineer in Edinburgh, my grandson, second son of the late **Lieutenant General John Cunningham** of Newton, and Andrew Davidson, writer in Perth, and to the survivors or survivor, and acceptors or acceptor of them, and to such other persons as they may assume into the trust aftermentioned, as trustees for the ends, uses and purposes aftermentioned and to their assignees;*

All and whole and all and sundry lands and heritages, goods and gear, debts and sums of money, and in general, the whole estate and effects heritable and moveable, real and personal, of what kind or nature soever or wheresoever situated, presently belonging or which shall pertain and belong to me at the time of my decease, with the vouchers and instructions, writs, titles and securities of and concerning any said estate and effects and all that has followed or may be competent to follow thereon, but in trust always for the ends, uses and purposes following, vizt.

First, for payment of all my just and lawful debts, deathbed and funeral expenses;

*Secondly, for payment to **Mrs. Euphemia Ritchie**, my daughter-in-law, wife of **Ruthven Ritchie**, my son, of the sum of £100 pounds sterling, which I legate and bequeath to her*

and to her heirs and executors, payable at the first term of
Martinmas or Whitsunday or as soon as possible thereafter as
may be, after my decease. But declaring that the said sum
shall be wholly exclusive of the Jus Mariti [the 'right of the
husband' to his wife's property] *of the said **Ruthven Ritchie**,*
both as respects the capital and interest thereof and that the
same shall not be liable to his debts or deeds nor to the
diligence of his creditors in any manner of way, the receipt or
*discharge of the said **Mrs. Euphemia Ritchie** by herself alone,*
being a sufficient quittance to my said trustees therefor;

Thirdly, for delivery, at the said term of Martinmas or
Whitsunday or as soon as conveniently may be thereafter, of
the following articles of household furniture and others in or
about my dwelling house or elsewhere, at the time of my
*decease, to or for behoof of my son **David Ritchie**, presently*
surgeon in the service of the East India Company, vizt. one
and a half dozen of my best silver table spoons, one and a
half dozen of my best silver dessert spoons, one and a half
dozen of my best silver forks, and two of my best silver
sliders, my sideboard, my French bed and bedding, two
parlour tables, my best set of dinner or table china, my
dessert set of the same, and any other of said articles of
furniture, which I may specify, in a list signed as relative
hereto;

*Fourthly, to **John Ritchie**, also my son, farmer of*
Cultmalundie, my silver tea set or equipage complete, and my
wardrobe, as also my carriage and harness, and any horse or
horses, cows and other cattle, which I may be possessed of at
my decease;

Fifthly, as to the whole remaining household furniture as
aforesaid bed and table linen, silver plate, china, books,
pictures, and in general, the whole moveable articles or effects
of that nature belonging to me, or which may be in or about
my dwelling house or elsewhere at the time of my decease, I

leave and bequeath and appoint my said trustees to deliver
the same, or in the event of any dispute, the proceeds thereof
on being sold by my said trustees, to, among or for behoof of
my son **Thomas Ritchie**, my said son **John Ritchie**, my said
son **Ruthven Ritchie**, my daughter **Mrs. Ann Ritchie or Scott**,
and my daughter **Mrs. Marjory Ritchie or Cunningham**, and
to their respective heirs or executors per stirpes;

In witness whereof, these presents written on the face of this
one sheet of paper by the said Andrew Davidson, writer in
Perth, are subscribed by me at Perth this 25th day of March
1852 years, before these witnesses: George Black and
Alexander Torrie, both apprentices to the said Andrew
Davidson.

2 (a). Codicil

I, the within-named and designed **Mrs. Euphemia Dick or
Ritchie**, being desirous, in consequence of certain changes
which have occurred in my family, of making certain
alterations on the within-written Trust Disposition and Deed
of Settlement, do hereby, in the first place, revoke and recall
the legacy and bequest of £100 pounds to **Mrs. Euphemia
Ritchie**, my daughter-in-law, wife of **Ruthven Ritchie**, my son,
and I do hereby legate, bequeath and appoint my said trustees
and executors to pay the said sum of one hundred pounds to
Mrs. Janet Morrison or Ritchie, spouse of **Thomas Ritchie** at
Bowhouse of Alloa, my son; Secondly, I do hereby legate,
bequeath and direct my said trustees, as a slight memorial
and remembrance of me, to pay to each of my grandchildren
afternamed the following sums, vizt.

To **George Cunningham**, within-named, now of Newton, the
sum of twenty pounds;

to each of his sisters, **Mrs. Euphemia Dick Ritchie or
Moncrieff**, wife of **Alexander Moncrieff**, writer in Perth,

Alison Cunningham, Ann Cunningham and Marjory
Cunningham, the sum of ten pounds; to each of **Isabella**
Scott and Ann Scott, daughters of the within-named **Ann**
Ritchie or Scott, *my daughter, the like sum of ten pounds;*
and to each of **Marjorie Ritchie** *and* **Euphemia Ritchie,**
daughters of the within-named **Ruthven Ritchie,** *my son, the*
like sum of ten pounds. In witness whereof, these presents
written on the back of the said Trust Disposition and Deed of
Settlement as a codicil thereto by the said Andrew Davidson,
writer in Perth, are subscribed by me at Perth the 4th day of
July 1854 years, before these witnesses: Thomas Gray,
apprentice to the said Andrew Davidson, and Laurence
Craigie, apprentice to Horace Skeete, writer in Perth.

3. Inventory

The third part of the testament is an itemized inventory of
Euphemia Ritchie's personal estate, which had a value of
£1,093.

4. Confirmation clause

The final part is a clause confirming that George Cunningham,
as Euphemia's only surviving trustee and executor, had entered
into possession and management of her estate, after her death
on 24 November 1856 (at the age of eighty-five).

Tip: Extend your search for a will or inventory

A testament dative (and even a testament testamentar) might
come before a court much later than you would expect
(because of a dispute, or as a result of the death of an
executor, trustee or heir), so it's worthwhile to search over
a good number of years.

Scots law and the courts in Scotland

Although Scotland has shared the same monarch with England since 1603 and the same parliament since 1707 (until 1999), the country continues to have its own legal system. Since 1999 Scotland has once again had its own parliament (which deals with and can pass laws on agriculture, education, health and justice), but is still part of the United Kingdom.

Scots law sits midway between the two main types of legal system in the Western world, Common Law (of England, North America and the Commonwealth) and Continental Law (of France, Germany, Italy, Spain and South America), and has borrowed from both of them.

The Court of Session is the supreme civil court in Scotland, while the High Court of Justiciary is the supreme criminal court, dealing with murder, armed robbery and drug trafficking. The forty-nine sheriff courts handle criminal cases and also most of the civil cases in Scotland (like the crown and county courts respectively in England and Wales). Lesser crimes (such as assault, vandalism, theft (but not by housebreaking) and traffic offences) are dealt with by the thirty district courts, which are lay courts with a Justice of the Peace rather than a judge, similar to English and Welsh magistrates courts.

In the late sixteenth century and in the seventeenth it was the commissary courts that dealt with inheritance, and testaments in particular. A commissary had originally been a bishop's official, and the commissary courts had taken over their functions from earlier church courts. This happened at the time that Scotland changed from Roman Catholicism to Presbyterian Protestantism, with the first commissary court established in Edinburgh in 1564. The early commissary court records of Aberdeen were unfortunately destroyed by fire in 1721.

A commissary court had jurisdiction over an area known as a commissariot, whose boundaries were similar to those of the medieval Scottish dioceses, and differed from the county boundaries. Responsibility for confirming testaments passed in 1824 to the existing sheriff courts, although some of the commissary courts continued in existence for several more years. The Edinburgh

Commissary Court, the last to go, didn't close until 1836. Some of the testaments dealt with by the Edinburgh Commissary and Sheriff Courts relate to Scots who died elsewhere in Scotland, as well as those who died abroad.

Glossary of some Scottish legal terms you may find in testaments

Allenarly	Exclusively
Anent	Regarding
Compear	Appear before the court
Compone	Make a payment to a feudal superior
Decern	Pronounce judicially
Decreet	Award by the court
Depone	Make a written statement to the court
Dispone	Convey or make over
Executor dative qua creditor	Creditor appointed by the court as executor
Guids and geir (goods and gear)	Movable estate
Intromit	Take up possession and management of an estate
Liferent	Right entitling someone to use and enjoy another person's property for life
Per stirpes	Latin for 'per branch' of the family, each of which is to receive the same amount, irrespective of the number of people in it
Petitioner	Person bringing an action before the court
Procurator	Person authorized to act on someone else's behalf
Relict	Widow

15

Records online

Scotland's People

The great advantage for people with ancestors from Scotland is that many Scottish family history records have already been digitized and made available over the Internet, with more records to follow over the next few years. The main website for Scottish family history research is Scotland's People (*www.scotlandspeople.gov.uk*), where birth, marriage and death records from the Scottish civil registration can be viewed, saved and printed. You can use both married and maiden surnames in a female death search (I tried it out and found two deaths that had previously eluded me).

At the same site you'll find the Scottish census records for 1841–1901. You can view digital images of the enumerators' returns for 1841–71 and 1891–1901, while the returns for 1881 can be seen in a transcription made by the LDS Church. Images of the actual records for the 1881 census are expected to become available online at some point in the future.

You can also view images of the baptisms and marriages (or proclamations of banns before the marriages) contained in the Old Parish Registers (OPRs) of Scotland. The register entries cover the period from 1553 (for the parish of Errol in Perthshire) – although many registers were not started until much later – until 1854.

You have to pay to view the records on Scotland's People, or even to search the indexes (see Appendix B). You pay for a session of thirty credits, which you buy through the website using a credit or debit card. To view each page of search results (up to twenty-five names) uses up one credit, while viewing the image of a record costs five credits. Each session lasts for ninety days, but any unused credits are saved until you buy another session.

Ancestry.co.uk

The censuses of Scotland have now been added to the censuses of England, Wales, the Isle of Man and the Channel Islands that are available at Ancestry's subscription/pay-per-view website *www.ancestry. co.uk*. The company doesn't have the right to use images, so it's made transcriptions of the Scottish censuses available online.

Free Census Project (FreeCEN)

The Free Census Project (*http://freecen.rootsweb.com*) has been making transcriptions accessible online free of charge for several years. The 1841 census returns for most of the thirty-three historic Scottish counties are now available online, plus returns for many of the counties for 1851, and for some counties for 1861 and 1871.

International Genealogical Index

The International Genealogical Index (IGI) on the LDS Family Search website (*www.familysearch.org*) is particularly useful for Scottish research, as almost all baptisms and marriages/banns listed in the OPRs are indexed in the IGI – and it's free of charge. The IGI also holds births and marriages from the Scottish statutory records for the period 1855–75. In addition, you can carry out a search for all the children of a couple by specifying the forenames and surnames of the parents. This is something you can't do on Scotland's People, although you can specify the father's and mother's surnames.

Although the Family Search website allows you to search the 1881 census free of charge, this applies only to the censuses of England, Wales, the Isle of Man and the Channel Islands. For the Scottish 1881 census, you have to go to Scotland's People and pay for access.

McKirdy Index

In New Zealand Wayne McKirdy is compiling a subscription database (*www.mckirdyindex.co.nz*) of Scottish civil registration death records, covering the period 1855–75. Different levels of membership are available, ranging from a basic Bronze level up to Gold, which allows searching by location and provides detailed search results. The official Scotland's People database holds in its index only the names of those who have died. The McKirdy Index, in contrast, contains the names of all those mentioned on the death record, including spouse, parents, informant and (on the 1855 records only) children. Searching using one of those names, you may discover that they occur on the death record of someone you were previously unaware of.

The index is a work-in-progress, and at the time of writing Wayne has covered only Bute, Clackmannanshire, Kinross-shire, Peeblesshire, Selkirkshire and Sutherland for the full twenty-one-year period, with fewer years included for Lanarkshire and Perthshire. He intends to cover the deaths in the rest of Scotland in due course, and eventually marriages too. Wayne points out that he's extracted the names from the registers in the way they were written by the registrars, who may not have spelled forenames and surnames in the way you expect. He therefore warns that you may not find the person you're looking for, if you don't try using variant spellings of names.

Tip: Use the LDS 1881 CD set

Rather than pay out to Scotland's People every time you want to view the 1881 census, you can make a one-off payment to buy a set of 1881 census CDs for Scotland, England and Wales from the LDS Church. As well as searching for a person by name, you can search for all the gamekeepers, or all the coachmen named Henderson.

Scots Origins

Until September 2002, the Scots Origins website (*www.scotsorigins. com*) provided access to the GROS records, which are now available through Scotland's People. The Scots Origins site still exists and provides a free placename search, as well as chargeable transcriptions of OPR (1700–1854), civil registration (1855–1990) and census records (1861 and 1871) through a partnership with the Scottish Roots Ancestral Research Service. Scots Origins also allows you to search on the IGI by parish, which isn't possible using Family Search.

Another website that lets you do this is that of Hugh Wallis (*free pages.genealogy.rootsweb.com/~hughwallis*). His site also features an interesting middle-name index, which lets you search for middle names that are probably surnames.

Scottish Strays Marriage Index

A useful free online source for tracing Scottish ancestors is the Scottish Strays Marriage Index, provided by the Anglo-Scottish Family History Society, a specialist branch of the Manchester & Lancashire Family History Society. The index, which is at *www.mlfhs.org.uk*, lists marriages that took place mainly outside Scotland, and where at least one spouse was born in Scotland. A reference number is usually given, so that if you want to make contact with the person who supplied the information, you can do so through the society.

Statistical Accounts of Scotland

You can find a lot of useful background information for the lives of your Scottish ancestors at the website of the Statistical Accounts of Scotland (*http://edina.ac.uk/statacc*), which you can view online free of charge. The Statistical Accounts contain descriptions of each of the *c.* 900 Scottish parishes in both the 1790s (the 'Old' Account) and the 1830s–1840s (the New Account).

Calling the accounts 'statistical' makes them sound dull and dry, but that's certainly not the case. Written by the local Church of Scotland ministers, the accounts describe the landscape, the people and how they lived. Their authors covered everything from the cost of living to local superstitions and whether the people spoke English, Gaelic or broad Scots (see Chapter 26).

Other useful Scottish websites

- Ayrshire Ancestors (*www.ayrshireancestors.co.uk*) – pay-per-view database of monumental inscriptions and birth, marriage and death extracts from the *Ayr Advertiser* newspaper;
- Ayrshire Roots 1851 census extracts (*http://fp.ayrshireroots.plus. com/Genealogy/Records/Census/1851/1851.htm*);
- Broadsides (*www.nls.uk/broadsides*) – the NLS's sites about broadsheets;
- Drew's Genealogy and Ancestor Search (*http://members.aol.com/ drewhss/drew.htm*) – many transcriptions here, especially for Fife and Angus;
- Dumfries and Galloway indexes (*www.dumgal.gov.uk/dumgal/ MiniWeb.aspx?id=86&menuid=921&openid=921*) – transcription of the 1851 census for Dumfriesshire, Kirkcudbrightshire and Wigtownshire, plus other records;
- Friends of Dundee City Archives (*www.fdca.org.uk/databases. htm*) – baptisms, burials and vehicle registrations;
- Glasgow Southern Necropolis (*www.southernnec.20m.com*) – alphabetical list of some of the burials;
- Highland Archives (*www.internet-promotions.co.uk/archives/ index.htm*) – all about Caithness, particularly military matters;
- Inveraray jail (*www.inverarayjail.co.uk/Former_prisoners/index. asp*) – database of nearly 4,500 former prisoners in this jail in Argyll;
- Lieutenancy Book for the County of Roxburgh 1797–1802 (*www.scan.org.uk/researchrtools/lieutenancy.htm*) – militia lists for all thirty-one Roxburghshire parishes of the time;
- Mull Genealogy (*www.mullgenealogy.co.uk*) – includes birth and (worldwide) burial indexes, and a search of 1841–1901 censuses and other population listings;
- North Perthshire Family History Group (*www.npfhg.org/ resources.htm*) – with some census, death and burial transcriptions;
- Orkney Genealogy (*www.cursiter.com*) – contains baptisms and marriages from the International Genealogical Index (IGI) for many surnames for Caithness and Shetland, as well as Orkney;

- Roots Hebrides (*www.rootshebrides.com*) – information on tracing your ancestry in the Western Isles, with many contact details (including the *Co Leis Thu?* genealogy centre, which has 30,000 detailed family trees);
- Scots at War Trust (*www.fettes.com/scotsatwar*) – includes a roll of honour, and links to others;
- ScotsFind (*www.scotsfind.org*) – includes transcriptions of Edinburgh marriages, burials and monumental inscriptions, Leith kirk session records, etc.;
- *The Scotsman* Digital Archive (*http://archive.scotsman.com*) – pay-per-view site with every issue of the newspaper from 1817–1950;
- Scottish Association of Family History Societies (*www.safhs.org.uk*) – with links to all the societies, both in Scotland and worldwide;
- Scottish emigration database (*www.abdn.ac.uk/emigration*) – contains the records of over 21,000 emigrants;
- Scottish maps at the National Library of Scotland (*www.nls.uk/digitallibrary/map/index.html*) – a large digital collection of maps of Scotland from 1560–1928, plus town plans from 1847–95;
- Scottish resources at Burke's Peerage and Gentry (*www.burkes-peerage.net/sites/common/sitepages/lisco.asp*) – links to family history and other Scottish websites;
- Talking Scot (*www.talkingscot.com*) – family history discussion forum;
- Virtual Mitchell (*www.mitchelllibrary.org/virtualmitchell*) – old photographs of Glasgow.

Future Scottish online records

Other NAS records that are currently being digitized and indexed are those of the kirk sessions (local church courts dealing with moral transgressions, among other things) of both the Church of Scotland parishes and some of the secession churches. In addition, the NAS intends to put High Court of Justiciary records and Roman Catholic registers online, and is also digitizing nineteenth-century poor relief registers (beginning with those of the historic counties of Caithness, Ross and Cromarty and Wigtownshire). Other records in the NAS that may be digitized in the future include 'sasines' (land records going back to 1599), fatal accident inquiries and taxation records, although these are all longer-term projects.

The Court of the Lord Lyon King of Arms, Scotland's heraldic authority, has digitized its 'Public Register of All Arms and Bearings in Scotland', which dates back to 1672. This is known as the Lyon Register and lists all the coats of arms that the Lord Lyon has authorized, together with their genealogies. These records were expected to become available at the Scotland's People website by 2008.

Ireland

16

Historical introduction

Ireland historical timeline

795	Vikings (Norwegians and Danes) begin raiding Ireland
12th–13th centuries	Anglo-Norman conquest of Ireland
1348–50	'Black Death' kills a large part of the population
16th century	English and Scottish plantations (settlements) in Munster and Ulster
17th century	Scottish and English plantations in Ulster
1641	Uprising in Ulster
1649–50	Oliver Cromwell invades Ireland, makes it part of his British republic, and transports 100,000 Irish to North America
1652–7	Land confiscated by Cromwell for his Parliamentary Army veterans
1798	Rebellion by United Irishmen and Catholic Defenders
1801	United Kingdom of Great Britain and Ireland created
1807	Abolition of the slave trade on United Kingdom ships
1833	Abolition of slavery in the British colonies
1845–9	Great Famine (failure of the staple potato crop in four years out of five)
1914–18	First World War
1918–19	Influenza epidemic kills over 40 million people worldwide
1922	Partition of Ireland, creating Northern Ireland and the Irish Free State
1937	Irish Free State officially named Éire (or Ireland)
1939–45	Second World War

1949	Éire becomes the Republic of Ireland
1973	United Kingdom and Republic of Ireland join what is now the European Union

A short history of Ireland

At the time of the Roman occupation of England and southern Scotland (AD 43–410), fourteen tribes lived in Ireland, according to Ptolemy, the ethnic Greek geographer who lived in Alexandria in Egypt in the second century AD. The Brigantes of southern Ireland were related to those of County Durham and Yorkshire, while the Gangani and Coriondi may have been related to people who lived in north Wales. The Manapii were also found in Gaul (modern France). There were also the Cruithin (or Dàl nAraide) in County Armagh and the Domnainn in the area around County Laois. The Cruithin (meaning Britons) are the Picts of Scotland, while the Domnainn are probably the same people as the Dumnonii of Devon and Cornwall.

As well as British tribes settling in Ireland, there were also a number of Irish settlements in Britain, most notably that of the Scots of Dàl Riata (or Dalriada) in Argyll in the sixth century. In addition, the Déisi of County Waterford settled in south Wales, the Laigin (who gave their name to Leinster) in north Wales, and the Uí Liatháin of eastern County Cork in Devon and Cornwall.

From 795, Norwegian Vikings began attacking Irish monasteries. In the ninth and tenth centuries the Vikings established bases at Dublin, Cork and Waterford, and founded the cities of Wexford (around 921) and Limerick (in 922). In the tenth century, the Norse kings of Dublin also ruled the Kingdom of York in England. In the twelfth century, Anglo-Norman adventurers conquered Leinster, the eastern province of Ireland. King Henry II of England arrived in Ireland in 1171 and was acknowledged as overlord by the conquerors and several Irish kings. In the following century, many settlers travelled to Ireland from the west Midlands and south-west of England.

The area under direct English control up to the mid-sixteenth century was known as the 'Pale', consisting of the counties of Dublin, Kildare,

Louth and Meath. During the rest of the century English control was extended over the whole island. Large-scale English settlements ('plantations') were established in King's County (now known as Offaly) and Queen's County (Laois) in 1556. Parts of the Munster counties of Cork, Kerry, Limerick, Tipperary and Waterford were also planted with English settlers around the same time (with a population estimated at around 22,000 by 1641). In Ulster, County Antrim and the Ards area of County Down were also planted, but with Scottish settlers. Scots also formed about two-thirds of the settlers in the 1609 plantation of the Ulster counties of Armagh, Cavan, Coleraine (enlarged and renamed Londonderry), Donegal, Fermanagh and Tyrone. An estimated 15,000 Scottish and English settlers had arrived in Ulster by 1641 (the ancestors of today's Northern Ireland Protestants).

About 10,000 Huguenots (French Protestants) came to Ireland at the end of the seventeenth century, a large number settling in Queen's County. In the early years of the following century, around 3,000 Palatines (German Protestants from what is now Rheinland-Pfalz) settled in Counties Limerick, Wexford and Cork and Dublin City. By this time, around a quarter of the total population of Ireland were Protestants descended from the immigrants of the previous two centuries.

From 1801, Ireland was combined with England, Scotland and Wales as the United Kingdom of Great Britain and Ireland. There was no longer an Irish parliament, but instead Ireland sent representatives to the British parliament in London.

From the end of the Napoleonic Wars in 1815 until the start of the First World War in 1914, around 8 million men, women and children left Ireland. Irish emigration increased considerably as a result of the Great Famine, when the staple potato crop failed in four seasons out of five between 1845 and 1849. The Irish population of 8.2 million in 1841 had dropped to 6.5 million ten years later, around half of the decrease being due to emigration and half to death through starvation and disease. Before the famine, most Irish emigration was to Canada; from 1850–1914, to the USA; and after the First World War, to Britain.

During the First World War, an abortive republican rising took place in Dublin in 1916. In 1919, nationalist MPs set up a republican parliament in Dublin, which led to a war of independence until 1921, when Ireland was partitioned between Northern Ireland (which remained within the United Kingdom) and the Irish Free State (which became a dominion within the Commonwealth on the same basis as Canada, Australia, New Zealand and South Africa).

From June 1922 to May 1923, a civil war was fought in the Irish Free State between those who accepted dominion status and those who wanted a republic over the whole island (who lost the war). It was during this war that the Four Courts complex in Dublin (including the Public Record Office of Ireland) was badly damaged, causing the destruction of the 1821–51 censuses, virtually all Irish wills and administrations, and half of the (Protestant) Church of Ireland parish registers.

In 1937, a new constitution gave the Irish Free State a president as head of state, and named the country Éire (in Irish) or Ireland (in English). In 1948, the country left the Commonwealth, becoming the Republic of Ireland in the following year. In 1973, both the Irish Republic and the United Kingdom became members of what is now the European Union.

Ireland genealogical timeline

1634	Parish registers are required to be kept in Ireland
1752	Changeover from Julian to Gregorian calendar with the 'loss' of eleven days (3–13 September)
1821	First official census of Ireland – with individual names
1823–38	Tithe Applotment Books produced in Ireland
1845	Civil registration of non-Catholic marriages in Ireland
1847–64	Griffith's Valuation carried out in Ireland
1858	Civil probate of Irish wills and administrations
1864	Civil registration of births, deaths and Catholic marriages in Ireland
1922	Explosion and fire at Public Record Office in Dublin, resulting in the destruction of many census returns, parish registers and wills

---

17

Births, marriages, deaths and census returns

Civil registration

Civil registration began in Ireland rather later than in England and Wales, with non-Roman Catholic marriages registered as from 1845, and births, deaths and Catholic marriages from 1864. At that time, there was a single registration system for the whole island, which was then part of the United Kingdom. From 1 January 1922, however, Ireland was divided administratively into Northern Ireland (with Belfast as its capital) and the Irish Free State (with its capital in Dublin), which became the Republic of Ireland in 1949. Since then, each part of Ireland has administered its civil registration system separately.

The General Register Office (GRO) in the Irish Republic holds the civil registration for all of Ireland up to the end of 1921 and for the Republic alone from 1922 onwards. In 2005, the GRO moved its headquarters from Dublin to Roscommon in the centre of the island, although it still has a research room in the Republic's capital.

The registrations of births and deaths that have taken place in the six counties of Northern Ireland from 1864, as well as marriages from 1922, are held in the General Register Office of Northern Ireland (GRONI) in Belfast. District registrars in Northern Ireland hold the registrations of pre-1922 marriages for the province.

What's on the certificates

An Irish birth certificate gives:

- date and place of birth;
- forenames and sex of child;
- father's name, address and occupation;
- mother's name, maiden surname and address;
- name and address of the person registering the birth.

From 1997, the mother's occupation and both parents' former surnames (if any) were added to the birth certificate in the Irish Republic. The current Northern Ireland birth certificate also states the mother's surnames at marriage, if different from her maiden name.

Irish birth certificate.

On an Irish death certificate, you'll find the deceased person's:

- date and place of death;
- name and sex;
- marital status;
- age at last birthday;
- occupation;
- cause of death;
- the name and address of the person registering the death.

An Irish marriage certificate states the:

- date and place of marriage;
- both spouses':
  - age;
  - name;
  - marital status;
  - occupation;
  - address before marriage;
  - father's name and occupation.

From 1957, the intended address of the newly married couple was added to the certificate in the Republic of Ireland.

Searching in Northern Ireland

In the public search room at the GRONI, you can either carry out an 'assisted search' or an 'index search'. With an assisted search, for a fee, members of staff help you to search the records for any number of entries over any number of years.

Alternatively, you can search in computerized indexes to the registers for up to six hours for about half the cost of an assisted search. The birth and death indexes start in 1864 and the marriage index in 1845 (although the GRONI holds marriage records only from 1922 onwards). You're recommended to book a terminal in advance.

Once you've found your references, you can have four of them verified by the GRONI staff as part of your index search payment. There is a charge for each further verification. The charge for a marriage, death or full birth certificate is halved if you can supply the appropriate reference number.

Searching in the Republic of Ireland

You can either carry out a 'general search' in the GRO's search room in Dublin, or a 'particular search' to find an entry over a five-year period. Unlike in Northern Ireland, you're not able to book a place in the search room in advance.

Tip: Get a photocopy of a certificate in the Irish Republic

You can buy a photocopy of a microfilmed birth, marriage or death record in the Irish Republic for one-fifth of the charge for a legally accepted certificate.

Civil registration records online

Under the Irish Republic's Civil Registration Modernisation Programme (see *www.groireland.ie/groproject.htm*), births began to be registered electronically in 2003. Existing birth records are also being computerized. Although this is not being done for the benefit of family historians, the technology used will allow the records to become available online at some point in the future.

Also in 2003, the GRONI carried out a consultation exercise on the modernization of the registration service in Northern Ireland, the results of which have not yet been published. The consultation document did suggest, however, that future developments might lead to public access to electronic versions of Northern Ireland's records. At present, you can order certificates for births, marriages (from 1922) and deaths online at the GRONI website (*www.groni.gov.uk*).

Irish death certificate (Republic of Ireland).

Free of charge at Waterford County Library's website (*www. waterfordcountylibrary.ie/library/web*), you'll find a searchable database of civil registration deaths in the county from 1 January 1864 to 31 December 1901.

At the Ulster Historical Foundation site (*www.ancestryireland.*

co.uk), you can search databases of the birth, marriage and death records for counties Antrim and Down. As well as transcriptions of civil registration records from 1864–1921, the databases hold earlier records from church registers. Basic searching is free, but there is a charge to use the advanced index (which shows the full date and father's forename) and view five transcriptions of the records. Members of the Foundation's Ulster Genealogical Historical Guild receive a discount.

Tip: Try using LDS Church facilities

The LDS Church's International Genealogical Index (IGI) includes Irish births from 1864–6 and non-Catholic marriages from 1845–9. You can view the IGI on microfiche in many record offices and family history societies, or online at the Family Search website (*www.familysearch.org*). You can then order a certificate by post. The LDS Church has microfilmed most of the Irish civil registration records and indexes, which you can order and view at any of its Family History Centres, of which there are ninety-six in Britain, three in Northern Ireland and three in the Irish Republic.

Census returns

Tracing ancestors in Ireland can be a bit trickier than finding them in England, Scotland or Wales, as many Irish records (including the nineteenth century censuses) are no longer in existence. The 1821–51 censuses of Ireland were mostly destroyed in a fire in Dublin in 1922 at the Public Record Office of Ireland. The 1861 and 1871 records were destroyed soon after the censuses were taken, while those for 1881 and 1891 were pulped during the First World War.

The first Irish census wasn't taken until 1821, but unlike those for Britain at that time, it listed all the inhabitants by 'townland' (subdivision of a parish), and gave their relationships to the head of the household. Name, age and occupation were specified, together with the number of storeys of the house, and the size of the family's land-holding in acres. People were not asked about their place of birth, however.

There are some surviving fragments of the 1821 census in Dublin at the National Archives of Ireland (NAI), the successor to the Public Record Office. These fragments cover parts of the counties of Cavan, Fermanagh, Galway, Meath and Offaly (formerly known as King's County). You can also find the surviving Fermanagh records in Belfast at the Public Record Office of Northern Ireland (PRONI).

Irish 1821 census fragment.

The Irish 1831 census contained similar information to that of the 1821, without the number of house storeys, but with a person's religion (i.e. Roman Catholic, Church of Ireland or Presbyterian). The only full 1831 records still in existence are those for County Derry (or Londonderry), which you can find at both the NAI and the PRONI.

The 1841 census was recorded by the householders themselves, rather than enumerators, and omitted the question on religion. This census did, however, collect additional information on date of marriage, ability to read or write, and members of the family who were absent or had died since the previous census. Unfortunately, the original 1841 returns have survived for only one parish in the whole of Ireland (Killeshandra in County Cavan). These records and some transcripts are in the NAI, as are the results of official searches made in the census returns when old age pensions were introduced much later on.

In 1851, information on religion was again provided, together with all the other details listed in 1841. Many of the original returns for County Antrim have survived (and are at the NAI and the PRONI), as have various transcripts for other areas.

All that remains of the 1861–91 censuses are transcripts for the parish of Enniscorthy in County Wexford in 1861 (Roman Catholics only), and for the parishes of Drumcondra and Loughbraclen in County Meath in 1871. The 1901 census returns do still exist, and you can view them at the NAI, where you can also see the returns for 1911, with both censuses covering the whole of Ireland. The 1911 census has been released early in the Irish Republic because of the loss of the nineteenth century censuses. The 1901 census for the six counties of Northern Ireland is also available at the PRONI, but not the 1911 census.

The details recorded in the 1901 census are: name, relationship to the head of the family, religion, ability to read or write, age, sex, marital status, place of birth, occupation, ability to speak the Irish language, and whether deaf, dumb, blind, 'imbecile', 'idiot' or 'lunatic'. Unfortunately, only the county or city was asked for in the question on birthplace. The 1911 census is similar, but with extra information about the length of a woman's marriage and the number of her children.

Irish 1911 census return.

The Irish language

In the 1840s Irish Gaelic was spoken by about 4 million people in Ireland, about half the total population. By the 1920s Irish was still the first language in parts of Counties Waterford, Cork, Kerry, Galway, Mayo and Donegal (the *Gaeltacht*, or Gaelic-speaking area), with scattered groups of Irish speakers in Counties Louth, Kilkenny and Clare. Despite compulsory Gaelic lessons in schools in the Irish Free State and its successor the Irish Republic, the number of native speakers of the language continues to drop. Although official Irish census figures show 1.5 million Irish speakers in 2002, UNESCO listed Irish as an endangered language in 1993, with fewer than 20,000 fully competent native speakers.

Census records online

The 1901 and 1911 census records are in the process of being digitized and indexed and will be made accessible over the Internet free of charge. The project is being carried out by the NAI in partnership with Library and Archives Canada, and is hoped to be completed by the middle of 2009. The 1911 census returns for the city and county of Dublin are scheduled to be the first records to go online.

The free Leitrim-Roscommon Genealogy Website (*www.leitrim-roscommon.com*) already holds an indexed transcription of the 1901 census for the complete counties of Leitrim, Mayo, Roscommon and Sligo, plus around 25 per cent of Wexford. You can find an indexed transcription of the 1901 census for County Clare at the free website of Clare County Library (*www.clarelibrary.ie*). The subscription-based site Irish Origins (*www.irishorigins.com*) includes the 1901 census for the 13,500 people living in the Rotunda ward in Dublin, as well as an index of 60,000 Dublin heads of household, extracted from the 1851 census. At the Irish part of the Census Finder site (*www.censusfinder.com/ireland.htm*), there are links to various census fragments.

Tip: Use census substitutes

Although very little remains of the Irish 1821–91 censuses, there are other records that you can use to take their place (to a certain extent). The principal census substitutes are land records: the Primary Valuation of Ireland (better known as Griffith's Valuation) carried out in the middle of the nineteenth century, and the Tithe Applotment Books from about thirty years earlier.

Griffith's Valuation

Between 1847 and 1864, Richard Griffith (Director of the Valuation Office in Dublin) had a land survey of Ireland carried out, so that liability for the Poor Rate (to support the poor and destitute of each area) could be calculated. Griffith's Valuation lists all tenants and

VALUATION OF TENEMENTS.   13

PARISH OF AGHADOWEY.

No. and Letters of Reference to Map.	Names		Description of Tenement.	Area.	Rateable Annual Valuation.		Total Annual Valuation of Rateable Property.
	Townlands and Occupiers.	Immediate Lessors.			Land.	Buildings.	
	GORRAN—continued.			A. R. P.	£ s. d.	£ s. d.	£ s. d.
6 h	. . . .	Rep. Hugh Lyle,	EXEMPTIONS: Wesleyan Methodist school-house, .	—	—	1 10 0	1 10 0
			Total, including Exemptions, .	395 2 37	178 0 0	18 0 0	196 0 0
	DRUMACROW. (Ord. S. 18.)						
1 A			Land, . . .	3 0 0	2 6 0		
— B			Land, . . .	7 0 15	2 8 0		
— C a	John Miller, . .	Rep. Hugh Lyle.	House, offices, and land,	1 2 20	1 6 0	1 10 0	10 15 0
— D			Land, . . .	6 0 15	3 0 0		
2			Bog, . .	3 0 22	0 5 0		
3 A B a	Robert Thompson, .	John Miller,	House & small garden, House, offices, and land.	10 0 35	6 0 0	0 15 0	6 15 0
— B a	James Browne, .	Rep. Hugh Lyle.	Land, . . .	4 0 0	2 4 0	1 0 0	9 10 0
4			Bog, . .	5 0 35	0 0 0		
5 A B a	John Browne, .	Free, . .	House & small garden, House, offices, and land.	10 2 25	6 10 0	0 15 0	6 10 0
B A a	David Woodend, .	Rep. Hugh Lyle,	Land, . . .	4 3 20	2 0 0		6 15 0
— B			Bog, . .	5 2 10	0 5 0		
7 A a	William Williamson, .	Same, . .	House, offices, & land.	17 3 35	12 10 0	1 5 0	14 10 0
— B			Land, . . .	0 2 20	0 15 0		0 10 0
— a	Thomas White,	William Williamson, .	House, . .			0 10 0	0 10 0
8 A a	John Kelly,	Rep. Hugh Lyle,	House, offices, & land.	35 1 25	23 10 0	1 0 0	23 15 0
— B				2 2 20	2 5 0		
— b	John Doolish,	John Kelly,	House, . .	—		0 5 0	0 5 0
— c	John Thompson,	Same, .	House, . .	—		0 10 0	0 10 0
— d	William Miller,	David Woodend,	House and garden,	0 0 30	0 5 0	0 10 0	0 15 0
— e	James Baxter,	John Kelly,	House, . .	—		0 5 0	0 5 0
9	John Kelly,	Rep. Hugh Lyle,	Bog, . .	3 2 0	0 5 0		0 5 0
10	Alexander Pattison,	Same, .	House, office, and land.	16 1 5	9 0 0	1 1 0	10 10 0
11			Bog, . .	3 3 10	0 2 0		
12	Samuel Pattison,	Same, .	House, offices, and land.	13 3 25	7 5 0	0 15 0	8 0 0
13			Bog, . .	3 0 20	0 5 0		
			Total, .	126 3 7	79 15 0	11 2 0	90 15 0
	CLAREHILL. (Ord. S. 11 & 12.)						
1 A	John Knox,	Worshipful Company of Ironmongers.	House, offices, & land.	3 2 30	6 5 0	—	16 15 0
— B				3 1 5	2 15 0		
— C b	Mary Stewart, .	John Knox,	House, . .	3 0 29	5 15 0	2 0 0	0 5 0
2 A a	Ellen M'Alister,	Worshipful Company of Ironmongers.	House, offices, & land.	3 0 10	3 9 0	0 15 0	11 5 0
— B				11 0 30	6 10 0		
3	James O. Locke,	Same, .	Land, . .	1 2 0	0 15 0		0 15 0
4	Alexander Archibald,	Same, .	House, offices, and land.	16 2 25	10 10 0	1 0 0	11 10 0
5	Thomas Moore,	Same, .	House, offices, and land.	15 0 10	12 10 0	1 10 0	12 0 0
6 a	John Wilson,	Same, .	House, offices, and land.	22 2 30	16 3 0	1 0 0	16 10 0
— b	Robert Wilson, .	John Wilson,	House, . .			0 5 0	0 5 0
7 a	Robert Knox, jun.	Worshipful Company of Ironmongers.	House, offices, and land.	43 0 0	28 5 0	3 15 0	31 0 0
— b	William Miller, .	Robert Knox, jun.	House, . .			0 10 0	0 10 0
8	Hugh Knox,	Worshipful Company of Ironmongers.	House, offices, and land.	34 1 20	21 0 0	2 10 0	23 10 0
9 a	Robert Knox, sen.	Same, .	House, offices, and land.	22 1 31	20 15 0	1 5 0	21 0 0
— b	John Chambers, .	Robert Knox, sen.	House, . .	—		0 5 0	0 5 0
— c	James Kane,	Same, .	House, . .	—		0 5 0	0 5 0
10	Mary Hempsey, .	Worshipful Company of Ironmongers.	House and land.	3 1 35	2 0 0	0 10 0	2 10 0
11	John Moon,	Same, .	House, offices, and land.	3 1 35	1 5 0	0 15 0	2 0 0
12	John Cunningham,	Same, .	House, offices, and land.	14 0 20	9 15 0	1 0 0	10 5 0
13	James Gilmore,	Same, .	House, offices, and land.	7 0 30	4 10 0	1 0 0	5 10 0
14	John Hegg,	Same, .	House, offices, and land.	14 0 30	7 15 0	1 0 0	8 15 0
15	James Hull,	Same, .	Land, . .	9 0 0	6 0 0		6 0 0
16	James Mooney,	Same, .	House, offices, and land.	8 3 0	6 15 0	1 5 0	7 0 0
			Total, .	227 9 27	165 15 0	20 0 0	188 15 0

Page from Griffith's Valuation.

landlords, both in towns and on the land. It is essentially a list of heads of household for the whole of Ireland, and consequently includes few women and no children. The information you'll find in Griffith's is listed by parish and consists of:

- Ordnance Survey map reference number;
- location of the property (either a street in a town, or a townland – subdivision of a parish – in the country);
- name of the occupier;
- name of the person from whom the property was leased;
- description of the property (such as 'house, offices and land');
- area (in acres, roods and perches);
- the annual valuation of the land and of the buildings.

You can consult Griffith's Valuation for the whole of Ireland at the National Library of Ireland (NLI) and at the Valuation Office (which have the largest holdings), as well as at the National Archives of Ireland (NAI). All these bodies are in Dublin. Griffith's is also available at the Public Record Office of Northern Ireland (PRONI) in Belfast, and online at Irish Origins (*www.irishorigins.com*).

Tithe Applotment Books

From 1823, tithes to the established (Protestant) Church of Ireland became payable in money rather than in kind. As a result, a valuation of the whole country was carried out from that time until 1838. In the Tithe Applotment Books you'll find the names of occupiers of titheable land, but no labourers or town-dwellers.

The books, organized by parish, contain the following information:

- occupier's name;
- townland;
- area in acres;
- land classification;
- tithe amount due.

You can see the Tithe Applotment Books in Dublin at the NAI and the NLI, or those for the nine counties of Ulster in Belfast at the PRONI. From the NLI's website, you can download its leaflet *Valuation Records*, which covers both Griffith's Valuation and the Tithe Applotment Books. The Tithe Applotment Books for Northern Ireland are also available on CD.

Census substitutes online

You can view indexed digitized records of Griffith's Valuation (including maps and town plans) online at the Irish Origins subscription website (*www.irishorigins.com*), as well as a census of the Diocese of Elphin (most of County Roscommon and parts of Galway and Sligo) carried out in 1749.

The site also contains the William Smith O'Brien petition, signed by over 80,000 people (both in Ireland and in Britain) between October 1848 and May 1849. The petitioners successfully asked for clemency for O'Brien, a member of parliament who had been sentenced to death for leading an abortive uprising against the British government.

At Ulster Ancestry (*www.ulsterancestry.com/search.html*), you can carry out a free search in Griffith's Valuation for the nine counties of Ulster: Antrim, Armagh, Cavan, Derry, Donegal, Down, Fermanagh, Monaghan and Tyrone. The site also contains a transcript of remnants of the 1851 census for thirteen areas of County Antrim.

At the PRONI website (*www.proni.gov.uk*), you can search free of charge in a database of freeholders in Ulster (mainly in the six counties of Northern Ireland). The names have been taken from electoral rolls (listing those entitled to vote) and poll books (showing those who had actually voted). The records in the database include some of the following information:

- name of freeholder;
- address of freeholder;
- location of freehold;
- description of freehold;
- name of landlord;
- address of landlord;
- value of freehold;
- names of other 'lives' (people to whom a lease would pass in the event of the holder's death);
- date and place of freeholder's registration;
- occupation of freeholder;

- religion of freeholder;
- for whom the freeholder voted.

The free Leitrim-Roscommon Genealogy Website (*www.leitrim-roscommon.com*) contains a database of information from Griffith's Valuation for parts of Galway, Leitrim, Mayo, Roscommon and Limerick. At the site, you can also view a partial database of the 1749 Elphin census.

Clare County Library's free website (*www.clarelibrary.ie*) contains indexes to Griffith's Valuation for the county, as well as transcriptions of the local Tithe Applotment Books. At Waterford County Library's free site (*www.waterfordcountylibrary.ie*), you can search and view a full online transcription of Griffith's for the county, and area trade directories from 1824–1909.

The website of the subscription-based Ulster Historical Foundation (*www.ancestryireland.co.uk*) has many population databases, mainly for counties Antrim and Down.

Tip: Use the various population listings that are online

Don't give up on your nineteenth-century (and earlier) Irish ancestors because the censuses have been destroyed. Take a look at the many census substitutes that do exist, not only Griffith's Valuation and the Tithe Applotment Books. Either at home or in your local library, try the many Irish websites that have been set up by public bodies, commercial companies and enthusiasts.

At the free Census Finder website (*www.censusfinder.com/ireland.htm*), you can find links to a variety of mainly free early censuses, trade directories, lists of tenants, tithe defaulter lists, muster rolls, hearth money rolls and other population lists.

18

Church registers and wills

Church registers

Up to 1869, Ireland's established church was the (Anglican) Church of Ireland, although most people in what is now the Irish Republic were Roman Catholic. Although Church of Ireland ministers received instructions to keep parish records as early as 1634, most of its registers didn't start until the end of the eighteenth century. The earliest surviving Catholic register is that of Wexford, which begins in 1671, but many Catholic registers didn't start until as late as the mid-nineteenth century (especially in the rural north and west).

The province of Ulster had been 'planted' in the sixteenth and seventeenth centuries with Scottish (Presbyterian) and English settlers, the ancestors of today's Northern Ireland Protestants. Presbyterian churches in Ulster began to keep registers from around 1700.

After the partition of Ireland between Northern Ireland and the Irish Free State (now the Irish Republic) in 1922, a civil war took place in the Free State. During this, the Public Record Office of Ireland (PROI) was set on fire, causing the destruction of about 60 per cent of the Church of Ireland registers, which had been called in for safe-keeping! Luckily, many had been copied or were still in the parish church.

The National Archives of Ireland (the successor to the PROI) holds copies of nearly all the pre-1870 Church of Ireland registers that still exist (about 50 per cent), as does the Representative Church Body Library. The National Library of Ireland contains copies of almost all the Catholic registers up to 1880. All of these repositories are in Dublin. The Public Record Office of Northern Ireland (PRONI) in Belfast holds copies of Church of Ireland and Presbyterian registers for Northern Ireland.

Tip: Look in the PRONI online parish register indexes

The PRONI website (*www.proni.gov.uk*) has online indexes showing which Church of Ireland and Presbyterian parish registers have been microfilmed and are available to view in Belfast.

Wills and administrations

Irish wills were proved in church courts until 1858, when responsibility passed to new civil probate registries. The wills proved in Ireland prior to that year were then transferred to the PROI, and were destroyed in the 1922 fire. The PROI immediately began to collect copies, transcripts, extracts and abstracts of the wills that had been destroyed. A card index of these was created, and this is now available at the NAI, as well as on CD and online.

The NAI also holds a consolidated index of wills proved from 1858–77, and calendars of wills proved after 1877 (excluding Northern Ireland after 1918). The PRONI holds all probated wills for Northern Ireland from 1900–1994.

Tip: Look for an Irish will in the English records too

Where a person left property in England and Wales, as well as Ireland, then the will would be proved not only in Ireland, but also in England at the Prerogative Court of Canterbury (PCC). The PCC's records are available to view at the National Archives (TNA) and the Family Records Centre (FRC), both in London. You can search free of charge in the online index of PCC wills (1384–1858) at TNA's Documents Online website (*www.nationalarchives.gov.uk/documentsonline*), and then download the digitized image of a will on a pay-per-view basis.

Church registers and wills online

A large number of church registers have been transcribed and indexed by Ireland's county-based family history research centres, as part of the Irish Genealogical Project, set up to create a database of all Irish family history records. One useful result is an online 'Central Signposting Index' created by Irish Genealogy Ltd (IGL), the company that coordinates the project.

The website of the Ulster Historical Foundation (*www.ancestry ireland.co.uk*) includes an index to Printed Irish Will Calendars (1878–1900) covering the whole of Ireland. This and nearly eighty other Foundation databases can be searched online free of charge by members of the Foundation's Ulster Genealogical Historical Guild.

The NAI's *Index of Irish Wills (1484–1858)* is accessible online at the subscription website Irish Origins (*www.irishorigins.com*). At the NAI's own site (*www.nationalarchives.ie/research/probate.htm*), you can view lists of wills and administrations proved at the main Probate Office in Dublin in 1983 and at various District Probate Offices in the Irish Republic from 1983–5.

Printed church registers

The Representative Church Body Library has published eight early Church of Ireland (Protestant) registers for the churches of:

- Cathedral Church of St Columb, Derry, 1703–32 and 1732–75;
- Holy Trinity, Cork, 1643–68;
- Leixlip, County Kildare, 1665–1778;
- St Catherine, Dublin, 1636–1715;
- St John the Evangelist, Dublin, 1619–99;
- St Thomas, Dublin, 1750–91;
- St Thomas, Lisnagarvey, County Antrim, 1637–46.

Irish Genealogical Project

Ireland has no county record offices as such, but it does have thirty-four family history research centres (four of which are currently closed), most of which are members of the Irish Family History Foundation (IFHF). The centres are mainly county-based, although counties Antrim and Down share a centre, as do Fermanagh and Tyrone, and Laois and Offaly (formerly known as Queen's and King's County respectively). The large counties of Cork, Galway, Mayo and Tipperary have two centres each, as has County Dublin.

You can download a leaflet from the IFHF's website *(www.irish-roots.net)* that contains contact details for the research centres, as well as a map showing their location. The website also has information on which Roman Catholic, Church of Ireland and Presbyterian registers are available at the centres.

As part of the Irish Genealogical Project, the research centres have transcribed and compiled computer indexes of local records, such as church registers, civil registration marriage records (non-Catholic from 1845; Catholic from 1864), civil birth and death records (from 1864), land records (such as Griffith's Valuation 1848–64 and Tithe Applotment Books 1823–38), the 1901 census (and the 1911 in the Republic of Ireland) and monumental inscriptions.

The project originated in the Irish Republic in the early 1980s as an attempt to attract tourists (mainly American) to return to their roots in Ireland; it also provided work for young people in transcribing and indexing the records. The family history centres in the Republic were later joined by those in Northern Ireland in 1990. Unfortunately, although the staff of the centres will carry out a search for you, members of the public are not allowed to search the records and indexes by themselves.

The Ulster Historical Foundation (UHF), the research centre for the counties of Antrim and Down, was the first centre to make its records accessible via the Internet. At present, over 400,000 civil birth and church baptism records and nearly 900,000 marriage records for the two counties are included in the UHF's index, with around 350,000 death records to be added in the future.

The IFHF is setting up an online pay-per-view system on its website for all the research centres, allowing you to search their indexes and view records online (in particular, those of births, marriages and deaths). The IFHF hopes that all centres will be online by the spring of 2008.

Irish Genealogy Ltd

At the website of Irish Genealogy Ltd (*www.irishgenealogy.ie*), a company set up to coordinate and market the Irish Genealogical Project, you can carry out a free search for your ancestors in what is referred to as a Central Signposting Index (CSI). This indexes the records of eleven participating counties: Armagh, Cavan, Derry (or Londonderry), Donegal, Fermanagh, Leitrim, Limerick, Mayo, Sligo, Tyrone and Wexford. You can search in the index for a specific county, or in the entire index, if you don't know where your ancestor came from. Unfortunately, only about a third of the counties of Ireland are covered by the CSI. Unless the name you're looking for is uncommon, you'll probably get search results from several counties, with little to indicate which (if any) is your ancestor. You can then buy a transcription of the record online.

In addition, you can search in a database of nearly 400,000 Irish monumental inscriptions (MIs) from the counties of Antrim, Armagh, Derry, Donegal, Down, Dublin, Fermanagh, Louth, Monaghan and Tyrone. Searching is free of charge, but you have to pay for a transcription and (if you wish) for a graveyard plan showing the location of the gravestone.

At the IGL website, you can download a 22-page booklet entitled *Tracing Your Ancestors in Ireland*, which provides information on what the main record offices and libraries contain, as well as their contact details and those of sixteen professional genealogists.

Tip: You can commission a search for a birth or baptism through IGL

At the IGL site, you can commission a chargeable search for the record of a baptism or birth in the appropriate research centre for any of the thirty-two counties of Ireland. Baptisms as well as births can be searched for in the counties of Antrim, Armagh, Cavan, Derry, Donegal, Down, Galway, Leitrim, Mayo, Roscommon, Sligo, Tyrone and Wicklow, but for the remaining counties only a birth search (i.e. from 1864 onwards) is available.

More Irish websites

Although many of Ireland's major family history records have been destroyed, other local records have been transcribed and made available online. The free Fianna Guide to Irish Genealogy (*www. rootsweb.com/~fianna*) contains links to many transcriptions, as well as a good deal of information by county about church records, censuses and substitutes, with contact details for local archives, libraries and societies.

Celtic Cousins (*www.celticcousins.net/ireland*) is a free American site with links to transcriptions of many directories, some parish records and a few will abstracts mainly for the western counties of Clare, Galway, Limerick, Mayo and Roscommon.

The professional genealogist John Grenham's Irish Ancestors site (*scripts.ireland.com/ancestor/index.cfm*), established in partnership with the *Irish Times*, has a very useful free surname search facility, which will show you by county the number of households of that name in Griffith's Valuation.

There's a good deal of information at island, county and (in some cases) parish level, with links to many websites, in the Ireland section of GENUKI (*www.genuki.org.uk/big/irl*), while Cyndi's List of Genealogy Sites on the Internet has nearly 2,000 links to Irish sites at *www.cyndislist.com/ireland.htm*. These include mailing lists and books on Irish family history available from Amazon.com.

There are GenWeb project sites for the Irish Republic (*www. irelandgenweb.com*) and Northern Ireland (*www.rootsweb. com/~nirwgw*), both of which are part of a worldwide volunteer network. The two sites lead to county pages with much information and links to transcriptions, mailing lists, etc.

There are various county-based Irish family history sites, such as the CMC (christening, marriage and cemetery) Record Project (*www. cmcrp.net*). This contains searchable transcriptions of birth, marriage, death, cemetery, land and property records mainly for counties Clare, Cork, Dublin, Kerry, Limerick, Mayo, Tipperary, Waterford, Wexford and Wicklow that have been submitted by family historians.

IGP (Ireland Genealogical Projects) is a group of county-based websites with transcriptions of family history records. You can find links to all the sites at the Galway IGP site (*www.rootsweb. com/~irlgal2/index.htm*).

Irish Family Research (*www.irishfamilyresearch.co.uk*) is a subscription site with databases covering all thirty-two counties of Ireland.

CDs

Eneclann (*www.eneclann.ie*), Unit 1b, Trinity College Enterprise Centre, Pearse Street, Dublin 2, Ireland (Tel: +353 (0)1 671 0338) has published a number of Irish family history CDs, including:

- *The 1851 Dublin City Census* heads of household index (with 60,000 names and addresses);
- *The 1798 Rebellion: Claimants and Surrenders* (with 8,000 names);
- *The 1831 Tithe Defaulters* (30,000 people who refused to pay tithes to the Church of Ireland);
- *The William Smith O'Brien Petition* (80,000 names);
- NAI's *Index of Irish Wills (1484–1858)* (over 70,000 records).

The company has also published CD versions of the genealogical journals:

- the *Irish Ancestor 1969–86* (thirty-three issues, plus four supplements);
- the *Irish Genealogist 1937–93* (eight volumes);

as well as two CDs entitled *Memorials of the Dead*. The first of these covers inscriptions from gravestones on the western seaboard of counties Mayo and Galway, and the second from graveyards in the counties of Wexford and Wicklow (both complete), large parts of south County Dublin and west County Clare, and parts of counties Cork, Kildare, Galway and Sligo.

Grenham's Irish Surnames is a particularly useful resource from Eneclann, which shows at parish level where you'll find a surname listed in Griffith's Valuation. In addition, the CD gives details of the years covered in the various denominations' registers for each parish (Roman Catholic, Church of Ireland, Presbyterian and Nonconformist), showing where the registers can be viewed. Both these facilities are chargeable at John Grenham's Irish Ancestors website (*www.ireland.com/ancestor/index.cfm*).

Irish World *(www.irish-world.com)* and the Genealogical Publishing Company in the USA are joint publishers of CDs of Griffith's Valuation and a list of flax growers in 1796 (both all-Ireland), as well as the Tithe Applotment Books for Northern Ireland.

Isle of Man and Channel Islands

19

Manx and Channel Islands records

Isle of Man

According to the website of the Isle of Man Government, the island is 'an internally self-governing dependent territory of the Crown which is not part of the United Kingdom'. With a population of just over 76,000, the island has its own 1,000-year-old parliament called Tynwald, which claims to be the oldest parliament in continuous existence. Tynwald dates back to when the Isle of Man was ruled by Norwegian Vikings (c. 800–1266) as part of the Lordship of the Isles. Rule over the island passed to the kings of Scotland, the Stanley family of Lancashire (1406–1736), and the Dukes of Atholl (in Perthshire). In 1765, the Isle of Man was bought by the British Parliament and the British monarch became head of state.

The Manx language

Up to the beginning of the eighteenth century, English was not understood by most of the island's people, who spoke the Manx language, closely related to Irish and Scottish Gaelic. By 1901, however, there were just under 4,500 Manx speakers left (out of a total population of nearly 55,000), all of whom also spoke English. A hundred years later, the Manx-speaking population had dwindled to just over 1,500.

Civil registration (births, marriages and deaths)

In 1849, non-compulsory civil registration marriage certificates began to be issued for Nonconformists, who didn't want to be married in a parish church. Compulsory registration of births and deaths was introduced in 1878, with compulsory registration of marriages following in 1884. The Manx National Heritage Library (MNHL, *www.gov.im/mnh*) in Douglas, the island's capital, has a microfiche copy of the indexes of births, marriages and deaths from 1878–1993. You can purchase a birth, marriage or death certificate from the Civil Registry section of the General Registry (*www.gov.im/registries*), which is also in Douglas. From the website, you can download the appropriate form to apply for a certificate.

Census returns

The first census was held on the island in 1811, but as in England, Scotland and Wales, individual names were not listed until 1841. The MNHL has copies of the 1841–81 censuses on microfilm and the 1891 and 1901 on microfiche. From 1901, Isle of Man census entries indicate whether someone could speak Manx, English or both languages.

Parish registers

The Isle of Man forms the whole of the Diocese of Sodor and Man, within the Anglican Province of York. The name 'Sodor' is a corruption of the Norse *Suðreyar*, meaning 'Southern Islands' (i.e. the southern Inner Hebrides), which were southern compared to the Outer Hebrides and Skye.

Microfilm copies of the registers of the seventeen Manx parishes (plus the towns of Douglas, Ramsey and Castletown) from the early seventeenth century up to 1883 are held by the MNHL. The baptisms and marriages from these registers are included in the LDS International Genealogical Index (IGI). Some Nonconformist registers are also held by the MNHL, although Roman Catholic registers are usually held by the parish priest. Nonconformists had to marry in the (Anglican) parish churches until 1849.

Wills and administrations

Up to 1884, Manx wills and administrations (of the estates of those who left no will) were proved by the church courts (the Consistory Court of Sodor and Man and the Archdeaconry Court of the Isle of

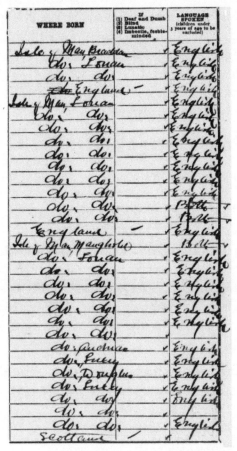

*Isle of Man 1901 census return, showing languages spoken
in right-hand column.*

Man), and after that time by the civil court (the High Court of
Justice). The MNHL holds original wills from around 1600–1910
and microfilm copies up to 1916, while later wills are at the General
Registry. Most of the wills have been indexed, apart from some in
the seventeenth century.

Other records

In addition to the records mentioned above, the MNHL holds nine-
teenth- and early twentieth-century trade directories, Manx
newspapers from the late eighteenth century, microfilmed land and

property records from the early sixteenth century, deeds from the late seventeenth century to 1910 (with later deeds at the General Registry) and monumental inscriptions transcribed by the Isle of Man Family History Society.

Isle of Man records online

Digitized images of the censuses of the Isle of Man from 1841–1901 are accessible at Ancestry.co.uk (*www.ancestry.co.uk*) on a subscription or pay-per-view basis. You can view a transcription of the 1881 census free of charge at the LDS Family Search site (*www.family search.org*), which also holds the IGI for the Isle of Man parishes.

Images of the 1841, 1861, 1871 and 1891 censuses for the island are available on the pay-per-view site Find My Past (*www.findmypast.com*), while the 1901 census is at the Genes Reunited census site (*www.1901census.nationalarchives.gov.uk*). S&N Genealogy's 'The Genealogist' website (*www.thegenealogist.co.uk*) has online transcripts of and also name indexes for the 1841–71 and 1891 censuses.

Isle of Man and Channel Islands genealogical timeline

1540	Earliest Jersey parish register
1563	Earliest Guernsey parish register
1801	First official ten-yearly census of the Channel Islands
1811	First official census of the Isle of Man
1840	Civil registration of births, marriages and deaths in Guernsey
1841	Probate of real estate wills passes to civil court in Guernsey
1842	Civil registration of births, marriages and deaths in Jersey
1849	Non-compulsory civil registration of marriages on the Isle of Man
1878	Civil registration of births and deaths on the Isle of Man
1884	On the Isle of Man, compulsory civil registration of marriages, and wills now proved by civil court
1949	Probate passes to civil court in Jersey

Channel Islands

The Channel Islands are also Crown dependencies, with the Bailiwicks of Jersey and Guernsey (which includes Alderney, Sark, Herm, Jethou, Lihou and Brecqhou). Previously part of Brittany, the islands and adjacent mainland were held by the Normans from 933 until 1204, when the rest of the Duchy of Normandy became part of France. During the Second World War, the islands were occupied by Germany from 1940–45. The population of Jersey is about 88,000, and that of Guernsey around 66,000.

Channel Islands' languages

The official languages of Jersey and Guernsey are English (the dominant language) and French. Until 1948, French was the official language of both bailiwicks. Norman French is still spoken by small numbers of people on the Channel Islands and mainland Normandy, and was the everyday language of most of the islanders until the nineteenth century.

The version spoken on Jersey is known as Jèrriais, and is still spoken by about 3,000 people. The Guernsey equivalent is Guernesiais, spoken by only 2 per cent of the island's population. Sercquiais, spoken on Sark, is derived from Jèrriais, as Sark (although nearer to Guernsey) was colonized by people from Jersey. Only about twenty people speak it today. Auregnais, the version of Norman French spoken on Alderney, died out in the twentieth century.

Jersey

Civil registration (births, marriages and deaths)

In August 1842, civil registration of births, marriages and deaths began in Jersey, with the records and their indexes held by the Superintendent Registrar in St Helier, the capital. Copies of the indexes from 1842–c. 1900 are also held by the Société Jersiaise and the Jersey Archive, both in St Helier.

Census returns

The Société Jersiaise, the Jersey Archive and the Jersey Library hold copies of the census returns for 1841–91 on microfilm and for 1901 on microfiche. As in England, Scotland and Wales, the 1801–31 censuses don't include individual names. General Don's militia census was carried out in French in 1806 and 1815, and you can see it at the Société Jersiaise.

Parish registers

The Channel Islands have been part of the Diocese of Winchester since the reign of King Henry VIII. Prior to that time, they were included in the Diocese of Coutances in France.

Jersey consists of twelve parishes, with the earliest register (for the parish of St Saviour) dating back to 1540. Early registers were written in French. As in France and Scotland, a woman retained her maiden surname after marriage, and she may even be buried in that name.

The original parish registers are still with the ministers of the individual churches, with copies at the Jersey Archive dating up to the late twentieth century. Indexes to and transcriptions of the registers (up to 1842) have been produced by the Channel Islands Family History Society (which covers only Jersey), and are held by the Jersey Archive and the Société Jersiaise.

The society has copies and indexes for Nonconformist and Roman Catholic registers, as well as some monumental inscriptions. The Jersey Archive holds baptism, marriage and burial registers for the island's Methodist chapels from 1836–1989, and other Nonconformist records from the early nineteenth century up to the mid- or late twentieth century.

Wills

Until 1949, probate was handled by the Ecclesiastical Court of the Dean of Jersey, after which the (civil) Royal Court at the Judicial Greffe (office of the clerk of the court) was responsible. Wills from 1660–1948 are held by the Jersey Archive, and are indexed by name on its database. The archive also has an index of wills from 1948–60.

Other records

Other records at the Jersey Archive include almanacs (directories), rate lists (1880–1970, with some up to 1988), militia nominal rolls (1902–38) and attestation papers (1929–40), telephone directories (1931–2002) and land records from 1602–1963, together with business and estate records. Registration cards for 33,000 inhabitants from 1940 are also indexed on the Jersey Archive database.

Guernsey

Civil registration (births, marriages and deaths)

In Guernsey, civil registration of births, marriages and deaths began in 1840, with the original records held at the Greffe in the capital, St Peter Port. Microfilm copies of the births and deaths from 1840–c. 1980 and marriages from 1840–1901 are held at the Priaulx Library (*www.priaulx.gov.gg*), also in St Peter Port, which has indexes for all three types of record from 1840–c. 1963.

Census returns

The Priaulx Library holds copies of the census returns for Guernsey from 1841–1901, as well as many for Jersey too.

Parish registers

The oldest registers of the ten parishes of Guernsey are those of St Peter Port Town Church, with baptisms from 1563 and marriages from 1565. Copies of these, many of which are indexed, are held by the Priaulx Library, which also has copies of some Nonconformist, Roman Catholic and cemetery records (some of which are indexed).

Wills and administrations

The Court of the Commissary of the Bishop of Winchester in the Bailiwick of Guernsey is still responsible for proving wills and granting letters of administration for personal estate only. Wills relating to real estate (land and buildings) have been proved by the (civil) Royal Court at the Judicial Greffe since 1841. Indexed books of wills and administrations from 1660 are held at the Greffe.

Other records

The Priaulx Library holds Guernsey newspapers (many of which were published in French) from their first publication in 1791, as well as copies of the official *Army List* and the unofficial *Hart's Army List* from 1756–1913, an incomplete run of the *Navy List* from 1847, and various regimental and campaign histories.

Channel Islands records online

The Jersey Archive database is at *www.jerseyheritagetrust.org/sites/archive/archive.html*, where you can search free of charge by name, place, subject and collection reference number, or carry out a combined search. In addition, you can browse the database by theme: church registers, German occupation, maritime, Royal Court, agriculture, education, businesses and military. You can find brief abstracts of wills by browsing under 'Royal Court'.

As with the Isle of Man, you can view images of the censuses of the Channel Islands from 1841–1901 at the subscription/pay-per-view site Ancestry.co.uk (*www.ancestry.co.uk*), as well as a free transcription of the 1881 census at the LDS Family Search site (*www.familysearch.org*). All ten Guernsey parishes (but no Jersey parishes) are included in the IGI for the period *c.* 1840–75.

The pay-per-view Find My Past (*www.findmypast.com*) has images of the 1861 and 1891 censuses for Jersey and Guernsey, as has the 1901 census site (*www.1901census.nationalarchives.gov.uk*).

You can obtain more information about finding your ancestors in Jersey and Guernsey at family historian Alex Glendinning's Channel Islands pages (*http://user.itl.net/~glen/CIintro.html*).

The Story of You: Dennis Craddock

Dennis Craddock became interested in family history in 1945 at the age of sixteen, when he had a chat about his family to his maternal grandfather, George Brummell, who was then aged eighty-one. 'He'd lived in Bedford for many years, but was born in 1864 in the Cambridgeshire village of Longstowe, on the Old North Road,' says Dennis. 'One thing he told me on that occasion that really fired my imagination was that he had an aunt who married a Mormon, went to America and was never heard of again. My mother, her sisters and her brothers all said, "Rubbish, Dad, you're making it up in your old age," as none of them had heard this story before.'

Family history research in the past

It's now over sixty years since Dennis began tracing his family history, although he confesses to long periods of inactivity. 'When I married in 1956, this stimulated an interest in my wife's family history,' he says. 'This was largely thanks to her grandmother's marvellous memories and family stories of their origins in Cornwall. She was then nearing her eightieth birthday. As her father was born in 1832 and lived until 1924, she was able to tell me many tales that her father had told her about his father and grandfather.'

Dennis's researches on the maternal side of his family began in the 1950s. In those days, to search in parish registers, he needed to make appointments with the vicars of various Cambridgeshire parishes, to which he travelled by bus. Dennis was lucky that some vicars saved him a journey by replying by post to specific enquiries about dates of baptisms, marriages or burials.

'This was long before the days of microfiche and computers, or the availability of the Mormon Index [IGI],' says Dennis. 'As the family searches spread wider, I began to spend the occasional day at the General Register Office in Somerset House [the predecessor of St Catherine's House and the Family Record Centre], humping heavy hand-written registers up and down from the shelves, and copying down every entry for the surname in question and its reference number. Back at home, I'd spend hours deciding which references to use to apply for actual certificates.'

Mormon pioneers in the family

In 1963, once Dennis had found most of the members of his mother's family, he wrote to the Church of Jesus Christ of Latter-day Saints (LDS) Family History Library in Salt Lake City, asking if any of those names appeared in their immigrant records. Dennis received an immediate reply, with confirmation that Anne Brummell Cooper, his maternal grandfather's aunt, had emigrated in 1856 from Orwell in Cambridgeshire with her three young daughters. 'They were in the Second Handcart Expedition,' says Dennis. 'They set out from Iowa City, where the railway ended, to walk the 1,300 miles to Salt Lake City pushing their young children and baggage on handcarts. There were 440 in that group, seventy-seven of whom died of starvation or froze to death on the journey, including Anne's two-year-old daughter.'

The information from Salt Lake City included the name and address of a family historian who was researching information for Anne Brummell Cooper's great-grandchildren in Southern Utah. Dennis was soon in touch with them, and in 1973, made the first of many visits to America. 'Bearing in mind that my grandfather George Brummell was born in 1864, and that his aunt and her three girls emigrated in 1856, it appears that this was something he had learned as a child,' says Dennis. 'It shows how important it is to seek out information from the oldest members of your family when you start to research.'

In fact, although Dennis's grandfather had said his Aunt Anne was never heard of again, after twenty years in Utah Territory, she wrote home to Cambridgeshire in 1876. Anne's descendants in Utah kept the replies she received from one of her brothers and two of her sisters, and Dennis has seen the originals, of which he has photocopies, in the archives in Salt Lake City.

Using the Internet

'I have used the Internet, but not a great deal,' says Dennis, 'as my basic family trees were already built up before it became available. The Local Studies Centre at my local reference library has been invaluable for its information, such as the censuses, the Mormon Index [IGI] and the Births, Deaths and Marriages Index.'

Dennis did use the Internet a few years ago to link up with descendants of Richard Brummell (an uncle of his maternal grandfather), who emigrated to Australia in 1882 with his wife and children.

'I was also very pleased to find the *Immigrant Ships Transcribers Guild* on the Internet,' says Dennis. 'From this, I obtained details of Anne Brummell Cooper's voyage with her three children, along with about 350 other Mormon emigrants from Liverpool on the ship *Thornton*, which arrived in New York on 15 June 1856. Anne, aged thirty-seven and her three children, aged six, four, and two, are listed on the 'Lower Deck' with their destination as 'Utah, USA', for which all the passengers were bound. About ninety of them were Danish and the rest British.'

Surprising and interesting ancestors

In 2002, Dennis was idly looking through the Register of Bedford Gaol (now online at *http://apps.bedfordshire.gov.uk/grd*), which has details of 20,000 nineteenth-century prisoners. For the period 1859 to 1877, there are photographs of the convicted criminals, as well as written details of the offences and the physical appearance of the prisoner.

'Suddenly I was brought up short,' declares Dennis. 'There was a portrait of an older brother of one of my great-grandfathers, sentenced in 1863 to seven years for manslaughter. He'd been arrested with six others following an affray in Castle Lane, Bedford that led to the death of a solicitor.' Dennis's great-great-uncle was tried at Bedford Assizes and sent to Millbank Prison in London to serve his sentence. To learn further details of this previously unknown event, Dennis was able to find extensive newspaper coverage in the *Bedford*

Times and *Bedford Mercury*, local newspapers available on microfilm at Bedford Reference Library.

Sensitive information

Although the prison sentence could have been a sensitive matter, Dennis was already seventy-two when he made the discovery, and there was no earlier generation of family members to feel embarrassed about it. 'A more sensitive issue arose about 1960 in researching my wife's family,' says Dennis. 'I was trying to find a death date before 1880 for her great-grandfather's first wife. My wife's grandmother, who in 1960 was much loved and active, was born in 1880 and was the first child of the second marriage. When I eventually found that the first marriage had ended not in a death, but in a divorce that didn't happen till grandmother was aged five, my wife and I decided not to tell either her mother or her grandmother.'

People are still the same

Dennis says his discoveries have confirmed to him that however different the times we live in, basically people are still the same, with the same worries about jobs and their health, the welfare of their children and the upheavals of wars or other unexpected events.

PART TWO

Extra Branches

20

Immigration to Britain and Ireland

One way or another, we're all immigrants to Britain and Ireland, whether our ancestors came before Britain became separated from the continent of Europe about 8,000 years ago (and from Ireland even earlier), or much more recently. Even the people who made cave paintings found in Nottinghamshire and dated to about 15,000 years ago, had come from elsewhere in Europe after the last Ice Age. The people of Wales have long been thought to descend from the ancient Britons. Recent DNA studies suggest, however, that they and most of the population of England, Scotland and Ireland are descended from immigrants from the Iberian Peninsula in the middle and new stone ages, rather than from later invaders.

Although the Romans occupied Britain for about 350 years, they made only a very minor contribution to its population. The Angles, Saxons and Jutes (who arrived in the fifth century), as well as the Danish and Norwegian Vikings (who came about 300 years later) had a much bigger effect on the population, although perhaps not as big as we'd previously thought. The Normans, however, simply replaced the Anglo-Saxon aristocracy after 1066.

William I's Conquest brought Normans, Frenchmen, Bretons and Flemings to Britain and Ireland. Although they became the new ruling class, their actual numbers were not large, and they didn't pass on their language (French) to the rest of the population.

During the reign of Henry I in the twelfth century, a colony of Flemings was set up in Pembrokeshire, while in the fourteenth century, Edward III brought seventy families from Wallonia (now the French-speaking part of Belgium) to promote woollen manufacture. In the seventeenth century, the engineer Cornelius Vermuyden brought Dutch workers with him to drain Hatfield Chase in Yorkshire.

A fleet was sent to Rotterdam in 1709 to bring Protestant refugees from the Palatinate (now part of the state of Rheinland-Pfalz in Germany) to England. Over 3,000 sailed to America, the so-called 'Pennsylvania Dutch', while a similar number settled in County Limerick in Ireland.

As well as the movement of peoples into Britain and Ireland from elsewhere in Europe, there has also been the colonization of Argyll by Irish Scots in the sixth century, the plantation of Ireland by English and Scots (particularly in the sixteenth and seventeenth centuries), and the movement of many Irishmen and -women to Britain in the nineteenth century.

In the last few hundred years, Huguenots, Jews and various other Europeans have settled in Britain, while large numbers of West Indians and South Asians arrived in the late twentieth century.

Surnames

Round about the twelfth century, the upper classes began adopting surnames in England and southern Scotland, and this filtered down to everyone in the next few hundred years. In Wales and the Scottish Highlands, however, fixed surnames didn't become universal until the eighteenth and (in some areas) the nineteenth centuries.

Languages in Britain, Ireland, the Isle of Man and the Channel Islands

Although the entire native-born populations of Britain, Ireland, the Isle of Man and the Channel Islands can now all speak English, and in most cases do so as their first language, this was not the case a few hundred years ago.

As recently as 1901, over 230,000 Scots could speak Gaelic (out of nearly 4.5 million), while Welsh was spoken by half of Wales's population of 1.7 million (and 280,000 of those could speak only Welsh). Today there are fewer than 60,000 Gaelic and 580,000 Welsh speakers (about a fifth of the overall Welsh population).

The number of Irish speakers has dropped from around 4 million in the 1840s to a UNESCO estimate of as few as 20,000 fully competent native speakers, despite compulsory learning of Irish in the Republic of Ireland.

The last native speaker of Cornish (Dolly Pentreath) died in 1777. A movement to revive the language has resulted in there being a few hundred fluent speakers today.

Two hundred years ago, most of the population of the Isle of Man spoke Manx Gaelic (and understood no English), but by 1901, only about a twelfth of its people knew the language, and were all bilingual. The last native speaker of Manx (Ned Madrell) died in 1974. As with Cornish, there has been a revival movement, and in the 2001 census, over 1,500 people claimed to be able to speak Manx (around 45 per cent of whom were under the age of nineteen).

In the nineteenth century, the first language of most Channel Islanders was Norman French, which is still spoken by about 3,000 people on Jersey, over 1,000 on Guernsey and only twenty on Sark. It has died out on Alderney. Until 1948, standard French was the only official language. Now it shares this position with English, which is the dominant language in the islands. You can find out whether your ancestors could speak one of these languages as well as (or instead of) English, as this is indicated on census returns for:

- Welsh – from 1891;
- Scottish Gaelic – from 1891;
- Irish Gaelic – from 1901;
- Manx Gaelic – from 1901.

Huguenots

During the sixteenth century, the word 'Huguenot' was applied to French Protestants, particularly by their enemies. During the sixteenth and seventeenth centuries, about 50,000 Huguenots fled to Britain, mainly from France itself, but also from Wallonia (nowadays the French-speaking part of Belgium). The largest numbers arrived around 1572 (after the Massacre of St Bartholomew during the Wars of

Religion in France from 1562–98) and 1685 (when the Edict of Nantes, which had guaranteed religious freedom in France since 1598, was revoked).

The Huguenot refugees settled in London (in particular in Bethnal Green, Soho, Spitalfields, Wandsworth and Westminster), Edinburgh, Bristol, Canterbury, Norwich, Plymouth, Southampton and other smaller communities. A further 10,000 moved on to Ireland, settling in Dublin, Cork, Kilkenny, Lisburn, Portarlington and Waterford.

(Other destinations for the 200,000 Huguenots who left France were the Dutch Republic (50–60,000), Germany (25–30,000), Switzerland (22,000), America (10,000), Scandinavia (2,000) and South Africa (400).)

By 1700, there were about twenty-three French churches in London, and in 1718, a French Protestant Hospital (*www.french hospital.org.uk*), known as 'La Providence', was established. The French Hospital still exists today, providing sixty self-contained flats in Rochester, Kent for people of Huguenot descent.

In 1885, the hospital's directors founded what is now the Huguenot Society of Great Britain and Ireland (*www.huguenotsociety.org.uk*) to mark the bicentenary of the Revocation of the Edict of Nantes.

During the eighteenth century, the communities of Huguenots were gradually integrated into mainstream British society, attending local instead of French Protestant churches, which consequently closed as their congregations grew smaller.

Tip: Huguenot registers are available on CD

The Huguenot Society has published many of its *Quarto* series of publications on CD, particularly those covering the registers of the French churches in London, in England outside London, and in Ireland. In addition, there are CDs listing denizations (granting foreigners rights of residence, but without full citizenship) and naturalizations (allowing them to become British citizens) from 1509–1800, as well as inmates of the French Hospital from 1718–1957.

The Huguenot Library www.ucl.ac.uk/Library/ huguenot.shtml

The Huguenot Library, formed from the library and archive collections of the French Hospital and the Huguenot Society, is believed to contain the most complete body of Huguenot literature in the UK. Since 1957, the library has been housed within the Special Collections of University College London (UCL).

The library's collection focuses principally on the social history of Huguenots in the UK, and includes around 6,000 books and many periodicals, prints and engravings. The library holds records of French Protestant churches in London, together with details of the relief funds distributed to the Huguenot refugees and their descendants from 1686–1876. You'll also find records of the French Hospital, as well as those of other Huguenot institutions such as the Westminster French Protestant School and several Huguenot societies and charities. In addition the library holds many family papers, such as the Wagner Pedigrees, which contain information on around 1,000 Huguenot families, and other family history research files, many of which are available on microfiche.

You can search most of the library (as opposed to archive) holdings, including material on Huguenots in Ireland, through the UCL Library's online catalogue eUCLid (*http://library.ucl.ac.uk/F*). The archive holdings, however, are not catalogued online, but in the Huguenot Society's *Quarto* series of occasional publications, copies of which are held by the library.

Tip: Family collections in the Huguenot Library

In the Huguenot Library, you can view collections covering the following families:

- Allix;
- Armand;
- Aufrère;
- Barraud;
- Beuzeville;

- Boileau;
- Bosanquet;
- Caillouet;
- Chick;
- De Béranger;
- Daniel de Grangues;
- De la Balle;
- De Luc;
- De(s) Vignolles;
- Dubrée;
- Duroure;
- Fenhoulet;
- Fremeaux;
- Giraud;
- Hardy;
- Hill;
- Lamotte;
- La Roque;
- Layard;
- Lepine;
- Minet;
- Minett;
- Ott;
- Papillon;
- Pechell;
- Renouard;
- Roget;
- Ruvigny;
- Rybot;
- Serces;
- Teulon;
- Turquand.

Jews

Many Jews arrived in England after the Norman conquest, settling in large towns, but were expelled by Edward I in 1290. Jews were not officially allowed to return to England until the Commonwealth period, when Oliver Cromwell gave them permission to do so in 1656, although small numbers had lived in London illegally before that time.

Most of the Jews who came to Britain in the late seventeenth century were Sephardim (from Spain, Portugal and Italy), although some Ashkenazim (Eastern European Jews) moved to England from the Netherlands after 1680. Around 120,000 Ashkenazi Jews arrived from Russia and Poland between 1880 and 1914.

In the 1930s, many Jewish refugees came to Britain from Nazi Germany, its allies (such as Hungary) and German-occupied Europe (Austria, Poland, etc.). More Ashkenazi Jews from South Africa, Australia and New Zealand settled in Britain from the 1960s onwards.

Tip: Many Jewish records are held by London Metropolitan Archives *www.cityoflondon.gov.uk/Corporation/leisure_heritage/libraries_archives_museums_galleries/lma/lma.htm*

Since the seventeenth century, the largest Jewish community in the UK has lived in London, and many of their records are held by London Metropolitan Archives (formerly the Greater London Record Office). Some of the collections freely accessible are:

- British Women's International Zionist Organization (WIZO) – founded in 1918;
- Jews' Free School (JFS) Admission and Discharge Registers;
- Liberal Jewish Synagogue;
- London School of Jewish Studies (formerly Jews' College);
- Victoria Club (founded 1901);
- Westminster Jews' Free School.

To be able to see other record collections, however, you need the depositing organization's permission:

- Board of Deputies of British Jews;
- (Central British Fund for) World Jewish Relief;
- Federation of Synagogues;
- Food for the Jewish Poor;
- Jewish Bread Meat and Coal Society;
- Jewish Health Organisation of Great Britain;
- Jewish Memorial Council;
- Jews' Temporary Shelter;
- Kashrus Commission;
- London Beth Din;
- National Council for Jews in the former Soviet Union;
- New Road Synagogue;
- Office of the Chief Rabbi;
- United Synagogue and its predecessors (includes records of closed synagogues);
- West London Synagogue;
- Western (Marble Arch) Synagogue.

Scottish Jewish Archives Centre www.sjac.org.uk

The Scottish Jewish Archives Centre was opened in 1987 as a national heritage, information and research centre. It has information on 23,000 Jews living in Scotland before the Second World War, including details from cemetery records, synagogue registers, naturalizations, charity subscription lists, school admission registers and many other records.

The centre contains an exhibition of Jewish history in Scotland since the seventeenth century, and records of the larger Jewish communities in Scotland:

- Edinburgh (founded in 1816);
- Glasgow (founded in 1823);

- Dundee (founded in 1878);
- Aberdeen (founded in 1893);

as well as those of the former small communities in Ayr, Dunfermline, Falkirk, Greenock and Inverness.

Jewish Genealogical Society of Great Britain
www.jgsgb.org.uk

The Jewish Genealogical Society of Great Britain (JGSGB) holds regional meetings in England, special interest group meetings on Jewish ancestry from different parts of Europe, and an online discussion group. The society has a members' library in north London, whose holdings include family histories and several hundred reference books. The JGSGB has a collection of family trees, whose index you'll find online at *www.jgsgb.org.uk/libtree.shtml*.

As well as a large collection of Yizkor (memorial) books, the library also has microfilm and microfiche copies of papers from many of the major Anglo-Jewish genealogy collections, and maps. You can view the library catalogue online at *www.jgsgb.org.uk/download/ LibraryList.doc* (for a Word file) or *www.jgsgb.org.uk/download/ LibraryList.pdf* (for a PDF file).

Romanies ('Gypsies')

The Romany or Roma people originated in northern India, from which they migrated to south-west Asia around 1,000 years ago. They speak Romany, a language within the Indo-Aryan branch of the Indo-European language family, related to Hindi/Urdu, Punjabi and other Indian languages, but with borrowings from the languages of the areas the Romany people passed through: Iranian and Slavonic languages, Armenian, Greek, Hungarian (Magyar), Romanian, German, Italian and other European languages.

The Romanies may have originated in the non-Aryan troops recruited by the Aryan rulers of India to defend it against Muslim invaders. In a second migration, Romanies moved into Europe in the fourteenth century, arriving in western Europe in the fifteenth. Because they had come from the east, they were called Egyptians or

'Gypsies' (which is now considered to be a derogatory name). In the late nineteenth and early twentieth centuries, a third migration to North America took place.

Romany and Traveller Family History Society www.rtfhs.org.uk

The Romany and Traveller Family History Society (RTFHS) publishes a quarterly journal, *Romany Routes*, as well as various research guides, transcripts, and other books on Romany families and Romany life. The society runs a mailing list through Google Groups, details of which you'll find on its website. There you'll also find information on the Robert Dawson Romany Collection, which is held by the Museum of English Rural Life at the University of Reading, as well as links to a number of websites with information on Romanies.

Immigration records and information online

Moving Here www.movinghere.org.uk

Set up by a number of museums and archives (and also funded with Lottery money), this free site describes the arrival in Britain and subsequent settlement of various recent immigrants. At present, only those who came in the last 200 years (Jewish, Irish, West Indian and South Asian immigrants) are covered. You can read about why people came, their journeys, and also the hardships and prejudice they faced after they arrived in their new country. In addition, there are images of documents and photographs, as well as sound and video clips.

The Moving Here site also contains a section on family history, with a good deal of information that can help you if your family is Jewish or came from Ireland, the West Indies or the Indian subcontinent.

JewishGen UK Database www.jewishgen.org/ databases/UK

The JewishGen UK Database, a joint project between the US-based website JewishGen and the Jewish Genealogical Society of Great

Britain (JGSGB), contains over 60,000 records relating to Jewish ancestry in the United Kingdom.

The information in the database, which you can search free of charge, has been contributed by Jewish Communities and Records – United Kingdom (JCR-UK, *www.jewishgen.org/jcr-uk*) and the JGSGB, as well as by a number of individuals. The database includes 3,500 Jewish marriages that took place between 1838 and 1972, including over 2,600 from the West London Synagogue from 1842– 1952.

There are over 30,000 Jewish burial records from England, Scotland and Wales, and details of Jews who were in business in London (9,000 in the first half of the nineteenth century, and 5,000 in the period 1769–1839). The database contains over 12,000 names being researched by Jewish family historians, as well as over 1,800 Jewish entries from the 1851 and 1891 censuses for Wales.

As well as the JewishGen UK Database, the site also lets you search in a supplementary database, containing Jewish records from the JGSGB that haven't yet been added to the main database. This includes 10,000 marriages and over 43,000 burials from all over Britain.

There are also over 1,300 Jewish records from Manchester directories for 1855, 1884, 1927 and 1934; 2,000 records from the Hull Hebrew School; and over 14,000 records from the Salford Police Register of Aliens 1916–65 (which includes non-Jews). In addition, the database includes Jews on census returns from:

- Exeter, Torquay and Devonport – 1841–61;
- Falmouth and Penzance – 1851;
- Manchester – 1871;
- Plymouth – 1841–91;
- Spitalfields – 1861;
- Stroud – 1881 and 1901.

Yad Vashem Holocaust Memorial Museum
www.yadvashem.org

At the website of the Yad Vashem Holocaust Memorial Museum in Jerusalem, you can search the Central Database of Shoah Victims'

Names for information on the Jews killed by the Nazi government of Germany. The database contains information from pages of testimony submitted by relatives, historical documentation and other sources. So far, information is available on about 3 million of the estimated 6 million people who died.

Tip: The National Archives hold many records of foreigners
www.nationalarchives.gov.uk

Foreigners are mentioned in various types of record at the National Archives (TNA), including:

- Records of the Chancery (record class C47) and the Exchequer (E106);
- Exchequer Subsidy Rolls (E179) – the Huguenot Society has extracted the names of foreigners living in and around London and published them on its CD No. 3 (Denization and Naturalization);
- Exchequer Accounts Various (E101);
- Parliament Rolls (C65) – including naturalizations from c. 1400;
- Patent Rolls (C66 and C67) – including denizations (c. 1400–1844);
- Close Rolls (C54) – including naturalizations (1844–73);
- State Papers, Domestic (SP10–16, 18, 29 and 30) – names also included on the Huguenot Society's CD No. 3;
- non-parochial registers (RG4) – original registers of baptisms/births, marriages and burials from Dutch, French, German and Swiss refugees' churches for periods between 1567 and 1857;
- oath rolls (KB24) – including Oath Rolls of Naturalization (1708–12);
- Treasury In-Letters (T1) – including embarkation lists for German Palatine emigrants sailing from the Netherlands to England in 1709;
- denizations (C97) 1751–93 and (HO4) 1804–43;

- duplicate certificates of naturalization kept by the Home Office (HO334) 1870–1987;
- certificates of aliens arriving in England and Scotland from 1836–52 (HO2) – earlier certificates (from 1826) no longer exist, but indexes to them do;
- Registered Papers (HO45) for denizations and naturalizations from 1841–78 and (HO144) for denizations and naturalizations from 1879–1922 – later records are not open to the public;
- passenger lists, inwards (BT26) from 1878–88 and 1890–1960 – generally passengers from outside Europe and the Mediterranean area;
- Alien Registration Cards (MEPO35) for the London area – only 1,000 cases survive out of tens of thousands;
- Internment Tribunal Cards (HO396) – 307 records of Germans, Austrians, Italians and their spouses interned or considered for internment.

You can find other records of foreigners in the UK at:

- Guildhall Library, London;
- Bodleian Library, Oxford;
- Cambridge University Library;
- Lambeth Palace Library, London.

21

Emigration from Britain and Ireland to the United States, Canada, Australia, New Zealand and South Africa

As well as the 64 million people who live in Britain and Ireland, a further 150 million people around the world are said to be descended from emigrants from the British Isles. Most of them live in five countries:

- the United States of America – where the first successful settlement was established at Jamestown in 1607;
- Canada – whose colonization by Britain began in the late eighteenth century (after about 150 years of settlement by the French);
- Australia – where a penal colony was set up at Sydney in 1788;
- New Zealand – where the first British settlements were made around 1820;
- South Africa – which had been first colonized by the Dutch in 1657, and the British from early in the nineteenth century.

Online databases

There are several online databases recording immigration to those countries, or emigration or transportation from Britain or Ireland. The Generations Network has a large number of immigration databases that you can search at its *www.ancestry.com, www.ancestry. co.uk, www.ancestry.ca* and *www.ancestry.com.au* websites. The University of Aberdeen has set up a Scottish Emigration Database (*www.abdn.ac.uk/emigration/index.html*), and Find My Past (*www. findmypast.com*) is digitizing the National Archives' departure passenger lists from 1890–1960.

The Ships List website (*www.theshipslist.com*) also contains many lists of passengers travelling to the USA, Canada, Australia, New Zealand and South Africa, as does the website of the Immigrant Ships Transcribers Guild (*www.immigrantships.net*).

There are several online databases and indexes of people convicted of crimes who were transported from the UK, mainly to Australia. As well as holding its own transportation database, Lincolnshire Archives has links to other convict websites at *www.lincolnshire.gov. uk/section.asp?catId=6724*.

The Commonwealth War Graves Commission's Debt of Honour Register (*www.cwgc.org*) of servicemen and -women who died in the First and Second World Wars includes Canadians, Australians, New Zealanders and South Africans.

You'll find many useful links to websites in the US, Canada, Australia, New Zealand and South Africa at Cyndi's List (*www. cyndislist.com*) and the various GenWeb sites:

- US GenWeb (*www.usgenweb.org*);
- Canada GenWeb (*www.rootsweb.com/~canwgw*);
- Australia GenWeb (*www.australiagenweb.org*);
- New Zealand GenWeb (*www.rootsweb.com/~nzlwgw*);
- South African Genealogy (*http://home.global.co.za/~mercon*).

Archives in Britain and Ireland

The main archives covered in Chapter 2 hold records on emigration from Britain or Ireland:

- The National Archives in London;
- The National Archives of Scotland in Edinburgh;
- The Public Record Office of Northern Ireland in Belfast;
- The National Archives of Ireland in Dublin.

Emigration to the USA

Although emigration from Britain to what is now the United States began as early as 1585, the first settlement to be successful was established in 1607 at Jamestown by the London Virginia Company.

Many thousands of emigrants went to Virginia to work in the tobacco plantations as indentured servants.

Many of the Europeans who colonized America went in search of a place where they could practise their religion in freedom. Emigration for religious reasons began in 1620, when the *Mayflower* sailed from Plymouth to New England carrying the 102 Puritan settlers known as the 'Pilgrim Fathers'. The state of Maryland was settled by English Roman Catholics, Pennsylvania by Quakers (the Religious Society of Friends) and, much later, Utah by Mormons (the Church of Jesus Christ of Latter-day Saints).

Shortly after England and Scotland were united in 1707, Scots took advantage of the new union by emigrating to America. By the time of the American Revolution in 1776, as many as 150,000 Scots who had previously settled in Ireland (the 'Ulster Scots' or 'Scots-Irish') had emigrated to America, as well as about 50,000 who had come from Scotland itself.

Transportation of criminals to the American colonies was first used as a punishment in 1615, but didn't become common until after 1660. Before 1718, most of those transported were sent to sugar plantations in the West Indies, but after that time the majority went to Virginia and Maryland. After serving their seven- or fourteen-year sentences, many of those transported remained in their new home, although some returned to Britain and Ireland. After the Revolutionary War, Britain was not able to transport criminals to the new United States, and began to send them to Australia instead. An estimated 30,000 people had been transported to America and the West Indies by that time.

Of the estimated 650,000 immigrants who arrived in America before 1820, just under 400,000 were from England and Wales, together with smaller numbers of Irish, Scots-Irish and Scots. During the nineteenth and twentieth centuries, many English, Scots, Welsh and Irish were among the 35 million immigrants to the United States, with over a million leaving Ireland because of the Great Famine in the late 1840s.

Tracing your ancestors in the USA

Vital records (civil registration)

The larger cities were the first civil governments to record births, marriages and deaths in the USA: Boston (from 1639), New Orleans (1790), New York (1847), Philadelphia (1860) and Baltimore (1875).

Record-keeping began early in New England, with New Hampshire recording marriages from 1640, and most states registering vital events between 1841 and 1897. The Mid-Atlantic states began birth and death registration between 1878 and 1915, although Delaware and New Jersey have some marriage records that date back to the 1660s. In the South marriages were recorded from the early eighteenth century, although in South Carolina there was no civil registration of marriages until 1911. Midwest states began registration of births and deaths in many counties in the 1860s, although this was not carried out state-wide until the period from 1880–1920. Most western states didn't start registration until the first two decades of the twentieth century. Hawaii, however, began registering births, marriages and deaths in the 1840s.

Vital records are usually held locally at the courthouse of one of the US's 3,066 counties (which are called boroughs in Alaska and parishes in Louisiana). You can find contact details for each county's administration building at the website of the National Association of Counties (*www.naco.org/Template.cfm?Section=Find_a_County& Template=/cffiles/counties/usamap.cfm*). At state level, there are vital records offices, whose addresses you can find at *www.vitalrec.com*.

Some states provide online access, e.g. images of Arizona's births and deaths are at *http://genealogy.az.gov*. You can find links to similar websites listed by state at Cyndi's List (*www.cyndislist.com*) and at the US GenWeb Project website (*www.usgenweb.org*). The births (or baptisms) and marriages of over 48 million Americans are indexed in the LDS International Genealogical Index (IGI), which you can search online at *www.familysearch.org*.

Another source of information on deaths is the Social Security Death Index (SSDI), which contains over 50 million deaths reported to the US Social Security Administration from 1937–95. The SSDI is available online at several websites, and you can search several of them (and do much more besides) from *www.stevemorse.org*.

Census returns

The federal censuses taken by the US government every ten years since 1790 are open to the public up to and including the 1930 census. The early censuses for the states of Delaware, Georgia, Kentucky, New Jersey, Tennessee and Virginia were destroyed in the war of 1812. Much later, most of the 1890 census was destroyed by fire in 1921. The 1790–1840 censuses name heads of household only, the 1850–70 censuses list each person in a household, and the 1880 and later censuses state their relationships to the head of the household.

US federal census record 1930.

The National Archives in Washington and the LDS Family History Library in Salt Lake City hold copies of the federal censuses. State archives also hold copies (sometimes for their area only), as well as state and colonial censuses and local population listings.

All the federal censuses are fully indexed and accessible online at the subscription-based website Ancestry.com (*www.ancestry.com*). The census returns are available in public libraries (and often remotely to library users at home) through Heritage Quest Online, but not all years are indexed. You can find links to transcriptions of parts of the federal censuses, as well as local lists, at the Census Finder site (*www.censusfinder.com*).

Church registers

The United States has never had an official national church in the way the Anglican Church is the 'established' Church of England. In the mid-seventeenth century, three-quarters of the population of the original thirteen colonies were Anglican or Congregationalist. The Anglican Church was strong in Virginia, while the Puritan settlers in New England were Congregationalist. In the seventeenth and eighteenth centuries, so many Presbyterians from Scotland and the north of Ireland emigrated to Pennsylvania, that by the mid-eighteenth century there were almost as many of them in the American colonies as Anglicans and Congregationalists.

In 1681, William Penn, a Quaker (member of the Religious Society of Friends), had founded Pennsylvania (named after his father), and the constitution he drew up for the colony ensured freedom of worship. Many Quakers settled in the colony, as did Protestants and various minority groups from Germany (including Mennonites and the Amish).

In the early nineteenth century and again after 1920, the Baptists became the largest Protestant denomination. In the intervening period, the Methodists were the largest Protestant group, and by 1850, formed about a third of the Protestant population.

By this time, Roman Catholics were the largest Christian group in the United States, having begun to settle in Florida and the western and southern states that were formerly part of Mexico in the sixteenth century. Catholics had also settled in Maryland (having emigrated from England) and Louisiana (from Spain and Acadia in French Canada). In the nineteenth century, many Catholics arrived in the US from Ireland and southern and eastern Europe.

Also in the nineteenth and early twentieth centuries, many Jewish immigrants arrived in the major American cities from Austria, Germany, Russia and other eastern European countries.

The Mormon Church (Church of Jesus Christ of Latter-day Saints, LDS) was founded in New York in 1830, moving west to what became the state of Utah and neighbouring areas in 1846–7. Members of the LDS Church wish to 'seal' their ancestors into their religion, but first they need to trace them. For this reason, the LDS Family History Library in Salt Lake City was founded in 1894. The library holds genealogical records from around the world that have been copied in the LDS Church's microfilming programme. The microfilms are made freely available to all by means of the library and its worldwide network of over 4,000 Family History Centres in eighty-eight countries.

American church records are often still held in the church, or have been collected by a state or denominational archive. The LDS Family History Library holds microfilm copies of many church records from the US and around the world, which it is currently in the process of digitizing. These will then be made available on-line in the future.

At present, many US church records are indexed in the IGI. You can find many transcripts of the records at the US GenWeb Project website and links to other transcription sites at Cyndi's List.

Wills and administrations

Wills and administrations (granted when the deceased person left no will) are proved in County Probate Courts and held in county court-houses and state archives. The LDS Family History Library holds transcripts of probate records for many states and for the District of Columbia.

Many wills of British settlers (particularly in the colonial period) were proved in London at the Prerogative Court of Canterbury (such as the will of William Penn) or in Edinburgh at the Commissary and (later) Sheriff Courts.

Immigration records

The National Archives in Washington and the LDS Family History Library have large collections of customs and immigration passenger lists from 1820 to the 1950s. These include 24 million arrivals in

New York, 2 million in Boston, 1.5 million in Baltimore, 1.2 million in Philadelphia, 700,000 in New Orleans and 4 million in other ports (including Charleston, Galveston, Key West, New Bedford, Passamaquoddy, Portland, Providence, San Francisco and Seattle).

From 1820–92, Castle Garden in New York was the main centre for immigrants arriving in the US. At Castle Garden's website (*http:// castlegarden.org/index.html*), you can search a database containing information on the 10 million immigrants who arrived there from 1830 onwards. A further 2 million records, covering those who arrived in the preceding ten years, have still to be digitized.

In 1892, Ellis Island was opened as the new federal immigration station in New York, replacing Castle Garden, which had been state-run. From that time until 1924, when immigration to the US was severely curtailed, over 12 million immigrants entered America via Ellis Island. You can search an online database of its records at *www. ellisisland.org*.

Ancestry.com (*www.ancestry.com*) has over 100 US immigration and naturalization databases on its website. Other immigration websites include the Ship's List (*www.theshipslist.com*) and the Immigrant Ships Transcribers Guild (*www.immigrantships.net*).

General

You'll also find many useful links to websites in the US at Cyndi's List (*www.cyndislist.com*) and US GenWeb (*www.usgenweb.org*).

Emigration to Canada

Eastern Canada was claimed from the mid-sixteenth century by the French, who established settlements in Acadia (now Nova Scotia, which changed hands between France and England several times during the seventeenth century), New France (between the city of Quebec and Lake Ontario) and the Detroit area. After seventy years of rivalry between Britain and France ending in the French and Indian War (or Seven Years War), in 1763, the French were forced to surrender their colonies on the American mainland. By this time, there were 70,000 French colonists living in what later became the eastern part of Canada.

After the American Revolution, around the same number of British 'United Empire Loyalists' (many of them Scots-Irish) fled to Canada from the newly independent United States. Few emigrants went to Canada directly from Britain, although by 1814, about 200,000 Americans had moved there from the US.

By 1806, the population of what is now Canada had grown to 250,000 in Lower Canada (now Quebec), 70,000 in Upper Canada (now Ontario), 65,000 in Nova Scotia, 35,000 in New Brunswick (mainly loyalists), 26,000 on Newfoundland and nearly 10,000 on Prince Edward Island. Until 1830, the numbers of emigrants were small, but from then on, thousands of English, Scottish and Irish settlers arrived each year. About 100,000 child migrants (mainly orphans) known as the 'Home Children' were sent to Canada from 1869 to the early 1930s.

Tracing your ancestors in Canada

Civil registration

Canada's provinces and territories started to record births, marriages and deaths in the late nineteenth and early twentieth centuries. Library and Archives Canada's Canadian Genealogy Centre has information and contact details for obtaining certificates from provincial archives and vital statistics agencies (*www.collectionscanada.ca/genealogy/022-906.006-e.html*). You can search vital event indexes online for British Columbia at *www.bcarchives.gov.bc.ca/textual/governmt/vstats/v_events.htm#indexes*, for Manitoba at *http://web2.gov.mb.ca/cca/vital/Query.php*, for New Brunswick at *http://archives.gnb.ca/APPS/GovRecs/VISSE/?L=EN*, and for Saskatchewan at *http://vsgs.health.gov.sk.ca/vsgs_srch.aspx*.

Census returns

Federal censuses prior to 1851 are incomplete and list only heads of household. The 1851–1911 censuses for the provinces and territories, listing each person by name, are publicly available. You can find links to the many Canadian censuses accessible online at *www. collectionscanada.ca/genealogy/022-911-e.html*.

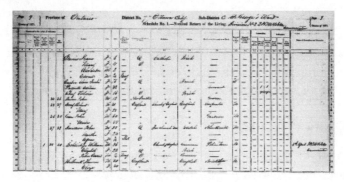

Canadian census record 1871.

As Newfoundland didn't become a Canadian province until 1949, it isn't included in the publicly available Canadian censuses. Labrador was enumerated with the North-West Territories in 1871 and 1911. The Newfoundland censuses of 1921, 1935 and 1945 are open to the public, and are being indexed. You can search these censuses online (and many other earlier Newfoundland censuses) at *http://ngb. chebucto.org/census.shtml*.

Church registers

The oldest surviving Canadian register begins in 1621. Unfortunately, there's no central repository of church registers: some are still in the churches, while others are held in provincial or religious archives. You'll find links to provincial and territorial archives at *www.collec tionscanada.ca/genealogy/022-802-e.html* and to church archives at *www.collectionscanada.ca/genealogy/022-806-e.html*. Many Canadian baptisms and marriages are listed in the LDS International Genealogical Index (*www.familysearch.org*). You can find some Ontario Wesleyan Methodist baptisms online at *http://freepages. genealogy.rootsweb.com/%7Ewjmartin/wm-index.htm*.

The University of Montreal has an online database at *www.gene alogie.umontreal.ca/en/acces.htm* including over 750,000 Roman Catholic baptisms, marriages and burials that took place between 1621 and 1799 in 153 parishes in the province of Quebec, 45,000 burials from 1800–1850, various censuses from 1666–1744, marriage contracts and migrant lists.

Wills and administrations

Wills are dealt with by provincial and territorial governments. You can find information on the records held by them, as well as contact details, at *www.collectionscanada.ca/genealogy/022-907.003-e.html*.

Immigration records

You can find information on early immigrant records and online databases at *www.collectionscanada.ca/genealogy/022-908.002-e. html*. The databases include a consolidated list of immigrants from the British Isles who settled mainly in Quebec and Ontario between 1801 and 1849. You can search this database online at *www.ingeneas. com/free/index.html*.

Information on the passenger lists held by Library and Archives Canada covering the period 1865–1935, as well as links to various online databases, is at *www.collectionscanada.ca/genealogy/022-908.003-e.html*. You can search the records for 1925–35 online at *www.collectionscanada.ca/archivianet/020118_e.html*. Ancestry.ca (*www.ancestry.ca*) provides access to Canadian immigration databases, birth, marriage, death, census and various other records.

General

You can find more information and links to Canadian websites at Cyndi's List (*www.cyndislist.com*), Canada GenWeb (*www.rootsweb. com/~canwgw*), and Canadian Genealogy and History Links (*www. islandnet.com/~jveinot/cghl/cghl.html*).

Emigration to Australia

British colonization of Australia began when the 'First Fleet' arrived in 1788 with 730 prisoners (570 men and 160 women) and 250 free people (most of them the Royal Marines guarding the convicts), and established a settlement at what was to become Sydney.

Australia became the main destination for transportation of British and Irish criminals once the United States achieved independence as a result of the American Revolutionary War (1775–83). By 1830, around 58,000 convicts (8,000 of them female) had been transported. Transportation to the eastern part of Australia was ended by the British government in 1852, after a total of 151,000 criminals had been sent there. A further 10,000 convicts were sent to Western Australia, where transportation began in 1850 and ended in 1868.

Most of the transported prisoners stayed on in Australia after they'd served their sentences. In many cases, their wives and families had travelled out to join them. There were also large numbers of free settlers, many of whom had their passage paid by the British government. By 1851, the number of Europeans in Australia had reached 450,000, which had grown to over a million ten years later.

There was assisted emigration to Australia from Ireland at the time of the Great Famine in the 1840s, and the Highlands and Islands Emigration Society helped poor Scots to emigrate between 1852 and 1857. In the twentieth century, many British families emigrated under the Australian government's assisted passage schemes, while over 3,000 child migrants went to Australia from 1947–53.

Tracing your ancestors in Australia

Civil registration

Civil registration of births, marriages and deaths in Australia was carried out first by the individual colonies and then by the states and territories. Registration began in 1838 in Tasmania, in 1841 in Western Australia, in 1842 in South Australia (which included the Northern Territory until 1911), in 1853 in Victoria, and in 1856 in New South Wales (which included Queensland until 1859 and the Australian Capital Territory until 1930).

Birth certificates issued in Victoria, New South Wales and Queensland include the father's name, age, occupation and birthplace, the mother's name, maiden surname, age and birthplace, the date and place of marriage, the names and ages of other living children, and the sexes of children who had died. Marriage certificates in those states include the ages and birthplaces of the bride and groom, father's name and occupation, and mother's name and maiden surname.

You'll find the following information included in the same states' death certificates: date and place of death and burial, father's name and occupation, mother's name and maiden surname, birthplace of the deceased person, length of time he or she had lived in Australia, in which colony or state, name of the deceased's spouse, date and place of marriage, age of the deceased at marriage, and names of the deceased's children (with their ages and indicating whether living or dead). The birth, marriage and death certificates of Tasmania give fairly basic information, as do those of Western Australia up to 1896 and South Australia up to 1907, after which more details were added.

You'll find contact details for the various registrars of births, marriages and deaths in Fact Sheet 89 from the National Archives of Australia (*www.naa.gov.au/publications/fact_sheets/fs89.html*). All of the states have made copies of their birth, marriage and death indexes available for sale on microfiche or on CD (except the Northern Territory indexes, which are available on microfiche only).

Both Victoria's church records from 1836 and civil registration records from 1853 have been indexed and digitized and are available online at the state's Births, Deaths and Marriages Online Shop (*http://online.justice.vic.gov.au/servlet/bdm_home*). There are cut-off points of eighty-one years for births, sixty-three years for marriages and twenty years for deaths. You can also search the Marine Index online for births, marriages and deaths that took place on ships bound for Victoria between 1853 and 1920. These have also been digitized. There is a charge for both searching the indexes and downloading the image of a certificate.

New South Wales has made an index (but no images) of both its church and civil registration records available online at *www.bdm.nsw.gov.au/familyHistory/searchHistoricalRecords.htm*. The indexes cover a period beginning in 1788, with cut-off points of 100 years for births, fifty years for marriages and thirty years for deaths.

Searching the indexes is free, and there is a discounted charge for ordering a certificate online.

Western Australia also has an online index of its historical civil registration records (but no images) at *www.justice.wa.gov.au/portal/server.pt/gateway/PTARGS_0_2_323_ 201_0_43/http%3B/justicecontent.extranet.justice.wa.gov.au/F/familyhistory.aspx?uid=7603-9553-6410-6954*. The indexes run from 1841, with cut-off points of 100 years for marriages and deaths and eighty-seven years for births. You can obtain a discount, if you quote the appropriate reference information when you order a certificate.

Although South Australia has no online index, you can apply for certificates online at *www.ocba.sa.gov.au/bdm/applying/online/apply online.html*.

Census returns

Unfortunately, most of the Australian nineteenth-century census returns were destroyed after the statistical analyses had been compiled, but those that do survive are held by the state archives. You can find their contact details in Fact Sheet 2 issued by the National Archives of Australia (*www.naa.gov.au/Publications/fact_sheets/fs02.html*).

Some Tasmanian returns for 1837, 1838, 1842, 1843, 1848, 1851 and 1857 have survived, and you can search an index of them at *http://portal.archives.tas.gov.au/menu.aspx?search=10*. State Records New South Wales has put various indexes online at *www.records.nsw.gov.au/archives/indexes_online_3357.asp*, including the 1841 census.

Church registers

Most of the church registers used to record baptisms, marriages and burials before civil registration began are held by the registrars of births, marriages and deaths (see 'Civil registration' above). Many Australian baptisms and marriages are listed in the LDS International Genealogical Index (*www.familysearch.org*).

Wills and administrations

Australian state archives hold records of granting probate on wills, and of issuing letters of administration (when no will had been made).

The Archives Office of Tasmania has an online index to wills and letters of administration (*http://portal.archives.tas.gov.au/menu.aspx?search=9*) from 1824–1989. Queensland State Archives has an online index of wills proved between 1857 and 1900 at *www.archives.qld.gov.au/research/index/wills.asp*.

Immigration records

Records of immigration after 1923 and naturalization after 1904 are held by the National Archives of Australia, and prior to that time, by the state archives. You can find out more from the National Archives' Fact Sheet 227 (*www.naa.gov.au/Publications/fact_sheets/fs227.html*).

The Archives Office of Tasmania has set up an online Index to Tasmanian Convicts, which covers 76,000 convicts, including those transported between 1804 and 1853. At *www.archives.tas.gov.au/nameindexes* you can search an online index of convict applications for permission to marry (1829–57), as well as various other indexes.

Among the many databases that State Records New South Wales has made available online at *www.records.nsw.gov.au/archives/indexes_online_3357.asp*, are various convict, immigration, naturalization and land record indexes. Similarly, at the Public Record Office Victoria website (*www.access.prov.vic.gov.au/public/PROVguides/PROVguide023/PROVguide023.jsp*), you can search various online databases, including immigration and convict record indexes.

Several indexes (including immigration) are available online at Queensland State Archives' website (*www.archives.qld.gov.au/research/indexes.asp*). Some of these indexes are also available on microfiche.

The Highlands and Islands Emigration Society database (*www.scan.org.uk/researchrtools/emigration.htm*) covers emigration from Scotland to Australia between 1852 and 1857.

Australian military service record.

You'll find a database of Irish prisoners transported to Australia between 1836 and 1853 (with petitions covering the period from 1791) at *www.nationalarchives.ie/genealogy/transportation.html*.

Lincolnshire Archives also has a transportation database at *www. lincolnshire.gov.uk/section.asp?docId=27638&catId=6722* of 2,000 convicts sent to Australia, Gibraltar and Bermuda from 1788–1868. On the same website (*www.lincolnshire.gov.uk/section.asp?catId= 6724*), you'll find links to various other transportation sites, both in the UK and Australia.

Ancestry.com.au (*www.ancestry.com.au*) also provides access to several convict and immigration databases.

General

You'll find useful links to websites in Australia at Cyndi's List (*www.cyndislist.com*), Australia GenWeb (*www.australiagenweb.org*), and the Australian Family History Compendium (*www.cohsoft.com.au/afhc*).

Emigration to New Zealand

In the early nineteenth century, a few hundred British settlers arrived in New Zealand, which was never used as a penal colony. These were mainly traders, followed by missionaries from 1814. In 1841, New Zealand became a Crown Colony, with the Maori (who had settled in the country from Polynesia about 1,000 years earlier) guaranteed possession of their lands, although this didn't prevent friction and wars between them and the European settlers in 1845–7 and 1860–71.

The story of you: Pamela Ormerod

'My families all seem to have had the "have feet will travel" mentality,' says Pamela. 'So far, my paternal family has moved from Cheshire to Staffordshire, Derbyshire, Nottinghamshire, South Wales, London, Kent, Sussex, Hampshire, Devon and New Zealand. They've also served the Crown in the air and on the sea, as well as in India, North Africa, Egypt, St Helena and South Africa.'

No one had ever mentioned to Pamela's father, however, that his great-great-grandfather Joseph Cookson had emigrated from Cheshire to New Zealand, together with his wife Sarah and eight of his children and their families. 'The eldest son, John Cookson, stayed in England,' says Pamela. 'My father's grandmother Mary Ann lived with him – her father-in-law – on occasions, with not a hint of the momentous exodus of his father, mother and siblings.'

The British Government and private organizations assisted emigration to New Zealand in the nineteenth century, with most of the emigrants coming from the UK. Many Scots emigrated to New Zealand, beginning with Lowlanders from Ayrshire and Galloway. They were followed in 1854 by Gaelic-speakers dispossessed in the Highland Clearances. These Highlanders had originally emigrated to Cape Breton Island in Canada, but then moved to Australia and finally to the North Island of New Zealand. Most of the country's Highland immigrants lived in the South Island, however, particularly in Dunedin. In addition, two groups of settlers from the north of Ireland emigrated between 1875 and 1878.

Today, 80 per cent of New Zealand's million inhabitants are of European origin (principally from Britain and Ireland), with Maori making up about 15 per cent of the population.

Tracing your ancestors in New Zealand

Civil registration

Compulsory registration of the births and deaths of New Zealanders of European descent ('Pakeha') began in 1847, and of their marriages in 1854. Maori marriages had to be registered from 1911, and Maori births and deaths from 1913, although this didn't necessarily happen. You can obtain certificates or electronic printouts (cheaper, and with more information) from the Central Registry in Wellington. Full information and downloadable forms are available at *www.bdm. govt.nz*. Around 10 million registrations have been digitized and are expected to be made available online in the future. The cut-off points for historic records are expected to be 100 years for births, sixty years for marriages and fifty years for deaths.

Early Pakeha registrations hold only basic information, but from 1876, the following details were added to birth registrations: date and place of parents' marriage, and age and birthplace of each parent. From 1880, the following information was added to marriage registrations: names of each spouse's parents, fathers' occupations and mothers' maiden surnames. Also from 1876, the following information was added to death registrations: names of both parents of the deceased, father's occupation, mother's maiden surname, birthplace of the deceased and length of time in New Zealand. In addition, if the deceased had been married: place of marriage, age at time of marriage, name of spouse, sex and age of surviving children (but no names), and date and place of burial.

Archives New Zealand (*www.archives.govt.nz*) in Wellington hold copies of compulsory Notices of Intention to Marry (marriage licences) from 1856–1956.

You can find links to online databases indexing the burial records of a number of New Zealand cemeteries at *http://nzgenealogy.roots chat.net/cemetery.html*.

Census returns

Although country-wide censuses have been taken in New Zealand since 1851, the detailed returns have unfortunately not been kept. Archives New Zealand hold some other population listings, such as electoral rolls (from 1866 for some areas) and telephone directories (from the early twentieth century onwards).

An Auckland Area Police Census carried out annually between 1842 and 1846 is searchable online at *http://o-www.aucklandcity. govt.nz.www.elgar.govt.nz/dbtw-wpd/policecensus/census.html*. You can also find 1881 Auckland electoral rolls at *http://o-www.auckland city.govt.nz.www.elgar.govt.nz/dbtw-wpd/electoral/electoral.html*.

Church registers

Some baptism, marriage and burial records are still in the churches, although most are in the archives of the various denominations. The Central Registry for Births, Deaths and Marriages and Archives New Zealand also have some nineteenth-century parish registers. Many New Zealand baptisms and marriages are listed in the LDS International Genealogical Index (*www.familysearch.org*).

A register of all Presbyterian marriages in Otago and Southland provinces between 1848 and 1920 is being made available online at *http://archives.presbyterian.org.nz/marriageregisters/otagosouthland marriages.htm*.

Wills and administrations

Archives New Zealand have many probate records for wills and administrations, as well as other estate records. Each of their offices – the head office in Wellington and regional offices in Auckland, Christchurch and Dunedin – holds records for its own area.

Immigration records

There are many immigration records at Archives New Zealand, including: passenger lists (1840–1973), shipping records, the registers of the New Zealand Company (1839–50), lists of 'fencibles' (750 retired soldiers sent from Britain between 1847 and 1853), registers of immigrants to the Waikato area in 1864–5 – 2,000 from Britain and 1,000 from the Cape Colony – and registers of over 19,000 'nominated' immigrants (1871–91), as well as lists of unassisted and subsidized immigrants.

In addition, there are links to many immigration and other databases at the website of New Zealand's History Online (*www.nzhistory.net.nz/handsonhistory/genealogy-links*).

Cyndi's List contains a page of links relating to New Zealand ship and passenger lists at *www.cyndislist.com/newzealand.htm#Ships*. You can search an online database of Auckland Area Passenger Arrivals from 1838–86 and 1909–21 at *http://0-www.aucklandcity.govt.nz.www.elgar.govt.nz/dbtw-wpd/passengers/passenger.html*. Both the Ship's List (*www.theshipslist.com*) and the Immigrant Ships Transcribers Guild (*www.immigrantships.net*) contain passenger lists of ships that sailed to New Zealand.

General

You'll find many useful links to websites in New Zealand at Cyndi's List (*www.cyndislist.com*), New Zealand GenWeb (*www.rootsweb.com/~nzlwgw*) and New Zealand's History Online (*www.nzhistory.net.nz/handsonhistory/genealogy-links*).

The New Zealand Society of Genealogists (*www.genealogy.org.nz*) is making available online databases of sheep owners, freeholders,

'First Families' and Members' Interests, as well as downloadable short guides, each covering a different type of record.

Emigration to South Africa

The Dutch were the first Europeans to settle in South Africa, when the Dutch East India Company landed there in 1652 and established a small settlement of nine men and their families in the Liesbeek Valley in 1657. By 1707, there were over 1,700 settlers with over 1,100 slaves.

During the Napoleonic Wars, the Cape Colony was occupied by the British from 1795–1803, at which time there were 16,000 European settlers living there, and then again from 1806. The population of mainly Dutch and German immigrants had risen to 43,000 by 1820, when about 1,000 British families arrived as a result of the British government's Cape Emigration Scheme.

In 1835, several thousand Boers (farmers) and their families headed north from the Cape Colony to find land on which to settle, and in 1852 and 1854 respectively, the Boer states of Transvaal and the Orange Free State gained their independence from Britain.

By the mid-1870s, there were 240,000 European settlers and their descendants in the Cape Colony, two-thirds of whom spoke Dutch (now known as Afrikaans). After the South African (Boer) War of 1899–1902, the two British colonies of the Cape and Natal were united with the former Boer republics of Transvaal and the Orange Free State to form the Union of South Africa in 1910.

According to the 2001 census of South Africa, 8.2 per cent of the country's total population of just under 45 million speak English at home. This equates to 3.7 million people, compared to around 6 million Afrikaans speakers.

Tracing your ancestors in South Africa

Civil registration

Registration of births, marriages and deaths began at different times in South Africa's four historic provinces:

Province	Births	Marriages	Deaths
Cape	1895	1700	1895
Natal	1868	1845	1888
Transvaal	1901	1870	1901
Orange Free State	1903	1848	1903

Civil registration records are held by the Department of Home Affairs in Pretoria, but the indexes are not open to the public (which makes it difficult to obtain certificates), and marriage certificates contain no information about the parents of the bride and groom. Many of the earlier records are held by the repositories of the National Archives of South Africa (NASA) in the four historic provinces. You can find the addresses of the Department of Home Affairs and the NASA repositories (and other bodies) at *http://home. global.co.za/~mercon/address.htm* on the South African Genealogy website set up by Conrad Mercer, past president of the Genealogical Society of South Africa.

Census returns

No census returns are open to view, as these are unfortunately destroyed (as is the case in Australia and New Zealand) once statistical analyses have been carried out. There are, however, electoral rolls from 1870 that are held by the NASA.

Church registers

The earliest Anglican registers begin around 1806, with Roman Catholic registers starting about 1820. Although some registers of baptisms, marriages and burials are still at the individual churches, many are held by archives in South Africa's four historic provinces. Many South African baptisms and marriages are listed in the LDS International Genealogical Index (*www.familysearch.org*).

The University of the Witwatersrand in Johannesburg holds registers for Beaufort West, Cape Town, Johannesburg, Namaqualand, Natal, Pretoria, Transvaal, Victoria West and Zululand, as well as for the island of St Helena. You can download a guide to the university's holdings at *www.wits.ac.za/histp/collections.htm*.

The registers of St George's (Anglican) Cathedral in Cape Town from 1834–1900 are held by the Cape Town Archives, and more recent records are still held by the cathedral. Rhodes University's Cory Library in Grahamstown (*http://campus.ru.ac.za/index.php?action=category&category=2635*) holds most Methodist registers, as well as some Presbyterian, Congregational, Catholic, Baptist and Jewish registers.

The church registers for St George's Cathedral in Cape Town, St John's (Waterkant Street, Cape Town), St Paul's Rondebosch and St Francis in Simonstown are being made available online at *www.ancestry24.co.za*.

Among the databases you can search using the NASA's National Automated Archival Information Retrieval System (NAAIRS) at *www.national.archives.gov.za/index.htm* is an index of gravestones compiled by the South African Genealogical Society. Using NAAIRS you can also find death notices, which are the South African equivalent of a death certificate elsewhere, and are held by the provincial repositories.

Wills and administrations

The provincial archive repositories hold records of 'deceased estates', which usually contain a death notice, a will (if there was one) and the estate accounts. You can use NAAIRS to find estate papers.

Immigration records

Some information on immigration is held by the NASA. At *www.sagenealogy.co.za*, you can find many passenger lists online, mainly for 1880 and 1881, together with lists of survivors of shipwrecks. Another site with passenger lists is at *http://sa-passenger-list.za.net/ index.php*, which includes ships docking at Cape Town in 1852 and Durban from 1845–58, and Huguenots arriving in South Africa between 1683 and 1756.

At *www.geocities.com/settlers1820*, you'll find the genealogies of some of the British settlers who arrived in 1820, while information on the 'stamouers', the founders of South Africa in the seventeenth and eighteenth centuries (most of whom were Dutch or German) is at *www.stamouers.com*.

General

There are many useful links to South African websites at Cyndi's List (*www.cyndislist.com*), South African Genealogy (*http://home. global.co.za/~mercon*) and Ancestry 24 (*www.genealogy.co.za/ Ancestry24.aspx?page=content/home*).

22

The East India Company

The East India Company was founded in 1600 as an association of English merchants who received the exclusive right to carry out trade with 'the Indies', which covered the whole of south and east Asia, including India itself. During the second half of the eighteenth century, the Company changed from being principally a trading concern to a political power controlling ever-greater areas of India, with a large number of 'civil servants' (the origin of the term) and its own army to protect its interests. The Company's headquarters were at East India House in Leadenhall Street in the City of London, where it was controlled by a 'Court of Directors'. Its administrative headquarters in India were in Calcutta, the capital of Bengal, one of three 'presidencies' that the Company's territories were divided into. The other two presidencies were Madras and Bombay, ruled from those two cities respectively.

In 1784, a 'Board of Control' was set up in London to supervise the Company's activities in India, and from 1833, it no longer had a monopoly over British trade with India. After that, the Company withdrew completely from its trading activities, but continued to govern large areas of India until shortly after the Indian Mutiny in 1857, a major rebellion by native troops, which was confined to the north of India.

Most of the Company's army consisted of native Indian soldiers, under the command of British officers and non-commissioned officers. By 1857, many of the native troops were concerned that the grease being issued to them for rifle cleaning was made from the fat of animals their religions forbade them to touch (cows for Hindus, and pigs for Muslims). Unfortunately, their British officers paid no attention to the soldiers' worries about the grease, with the result that when the mutiny came, it took the Company by surprise. The mutineers massacred British men, women and children, and the troops sent to put down the mutiny were equally brutal. For many Indian historians, the mutiny is seen as the beginning of the struggle for independence from British rule.

The Company troops were put under the command of the British Army after the mutiny, and soldiers from the UK were given the opportunity to join the British Army or retire on a pension. The large areas of India controlled by the Company were placed under the British Crown from 1858 and Queen Victoria was crowned 'Empress of India'. By the time India regained its independence in 1947–8 as India, Pakistan (of which the eastern part later became Bangladesh) and Burma, the British had spent roughly the same length of time in India as Britain had been part of the Roman Empire (three and a half centuries).

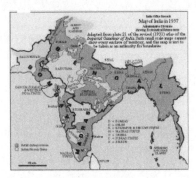

Map of India as it was in 1937.

The records of the East India Company

You can find the East India Company's records in the British Library in London. These include church registers, military records (such as muster rolls, discharge papers and embarkation records), wills, monumental inscriptions, pension records, ships' logs and letters to the Company. There are no civil registration records, however, or census returns with individual names.

Not all of the Europeans that you'll find in the East India Company's records were British. In particular, the French, Dutch and Portuguese had also set up trading posts on the Indian coast, with Goa remaining in Portuguese hands from 1510–1961 and Pondicherry under French administration from 1674–1954.

Ecclesiastical Returns

Copies of the baptisms, marriages and burials of Europeans recorded in the church registers in India and elsewhere were sent to East India House in London, and are known as 'Ecclesiastical Returns'. These are the Indian equivalent of the bishop's transcripts of England and Wales. The returns for Madras begin in 1698, for Bombay in 1709 and for Bengal in 1713, in all cases continuing up to 1947. Unfortunately, the British Library believes that 20–30 per cent of these records are missing.

There are also ecclesiastical returns for places outside India, including:

- St Helena 1767–1835;
- Fort Marlborough (Benkulen, Sumatra) 1759–1825;
- Prince of Wales Island (Penang), Malacca and Singapore 1799–1829 (and continued in the Bengal returns up to 1868);
- Macao and Whampoa (Canton) 1820–33;
- Kuwait 1937–61;
- Aden 1840–1948 (although most of the Aden entries also appear in the Bombay returns).

You won't find a great deal of information in the baptismal records of the eighteenth and early nineteenth centuries, and only slightly more by the mid-nineteenth century. A typical baptismal record from St Mary's Church, Madras (the main Anglican church, located inside Fort St George, the British military and administrative centre for the city) reads:

> Mary, daughter of Thomas Adamson and Ann his wife,
> October 30th [1790]

A later record gives you a little more information:

> Black Town, 13th December 1820
> John James, the son of John Wiltshire, writer, and
> Elizabeth his wife, born October 22nd 1820, was this
> day baptised by me.
> (Signed) Charles Church, Chaplain

Marriage records can give you names of witnesses:

> Mr Samuel Godfrey and Miss Mary Adamson (natives) were
> married in St. Mary's Church, Fort St. George on the 1st day
> of December 1808 by me.
> (Signed) Edward Vaughan, Chaplain
> This marriage was solemnised between us: Samuel Godfrey,
> Mary Adamson in presence of Geo. Stevens, Thomas
> Adamson, Jas. Rd. Hogg

The names of two of the witnesses confirm that the Mary Adamson marrying is the one baptized in 1790, as she had a brother Thomas and a sister Margaret, who had married a George Stevens in 1802.

Burial records also provide more information later. In 1810, we find:

> Mrs Anne Adamson, 11th May

Nine years later, we have:

> Madras 23rd May 1819
> Mary Catherine Wiltshire, clerk in the Military Auditor
> General's Office, aged 9 years and five months, was buried by
> the Revd. Thomas A. Lewis.

Thirty years after that sad entry, we have more information:

> 5th April 1848
> John Wiltshire who died on the 4th of April of lumber
> abscess aged 57 years, pauper, was buried at Madras by me,
> M.W.Wm. James MA, Assistant Chaplain.

Tip: Useful book

You'll find much helpful advice in the short book *Baxter's Guide: Biographical Sources in the India Office Records* (Families in British India Society, 2004). Now retired, Ian Baxter was a Curator of the India Office Records, and pointed me in the direction of several records I wouldn't have found otherwise.

Wills and administrations

Although the British Library holds wills proved and administrations granted in India, many wills of English and Welsh people who had lived in India were proved in the Prerogative Court of Canterbury (PCC) and are held by The National Archives (TNA) in London. Similarly, the National Archives of Scotland (NAS) in Edinburgh hold many wills of Scottish people who had lived in India.

Unfortunately, the wills of Irishmen and -women who had lived in India were destroyed in the major fire at the Public Record Office of Ireland (PROI) in Dublin in 1922. You can, however, find copies, transcripts, abstracts and extracts of some of those wills at the PROI's successor, the National Archives of Ireland (also in Dublin).

Muster rolls

In the 'List of military on board the ship *Royal George*, Captn Thomas Foxall, for Madras', we find a typical muster roll entry:

> John Wilsher, Private, London, labourer, age 16, size 5ft 2ins.
> Mustered on board the ship Royal George the 5th Jany. 1778

William Godfrey (*c.* 1750–1809), officer of the Company

William's career with the Company

In 1801, my 5× great-grandfather William Godfrey was an officer who had been invalided out of the Company's army and was on half-pay in command of a company of invalids. To get back on to the 'effective establishment', William petitioned the Company's Court of Directors, travelling to London with his family to do so. He was unsuccessful in his attempt, but did receive a promotion to Major.

Among the 'Auditor's References' in the India Office Records is a 'memorial' that William wrote to the directors, in which he describes his career with the Company:

> *After serving as an officer on board one of your ships for above eight years from 1765 to 1773 – during which time I had the misfortune to be shipwrecked in the* Falmouth *and was 42 days in an unexplored country before I reached Calcutta nearly starved to death – I was appointed an Ensign in your military establishment at Fort St. George the 31st December 1773.*
>
> *From that time until 1784 (when, from an injury received on service, I was obliged to return to Europe for a cure), I was constantly employed in the active duties of an officer:-*
> *In 1775, I was detached to Bombay to join the expedition in support of Ragobah;*
> *In 1777, served against the Poligars;*
> *[In] 1778 at the siege of Pondicherry;*
> *In 1780 against Hyder, when I volunteered in the Storm of Chittapet and received the thanks of Colonel Cosby.*

The Storm of Chittapet

In one of several testimonials that William submitted with his memorial, Lieutenant-Colonel (later Major-General Sir) Henry Cosby states that:

> *Captain William Godfrey of the Madras Establishment, making part of a detachment under my command when marching to reinforce General Sir Hector Munro at Conjeveram after the unfortunate defeat of Colonel Baillie, in a very handsome manner volunteered at the attack of Chitteput, a fortress of very considerable strength in the Carnatic, that had been recently surrendered to Hyder Allie, and which I was in hopes of retaking by surprise and, having a wet ditch to pass and two walls to surmount, was particularly hazardous, and that his conduct on this occasion met with my entire approbation.*

Hyder Ali was the ruler of the south Indian state of Mysore, which in 1780 was outside the area under Company control. Hyder had attacked the Carnatic, the area to the south of Madras, and seized a number of forts.

In the Orme Collection of manuscripts in the India Office Records, I found a letter by Colonel Cosby to an unknown person from 'Camp near Madras 15 Oct 1780', in which he describes the Storm of Chittapet:

> *I considered an idea that if Chitteput was attacked by escalade in the night, it might probably succeed (at any rate, it was worth the trial), and should it, it would of course be a great check on Hyder and afford me an excellent station to make excursion from towards the forts of Trinomally, Arnee, Powlour etc. in his possession and by which he drew his provisions.*

I therefore, having prepared four ladders, left my camp standing and marched at seven in the evening, and about half past two the next morning reached Chitteput, having previously made the disposition for the attack. We passed the ditch and mounted into the fause bray [a mound of earth forming a rampart]. *From the bottom of the ditch to the top of the wall is at least 30 feet, so that it proved a most laborious business to get the ladders (which being made for two abreast were heavy) into the fause bray. The great crowd which, anxious to get in after their companions, kept constantly getting up the ladders, it was above half an hour before two could be got over, and even these damaged. They were, however, planted against one of the bastions, but by this time, the enemy's whole force were collected to oppose us.*

Numbers of blue lights [were] *hoisted all along the face attacked, and rows of pikes presented through every embrasure, so that it now became impossible to enter. A man no sooner got to the top of the ladder than he was knocked down by a shot or a pike. Notwithstanding, we continued to persevere for one hour and a half, when, the day beginning to break and no further hopes of success remained, we retreated.*

East India Company records online

There are several websites dealing with the British and other European presence in India that you can view and search free of charge.

India Office Records

The section of the British Library's website that covers its Asia, Pacific and Africa collections includes a number of pages on India Office Records: Family History Sources (*www.bl.uk/collections/oiocfamily*

history/family.html). These describe the various records that you can find in the India Office Records at the new British Library building in London.

The site contains a glossary of terms found in India Office documents and records, as well as a description of occupations found in colonial India. Although the records themselves have not been put online by the British Library, you can find references to individual people in the index at the Access to Archives (A2A) website (*www.a2a.org.uk*). Under 'Location of Archives', select 'British Library, Asia, Pacific and Africa Collections'.

Families in British India Society (FIBIS)

The website of the Families in British India Society (FIBIS) at *www.fibis.org* includes a 'FIBIS search' facility that lets you carry out a search in or browse various East India Company records. Some of these are transcriptions of full records, including extractions from copies of the *East India Register* of baptisms in the three presidencies from 1809–44, marriages from 1807–44 and burials from 1809–44 in Bombay and Madras, but from 1809–1923 in Bengal. The events listed in the *Register* are for two years prior to the year listed, i.e. burials for 1809 will be found in the 1811 *Register*.

There are also indexes of the baptisms, marriages and burials for the three presidencies taken from the ecclesiastical returns. In the case of Madras baptisms, the index goes back as far as 1707, and for Bombay marriages back to 1714. Embarkation lists, military records, bonds, directories and other publications are also indexed.

Family History in India (http://members.ozemail.com.au/~clday)

The Family History in India website is a must for anyone whose ancestors spent time in the Indian subcontinent. Set up by an Australian family historian, Cathy Day, many of whose own ancestors lived in India, the site contains indexes of European marriages in Calcutta (1713–1800) and in the Bengal Presidency (1855–96), as well as an index of over 230,000 Europeans who lived in India before independence.

The site includes a number of lists and transcriptions of various church, civil and military records, with links to those on other sites too. There is, for instance, a French site with a census of surnames in Pondicherry in 1797 ('Patronymes du recensement anglais de Pondichéry en 1797'), together with the names of the town's voters in 1792 and the surnames of Europeans buried there.

You can also find on the site the embarkation list of the *Duke of Cornwall*, bound for Madras on 27 April 1843, on which my great-great-grandfather Alexander Stewart sailed under the name 'James Miller'!

As well as a considerable amount of information on the British involvement with India, Cathy provides several interesting web pages on the history of the relationship with India of other nationalities present there from the sixteenth to the twentieth centuries – French, Portuguese, Dutch, Danes, Armenians and Jews – as well as of the Indians themselves.

Cathy provides information on records microfilmed by the LDS Church and now available through the worldwide network of LDS Family History Centres, and details of other relevant websites, family history societies and books.

Genealogy in India

Bob Holland, an Australian genealogist, has made available an index of East India Company officer cadets (1789–1859) on his Genealogy in India website (*www.ans.com.au/~rampais/genelogy/india/indexes/index.htm*). Watch out for the idiosyncratic spelling of 'genealogy' in the web address.

Bob's index will provide you with an India Office Records reference number and an LDS Family History Centre microfilm number. You can then order the film with the record you want to see from the nearest LDS Family History Centre, and view it there.

Bob's site also contains a cemetery index complied by Sue Lally from an LDS microfilm of monumental inscriptions from St Mary's church, Fort St George, Madras. In addition, there is a list of Scots who went out to India from Glasgow and the west of Scotland, transcribed by Pauline McGregor Currien, who extracted names with a possible Indian connection from a series of booklets published by the Scottish Genealogy Society. There are also various other India-related indexes at the site.

International Genealogical Index

The LDS Church's International Genealogical Index (IGI), which you'll find at its Family Search website (*www.familysearch.org*), contains many baptisms and marriages, and even some burials of Europeans in India.

Wills online

Many wills of people who died in India (or had lived there) were proved (or confirmed) in the UK, and are among the digitized wills accessible at the Documents Online (*www.nationalarchives.gov.uk/ documentsonline*) and Scotlands People (*www.scotlandspeople.gov. uk*) websites.

At Irish Origins (*www.irishorigins.com*), you can search an index of the copies, transcripts, abstracts and extracts of wills proved in Ireland (and destroyed in 1922), in which you'll find some that were made by people who had lived in India.

23

Records of the British Army, Royal Navy, Royal Marines and Royal Air Force

Most of us are likely sooner or later to come across ancestors or relatives who were in the armed forces. The National Archives (TNA) are responsible for most of the historic records of the British Army, Royal Navy, Royal Marines and Royal Air Force.

British Army – other ranks

You'll need to look at different records at TNA, depending on whether your ancestor was an officer or one of the 'other ranks' (a private soldier or non-commissioned officer) in the Army. The main records for other ranks are the attestation and discharge papers in TNA's incomplete WO (War Office) 97 collection, which covers discharges between 1760 and 1913, but usually not those who died in service. Soldiers discharged before 1883 were normally only those who received a pension.

Records in WO97 covering the period 1760–1854 have been indexed and you can search those in the TNA Catalogue (see p. 289). For discharges from 1855–72, you need to know the soldier's regiment. You have to look under the relevant branch of the Army (e.g. Royal Artillery, Royal Engineers, Infantry, etc.) between 1873 and 1882.

The records of soldiers discharged from 1882–1900 are filed in A–Z order for the entire British Army, as are those discharged from 1900–1913. Some of the discharge papers were misfiled, and are now filed in two WO97 A–Z sequences, one covering the period 1760–1900 and the other 1900–1913. There are separate service records for soldiers in regiments raised in Ireland from 1783–1822

(WO118 and 119), as well as for the Royal Artillery from 1791–1855 and the Royal Horse Artillery from 1803–63 (both in WO69). More service records for soldiers discharged to pension between 1787 and 1813 are held in WO121, which are also indexed in the TNA Catalogue.

Tip: Guards' records are held separately

The Coldstream, Grenadier, Irish, Scots and Welsh Guards hold their own records, although some of these were destroyed by bombing during the Second World War. You can gain access to these through the relevant Guards Regimental Headquarters at Wellington Barracks in London.

The original records of the Household Cavalry are now held by TNA in WO400, with microfilm copies at the Household Cavalry Museum at Combermere Barracks in Windsor (*www.household cavalry.gvon.com/museum.htm*). These cover the period 1799–1920 (including the First World War), and contain records of the Life Guards, Royal Horse Guards and Household Battalion. There are also muster rolls and pay lists for other ranks that specify their enlistment dates, movements and discharge dates. You can use these records to find out about a soldier who didn't receive a pension, but to do so, you need to know his regiment.

The monthly or quarterly musters (used for pay and accounting) usually give the age, place of enlistment and trade in the first entry for a recruit. From 1730–1878, the muster rolls and pay lists for most regiments are in the series WO12, while those for the Artillery are in WO10, WO54 and WO69, the Engineers in WO11 and WO54, militia and volunteers in WO13 and WO68, and troops sent to the Scutari Depot during the Crimean War (1854–6) in WO14.

The story of you: Anne Simmonds

Anne found she had a soldier ancestor who lost his good conduct pay because he was found asleep on duty at Horse Guards Parade in London.

From 1878, there were no more pay lists. Muster rolls from then until they were phased out in the mid-1890s are in WO16. There are also regimental description books for soldiers in WO25, and depot description books in WO67. TNA holds various other collections of records that can help you to identify a soldier's regiment.

As well as the records of soldiers receiving a pension in WO97 and WO121, there are also pension admission books for disability (from 1715–1882) in WO116, and for length of service (from 1823–1913) in WO117. Soldiers in the Artillery have separate pension records from 1770–1834.

Records of pensioners in British regiments 'living in' at the Royal Hospital, Chelsea in London covering the period 1702–1933 are in WO23, while those of 'in-pensioners' in Irish regiments at the Royal Hospital, Kilmainham in Dublin (1704–1922) are in WO900.

The National Army Museum (*www.national-army-museum-ac.uk*) holds records of soldiers' effects from 1901–60, with those for 1901–14 on site at the museum. You can view the records there, although you need to obtain a Reader's Ticket in advance. The records are indexed by soldier's name, and the information specified includes full name, regimental number and rank, date and place of death, place of birth, date of enlistment, trade on enlistment and next of kin.

Tip: Lost First World War other ranks' records

Unfortunately, most of the records of the 6–7 million soldiers who fought in the First World War were destroyed by bombing in 1940, including those of soldiers who had enlisted prior to the war and were still in service or recalled to it.

The records for around 2 million soldiers either survived and are in WO363 (the so-called 'burnt documents'), or were reconstructed from pension records and are in WO364. All of the Household Cavalry records survived, as they were stored elsewhere.

Army discharge papers.

Records for soldiers serving in the Army after 1920 are held by the Ministry of Defence (the successor to the War Office) at the Army Personnel Centre in Glasgow, who will search the records for a fee.

British Army – officers

TNA holds manuscript lists of Army officers from 1702–52 in WO64, while a printed record of the officers in the British Army is contained in the official *Army Lists* first published in 1740. For the regular Army, TNA has annual (1754–1879), quarterly (1879–1922) and half-yearly (1923–50) *Army Lists*, as well as a continuing series of modern lists from 1951. TNA also holds a second official series of monthly (1798–1940) and quarterly (1940–50) *Army Lists*, as well as a Home Guard List (1939–45) and eighteenth- and nineteenth-century militia lists. In addition, TNA has a full set of the unofficial *Hart's Army List*, published from 1839–1915.

There are officers' commission books covering the period 1660–1873, and information on officers' families, both in WO25. TNA has regimental records of officers from 1764 to about 1915 in WO76, baptismal certificates from 1755–1908, details of widows' pensions in WO25, and several other collections of records.

Tip: Lost First World War officers' records

The main series of officers' service records covering the period of the First World War was destroyed in 1940, as were the other ranks' records. In the officers' case, however, there is still a supplementary series of records, although some of those had been destroyed by clerks. The records' content varies between, on the one hand, attestation papers, service record and personal correspondence, and on the other, a simple note of the date of the officer's death.

The record series WO339 holds almost 140,000 service records for officers who were either regular Army officers prior to the war, given a temporary commission or commissioned into the Special Reserve of officers. The WO374 collection contains nearly 80,000 records of officers with a Territorial Army or temporary commission. These can be searched for in the Catalogue (see below). Records for officers still serving after 31 March 1922 are at the Ministry of Defence in Glasgow.

Royal Navy – ratings

Royal Navy 'ratings' are the equivalent of 'other ranks' in the Army, in other words, sailors who are not officers. Ratings' service records include ships' musters (1667–1878) in the TNA collections ADM (Admiralty) 36–39, 41, 115 and 119. The musters usually contain the rating's age and place of birth from 1764 onwards, and may include description books from around 1800.

In addition, there are ships' pay books with ratings' names in series ADM31–35 and 117. Certificates of service (1802–94) were compiled from the pay books. The certificates are in ADM29 and can be searched using the TNA Catalogue (see p. 289). Ratings joining the Navy from 1853–72 are listed in Continuous Service Engagement Books in ADM139. From 1873–1923, ratings are included in the Register of Seamen's Services in ADM188, which is now searchable online (see Documents Online below). There are also pension records for ratings (1704–1926), mainly in ADM6 and 73, as well as widows' pensions (1675–1933) in ADM82, 106 and 166.

The records for ratings who joined the Navy between 1923 and 1928 are held either by the Directorate of Personnel Support (Navy) at Swadlincote, Derbyshire (if the rating has since died) or the Data Protection Cell (Navy) in Portsmouth, Hampshire (if still alive). Swadlincote holds records from 1928–38 as well, while those after 1938 are at Portsmouth.

Royal Navy – officers

The Royal Navy equivalent of the *Army List* is the official *Navy List*, published quarterly from 1814. Before this, *Steele's Navy List* was an unofficial publication from 1782. In addition, the *New Navy List*, which contains short biographies, was published unofficially from 1841–56. Registers of officers' services were kept from 1756–1966, although most cover the period 1840–1920. These are in the series ADM196 (with surgeons' records 1891–1919 in ADM104). There are also returns of some officers' service, made in 1817 and 1846, and held in ADM9. Passing (qualification) certificates for various ranks are held in ADM6, 13, 106 and 107.

The certificates of service (1802–1894) for ratings in ADM29 (and searchable through the TNA Catalogue) also include certificates for warrant officers. There are officers' full and half-pay registers (1697–1924) in series ADM6, 22–25 and PMG (Paymaster General) 15, widows' pension records (1673–1932) in various collections, 'black' (misconduct) books (1741–1815) in ADM11 and 12, and leave books (1783–1847) in ADM6.

Officers' pensions granted by the Admiralty before 1836 are recorded in ADM7, 18, 22, 23 and 181, while those granted after that year are in ADM23 and PMG15, 16, 19, 20, 24, 43 and 44. Pensions from the Royal Hospital, Chelsea (1704–1961) are in ADM22, 73 and 165, as well as PMG70 and 71. Wounds and disability pensions (1673–1931) are held in ADM6, 7, 18, 22, 23 and 181, as well as PMG16 and 42. There are similar records for Royal Navy warrant officers, with the records for wounds and disability pensions and widows' pensions beginning in 1653. Records for officers serving after the First World War are held at Swadlincote (if the officer has died) or Portsmouth (for those still living).

Horatio Nelson and his family

Horatio Nelson was born at the parsonage in Burnham Thorpe, Norfolk on 29 September 1758. He was the sixth of eleven children of the Reverend Edmund Nelson and his wife Catherine (née Suckling). You can find the story of the Nelson family (based on a talk given by the Reverend Cecil Isaacson, late vicar of Burnham Thorpe, at the University of California at Los Angeles in 1983) on the website of the Nelson Society at *www.nelson-society.org.uk/html/family_life.htm*.

Nelson joined the Royal Navy at the age of twelve, became a captain at twenty, and served in the West Indies, the Baltic and Canada. On 11 March 1787, on the West Indian island of Nevis, he married Frances Herbert Nisbet (née Woolward), a doctor's widow with a young son, Josiah; she was 'given away' by the future King William IV. Nelson lived with his wife at Burnham Thorpe from 1787 to 1793, when he was given command of HMS *Agamemnon* (Nelson's favourite ship, which was also at Trafalgar) on the outbreak of war with the French.

Nelson lost the sight of his right eye at the Battle of Calvi in 1794 (but never wore an eye-patch). He was appointed commodore in 1796, promoted to rear admiral and made a Knight of the Bath in 1797, and later that year lost his right arm (his stepson Josiah saved Nelson's life by applying a tourniquet). He was created Baron of the Nile and Burnham Thorpe in 1798, Duke of Bronte (in Sicily) in 1799 by King Ferdinand IV of Naples, and in 1801, was promoted to vice admiral and created Viscount of the Nile and Burnham Thorpe.

After the Battle of the Nile in 1798, Nelson began an affair with Lady Emma Hamilton, the wife of the British ambassador to Naples, Sir William Hamilton. Born Emily Lyon in 1765, the daughter of a Wirral blacksmith, Emma Hart (as she had become known) married the sexagenarian Sir William in London in 1791.

Horatia, the daughter of Nelson and Lady Hamilton, was born in January 1801, and Nelson separated from his wife shortly afterwards. Lady Nelson lived quietly in London until her death in 1831 at the age of seventy, a year after that of her son Josiah.

After her mother's death in Calais in 1815, Horatia went to live in Burnham Market with Nelson's brother-in-law, Thomas Bolton (who had married Susannah Nelson). On 19

February 1822, she married Philip Ward, the curate of Burnham Westgate, and about 1830 moved with him and their six children to Tenterden in Kent, where her husband had become vicar. There the couple had four more children. Horatia died on 6 March 1881 and is buried at Pinner, Middlesex.

Royal Marines – other ranks

The Royal Marines were first raised in 1664 and are, in effect, sea soldiers, but they're part of neither the British Army nor the Royal Navy. Marines' attestation forms (enlistment and discharge papers) from 1790–1925 are held in TNA class ADM157, description books (1755–1940) in ADM158 and service records (1842–1936) in ADM159. These records are held in divisional order. As well as the main divisions based in Chatham, Portsmouth and Plymouth (and Woolwich from 1805–69), there are also records for the Royal Marine (RM) Artillery, RM Engineers and RM Labour Corps (in Chatham and Deal).

Records of other ranks who enlisted after 1925 are held by the Directorate of Personnel Support (Navy) 2 (DPS(N)2) in Portsmouth.

Royal Marines – officers

Royal Marine officers are listed in the *Army List* from 1740, the *Navy List* from 1797, *Hart's Army List* and the *New Navy List* from 1840. As with Naval officers' service records, those of RM officers are held in the TNA series ADM196 and their pension records are also generally in the same series as those of Naval officers.

As with those of other ranks, the records of officers who were appointed after 1925 are held by the DPS(N)2 in Portsmouth.

Royal Air Force – airmen

The Royal Air Force (RAF) was created on 1 April 1918 from a combination of the Royal Flying Corps (RFC, an Army unit formed in 1912) and the Royal Naval Air Service (RNAS, formed in 1914), together with new recruits to the service.

The RAF equivalent of the Army's 'other ranks' and of the Navy's 'ratings' are known as 'airmen'. If an airman died or was discharged before the formation of the RAF, you'll find his service record in TNA series WO363 or 364 (if he served in the RFC), or in ADM188 (if in the RNAS). These records are covered in the parts of this chapter about 'British Army – other ranks' and 'Royal Navy – ratings'.

If he was still serving when the RAF was created, then his RFC or RNAS record would have been transferred to the new service. These records, together with those of airmen who joined up after the creation of the RAF, are in the series AIR79, with an index in AIR78.

In an airman's service record you're likely to find information on his birth date, birthplace, physical description, religion, next of kin, wife's and children's names, joining date, promotions, units served in, medals awarded and discharge date.

Records of airmen with a service number higher than 329000 (and of those with a lower number but who also served in the RAF in the Second World War) are still held by the Ministry of Defence at RAF Innsworth, near Gloucester.

Royal Air Force – officers

You can find service records of RAF and RFC officers in the TNA collection AIR76, which also holds those of RNAS officers still serving at the formation of the RAF. The records of RNAS officers who had died or were discharged before 1918 are in the series ADM273. From March 1919, RAF officers are listed in the official *Air Force List*, with lists from 1939–54 in the series AIR10.

24

Military records and memorials online

The National Archives

You can download many useful research guides from the TNA website (*www.nationalarchives.gov.uk*). Move your mouse pointer over 'Research, education and online exhibitions' on the TNA home page, and click on 'Research guides' on the pull-down menu. Then, on the page that appears on your screen, click on 'Records research guides'. You'll see a long A–Z list of all TNA's research guides, on everything from 'Diplomatic sources before 1509' to 'Unidentified flying objects (research notes)'. There are four general guides about the armed forces, eighteen on the British Army, four each on the Royal Air Force and the Royal Marines and eleven on the Royal Navy.

Ancestry.co.uk

Two and a half million records from TNA's collections of British Army Service Records (WO363) and Pension Records (WO364) are being put online at *www.ancestry.co.uk*. Information in the records includes date and place of enlistment, service history, tours of duty, medical history, conduct, former occupation, next of kin, physical appearance, employer's reference and other correspondence. The index is searchable free of charge, and you can view the images either on a subscription or pay-per-view basis. All the records are expected to be online by the end of 2008.

Documents Online

Documents Online (*www.nationalarchives.gov.uk/documentsonline*) provides access to various collections that TNA has digitized and made available online. You can search the following databases free of charge, and then download records on a pay-per-view basis:

- *Register of Seamen's Services*
  This database (in the series ADM188) contains information on around half a million ratings (i.e. non-officers), who joined the Royal Navy from 1873–1923, including year (and in some cases, also day and month) of birth, place of birth, ships served on and period of time served. From 1892 onwards, details are provided about occupation, any badges, comments on character and ability, physical appearance and wounds.

- *Soldiers' medal cards*
  This database holds images of about 5.5 million medal cards for soldiers who fought in the First World War and were awarded campaign medals such as the 1914 or 1914–15 Star, British War Medal (BWM), Victory Medal, Territorial Force Medal and Silver War Badge (SWB). You can also view cards for the following gallantry medals on the database: Distinguished Conduct Medal (DCM), Military Medal (MM), Meritorious Service Medal (MSM), Territorial Force Efficiency Medal (TFEM) and Territorial Efficiency Medal (TEM), as well as those Mentioned in Despatches (MiD).
  The Medal Index Cards were created towards the end of the First World War to allow the Army Medal Office to place on one card the details of a soldier's medal entitlement, his rank(s), unit(s) served in and first operational theatre served in. In addition, the card lists the AMO reference for the medal rolls (in the WO329 series) showing the soldier's entitlement to the medals.

- *Women's Army Auxiliary Corps/Queen Mary's Army
Auxiliary Corps*

  The Women's Army Auxiliary Corps (WAAC) was formed in
  1917, renamed the Queen Mary's Army Auxiliary Corps (QMAAC)
  in 1918, and disbanded in 1921; women served in either the
  Cookery, Mechanical, Clerical or Miscellaneous sections. Although
  around 57,000 women served in the WAAC/QMAAC, most of
  the records were destroyed in 1940, with only 7,000 surviving.

  The records include enrolment forms (stating name, age,
  address, parents' nationality, and marital status) and statements
  of service (recording grade, location, promotions, and the name
  and address of next-of-kin). You can view other documents,
  such as identification certificate, employer's and other references,
  application form, casualty form and clothing history sheet (with
  details of each woman's uniform).

- *Victoria Cross registers*

  The Victoria Cross was instituted in 1856, to be awarded to
  both officers and other ranks/ratings in the Army or Royal
  Navy for gallantry in the face of the enemy. It has since been
  awarded 1,356 times (including three bars) to soldiers, sailors
  and members of the other armed forces. In this database, you
  can search for information about 1,236 individuals who have
  been awarded the Victoria Cross. The names of a further 117
  winners of the award are listed on the Documents Online
  website at *www.nationalarchives.gov.uk/documentsonline/
  victoriacross.asp.*

Was your ancestor at the Battle of Trafalgar?

What many historians consider Britain's most important
naval battle was fought and won on 21 October 1805 at
Cape Trafalgar off the southern coast of Spain by a fleet of
twenty-seven British battleships (plus six other vessels)
commanded by Vice Admiral Viscount Horatio Nelson. His
objective was to destroy a combined fleet of eighteen French

---

and fifteen Spanish ships (under the command of Vice Admiral Pierre-Charles de Villeneuve) to prevent a French invasion of Britain planned by Napoleon Bonaparte.

After Nelson's famous signal: 'England expects that every man will do his duty,' the British fleet attacked in two columns, led by Nelson in HMS *Victory* and his second-in-command, Vice Admiral Sir Cuthbert Collingwood, in HMS *Royal Sovereign*. The battle was fierce, and resulted in the capture or destruction of twenty-two enemy ships. Nearly 450 British men were killed and over 1,200 wounded, compared to almost 3,400 Frenchmen and 1,000 Spaniards killed and 1,200 Frenchmen and 2,500 Spaniards wounded (with 7,000 taken prisoner, including Vice Admiral de Villeneuve).

Although Britain won the battle, Nelson himself was killed. His body lay in state at Greenwich Hospital, London and was then taken up the Thames in a procession of barges to a state funeral at St Paul's Cathedral on 9 January 1806, accompanied by forty-eight members of the crew of HMS *Victory*. In 1843, a statue of Nelson was placed on top of a 145-ft column in what had been named Trafalgar Square eight years previously.

Perhaps an ancestor of yours was one of around 18,000 men on the British side or 30,000 on the French/Spanish side who took part in the battle.

Battle of Trafalgar

TNA *Trafalgar database*

TNA holds a database of 18,000 men and one woman (Jane Townshend) who fought at Trafalgar on the British side (*www.nationalarchives.gov.uk/trafalgarancestors*). The records include 361 men from America and thirty-one from Canada, including Newfoundland. You can search the database (which was researched and compiled by Bruno Pappalardo, TNA's naval specialist) and view the results free of charge. The information was taken from the muster records for the thirty-three ships in Nelson's fleet, together with certificates of service, pension records, passing certificates and survey returns.

HMS Victory *Trafalgar Muster Roll*

On the Official HMS *Victory* website (*www.hms-victory.com*), you'll find the Battle of Trafalgar Muster Roll, which lists the 820 men and boys (thirty-one of them) who were on board the ship on the day of the battle, including Nelson and Captain Thomas Hardy, the commander of the ship. The crew of the *Victory* included nine commissioned officers, twenty-one midshipmen, and seventy-seven non-commissioned warrant and petty officers. The remainder were able and ordinary seamen, landsmen, supernumeraries and boys, plus 146 marines under the command of Captain Charles Adair. Although most were English, Scots, Welsh or Irish, 120 belonged to eighteen different nationalities: twenty-two Americans, nine Italians, seven Dutchmen, six Maltese and even four Frenchmen! Fifty-seven of *Victory*'s crew died in the battle or over the next few days, and 102 were wounded.

The Trafalgar Muster Roll lists the surname, forename, age, nationality and rank/rate of each man, e.g.:

Nelson	Horatio	47	English	Vice Admiral
Hardy	Thomas	36	English	Captain
Adair	Chas. William	29	Irish	RM/Capt.

GENUKI *Trafalgar Roll*

On a page on the GENUKI genealogical 'reference library' website entitled The Trafalgar Roll (*www.genuki.org.uk/big/eng/Trafalgar*), you can find a list of 1,640 men who took part in the battle on the British side and were awarded honours. The list, compiled by the Genealogical Computing Group of the New Zealand Society of Genealogists, gives the surname, forename, rank, ship, other medals awarded to the man, and any relevant notes, e.g.:

Abbott	William	Pte RM	Leviathan	
Aitken	James	Ord	Defence	Egypt, Camperdown
Brown	Geo	Lieut	Victory	(died 1856)

There are lists of officers killed and wounded in the battle, using information extracted from Volume 5 (pp. 157–160) of the seven-volume set *The Royal Navy: A History from the Earliest Times to 1900* by Sir William Laird Clowes (first published in the 1890s). Also taken from this book is a list of the British ships that took part in the battle, together with the names of their commanders and the numbers killed and wounded on each ship.

Nelson's captains

On the website of the Nelson Society, you can find brief biographies and portraits of twenty-seven of Nelson's captains at *www.nelson-society.org.uk/html/trafalgar_captains.htm*. The biographies have been taken from *The Trafalgar Roll: The Ships and the Officers*, which lists over 1,250 officers and describes the careers of most of them in detail.

Trafalgar Roll CD website

Pam and Derek Ayshford have compiled a Trafalgar Roll CD using documents at the National Archives, the Royal Naval Museum in Portsmouth, the National Maritime Museum in Greenwich and the Royal Marines Museum in Eastney. The CD contains the names and details of more than 21,000 men who were on the musters of the British ships on 21 October 1805. (The Ayshfords point out that, although still on the musters, some men had been discharged before the Battle.)

At *www.ageofnelson.org/TrafalgarRoll/index.html*, you can search the surnames on the CD, and see the results in the form:

Anderson	William	Midshipman	Stockton
Cole	Daniel	Landsman	County Down
Turner	Benjamin	Able Bodied Seaman	Philadelphia

The details on the CD include the ship on which the man served, his rank or rating, and in most cases his age and place of birth. A good deal of other information may also be given, such as former trade, pension, medals and awards, physical description, injuries and illnesses, and death date.

French muster rolls

On 4 November 1805, four French ships that had taken part in the Battle of Trafalgar (*Duguay-Trouin*, *Formidable*, *Mont-Blanc* and *Scipion*) were captured by a Royal Navy squadron in the Bay of Biscay. Among the items seized were the muster rolls of the ships, which list nearly 6,000 sailors, soldiers and passengers on board the four ships.

The information you're likely to find in this database at Documents Online (*www.nationalarchives.gov.uk/documentsonline*) includes an individual's name, rank, birthplace, nationality, monthly salary, dates of embarkation and disembarkation, offences committed, punishments, promotions, demotions and transfer from one ship to another.

The National Archives Catalogue

The purpose of TNA's free catalogue (*www.nationalarchives.gov. uk/catalogue*) is to provide general information on its holdings. Several military indexes have been added to it, however, so you can search the catalogue to find information on individual soldiers and sailors.

You can search using a name ('John Smith', for instance) and the record class (WO97 for soldiers' pension records, for example). This will produce a list of 469 soldiers named John Smith, stating where they were born, in which regiments they served, their periods of service, their ages and the TNA reference number for each man. You can also specify a year range, to cut down the number of results.

To find information on soldiers (not including officers) pensioned off between 1760 and 1854, you need to search in record classes WO97 and WO121. For Royal Navy officers and men serving between 1802 and 1919, the record series is ADM29, and for correspondence about prisoners of war from 1915 to 1919, it's FO383.

Other collections you can search via the catalogue include WO339 and WO374 (officers' service records). These are listed with surname first, so to find John Smith, you have to search for 'John AND Smith'. Once you've found the basic information in the catalogue free of charge, you can click on the details of the entry that you're interested in, then on 'Request this' and you'll be able to request an estimate for a copy of the record. The fee for the estimate covers up to five documents. TNA will send you an e-mail estimate of the cost of copying the records, and you can then place an online order for a paper copy of the actual record, which will be sent to you by post. Alternatively, you can order an electronic copy to download on to your computer.

Tip: Using The National Archives' Catalogue

According to the marriage entry for my 3× great-grandfather Alexander Stewart in the Edinburgh parish register for 1813, he was a soldier in the '9th R.V.B.' stationed at Edinburgh Castle. I searched in TNA's catalogue for an 'Alexander Stewart' with service between 1810 and 1820, which resulted in a list of seventeen men of that name with covering dates completely or partially within that period.

The list shows each soldier's TNA reference number, name, birthplace, regiments served in, age at discharge, and dates of service. My 3× great-grandfather's index entry reads:

WO 97/1135/256
ALEXANDER STEWART Born DURINESS, Inverness-shire
Served in 3rd Garrison Battalion; 71st Foot Regiment;
Lochaber Fencibles; 9th Royal Veteran Battalion
Discharged aged 36
Covering dates: 1798–1814
The 9th Royal Veteran Battalion is the '9th R.V.B.' mentioned

---

in his marriage record. I hadn't previously been aware that I had ancestors from Duriness (or, more correctly, Duirinish), which lies in the north-west of the Isle of Skye.

Naval Biographical Database

About seven years ago, Christopher Donnithorne began work on the major task of recording the men and women who have served in or supported the Royal Navy since 1660, estimated to be around 5 million people. Currently the database (*www.navylist.org*) contains information on about 14,000 people and 5,000 ships.

You can search the database for individual people and view results free of charge, which include the dates of the earliest and latest references to the person, his rank and the number of 'hits' (occurrences in the database). In addition, you can search for ships, places and organizations. Once you've found relevant results, you can send an online request for an estimate of the cost of further information.

Military Genealogy

The Naval and Military Press has set up a pay-per-view website at *www.military-genealogy.com*, which contains details of the soldiers in the British Army who died during the First and Second World Wars using data taken from the official lists published by the British government. This information is also available on CD as *Soldiers Died in the Great War 1914–19* and *Army Roll of Honour – World War Two*. About 41,000 officers and 662,000 other ranks died in the First World War, out of about 5.7 million British and Irish troops.

The website also contains the National Roll of the Great War, published shortly after the war, and originally intended to cover all the men and women who participated. Unfortunately, the project ran out of money, but 100,000 people were listed, most of whom survived the war.

An entry from the National Roll of the Great War

SYRATT, H.T., Pte., 7th Oxford. and Bucks. L.I.

He was mobilised with the Territorials in August 1914, and later in the same year was drafted to France. There he took part in much heavy fighting in the Ypres, Marne, Somme, Arras and Cambrai sectors, and was twice wounded. Eventually invalided home, he was in hospital about six months, and was demobilised in November 1919. He holds the 1914-15 Star, and the General Service and Victory Medals. 54, Spencer Street, Bradwell, Bucks.   Z4354/B

Before registering on the Military Genealogy site, you can search for a name free of charge, and you'll be shown the number of entries there are for that name in the First and Second World War databases. After you've registered, a free search will return a list specifying surname, forename, initials, place of birth and place of residence.

To see more details, you need first to buy credits. You can then buy a soldier's record or a memorial scroll. The record can tell you where the soldier enlisted, his rank and number, where and how he died, in which theatre of war, and any supplementary information, although you may find that not all of these details are present in the record.

Commonwealth War Graves Commission

The information on Military Genealogy is similar but complementary to that on the free Commonwealth War Graves Commission (CWGC) website (*www.cwgc.org*). Military Genealogy's databases contain information on only British and Irish soldiers, however, while that of the CWGC holds details of soldiers, sailors and airmen from the UK and also from other Commonwealth countries.

In 1917, the CWGC was founded as the Imperial War Graves Commission, principally due to the efforts of Fabian Ware. An educationalist and newspaper editor, Ware was considered too old for military service at the age of forty-five, and instead went to France in September 1914 in command of a mobile Red Cross unit. Having seen that soldiers' graves were not being marked or recorded, Ware's unit undertook this responsibility. The following year, the British government set up a Graves Registration Commission (GRC) within the Army. Ware commanded the GRC with the rank of major. By the end of the war, Ware had been promoted to major-general, and received a knighthood in 1920.

The CWGC's records of the 1.7 million members of the Commonwealth armed forces who were killed in the two world wars (together with the records of the Civilian War Dead of the Second World War) have now been made available for searching over the Internet.

In your search, you can specify the force (from 'Army', 'Air Force', 'Navy' and 'Merchant Navy') or 'Civilian' and/or nationality (from 'Australian', 'Canadian', 'Indian', 'New Zealand', 'South African', and 'United Kingdom'). Beware, however, that this is the nationality of the force, rather than of the individual.

The results you're likely to see displayed on screen are the individual's surname (with forename or initials), rank, service number, date of death, age, regiment/service, nationality, grave/memorial reference and cemetery/memorial name. Clicking on the deceased person's name brings up a page with the above details, plus the individual's military unit and any information such as parents' or wife's address.

From the casualty details screen, you can click on the name of the cemetery to view information on its history, location and layout, as well as a photograph of the cemetery and a complete list of all those buried there. If you click on the 'certificate' button on the casualty details page, a memorial certificate with the deceased's details and the cemetery photograph is displayed, which you can print out and frame.

In Memory of
Private JAMES ALFRED SMITH

201508, 4th Bn., Royal Scots
who died
on 19 April 1917
Private SMITH

Remembered with honour
JERUSALEM MEMORIAL

Commemorated in perpetuity by
the Commonwealth War Graves Commission

Commonwealth War Graves Commission memorial certificate.

Find My Past

Like Military Genealogy, the Find My Past website (*www.findmypast.com*) provides access to Soldiers Died in the Great War, the Army Roll of Honour 1939–45 and the National Roll of the Great War on a pay-per-view basis. The site allows you to search various other military indexes, including a list of Grenadier Guards 1656–1874, Peninsular Medal Roll 1793–1814, Army List 1798 and 1878, Waterloo Roll Call 1815, Hart's Army List 1840 and 1888, the East India Register and Army List 1855 and the Indian Army and Civil Service List 1873.

You can also search the indexes of armed forces births, marriages and deaths from 1761–1994, although the results show a surname range rather than the name searched for. Thus, searching for 'Freeth' produces a result with a surname range of 'Fisk to Green', with no guarantee that there are any Freeths within it.

Family Relatives

This pay-per-view website (*www.familyrelatives.org*) also holds Soldiers Died in the Great War. The site lets you search the General Register Office (GRO) war death indexes 1914–21 and 1939–48, including those for Army officers and other ranks, and Royal Navy officers and ratings. You can also search the GRO war death indexes 1939–48 for all ranks in the Royal Air Force.

There are also various GRO birth, marriage and death indexes that you can search (and view results from) free of charge. These include Army births 1881–1965; Army chaplains' birth, marriage and death returns 1796–1880; regimental births 1761–1924; Army marriages and deaths 1881–1955; service departments' marriages and deaths 1956–65; Army marriages within British lines 1914–25; and Natal and South African forces' deaths 1899–1902.

Lost Generation

This is a new searchable database of First World War memorials and the servicemen listed on them, set up by the Channel 4 television network to tie in with a television programme about war memorials and those commemorated on them. You can search the database and view results free of charge.

The site (*www.channel4.com/history/microsites/L/lostgeneration*) uses war memorial information and the names of over half a million men who died, which have been collected by volunteers for the UK National Inventory of War Memorials (*www.ukniwm.org.uk*), to whose website the online database may be transferred in the future. Users of the Lost Generation site are being encouraged to submit information on war memorials not yet covered by the site, or to add names to memorials already in the database.

To find information on someone who died in the First World War, you can search in the Lost Generation database for either a name or a war memorial (if you know where the person's death is likely to have been commemorated).

Roll of Honour

This site (*www.roll-of-honour.com*), which has been around for several years, has the same basic idea as Lost Generation: to provide a UK-wide register of servicemen commemorated on war memorials. Roll of Honour doesn't restrict itself to the First World War, however, but also covers the Second World War, the Boer (South African) War 1899–1902 and the Crimean War 1853–6.

You can search any of the site's twenty databases (or the entire site) and view results free of charge. Alternatively, if you know which town or village your serviceman ancestor came from, you may be able to find him by going direct to the war memorial information for that location.

The site has particularly good information on regiments from the historic counties of Bedfordshire, Cambridgeshire and Huntingdonshire. As well as covering many war memorials in these counties, the site has good coverage of memorials in Kent, Norfolk and Sussex. In addition, it has many useful links to other military, regimental and war memorial websites.

Soldiers' Memorials

At this free site (*www.angelfire.com/mp/memorials/memindz1.htm*), you can view information from various regimental and other memorials and rolls of honour, mainly related to British soldiers serving in India. The data on the site covers other ranks, but not officers, who are to be found on the Officers Died site below.

Officers Died

This is the companion website to Soldiers' Memorials above, but has a much broader coverage. As well as officers who died in India, this site (*members.tripod.com/~Glosters/memindex3.htm*) includes information on the deaths of British officers during the American Revolutionary War 1775–83 and the War of 1812, in the Peninsular

Campaign 1808–14 (in France, Spain and Portugal), at the Battle of Waterloo 1815, in Afghanistan 1838–42 and 1878–80, during the Crimean War 1853–6, in the Indian Mutiny 1857–9, in the Boer (South African) War 1899–1902 and in other conflicts in the late twentieth and early twenty-first centuries.

Scots at War

The Scots at War project is creating a roll of honour on its website (*www.fettes.com/scotsatwar/rollofhonour.htm*) to list Scots and those of Scots descent who fought in the wars of the twentieth and twenty-first centuries. The site has links to online 1914–19 Army and Navy rolls of honour for the county of Caithness. In addition, there is a link to a First World War roll of honour website for the county of Angus, which in turn has a link to similar roll of honour sites for Aberdeenshire (two memorials only) and Kincardineshire. All of these rolls of honour are accessible free of charge, and none of them is included in the Roll of Honour website mentioned above.

Maritime Memorials

The UK's National Maritime Museum (NMM) has set up this database, which is searchable free of charge through the NMM website (*www.nmm.ac.uk/memorials*). The database contains information on people killed in connection with the sea – many of them serving in the Royal Navy – and their memorials (over 5,000).

You can search by a person's surname, forename, rank or occupation, by a placename or by the name of a ship. A search for memorials to those who died in the sinking of the *Titanic*, for example, produces forty-two results. You can refine the search by specifying an area of the UK or the world.

In addition, you can browse the memorials by topic (such as exploration, piracy and vessel loss), maritime-related cause of death (such as infectious disease, maritime accident and war casualty) and event (including the American Revolutionary War, Napoleonic War and nineteenth-century conflicts in Asia).

World War One Cemeteries

This free website (*www.ww1cemeteries.com*) contains photographs of over 1,000 cemeteries (and their memorials) in the UK, France and Belgium. The site also has a roll of honour with photographs of fifteen men who were killed during the First World War and two who fell in the Second World War.

British War Memorial Project

This voluntary project is creating a free archive at *www.britishwar graves.org.uk* of the graves of and war memorials commemorating the British soldiers, sailors and airmen who were killed in service from 1914 up to the present. You can search the archive by name, unit (such as Grenadier Guards), service number, service (such as Royal Navy) or country.

You're then able to order a photograph of a headstone, war memorial or Commonwealth War Grave at no charge (although the project will gratefully accept a donation). The photographs (around 176,000 so far) and the information in the database are provided by volunteers.

25

Electoral rolls

It may seem surprising to us today, brought up on the principle of the secret ballot at elections, but in the past, lists were published in Britain and Ireland showing which electors voted for which candidates. Beginning mainly in the late seventeenth century, the votes of electors at parliamentary and local elections were recorded and published in 'poll books'.

This continued until the secret ballot was introduced in the United Kingdom in 1872. In addition, starting in 1832, 'registers of electors' were compiled to show who was entitled to vote at elections, and these have continued to be published up to the present day.

Electoral rolls can be a useful resource for tracing your family, particularly before and after the period of detailed census returns (1841–1901). If you're looking for confirmation of the whereabouts of an ancestor or other relative before 1841 or after 1901, then electoral rolls can be very helpful. Even within the period of detailed census returns, if you can't find someone in the census, but believe they were living in a certain area, then you can try looking at the electoral rolls.

Who will you find in the electoral rolls?

Unlike the census, however, poll books and electoral registers don't show everyone who lived in an area, but only those who were entitled to vote. It was only relatively recently, in 1928, that all men and women aged twenty-one and over were given the vote.

You'll find no women in any of the poll books, because from the time of their introduction up to the last non-secret parliamentary election in 1868, only men were allowed to vote. In the following year, women were entitled to vote in local elections for the first time.

Counties

Since 1429, men aged twenty-one and over in most English counties were able to vote, provided they owned property with a rental value of 40 shillings (£2) a year or more (Cheshire was not included until 1553, with Durham following in 1675). In 1536, men in Wales received the franchise on the same basis as England. (The towns of Berwick, Bristol, Exeter, Haverfordwest, Lichfield and Nottingham were treated as counties.)

Scotland too had had a 40 shilling property qualification in the thirteenth century, but the amount had been increased to allow for inflation, with the result that by 1788, the country had only 2,662 county voters.

Ireland had its own parliament from 1692 until 1801, when it became part of the UK. From 1727–93 only Protestants with a 40 shilling freehold were entitled to vote, after which Roman Catholics were also enfranchised, provided they too had a 40 shilling freehold. In 1829, however, the franchise level was increased to £10.

Boroughs

Who voted in borough elections varied according to local custom. There were boroughs where only the corporation voted, and others where freemen voted, or ratepayers, or all householders ('potwalloper' boroughs).

Among the towns in England that returned (usually two) members of parliament were fifty-six that had dwindled in size, but retained this ancient privilege, despite having very few electors. Such towns, known as 'rotten', 'pocket' or 'close' boroughs, included Old Sarum (the original site of Salisbury, with only eleven electors, who all lived elsewhere), Gatton in Surrey (with six electors), and Dunwich in Suffolk (once a sizeable port, but which had been eaten away by the sea, and had only thirty-two electors). In Ireland, Coleraine and Belfast had thirty-six and thirteen electors respectively. Other much larger towns, however, such as Birmingham, Manchester, Leeds, Sheffield, Brighton and Cheltenham had no representation other than as part of their counties.

The Great Reform Act of 1832

In 1832, the Representation of the People Acts (RPAs) for England and Wales, Scotland and Ireland introduced registers of electors, abolished the English 'rotten boroughs', enfranchised the industrial towns, and extended the right to vote to a further 300,000 men in Britain and Ireland. In England, Scotland and Wales, borough electors were now principally occupiers (either as owners or tenants) of property worth £10 a year. In the English and Welsh counties, the qualification was also £10 a year for property owners and holders of sixty-year leases, and £50 a year for tenants or holders of twenty-year leases.

The position was similar in the Scottish counties, with the proportion of men entitled to vote in Scotland increasing from one in 125 to one in eight. This was the same as in England before the Act, where the number had now increased to one in five.

In Ireland, the RPA had a similar effect to that in England and Wales, but with the county franchise being extended to £10 freeholders, copyholders and leaseholders for life or sixty years, as well as leaseholders with fourteen-year leases worth £20 a year.

Later voting reforms

In 1867 in England and Wales, and 1868 in Scotland, the borough franchise was extended to all male householders, as well as to lodgers in property worth £10 a year. The county franchise was extended to owners of land worth £5 a year and occupiers of land worth £12 (or £14 in Scotland). These changes added about 1.5 million men to the electoral rolls.

In Ireland, artisans received the vote in 1867, while the property qualification in Irish boroughs was halved the following year. This distinction between borough and county electors came to an end in 1884, when the franchise for voters in the county was made the same as for those in the boroughs. In addition, a new occupation qualification came into force for men with property worth £10 a year. As a result of all these changes, a further 3 million British electors were added to the registers, mainly in the counties. The Irish electorate was tripled by the changes.

The 1918 RPA extended the franchise to most men, and for the first time women were allowed to vote in a parliamentary election (see box). In Britain, this entitled a further 3 million men to vote, as well as 6 million women. In Ireland, over a million new electors were added to the registers.

In the UK, all men and women aged twenty-one or over were entitled to vote in 1928, and in 1969 (effective in 1971), the minimum age for voting was reduced to eighteen.

Information contained in poll books and registers of electors

Apart from the name of the voter and his voting preference, a poll book usually lists his address and occupation. Electoral registers before 1918 give the name of the voter, 'place of abode', qualification to vote, and the address of the property or name of the tenant. As the tenant was not necessarily the same person as the voter, you may find an ancestor in a register of electors, even though he was not entitled to vote.

Until 1918, electoral rolls were produced in alphabetical order within polling districts, as they still are in remote rural areas. In urban areas, however, electoral registers are compiled in alphabetical order of streets.

Absent Voters' List

Under the 1918 RPA, Absent Voters' Lists were compiled for each polling district, showing all the men serving in the armed forces, including those aged nineteen or twenty, who were exceptionally allowed to vote in the 1918 general election. The lists give the serviceman's full name, address, number, rank, and regiment or ship. Service registers were also produced from 1945 to 1948, as well as the usual civilian registers.

When women received the vote

In parliamentary elections, women were not allowed to vote until 1918, and even then, only those who were at least thirty years old and a householder, or married to one. Ten years later, the franchise was extended to all women of twenty-one years of age and over (eighteen since the 1969 RPA).

Nearly fifty years before they were able to elect MPs to Westminster, however, women were able to vote in local borough elections in England and Wales as a result of the Municipal Corporations Amendment Act 1869.

They were subject to the same property qualifications as men, which meant few married women were entitled to vote, as their property automatically passed to their husbands on marriage. This was rectified by the Married Women's Property Act of 1870. In 1888, the Local Government Act allowed women to vote in the elections for county and county borough councils.

In Scotland, the Householders of Scotland Act 1881 entitled unmarried women or married women living apart from their husbands to vote in burgh elections. Women could vote in county elections in Scotland from 1889.

Where to find poll books and electoral registers

You can usually find poll books and registers of electors for counties and boroughs in England and Wales at your local county record office, county reference library, archaeological society, museum, or university library. Other places where you can find some of the English electoral rolls are (in London) at the Society of Genealogists, the British Library, the Guildhall Library, the Institute of Historical Research at the University of London, (in Oxford) at the Bodleian Library, and (in Cambridge) at the University Library. In addition, some of the Welsh (and English border) records can be found at the National Library of Wales in Aberystwyth.

Before 1832, there were no poll books as such for Scotland, although printed books exist that list by county all the voters in Scotland (fewer than 3,000 of them) for the years 1788, 1790, 1811 and 1812. You can find all of these books in Edinburgh in the Central Library's Scottish Room, the National Library of Scotland (NLS) and the National Archives of Scotland (NAS, 1788 only), as well as at the Society of Genealogists in London (1788 only).

Poll books covering the forty years after 1832 are mainly in the NAS, while you'll find most of the registers of electors for Scotland in the NLS. Some of the electoral registers are also in the NAS, as well as in local archives in Aberdeen, Dumfries, Dundee and Glasgow.

Most of the electoral rolls for Northern Ireland are held in Belfast by the Public Record Office of Northern Ireland. Those for the Republic of Ireland are mainly in either the National Archives of Ireland or the National Library of Ireland (both of which are in Dublin), with a few rolls in local archives.

Two very useful booklets that list where electoral rolls are held have been published by the Federation of Family History Societies. *Poll Books c1696–1872: A Directory to Holdings in Great Britain* (3rd edition, 1994) and *Electoral Registers since 1832 and Burgess Rolls* (2nd edition, 1990) were both written by Jeremy Gibson and Colin Rogers.

The British Library has published *Parliamentary Constituencies and their Registers since 1832* by Richard H. A. Cheffins (1998), which lists the library's extensive collection of registers of electors, as well as poll books held by it.

Edited registers in the UK

Since 2002, two sets of electoral registers have been compiled for each area: a full register (containing the names of all voters) and an edited register (omitting the names of people who have chosen not to appear in it). You're allowed to inspect the full register, but only under supervision, whereas the edited version is available to anyone without restriction. After ten years, each full version will also be openly available.

Poll books and registers of electors available on CD and online

Archive CD Books (*www.rod-neep.co.uk*), S&N Genealogy Supplies (*www.genealogysupplies.com*), Stepping Stones (*www.stepping-stones.co.uk*), and a number of family history societies have made some electoral rolls available on CD.

Some historic electoral rolls are accessible online, including those for Barnsley (1835), Bedfordshire (1722 and 1784), Dorset (1807), Halifax (1835 and various other years), Liverpool (1832), Nottingham (1754), Wakefield (1865) and Westminster (1749).

The Public Record Office of Northern Ireland has digitized free-holders' records and made them available at *www.proni.gov.uk/freeholders*. The records cover eight of the nine counties of Ulster, but predominantly counties Armagh and Down.

You can see the current edited registers of electors for the UK on a pay-per-view basis at 192.com (*www.192.com*) and Tracesmart (*www.tracesmart.co.uk*).

26

Background information

Victoria County History of England

In 1899, the Victoria County History (VCH) series was founded, dedicated to Queen Victoria, with the intention of producing an encyclopaedic national history in a series of volumes. The aim was to cover, for every parish in every county, the general and detailed history of England from the earliest times up to the present. By 1914, six of the counties had been completed and eighty VCH volumes produced. By now, London and thirty-seven of the counties of England have been at least partially covered: Bedfordshire, Berkshire, Buckinghamshire, Cambridgeshire, Cheshire, Cornwall, Cumberland, Derbyshire, Devon, Dorset, County Durham, Essex, Gloucestershire, Hampshire, Herefordshire, Hertfordshire, Huntingdonshire, Kent, Lancashire, Leicestershire, Lincolnshire, London, Middlesex, Norfolk, Northamptonshire, Nottinghamshire, Oxfordshire, Rutland, Shropshire, Somerset, Staffordshire, Suffolk, Surrey, Sussex, Warwickshire, Wiltshire, Worcestershire and Yorkshire.

The VCH volumes divide the history of each area into topics such as settlement, religious history, social and economic history, and buildings. To compile a parish history, researchers explore the area on the ground, contact local people, and consult standard printed and manuscript sources, a process that can take several weeks.

Documents are studied in local record offices and The National Archives (TNA), as well as archaeological data, printed and manuscript maps, buildings information and visual evidence, including photographs and topographical drawings. The researchers then locate and investigate other archives, do more intensive fieldwork, and investigate buildings with the permission of local householders. Draft accounts are often made available on VCH county websites in advance of publication.

VCH online

London University's Institute of Historical Research and the History of Parliament Trust have combined to create the British History Online website (*www.british-history.ac.uk*) to provide British historians with digital access to various resources. Among these are many volumes of the Victoria County History series, in which many individuals are named. The volumes online cover parts of the counties of Bedfordshire, Berkshire, Buckinghamshire, Cambridgeshire, Cheshire, Cumberland, Derbyshire, Dorset, County Durham, Essex, Gloucestershire, Hampshire, Hertfordshire, Huntingdonshire, Kent, Lancashire, Leicestershire, Lincolnshire, London, Middlesex, Norfolk, Northamptonshire, Nottinghamshire, Oxfordshire, Rutland, Shropshire, Somerset, Staffordshire, Suffolk, Surrey, Sussex, Warwickshire, Wiltshire, Worcestershire and Yorkshire.

The site contains a good deal of information about London, including an index of inhabitants living within the walls in 1695, and extracts from various books, directories and censuses. In addition, you can view digitized copies of London maps from the sixteenth and seventeenth centuries, as well as nineteenth-century Ordnance Survey maps of the whole of Britain. The site has a good search facility, and all the information can be viewed free of charge.

Extract from the VCH of Gloucestershire Vol. 10: Westbury and Whitstone Hundreds: Westbury-on-Severn, Manors and other estates

BAYS COURT at Bollow was recorded by that name in 1423 when it also belonged to Rodley manor. (fn. 40) In 1560 it was on lease to Richard Hunt (fn. 41) and in 1582 it was leased with 28 a. to John Bayse and his son Thomas; (fn. 42) Thomas Bayse was the tenant in 1614 (fn. 43) and it was sold with the

---

> *manor in 1625. (fn. 44) It was probably owned by John Bayse
> of Bollow who was a freeholder of the manor by purchase in
> 1658, (fn. 45) and by James Bayse of Bollow who was a free-
> holder in 1691; (fn. 46) he or another James Bayse was
> succeeded in the Bays Court estate before 1737 by his daugh-
> ters, Elizabeth who married Daniel Lea and Mary who married
> James Sandford. (fn. 47)*
>
> The 'fn.' numbers are footnotes giving the sources of the
> information.
>
> The James Sandford and Mary Bayse mentioned at the end
> of the extract were my wife's 7× great-grandparents.

There are a number of other county websites for the VCH, many
of which contain drafts of some of the text of volumes to be published
in the future. These sites cover:

- Cornwall (*www.cornwallpast.net*);
- Derbyshire (*www.derbyshirepast.net*);
- County Durham (*www.durhampast.net*);
- Essex (*www.essexpast.net*);
- Gloucestershire (*www.gloucestershirepast.net*);
- Middlesex (*www.middlesexpast.net*);
- Northamptonshire (*www.northamptonshirepast.net*);
- Oxfordshire (*www.oxfordshirepast.net*);
- Somerset (*www.somersetpast.net*);
- Staffordshire (*www.staffordshirepast.net*);
- Sussex (*www.vchsussex.net*);
- Wiltshire (*www.wiltshirepast.net*);
- Yorkshire (*www.yorkshirepast.net*).

The Statistical Accounts of Scotland

Scotland has no Victoria County History series, but it does have the
Statistical Accounts of Scotland. In 1790, Sir John Sinclair of Ulbster
(1754–1835), Member of Parliament for Caithness and a lay member
of the General Assembly of the Church of Scotland, wrote to the

ministers of all 938 parishes in Scotland asking each of them to write a 'statistical account' of his parish.

To assist the ministers, Sir John sent them a list of 160 questions to answer. The first forty questions covered the geography and topography of the parish, including its climate, natural resources and natural history. The next sixty were on different aspects of the parish's population, followed by sixteen on agriculture. The remaining forty-four questions dealt with miscellaneous topics, ranging from whether the wages a labourer received were enough to bring up a family, to any 'Roman, Saxon, Danish or Pictish . . . remains of antiquity' that had been found in the parish.

Although to us, a 'statistical account' may sound like a dull and dry set of figures, the accounts that Sir John received are fascinating documents. The ministers wrote about the landscape, the crops that were grown, the fish to be found in the rivers and the sea, the price of food and clothing, the numbers of people living in the parish (according to their sex, age group and occupation), and whether they spoke Gaelic or broad Scots.

After a fair amount of cajoling by Sir John of some reluctant authors, the Statistical Account of Scotland was published in twenty-one volumes between 1791 and 1799 in the order that the parish entries were received. A New Statistical Account was published between 1834 and 1845. This time, the parish entries, although still mainly written by the ministers, also included contributions from local doctors, teachers and landowners. Between 1951 and 1992, a Third Statistical Account appeared.

Sir John did not insist that all his questions were answered, and as a result the accounts vary greatly in length and detail. As you might expect, the accounts of Glasgow and Edinburgh are much longer than the typical account of a country parish, and include much more information on general Scottish history.

The entry in the New Statistical Account for the City of Glasgow, written by the Very Reverend Duncan MacFarlan, Principal of Glasgow University, described church discipline in the past:

On 16th August 1587, the kirk session appointed harlots to be carted through the town, ducked in [the] Clyde, and put in the jugs at the cross, on a market day. The punishment for adultery was to appear six Sabbaths on the cockstool at the pillar, bare-footed and bare-legged, in sackcloth, then to be carted through the town, and ducked in [the] Clyde from a pulley fixed on the bridge.

King Charles I's introduction of the Anglican prayer book to Scotland was not a success. The Revd William Robertson, minister of New Greyfriars, wrote in the 1845 entry for Edinburgh that in St Giles's Cathedral on 23 July 1637:

All was profound silence till the Dean of Edinburgh arrayed in his surplice opened the service book. On this, one of the old women near the pulpit exclaimed, 'Out, out, ye fause thief, do ye say the mass at my lug?' This was followed by clapping of hands, hisses, imprecations, and yellings of scorn. Lindsay, Bishop of Edinburgh, with a view to appease the tumult, ascended the pulpit, but immediately a stool was hurled at his head by Janet Geddes. The Archbishop of St Andrews, the Lord Chancellor, and others attempted but in vain to stem the torrent of popular indignation; the greater part of the multitude now left the church at the persuasion of the magistrates, and the service was hurried over amid much interruption both from within and the crowd without. In the adjoining church the disapprobation to the liturgy was as marked though not so violent; while in the Greyfriars the service was given up. In the College Church the minister laid aside the prayer book and gave his usual extempore prayer. The opposition during the afternoon's service was nearly as great as before, and the bishop was rudely assaulted in going home.

Of the union with England in 1707, Mr Robertson wrote that:

The union of the two kingdoms was so unpopular that all parties joined in deprecating it. The articles had been industriously concealed from the people, but on their being printed a universal clamour ensued. The Parliament Square, in which the parliament at that time was sitting, was filled with an immense multitude of people who, with booings and execrations, attacked the Duke of Queensberry, the Commissioner, and every partizan of the Union, while those who headed the opposition were followed with the loudest acclamations.

A century later, thousands of workers paraded the streets of Glasgow demanding employment or bread:

The distress and dissatisfaction continued during the greater part of 1820, when large distributions of clothing, meal, and coals were given to such persons as could not find employment. The distress was such that 2040 heads of families were under the necessity of pawning 7380 articles, on which they received £739, 5s. 6d. Of the heads of families, 1943 were Scotch, and 97 English, Irish, or foreigners; 1372 had never applied for nor received charity of any description; 474 received occasional aid from the committee, and 194 were paupers.

For family historians, the accounts are a wonderful source of background material, and although your ancestors are unlikely to be mentioned in them by name, individual parishioners are occasionally described.

In the combined parish of Mid and South Yell in the Shetland Islands, for example, John Williamson, who carried out inoculation against smallpox, was described in the Old Statistical Account by the Revd Andrew Dishington as someone:

who, from his various attainments and superior talents, is called Johnny Notions among his neighbours. Unassisted by education, and unfettered by the rules of art, he stands unrivalled in this business. Several thousands have been inoculated by him, and he has not lost a single patient.

Also in the Old Account, the Revd John Garlies Maitland stated that in Minnigaff in the Stewartry of Kirkcudbright:

Instances of longevity are frequent in this parish. One man, still alive, is said to be 118 years of age. This, however, rests chiefly on his own testimony, as no authentic record of his birth has ever been produced. His name is William Marshall; he has the remains of an athletic frame. In his youth he was a soldier; he says he served under King William in Ireland. If this was the case, he certainly does not exaggerate his age; but of this part of his history there is no better evidence than that of his age itself. That his age, however, is very great, there is this presumptive proof, that none of the oldest people in the country have ever contradicted his assertion.

The longevity of three sisters, who lived to the ages of ninety-eight, eighty-eight and eighty-seven, was mentioned by Robert Thomas, 'Preacher of the Gospel', in his account of Scone in Perthshire in the 1790s, although he gave no names.

The Revd Dr Moir, in his account of Peterhead in Aberdeenshire, described how:

There was alive in 1790, and she is not yet dead, a poor woman, who declared she was then 105 years old, and a few days ago told me she was now 109 years of age. This declaration appears to be sufficiently authenticated from answers she gives to questions respecting past events, and other collateral circumstances. She is by no means decrepit, as one might naturally expect; she still continues to travel through the country as a beggar, and says, the only uneasiness she feels, is a small degree of weariness from carrying her meal bag, which is generally pretty full. She has the appearance of being only betwixt 70 and 80 years of age. When the last list of the inhabitants of the town of Peterhead in 1790 was taken, there were two persons from 90 to 95 years of age, one person of 87, one of 86, two of 85, and 21 from 80 to 85.

Although some of the ministers wrote sycophantic reports about their patrons and their families, others took advantage of the opportunity to air their views on a variety of subjects. Dr Moir described the town of Peterhead as being in a very thriving state, but believed it would be improved if there were 'a firm and steady police', some nuisances removed, greater exertions made to improve the harbour, soft spring-water brought into the town, the streets better paved, and illuminated with lamps in winter. In addition, he felt that:

It would likewise contribute much to the ornament of the town, if some regular plan could be adopted as to the size of the houses in the new streets that are lately opened. There is no greater defect than the want of a proper schoolmistress of education, manners, and character, to teach the young girls such branches of education as are only to be found in larger towns at a very high expence.

In the Old Statistical Account entry for Harris in the Outer Hebrides, the Revd John MacLeod was outspoken about the 'aristocratical influence' of a few families, which he felt was 'entirely incompatible with the liberty of British subjects':

While the mutual attachment of the chieftains and their clans subsisted, this evil was neither felt nor complained of. The chief reigned in the hearts of his vassals, who bore his exactions, and followed his fortunes with zeal and alacrity. At that time his object was men, now it is money. The inhabitants of these countries had then a degree of security in their possessions, arising from claims either of kindred or services to the chief. Now they consider themselves as mere birds of passage. When a tenant is dispossessed, in consequence of the proprietors demanding more rent than he is able to pay, or, as has often happened, in revenge of a slight offence, to which an unguarded spirit of independence, deserving better treatment, may have led, he has no resource left him but to emigrate out of the kingdom.

Dr James Cleland (co-author of the 1845 Glasgow entry) wrote to each of Glasgow's seventy-five clergymen asking how many children they had baptized in 1830:

It appeared that in the city and suburbs, there were 6397 children baptized, and of that number there were only 3225 inserted in the parochial registers, leaving unregistered 3172.

He described the situation in Edinburgh as similar:

While the great importance of accurate Parochial registers is admitted by all, it is astonishing how little they have been attended to in this country. In Edinburgh, the metropolis of Scotland, a city distinguished for its erudition, and for its numerous and valuable institutions, the baptismal register is miserably defective. It appears from a printed report of a Committee of the Town Council of that city, of date 20th February, that in 1834, the baptismal register for the thirteen parishes contained only the names of *four hundred and eighty* children.

Now you know why you can't find your ancestors in Scotland's Old Parish Registers.

Reading the Statistical Accounts

Although the Third Statistical Account is now out of print, you can purchase county and major city volumes through antiquarian booksellers or online at Amazon.co.uk (*www.amazon.co.uk*) or

Abebooks.co.uk (*www.abebooks.co.uk*), which also offers complete sets of the Old and New Accounts.

You can read the Old and New Statistical Accounts online free of charge at *http://edina.ac.uk/statacc*, or subscribe on an annual basis to an enhanced version of the service. The subscription service allows you to search for information in either or both sets of accounts, and also lets you see the accounts as text (rather than images of the original printed pages) that can be cut and pasted. You can also download up to ten individual parish accounts as portable document format (PDF) files.

A useful book on the subject is *Parish Life in Eighteenth-Century Scotland: A Review of the Old Statistical Account* by Maisie Steven (Scottish Cultural Press, 2002). Ms Steven describes how the Account came to be written, and quotes examples from the individual accounts on dress, lifestyle, food, fuel, customs, games and amusements, character, education, poor relief, diseases and health, fishing, industry and occupations, agriculture, emigration, and the Church and its ministers.

Directories

Directories of counties and large towns began to be published around the middle of the eighteenth century, and by the late nineteenth and early twentieth centuries, all parts of Britain and Ireland had been covered. A county directory will typically contain an introduction to the county as a whole, followed by a short description of each town (or even each parish in the later directories).

Pigot's 1839 Directory of Suffolk

This is a good example of what you can find in a directory. Pigot's Directory lists the inhabitants of the main places in Suffolk under various headings. For the town of Beccles, for instance, the lists cover:

- nobility, gentry and clergy;
- academies and schools (identifying boarding and day schools);

- attorneys;
- auctioneers and appraisers;
- bakers and flour dealers (identifying those who were also confectioners);
- bankers;
- basket makers;
- blacksmiths;
- boat builders;
- booksellers and stationers (identifying those who were also binders);
- boot and shoe makers;
- braziers and tinmen;
- brewers;
- brick and tile dealers (identifying those who were also brick and tile makers);
- bricklayers;
- butchers (identifying pork butchers);
- cabinet makers and upholsterers;
- carpenters and builders;
- chemists and druggists;
- china, glass, etc. dealers;
- coach makers;
- coal merchants;
- coopers;
- corn and coal merchants;
- corn chandlers (identifying those who were also seedsmen);
- curriers and leather cutters (identifying those who were also tanners);
- dyers;
- fellmongers (identifying those who were also bone merchants);
- fire, etc. office agents;
- fruiterers;
- furniture brokers;
- glovers;
- grocers and tea dealers;
- gunsmiths;

- hair dressers;
- horse dealers;
- inns;
- ironmongers;
- lime burners;
- linen and woollen drapers (identifying those who were also silk mercers);
- maltsters;
- millers;
- milliners and dress makers;
- nursery and seedsmen;
- painters, plumbers and glaziers;
- printers – letter-press;
- pump makers and well sinkers;
- saddlers and harness makers;
- shopkeepers and dealers in groceries and sundries;
- silversmiths and jewellers;
- stone and marble masons;
- straw hat makers;
- surgeons;
- surveyors;
- tailors (identifying those who were also drapers);
- taverns and public houses;
- timber merchants;
- tobacco pipe makers;
- upholsterers and paper hangers;
- watch and clock makers;
- wheelwrights;
- whitesmiths;
- wine and spirit merchants (identifying those who also sold porter and ale).

In addition, you'll find information on coach services (to London, Bury St Edmunds, Lowestoft, Norwich and Yarmouth), carriers (to London, Bungay, Eye, Halesworth, Lowestoft, Norwich, Southwold, Wrentham and Yarmouth), and conveyance by water (to London and Yarmouth).

There is, as you'd expect, less information on smaller places, and even more on Ipswich, the county town of Suffolk, and its inhabitants.

Additional occupations listed for Ipswich include:

- agricultural implement and patent plough manufacturers;
- barristers;
- cheesemongers (retail);
- eating-house keepers;
- iron founders and merchants;
- music and musical instrument sellers;
- newspapermen;
- pawnbrokers;
- professors and teachers (identifying those who were teachers of music);
- tea and coffee dealers.

By the late nineteenth century, town directories listed virtually all householders street by street.

Directories online

The University of Leicester has created the Historical Directories (*www.historicaldirectories.org*) website (funded by the National Lottery). The university describes this as 'a digital library of local and trade directories for England and Wales'. The project's aim is to make available online at least one directory for each historic English county and for all of Wales for the 1850s, 1890s and 1910s. In practice, far more directories have been made available online. For Leicester itself, forty-two directories have been digitized, for London seventy-four, Yorkshire thirty-two, Lancashire forty-nine and Wales fifty-three. Some of the directories date from the eighteenth century, including Cardiff (1766), Leeds (1798), Leicestershire (1794), Liverpool (1766), Manchester (1794), Nottinghamshire (1783–84) and Sheffield (1787).

You can search within the directories free of charge. By using the many advanced searching methods that are explained on the website, it's fairly simple to locate individuals and their professions within the directories.

Despite its name, the Census Finder website (*www.censusfinder. com*) is another good site for finding directories online. The site contains links to English, Scottish and Welsh directories, but is probably most useful for Irish directories and other population lists (as only a few fragments of the nineteenth-century Irish censuses are still in existence). In most cases, these are directory extracts, rather than the entire directories.

More online background resources

Old Towns of England

The Old Towns of England website (*www.oldtowns.co.uk*), set up by Chris Peen, contains descriptions of the cities, market towns and larger villages of England. These have been transcribed from the *Penny Cyclopaedia*, published in parts between 1833 and 1848 by the Society for the Diffusion of Useful Knowledge. London is divided into ten sections on different topics.

Old Towns of England: extract from *Tewkesbury 1842*

The town principally consists of three good streets, well-built, with a number of smaller ones branching from them. According to the census of 1831, the population amounted to 5,780. The principal manufacture is the cotton and lambs'-wool hosiery.

In 1810 the number of stocking-frames in the town was 800; and in 1833 there were 600. The wages averaged 12 shillings in the former year, and 7 shillings in the latter. The number of men, aged 20 and upwards, employed in the stocking manufacture in 1831 was 300, and 44 were engaged in the lace manufacture. Nail-making formerly employed a considerable number, but in 1833 there were only 50 persons so occupied.

Tewkesbury was and is still the centre of an extensive

---

carrying-trade on the Severn and Avon; but the improvement of the navigation of the Severn to Gloucester, by means of a ship-canal, is said to have been injurious to Tewkesbury, and to the improved means of intercourse with other towns in the same district is also ascribed some decline in the attendance at the corn-market.

The iron bridge across the Severn, which opened a communication with Hereford and Wales, counterbalances on the other hand the effects of the above-mentioned improvements. There is a branch railway from Tewkesbury rather more than two miles in length, which joins the Birmingham and Gloucester Railway.

Proceedings of the Old Bailey

Funded by research and Lottery money, the Proceedings of the Old Bailey website (*www.oldbaileyonline.org*) was set up by academics at Hertfordshire and Sheffield universities. It contains the digitized records of trials at London's Central Criminal Court (which is situated in a street called Old Bailey).

At present the site contains information on over 100,000 trials, which took place between April 1674 and October 1834. The project team has obtained funding from the Arts and Humanities Research Council to extend the period covered to April 1913. A further 100,000 trials will be added to the site by September 2008, with the first of this tranche of trial records expected to be added early in 2008.

You can search the trials free of charge to see if one of your ancestors is mentioned. This doesn't necessarily mean he or she was accused of a crime: many of the names mentioned in the trials are those of witnesses and victims. As well as recording the statements made to the court, the proceedings state the verdict and punishment (if guilty). This might be transportation, hanging, imprisonment, branding or whipping, often for what we would consider petty offences.

Workhouses

'Poor relief' started in England and Wales around the beginning of the seventeenth century. The first mention of a workhouse (in which paupers lived and had to work) was of one in Abingdon (formerly in Berkshire, and now in Oxfordshire) in 1631. At that time, most help for poor people was through money, clothing, food or fuel given to people who continued to live in their own homes. This parish-distributed 'out-relief' was gradually replaced by 'in-relief' in workhouses, and in 1834, a Poor Law Amendment was enacted. The Act replaced all out-relief in England and Wales with a system in which parishes were combined in Poor Law Unions, each required to set up its own union workhouse. A similar system was introduced in Ireland in 1838.

Between 1834 and 1930, people in England and Wales who were unable to support themselves could receive relief only within one of the many workhouses that were built during this time. Many of our ancestors entered a workhouse at some point in their lives, either because they had become old and infirm, were unemployed, or were single mothers. Many illegitimate children were born in the work-house.

With the intention of making life in the workhouse as unpleasant as possible, inmates were given soul-destroying tasks such as breaking stones or unpicking 'oakum' (old tarry ropes). Men, women and children were kept separate in the workhouse, and food consisted largely of gruel (watery porridge). In 1930, the system was abolished, with most of the workhouse buildings becoming hospitals, many of which are still in use today.

In Scotland, workhouses were often known as 'poorhouses'. As in England, before the nineteenth century, most poor relief came in the form of out-relief, although Scottish workhouses existed from at least the early eighteenth century. In 1845, Scotland had its own Poor Law Amendment Act, which differed from the English/Welsh Act in keeping parish-based poor relief, although allowing for joint poorhouses in towns.

In addition, the sick and destitute could receive either out-relief or live in a poorhouse. Unlike the system in England, Wales and Ireland, the Scottish parishes were not required to build workhouses. The able-bodied poor not only didn't have to live in a workhouse, they were not allowed to do so. Most of the poor in Scotland received out-relief, and those poorhouses that were built were only half full.

Peter Higginbotham has created a comprehensive website (*www. workhouses.org.uk*) that describes the workhouse system in England (and Wales), Scotland and Ireland. The individual workhouses are illustrated by many recent colour photographs taken by Peter, and accompanied by extracts from the 1881 census, listing both staff and inmates. There's also a photographic tour of the different parts of the workhouse.

Police, 'Black Sheep' and other indexes

Derek Wilcox is another family historian who has created a website (*www.lightage.demon.co.uk*) with various useful indexes. These have been compiled from newspaper reports of court cases and inquests that took place between 1860 and 1920, and involved murder, suicide, assault, accident, divorce, disaster, fraud, probate, cruelty and theft.

The Police Index contains over 70,000 entries for police officers mentioned in the reports, while the Black Sheep Index lists over 120,000 people (who were not necessarily criminals). You can print out forms from the site, fill them in, and send them to Derek to order copies of the reports.

The site also contains an index of over 35,000 officers and men who died in the First World War (taken from obituaries, medal citations, etc.), and 4,000 who fought in the Second World War (from British war magazines).

27

Online family history portals

There are several free portal websites that consist mainly or entirely of links to family history websites. The most useful of these are:

- Family Records – a guide to both the main family history records and the record offices and libraries that hold them;
- GENUKI (Genealogy United Kingdom and Ireland) – set up and run by volunteers based mainly in the UK;
- Cyndi's List – a US-based list of family history websites;
- Census Finder – a US-based listing site with links to much more than census sites;
- British Isles GenWeb – the UK and Ireland part of the US-based World GenWeb Project.

Rather than add so many web addresses to your lists of 'bookmarks'/ 'favourites' that they become completely unmanageable, it can be easier to use a portal.

Family Records www.familyrecords.gov.uk

The Family Records website contains information on the principal records you need to use in tracing your family history, where they're held, how you can obtain them, links to relevant websites, and books with further information. The English, Welsh, Scottish and Irish records covered are:

- birth, marriage and death records (civil registration);
- church records (parish, Nonconformist, Roman Catholic and Jewish registers);

- census returns (1841–1901);
- wills and administrations;
- immigration records;
- emigration (to the USA, Canada, Australia, New Zealand, South Africa, India and the Caribbean);
- military records;
- adoption.

You can print out all of the above information from the website. In additon, Family Records has brief information and contact details of the various partners responsible for the site:

- Access to Archives (A2A) *www.a2a.org.uk*
- British Library – India Office Records *www.bl.uk*
- Commonwealth War Graves Commission *www.cwgc.org*
- Family Records Centre *www.familyrecords.gov.uk/frc*
- General Register Office *www.gro.gov.uk*
- General Register Office for Scotland *www.gro-scotland.gov.uk*
- Imperial War Museum *www.iwm.org.uk*
- The National Archives *www.nationalarchives.gov.uk*
- National Archives of Scotland *www.nas.gov.uk*
- National Library of Wales *www.llgc.org.uk*
- Public Record Office of Northern Ireland *www.proni.gov.uk*
- Scottish Archive Network *www.scan.org.uk*

GENUKI *www.genuki.org.uk*

The GENUKI website was set up in 1995 by a group of volunteers to act as a virtual reference library of family history information for the British Isles. The site is organized in several levels: as well as general information at the top level, at the next level there are sections for England, Scotland, Wales, Ireland, the Isle of Man and the Channel Islands. At this level, there is information related to each country as a whole.

Within those country sections are pages devoted to the historic counties of Britain and Ireland (as they were before the 1974–5 reorganization), i.e. the forty English, thirty-three Scottish, thirteen Welsh and thirty-two Irish counties (including Northern Ireland and the Irish Republic). The Channel Islands section includes subsections on the islands of Jersey, Guernsey, Alderney and Sark. The Isle of Man page and the county pages lead in turn to pages about individual parishes.

GENUKI topics

The county and parish pages are divided into many subject areas, within each of which there are links to various websites. At the level for the whole of England, you'll find information on the following subjects:

- archives and libraries;
- bibliography;
- biography;
- business and commerce records;
- cemeteries;
- census;
- chronology;
- church history;
- church records;
- civil registration;
- correctional institutions;
- court records;
- description and travel;
- directories;
- emigration and immigration;
- gazetteers;
- genealogy;
- historical geography;
- history;
- land and property;
- language and languages;
- manors;

- maps;
- medical records;
- merchant marine;
- migration, internal;
- military history;
- names, geographical;
- names, personal;
- newspapers;
- obituaries;
- occupations;
- politics and government;
- poorhouses, Poor Law, etc.;
- population;
- probate records;
- public records;
- schools;
- social life and customs;
- societies;
- statistics;
- taxation;
- town records.

Similar information is provided at country level for Scotland, Wales and Ireland, as well as at county level for all four countries.

As well as links to external websites, GENUKI has over 60,000 pages of information specially written for the site, such as the pages about 'The Wills of Gloucestershire' (*www.genuki.org.uk/big/eng/ GLS/ProbateRecords/index.html*), with abstracts of many wills.

The amount of detail at each level of GENUKI varies according to what websites exist for the particular area. The pages for the city of Gloucester, for instance, link to more websites than the pages covering the remote rural parish of St Margarets in Herefordshire. As you would expect, the web links for large cities such as London, Liverpool, Manchester and Leeds lead to even more information.

Not every local site is covered by GENUKI, however, so it's worthwhile also running a general search for the parish name using Google or another search engine. Walsham-le-Willows in Suffolk, for example, has a community site at *www.walsham-le-willows.org* with an index of local wills from 1396–1798.

In addition, the site contains articles from the village history group's *Quarterly Review* (covering many local people, such as the Hawes family, who are traced back to the thirteenth century), as well as an illustrated history of the parish from *c.* 4000 BC to the twentieth century. You won't find a link to the Walsham site from GENUKI, however.

Cyndi's List www.cyndislist.com

In 1996, an American woman named Cyndi Howells created a personal website with over 1,000 links to family history sites. Ten years later, that free website has had hundreds of thousands of visitors, and now features links to around a quarter of a million other sites. Cyndi's List has become a family business, with Cyndi herself maintaining it on a full-time basis, her sister-in-law Michele Ingle working on it part-time, and Cyndi's husband Mark also putting in time on keeping the list up to date.

Because finding your way around is very important on such a large website, Cyndi's List has several indexes, including a main category index, an index of items within topics (such as 'Localities', 'Records' and 'Occupations'), an alphabetical category index, and a scaled-down 'No Frills' category index.

Cyndi's List has 12,500 family history links for England, over 6,000 for Scotland, nearly 3,000 for Wales, almost 2,000 for Ireland, and around 500 each for the Isle of Man and the Channel Islands. There are also more than 1,000 links to general UK websites, over 800 links to UK military sites, and over 400 to UK and Irish census sites.

Cyndi's List topics

The main topics at country level, and below that at county level, are:

- general resource sites;
- government and cities;
- history and culture;
- how to;
- language and names;
- libraries, archives and museums;
- locality specific;
- mailing lists, newsgroups and chat;
- maps, gazetteers and geographical information;
- military;
- newspapers;
- people and families;
- photographs and memories;
- professional researchers, volunteers and other research services;
- publications, software and supplies;
- queries, message boards and surname lists;
- records: census, cemeteries, land, obituaries, personal, taxes and vital;
- religion and churches;
- societies and groups.

Census Finder www.censusfinder.com/united_ kingdom.htm

The Census Finder website calls itself 'a directory of free census sites', but it contains links to many other lists of people besides the official censuses. Being an American site, most of its 31,000+ links lead to population listing sites for the USA. In addition, there are links to nearly 1,500 Canadian listings and to over seventy Native American censuses (including schedules of the Cherokee, Creek and

Seminole nations), as well as to Norwegian and Swedish censuses.

Census Finder also has links to over 2,000 population listing sites for Britain and Ireland, including over 1,000 English, over 750 Irish, over 300 Scottish and over 150 Welsh websites. You'll find the Channel Islands and the Isle of Man listed under England.

In addition to the transcriptions of census returns, Census Finder has some of the following records for some counties:

- apprenticeship lists;
- birth, marriage and death databases;
- cemetery burials;
- deeds lists;
- electoral registers;
- emigrant lists;
- flax grower lists (Ireland);
- freeholder lists;
- Griffith's Valuation (Ireland);
- hearth tax records;
- jury lists;
- land tax records;
- landlord and tenant lists;
- marriage bonds;
- militia lists;
- mining index;
- newspaper cuttings;
- overseers' accounts;
- parish registers;
- poll books;
- poll tax lists;
- poor relief accounts;
- prison records;
- pub and licensee names indexes;
- Quarter Sessions rolls;
- regimental lists;
- resident lists;
- rolls of honour;
- school records;

- strays;
- telephone directories;
- Tithe Applotment Books (Ireland);
- tithe defaulter lists (Ireland);
- trade directories;
- transportation records;
- vehicle owners' registrations;
- visitation records;
- war memorial lists;
- wills databases.

Because of the unfortunate destruction of the Irish 1821–91 censuses, many more types of population listing have been transcribed for Ireland than for England, Scotland and Wales.

British Isles GenWeb www.britishislesgenweb.org

The British Isles GenWeb pages are part of the World GenWeb Project, a non-profit, volunteer-based organization dedicated to providing family history records and resources for access worldwide. The project was founded in 1996 with the intention that there would be a website for every country in the world, and that the site would be run by family historians either living in the country or familiar with its resources. The World GenWeb Project was modelled on the US GenWeb Project, which had become available online earlier in the same year.

The British Isles GenWeb home page leads to subsidiary websites for:

- England (*www.rootsweb.com/~engwgw*);
- Scotland (*www.scotlandgenweb.org*);
- Wales (*www.walesgenweb.com*);
- Ireland (Republic of) (*www.irelandgenweb.com*);
- Northern Ireland (*www.rootsweb.com/~nirwgw*);
- Isle of Man (*www.britishislesgenweb.org/~iom*);
- Gibraltar (*www.britishislesgenweb.org/~gibraltar*);
- Caribbean Islands (*www.britishislesgenweb.org/carribbean.html*);

- Falkland Islands (*britishislesgenweb.org/~falklandislands*);
- St Helena (*website.lineone.net/~sthelena/familyhistory.htm*).

The sites for England, Scotland, Wales, Ireland and Northern Ireland lead, in turn, to county pages, while the Caribbean Islands site leads to pages on the individual islands or island groups. The county and island pages contain links to external websites with family history records or information.

The British Isles GenWeb group of sites tends to have less information than GENUKI, and has no parish pages. It's still worthwhile to take a look at what GenWeb does have, however, particularly on its Irish sites.

28

Making contact with your cousins online

The websites mentioned so far have been those where you can find family history records and more general background information. There are also contact sites, however, such as Genes Reunited (*www.genesreunited.co.uk*) and Lost Cousins (*www.lostcousins.com*). Through these you can make contact with distant cousins you didn't know about beforehand. Apart from the joy of discovering previously unknown relatives, you may find that they have information about some of your ancestors – and maybe even photographs of them.

There are many 'mailing lists' devoted to different aspects of family history. You can find a list of UK and Ireland mailing lists at GENUKI (*www.genuki.org.uk/indexes/MailingLists.html*). Through these you can send e-mail messages to other list members asking for help with your research.

Family historians are really nice people, who'll be only too happy to help. A fourth or fifth cousin may very well let you know that the reason you can't find your great-grandfather's death in Bristol, is because he ran off to San Francisco with one of his female employees!

There are also several family history message board websites, on which you can post queries or comments. They will notify you when you receive replies, so you can return to the site later to read them. The US-based RootsWeb carries over 130,000 message boards, while RootsChat is a major British discussion forum.

Genes Reunited www.genesreunited.co.uk

Genes Reunited (originally called Genes Connected) was set up by the reunion website Friends Reunited (*www.friendsreunited.co.uk*), which has since been taken over by ITV.

On the Genes Reunited website, you can search the 80+ million names submitted by its many members to see if any of the names are the same as those of your ancestors. On the search page, you must enter a surname, and you may narrow your search by entering a forename, year of birth (plus or minus so many years) and place of birth.

The results page will list the entries in the Genes Reunited database that match your search criteria, showing:

- forename(s);
- year of birth;
- place of birth;
- born in (name of country);
- prior contact;
- tree owner.

As a member, you can then click on a button on the listing, next to the tree owner's name, to send a message to that person. If you've already contacted that person, the results list will state 'Yes' in the 'prior contact' column.

Membership of Genes Reunited entitles you to put your own family tree online at the site, so that your ancestors can be listed when someone else carries out a search. You can either enter the details of your family tree members one at a time, or import an existing tree from a family history program in GEDCOM format. This is a standard format for family tree files, originally created by the LDS Church.

Genes Reunited will e-mail you regularly to let you know if any of your ancestors are 'hot matches' for those in other people's trees. Unfortunately, the comparison seems to be on name and date only, but not birthplace. The result is that, if you have a 'John Smith' in your tree (as I have), your ancestor is continually being matched with people born in a different part entirely of Britain (or the world).

Lost Cousins *www.lostcousins.com*

Lost Cousins has the same general aim as Genes Reunited: to connect you to distant relatives you didn't know about. It does this in a different way, however. With Lost Cousins, you enter details of your ancestors from censuses, and the website will check whether any of your entries match those of other users.

As with Genes Reunited, you can use the site free of charge, but have to join to be able to contact other members. Lost Cousins recommends that you enter not only your ancestors, but also all your relatives mentioned in the census, to increase your chances of being contacted.

RootsWeb mailing lists

Once you've joined a mailing list, every e-mail message that you send to it will be forwarded to all its other members. In turn, you'll receive all the messages that the other members send.

RootsWeb (*www.rootsweb.com*) hosts almost 30,000 family history mailing lists. If you click on 'Index' in the Mailing Lists section on the RootsWeb's home page, you'll be taken to the main index of mailing lists. This consists of sections for Surnames (for which there are a very large number of lists), the USA, International, and Other (mainly non-geographical) lists.

In the International section, the mailing lists for England range from 'BEDFORD' to 'YORKSGEN', for Scotland from 'ABERDEEN' to 'WGW-SURNAMES-SCOTLAND' (where 'WGW' stands for 'World GenWeb'), for Wales from 'BlaenauGwent' to 'WLS-USK-WYE-VALLEY', for Northern Ireland from 'County-TyroneIreland' to 'Unionist-Culture', and for the Republic of Ireland from 'BLACK-IRISH' to 'WEXFORD'.

Click on the name of the mailing list you want to see, and a page for that list will be displayed. This enables you to subscribe to the list free of charge (you can also unsubscribe when you don't want to receive messages any more). You can also search or browse the archived messages for a list without having to join it. In addition, there's a test version of a search across the archived messages for all the mailing lists. If you've subscribed to a popular list, you'll find you get a large number of e-mail messages arriving at your computer. You can instead subscribe to a digest version of the list, where several messages are grouped together. You'll have to read the digest, however, to see if it contains any messages that interest you, rather than simply looking for interesting message headers.

Yahoo! groups

You can also subscribe to various family history discussion groups at the *Yahoo! UK & Ireland* groups website (*http://uk.dir.groups. yahoo.com/dir/Family__Home/Genealogy*). There are three underscore characters between 'Family' and 'Home' in that address.

Usenet newsgroups

In 1979, the world's largest Internet bulletin board system, known as Usenet ('Users' Network') was created at Duke University in North Carolina in the USA. Users of the system post messages in forums known as 'newsgroups', which (unlike mailing lists) you don't join. Newsgroup postings can be read either using special 'newsreader' programs such as Outlook Express and Agent, or through the search engine Google's Groups section (*http://groups.google.co.uk*) using a web-browser program such as Internet Explorer or Firefox.

There are now many thousands of newsgroups, with over 250 dedicated to 'genealogy'. Google holds an archive of all the Usenet messages posted since 1981, which you can search in the same way you would web pages. You can also make postings to newsgroups, without the need for newsreader software, and create your own newsgroups.

Web-based message boards and forums

RootsWeb message boards

In addition to all its mailing lists, you'll find over 132,000 message boards at RootsWeb at *http://boards.ancestry.com/mbexec?htx=boa rd&r=rw&p=localities.britisles*. The boards are in groups according to surname, location or topic, and you can post queries to them free of charge. Messages posted to the boards are sent to people who subscribe to the equivalent RootsWeb mailing list. You can also find the same boards at Ancestry.com (the American forerunner of Ancestry.co.uk) at *http://boards.ancestry.com/mbexec?htx=board&r =an&p=localities.britisles*. (This is almost exactly the same address as for the RootsWeb version.)

For England, Scotland, Wales and Ireland, there is a message board for each of the historic counties, as well as a general board for each country. There are also boards for the Isle of Man and the Channel Islands (with sub-boards for Jersey, Guernsey, Alderney and Sark).

GenForum

Genealogy.com (which, like Ancestry.co.uk, Ancestry.com and RootsWeb, is owned by the American company The Generations Network) hosts a similar group of discussion forums. You'll find those for England, Scotland, Wales, Ireland and the Isle of Man at *http://genforum.genealogy.com/regional/countries*.

There are forums for all the counties of Ireland and nearly all those of England, but for only a small number of Scottish and Welsh counties, with no forums at all for the Channel Islands.

British Genealogy

The British Genealogy website was set up by Rod Neep, founder of the Archive CD Project to provide digital copies on CD of rare books. At *www.british-genealogy.com/forums*, you can find forums for all the counties of Britain, as well as general forums for Ireland, the Isle of Man, the Channel Islands and various other topics, including twelve historical periods from 'The Normans (1066 onwards)' to 'World War 2 (1939–45)'.

RootsChat

RootsChat (*www.rootschat.com*) is a similar website with forums for England, Scotland, Wales and Ireland (all with county sub-forums), as well as the Isle of Man, the Channel Islands and a large number of other topics. RootsChat has over 34,000 members.

Talking Scot

The Talking Scot forum (*www.talkingscot.com/forum*) was set up in 2004 in part as an independent replacement for the Scotland's People discussion group, which had become something of an embarrassment to the General Register Office for Scotland and was closed down in that year. Here you'll find many topics related to Scottish ancestry, posted by over 1,500 users.

In addition, there are other forums at:

- *Family Tree Magazine/Practical Family History* (*www. family-tree.co.uk/phpBB2/index.php*);
- Genealogy Marketplace (*www.genealogymarketplace.co.uk/ phpbb/index.php?c=3*);
- UK Genealogy Forum (*www.uk-genealogy.org.uk/phpBB2/ index.php*).

Blogs

Blog is an abbreviation of 'web log', a combination of online journal, newsletter and forum. An interesting family history blog is Dick Eastman's Online Genealogy Newsletter (*http://eogn.typepad.com/ eastmans_online_genealogy*). Dick is American, but features quite a lot of news from the UK.

You can search for other family history/genealogy blogs using Google's Blog Search facility (*www.google.co.uk/blogsearch?hl=en*).

29

Family history societies

Although you can find out more and more about your ancestors simply sitting at home in front of a computer, it's good to get out and meet other people who are also family history enthusiasts. The main way to do this is by joining a family history society (FHS).

It can be very useful to join your local society, so that you can attend meetings in your area, which are often talks given by experienced family historians. Many of the larger societies have a research or resource centre, sometimes located in the local record office or reference library. You can carry out a lot of ancestral research using the equipment in the centre, such as microfilm and microfiche readers, as well as computers with Internet access.

This is particularly helpful, if some of your ancestors lived in your local area. Even if none of them did, however, it's still good to meet and talk to other family historians about your shared interest. Nearly all the societies publish a regular journal, with family history news and articles, which can be a great help in your researches. Your local FHS will probably exchange journals with other societies, which you can then borrow from its library.

As well as joining your local society, you would do well to join some of the societies for the areas your ancestors came from, and receive your own personal copies of their journals. Most societies run projects creating indexes of baptisms, marriages, burials and monumental inscriptions, which they'll search for you free of charge (non-members have to pay for this service).

As a society member, you can also have the surnames you're interested in listed in the 'Members' Interests' published in the society's journal. Any other members who are researching the same names as you can then get in touch. You never know, you may discover some fourth- or fifth- or even more distant cousins.

A sample family history society: Gloucestershire FHS (GFHS)

The Gloucestershire Family History Society (*http://mysite. wanadoo-members.co.uk/gfhs/gfhs.htm*) holds monthly meetings in Gloucester, Bream (Forest of Dean branch), Caincross (Stroud branch), Cirencester and Chipping Campden. Each year, in April, the society holds its annual Open Day at the Crypt School in Gloucester.

Since 1999, the GFHS has had a resource centre in Gloucester, open to both members and non-members of the society. The centre contains a bookstall (with general family history and local books for sale), library (see the catalogue at *mysite. wanadoo-members.co.uk/gfhs/LibCat/LibCat.htm*) and main research room.

There you'll find six computers with free Internet access and ten microfiche readers, with print-outs available for a small charge. The research room has many resources on computer or fiche (not only for Gloucestershire), such as baptism, marriage and burial indexes, the national calendar of wills (1858–1943), criminal registers, Poor Law records, monumental inscriptions, parish register transcripts and trade directories. You can view the full list of resources at *mysite. wanadoo-members.co.uk/gfhs/ResourceList.htm*.

The GFHS provides online access to the databases of Ancestry. co.uk and British Origins. This is free of charge to members and non-members alike, although the society does ask for a donation to cover running costs. The society's own CD publications are also available on computer: Gloucestershire burials, marriages and Nonconformist records. The society is currently working on an index of births, as well as continuing to index Nonconformist records and memorial inscriptions, with further CDs expected to be published in the future.

Family history societies also publish various useful items, such as listings of cemetery inscriptions, census and parish register indexes, and parish maps. These come in various forms: booklets, microfiche, diskette and CD. Most societies have a website with information on meetings, services, publications, resources and location of the research centre (if there is one).

In addition, some societies' sites also provide access to free family history databases. The Herefordshire FHS, for example, has an online monumental inscription index (*www.rootsweb.com/~ukhfhs/miindex. html*), as does the Aberdeen and North East Scotland FHS (*www. abdnet.co.uk/mi-index*). The Bristol and Avon FHS has an online South Gloucestershire burials index (*www.bafhs.org.uk/burialindex/ burials.htm*), while at the City of York FHS site, you can view an index of prisoners brought to trial at York Assizes from 1785–1851 (*www.yorkfamilyhistory.org.uk/assizes.htm*).

Examples of some family history societies' projects

Family history societies undertake a variety of indexing and recording projects. The Northumberland & Durham FHS, for instance, has indexed the 1851 and 1891 censuses, both of which are now complete and available in paper and microfiche form. The society is adding entries from sixty burial registers to the National Burial Index (NBI), and also inputting all of its transcripts of baptisms and marriages into a common database.

The Suffolk FHS (SFHS) has completed a county-wide index of marriages from 1813–37 (available in booklet, microfiche or CD form), and volunteers are now indexing marriages from 1754. The society is also compiling a baptism index, which will be issued on CD in groups of parishes.

In addition, the SFHS is creating a 'Parish Finder' database of all surnames that occur in a parish's registers. At present, only a search service is offered, although you'll be able to buy CDs later. The society's Mildenhall Group is currently

---

working on what will become a CD of monumental inscriptions in Mildenhall Cemetery, with a digital photograph of each of the 800 gravestones.

The Manchester & Lancashire FHS (MLFHS) has completed a fourteen-year project in conjunction with The National Archives (TNA) transcribing water-damaged 1851 census returns for the Manchester and Salford area. These returns had never been microfilmed or digitized. The society's transcription is available on CD, can also be viewed at TNA, and is being made available through Family History Online (see below).

The MLFHS also has an ongoing project, in which its members are extracting information from obituaries in the *Manchester Guardian* for those cremated in Manchester up to 1940, as the original records were lost during the Second World War.

The Derbyshire FHS is busy recording monumental inscriptions from the county's churchyards. The society is also indexing the 1861 census, some cemetery and parish registers, and the civil registers of births, marriages and deaths.

For some time, the Dorset FHS (DFHS) has been transcribing the baptisms, marriages and burials in the parish registers held at the Dorset History Centre, and now holds a large number of such transcriptions. You can see which parishes have been covered, and for which time periods, by checking on the society's website.

The DFHS has transcribed most of the county's baptisms, as well as the marriages and burials from 1813–37. The society is now transcribing the earlier marriages and will then begin on the pre-1813 burials.

The Glamorgan FHS (GFHS) has compiled databases of over half a million baptisms and a similar number of burials, taken from the county's parish and chapel registers. In addition, the GFHS marriage database holds over 64,000 entries for the period before 1837.

The society offers a free search service to its members from these databases. The baptism and marriage indexes are available on CD, and the marriage and burial indexes are available online. The GFHS has also published indexed transcripts of the 1891 census of Glamorgan on seven CDs.

In a large project that has been running for several years in conjunction with the city's Mitchell Library, the Glasgow and West of Scotland FHS (GWSFHS) is helping to index the records of Glasgow's Southern Necropolis. Around a quarter of a million people were buried there between 1841 and 1947.

There are twenty-five volumes of burials to be indexed, of which eleven have been completed so far and are available for viewing at the GWSFHS research centre in Glasgow. The society's members are hopeful that once the indexing is finished, the Mitchell Library will allow them to release the index on CD.

The GWSFHS has completed several other Glasgow City Archives indexing projects in conjunction with the Mitchell Library, including Poor Law applications (1851–1915) for Glasgow City and Barony (with Govan still ongoing), Lanarkshire Poor Law applications up to 1900, Strathclyde area police registers from 1850–1930, and Glasgow militia records (1810–31). Various other indexing projects are continuing, including Glasgow Burgh Register of Sasines (land records). These indexes are expected to be made available online by the Mitchell Library at some point in the future.

Society of Genealogists (SoG) www.sog.org.uk

The Society of Genealogists, Britain's oldest genealogy society, founded in 1911, has published many books and booklets on different aspects of family history, runs educational courses and seminars, and holds a Family History Show each year in central London in the spring.

The society's library, also in central London, contains a large number of family history records and publications covering England, Scotland, Wales, Ireland, the Isle of Man, the Channel Islands and other countries (including Australia, Canada, India, the USA and the West Indies). The SoG's holdings include parish registers, marriage licences, censuses, monumental inscriptions, wills, local histories, poll books and directories.

You can search the society's catalogue online at *www.sog.org. uk/sogcat/sogcat.shtml.*

Scottish Genealogy Society (SGS) www.scotsgenealogy.com

The Scottish Genealogy Society (SGS) was founded in Edinburgh in 1953, as the first society in Scotland dedicated to family history. The society has published a large number of transcriptions of monumental inscriptions, among other publications. The SGS library, whose index can be searched online at the society's website, contains books, manuscripts and pedigrees, as well as parish registers, census returns and other indexes on microfilm, microfiche and CD.

Federation of Family History Societies (FFHS) www.ffhs.org.uk

The Federation of Family History Societies was founded in 1974, as an umbrella organization, and now has a membership of over 200 family history societies and similar organizations in the UK (except Scotland) and around the world. The federation has issued various family history publications, including a National Burial Index (NBI) on CD, using information compiled by its member societies. The FFHS website has links to the sites of all its members.

Family History Online *www.familyhistoryonline.net*

The FFHS is also the organization behind the pay-per-view Family History Online website, which holds databases compiled by family history societies. The databases include baptisms, marriages, burials, census returns, marriage bonds, memorial inscriptions, 'strays' (people found in the records away from their own county), wills, Quarter Sessions calendars, and army deserters, as well as civil registration births, marriages and deaths in Derbyshire.

Scottish Association of Family History Societies (SAFHS) *www.safhs.org.uk*

In 1986, the Scottish Association of Family History Societies was formed as an umbrella organization for family history societies in Scotland. Prior to this, Scottish societies had belonged to the FFHS. SAFHS has issued a number of publications, and now has twenty-six full-member societies (mainly in Scotland itself). There are also nearly twenty family history societies outside Scotland that are associate members of SAFHS. On the SAFHS website, you'll find links to all its member societies.

Association of Family History Societies of Wales (AFHSW) *www.fhswales.info*

The Association of Family History Societies of Wales was formed in 1981 as an umbrella organization for Welsh family history societies. There are links on the AFHSW website to the sites of its member societies, who are all also members of the FFHS.

Irish family history societies

In Ireland, the family history societies are national or regional, rather than county-based, and include the Genealogical Society of Ireland (*www.familyhistory.ie*), Irish Family History Society (*homepage. eircom.net/~ifhs*), North of Ireland Family History Society (*www. nifhs.org*) and Ulster Genealogical Historical Guild – part of the Ulster Historical Foundation (*www.ancestryireland.co.uk/guild.php*).

343

In addition, there is also a London-based Irish Genealogical Research Society (*www.igrsoc.org*), and The Irish Ancestral Research Association (TIARA). TIARA (*www.tiara.ie*) is based in the USA, but has a website with a large number of useful links.

Other societies

As well as geographically based family history societies, there are others that are more broadly based. You may find it helpful to join associations such as the Huguenot Society (*www.huguenotsociety. org.uk*), the Catholic FHS (*www.catholic-history.org.uk*), the Jewish Genealogical Society of Great Britain (*www.jgsgb.org.uk*), Quaker FHS (*www.rootsweb.com/~engqfhs*) and the Romany and Traveller FHS (*www.rtfhs.org.uk*).

There are family history societies catering for those with some ancestors from continental Europe: the Anglo-German FHS (*www. art-science.com/agfhs*) and Anglo-Italian FHS (*www.anglo-italianfhs. org.uk*), or who lived in the Indian subcontinent: the Families in British India Society (*www.fibis.org*).

The Guild of One-Name Studies (*www.one-name.org*) has almost 2,000 members studying over 5,000 individual names in 'one-name studies'. The guild's members are researching everyone with the surnames they're studying, rather than just their own family tree. You can find the names being researched at the guild's website.

Conclusion: the past, present and future of family history

The big change in family history over the last hundred years has been its democratization: tracing ancestors has developed from being a middle- and upper-middle-class pastime to a hobby for the millions. Technology, in particular, has helped to transform what used to be called 'pedigree-hunting' into today's worldwide family history. Where once ancestor-tracing was mainly concerned with trying to establish a link with royalty and the aristocracy, today's family historians simply want to know who their ancestors were, whether rich and famous or (more likely) poor and unknown. Pedigree-hunting, once the preserve of vicars, retired army officers and the leisured and academic classes, led to the foundation of the Society of Genealogists (SoG) in London in 1911.

How to Trace a Pedigree is a sixty-eight-page book by H. A. (Helen Augusta) Crofton that was published in the same year. Although Ms Crofton's book contains two chapters on wills, two more on 'published sources of information', and a chapter on 'miscellaneous manuscript documents' (the actual records), surprisingly (to us), she devotes only two paragraphs to parish registers and one to civil registration indexes. Although (with today's 100-year rule) you'd expect the censuses to be unavailable for public access in 1911, interestingly, Ms Crofton says, 'For nineteenth-century searches, census returns may be consulted.'

> ### Tip: Check your information is correct
>
> '. . . the golden rule to be most carefully observed by gene-alogists is
>
> ### *Verify your Information.*
>
> An honest researcher would never appreciate a 'faked' pedigree; but it is fatally easy to assume a certain point, and, working from that assumption, to have all future details more or less incorrect.'
>
> H. A. Crofton, *How to Trace a Pedigree* (Elliot Stock, 1911)

Technological change

The spread of interest in family history has largely been brought about by the use of technology. Although microfilming was first carried out as early as 1839, and used to send messages by pigeon post during the Franco-Prussian War of 1870–71, the technology wasn't adopted in earnest until the 1920s. In 1938, the LDS Church started to use microfilm technology to begin its programme of filming parish registers and other records worldwide, and six years later, had 2,000 rolls of microfilm. All archives and record offices now make many of their records available to the public on microfilm, and indeed, some are still carrying out microfilming programmes.

The introduction of microform (microfilm and microfiche, invented in 1961) helped to spread the availability of family history records. Microform meant not only that original records could be preserved from overuse, but that copies could be made available in other record offices and libraries. The LDS Church now has over 2 million rolls of microfilm stored in its granite vaults in the Wasatch Mountains, twenty-five miles from Salt Lake City, Utah. The microform records are available not only to the LDS Family History Library in Salt Lake City, but also to the more than 3,500 LDS Family History Centres around the world. In addition the SoG has a large collection of microform records in its library in London.

The LDS Church was also in the forefront in its use of mainframe computer technology. In 1973, the LDS Church converted its 30 million-record Temple Records Index Bureau (TIB) card index, begun in 1927, to a Computer File Index (CFI). Three years later, the CFI became available in the UK on microfiche, and in 1981, the database was renamed as the International Genealogical Index (IGI).

In the 1990s, the personal computer (PC), compact discs (CDs) and the Internet began to be used by family historians. A number of programs (such as *Family Tree Maker, Roots Magic, Family Historian* and *The Master Genealogist*) have been written for the PC that let you input information on your ancestors and other relatives. Rather than having to redraw your tree every time you find new family members, you can simply view your family file on-screen, print it (or a part of it) out as a family tree or genealogy report, and even exchange it with your cousins over the Internet.

Although many family history societies (see below) published transcriptions of censuses, monumental inscriptions and parish registers in booklet or microfiche form, it was the use of computer databases that made searching the records so much easier. You could simply enter your ancestor's name, run a search and see what results you get. Instead of transcriptions, many CDs contain digitized copies of the records, which removes the danger of errors creeping into the transcription process. The arrival of Windows-based web browser software around 1994 made many more records easily accessible to family historians all over the world. The LDS Church set up its free Family Search website *www.familysearch.org* in 1999, and the first commercial sites, Ancestry.com (*www.ancestry.com*) and Genealogy.com (*www.genealogy.com*), were established in the USA in 1996 and 1999 respectively. In 2003, Genealogy.com was acquired by Ancestry.com's parent company.

Although the Internet's effects have generally been beneficial to individual family historians, the spread of records online in the twenty-first century has brought with it lower attendance at family history society meetings and family history societies' fairs, and smaller sales of census CDs.

The use of computer technology has made transcriptions and indexes from the eighteenth, nineteenth and early twentieth centuries available to a much wider public than their creators would ever have imagined. *Historical, Monumental and Genealogical Collections Relative to the County of Gloucester* (published posthumously in 1786) includes transcriptions of many of the county's gravestones compiled over thirty years by Ralph Bigland, a herald and king of arms in the College of Arms, who rose to become Garter Principal King of Arms from 1780 until his death in 1784. Bigland's book has now been issued on CD by Archive CD Books *www.rod-neep. co.uk.*

William Phillimore (the founder of the local history publishing company) and his helpers extracted the marriages from around 1,200 parish registers in twenty-nine English counties and began to publish them from 1894 until his death in 1913. The counties best covered are Cornwall, Gloucestershire, Leicestershire, Lincolnshire, Norfolk, Nottinghamshire and Somerset, although none is complete. Phillimore's marriages have been made available on CDs from Archive CD Books, S&N Genealogy Supplies (*www.genealogysupplies.com*), Stepping Stones (*www.stepping-stones.co.uk* (for Worcestershire only)) and UK Genealogy Archives (*www.uk-genealogy.org.uk* (for eight counties)). Most counties are now accessible online at the pay-per-view site Family Relatives (*www.familyrelatives.com*), and some (including thirty parishes in Cornwall and thirty-nine in Derbyshire) are available free-of-charge at UK Genealogy Archives.

During the 1930s, Percival Boyd, a Fellow of the Society of Genealogists, and his assistants compiled a marriage index containing around 7 million names and covering (but not completely) sixteen counties from the start of parish registration until 1837. More than 400 parishes in Suffolk are included in Boyd's Marriage Index, 300 in Essex, 200 in Cornwall and Yorkshire, and 100 in Cambridgeshire, Devon, Gloucestershire, Lancashire, London and Middlesex, Norfolk, Shropshire and Somerset. The original index is available at the SoG, but you can now search it online at the British Origins website *www. britishorigins.com.*

In 1818, a similar index, but covering mainly marriages between 1780 and 1837 in almost all of the ancient parishes in the City of London, was begun by a firm of record agents. Among their successors were Pallot and Co., whose name has been linked to the index ever since. Today the Pallot Marriage Index is accessible online at the subscription and pay-per-view site Ancestry.co.uk (*www.ancestry.co.uk*).

Magazines and television

Magazines and television programmes have also helped to broaden the family history base. In 1984, issue number one of *Family Tree Magazine* (*www.family-tree.co.uk*) appeared on the news-stands. This was the first of the current professionally published magazines devoted to non-academic family history, and was followed by *Family History Monthly* (*www.familyhistorymonthly.com*) in 1996.

The following year, *Practical Family History* (a sister magazine to *Family Tree*) was aimed at newcomers to the subject. The National Archives began publishing its own magazine *Ancestors* (*www.ancestorsmagazine.co.uk*) in 2001, and two years later, the first issue of *Your Family Tree* (*www.yourfamilytreemag.co.uk*) was published. The latter came with a cover-mounted CD, which has since become obligatory for all the magazines except *Ancestors*.

The annual *Family and Local History Handbook* (*www.genealogical.co.uk*) was first published by Bob and Liz Blatchford (as *The Genealogical Services Directory*) in 1997. As well as listings of family and local history societies, libraries, archives, registrars of births, marriages and deaths, probate registries, cemeteries and museums, the handbook also contains over seventy articles on different aspects of family, local and military history.

Although the BBC broadcast a television series called *Family History* as long ago as 1979, it has only been in the last few years that TV shows on the subject have become really popular. The BBC's *Who Do You Think You Are?* series (first broadcast in 2004), with an audience of around 6 million viewers, has introduced a younger audience to family history. There have also been several other television programmes on the topic, but with smaller audiences.

Family history societies

Although the Society of Genealogists (SoG) had been founded in 1911 and the Scottish Genealogy Society in 1953, it was not until the sixties and seventies that county- and region-based societies were founded in Britain. (In the USA, the New England Historic Genealogical Society was founded in Boston, Massachusetts as early as 1876.) These newer societies tended to call themselves 'family history societies' rather than 'genealogy societies'. Members of the older societies had already carried out some record indexing, and the much larger numbers joining the county-based societies allowed extensive indexing projects to be tackled. The 1881 census, for example, was indexed by family history societies in conjunction with the LDS Church, which published the results in 1999 on a set of reasonably priced CDs and then in 2002 on the Family Search website.

In 1974, the Federation of Family History Societies (FFHS) was established as an 'umbrella' organization for both new and old societies. The Federation originally had some Scottish member societies, but these left when the Scottish Association of Family History Societies (SAFHS) was formed in 1986. Like the SoG, the FFHS has an extensive publication programme. Its main projects include the National Burial Index on CD, with a first edition containing 5.4 million burials published in 2001, and a second (with 13.2 million burials) in 2004. In 2003, the federation set up a pay-per-view website under the name Family History Online (*www.familyhistoryonline. net*), with indexed transcriptions of census returns, monumental inscriptions, parish registers, some wills and other records.

Most family history societies hold annual fairs at which you can get advice on your researches, and buy items including genealogical books, magazines, CDs and microfiche. Exhibitors usually include family history societies from neighbouring counties, record offices and commercial companies. The Society of Genealogists has been holding an annual family history fair/show in London in May since 1993. In 2007, the SoG show became part of a new larger *Who Do You Think You Are?* National History Show, which attracted an audience of around 12,000 over three days. In Gateshead, the National Family History Fair (originally known as the Great North Fair) has been held in the autumn since 2003, with over 2,000 people attending. The larger fairs and some of the smaller ones hold seminars on different aspects of family history, as well as workshop sessions.

> ### The story of you: Mary Wooldridge
>
> Mary managed to unite a friend with her birth siblings after she was adopted through Barnardo's. 'I found them using the basic research skills that I have learnt over many years,' she says. 'This is the most rewarding thing I have ever done, so I can positively say that family history is "life-changing".'

Finding distant cousins

Strictly speaking, we're all related. I always find it fascinating to walk along a busy street in a town, look around at the people of different races and colours and think: all of these people are my cousins. It is good, however, to meet those who are rather more closely related to you. The various family history magazines have pages to which you can send details of your family, in the hope that people who are related to you will make contact. In Australia Keith Johnson and Malcolm Sainty publish an annual Genealogical Research Directory (GRD) (*http://members.ozemail.com.au/~grdxxx*) dedicated to this task. The GRD has been published in book form since 1981, and on CD since 2003 (with back issues since 1990 also available on CD).

Now, however, through websites such as Genes Reunited (*www.genesreunited.co.uk*) and Lost Cousins (*www.lostcousins.com*) and via Internet mailing lists, it's easier and cheaper to make contact with fourth or fifth cousins.

DNA, chromosomes and genes

The human body is composed of several trillion cells. Each of these has a nucleus that consists of forty-six string-like structures called chromosomes, which were discovered in the mid-nineteenth century by Gregor Mendel, an Augustinian monk living in what is now the Czech Republic. The chromosomes come in two sets, one set being inherited from each parent. Twenty-two of the twenty-three chromosomes in each set are single chromosomes, while the remaining one is either the X or Y sex chromosome. A woman's cells contain two X chromosomes, while a man's contain an X and a Y chromosome. A man inherits the Y chromosome from his father, which is significant for family history.

Each chromosome contains tightly coiled threads of DNA and associated protein molecules. DNA was first identified in 1869 by a Swiss biochemist named Friedrich Miescher (and named 'nuclein'), and contains the instructions to our bodies for our physical characteristics, which may be passed on to future generations. It was only after further research by the bacteriologists Fred Griffith of the UK (in the 1920s) and the American Oswald Theodore Avery (in the 1940s), however, that the scientific community accepted that DNA (rather than protein, as biochemists had thought) transmitted inherited characteristics.

A DNA molecule in humans and other higher organisms comprises two strands wrapped round each other like a twisted ladder (the double-helix). Its 'rungs', consisting of chemicals containing nitrogen, are called bases. There are four bases in DNA: adenine (A), thymine (T), cytosine (C), and guanine (G).

The Briton Francis Crick and the American James Watson discovered the double-helix format of DNA in Cambridge, England in 1953. Their findings were based on earlier work by Rosalind Franklin and Maurice Wilkins. A Nobel Prize was awarded to the three men in 1962, but Franklin was unable to share the award as she had died of cancer in 1958, aged only thirty-seven.

Genes are discrete stretches of these bases that code the instructions for the body. In humans, the genes take up only about 5–10 per cent of the DNA. The genes are, in effect, units of heredity information. All of the heritable genetic material in the chromosomes, taken together, is known as the genome. There are around 24,000 genes in the human genome, each of them having a fixed position on a chromosome. The sequencing of the human genome was completed in 2003.

The Human Genome Project aimed to locate every human gene, find out its precise chemical structure and how it functioned in health and disease, so that the genetic basis of human disease could be determined. The project's collected information will form the basic reference for research in human biology and medicine.

The Y chromosome

When you're conceived, you receive one of your sex chromosomes from your mother. This is always an X chromosome, because women have two X chromosomes, but no Y chromosome. You also receive a sex chromosome from your father. This one may be either an X or a Y, as men have one of each. The Y chromosome contains a gene that makes a human embryo become male, whereas it would otherwise be female. If you're a man, then you'll have inherited your Y chromosome from your father, who inherited it from his father, and so on back to the earliest modern humans about half a million years ago and beyond.

Over the generations, as the Y chromosome is passed on, it gradually mutates, so that not all men have it in exactly the same form. Segments of the chromosome (known as markers) can be detected in DNA tests, and compared to those of other men. When there is a close match in the results, it will give some indication (but not an exact measurement) of how long ago the two men shared a common ancestor.

Mitochondrial DNA

Women have no Y chromosome that can be tested, but do have mitochondrial DNA (mtDNA). Unlike the sex chromosomes, the mitochondria are not part of the nuclei of the several trillion cells of the body, but are tiny structures found in a different part of the cell. Both men and women have mtDNA, but you always inherit it from your mother (although mtDNA inherited from his father was found in the muscle of a man who had inherited the mtDNA in his blood from his mother). In a similar way to the Y chromosome, mtDNA mutates over the years (although more slowly). Although mtDNA can also serve to determine relationships, Y-chromosome testing is generally used for family history research, as surnames are usually passed down the male rather than the female line.

DNA and family history

The use of DNA testing for family history is often described as a major breakthrough that can help you to get further back in time with your genealogy than paper records can take you. A number of companies, particularly in the USA, are providing tests aimed specifically at family historians.

The initials DNA stand for DeoxyriboNucleic Acid. According to James Watson (one of the two scientists who discovered DNA's double-helix structure), DNA holds the key to the nature of living things. 'It stores the hereditary information that is passed on from one generation to the next, and it orchestrates the incredibly complex world of the cell,' says Professor Watson in his book *DNA: The Secret of Life*.

In family history DNA projects, often two or more groups of people with the same or similar surnames will be tested to try to find out if they belong to different lines of the same family. If two test results match exactly, this indicates that the two people are fairly closely related.

When genealogical DNA testing began around 2001, only ten or twelve Y-chromosome markers were tested. In his book *DNA and Family History*, Chris Pomery warns that tests on a small number of markers will lump together many families that are unlikely to be directly related as part of a single family within a genealogical time-frame.

Several companies now offer DNA tests on larger numbers of markers. According to Family Tree DNA, one of those companies, an exact match of the results of a test carried out on sixty-seven Y-chromosome markers indicates that there's a 50 per cent likelihood that the 'time to the most recent common ancestor' (TMRCA) is two generations or less, a 90 per cent likelihood that TMRCA is four generations ago or less, and a 95 per cent likelihood that TMRCA is six generations ago (i.e. 180 years ago, if we take an average generation to be thirty years).

So does DNA testing mean the end of traditional family history? By no means. DNA testing can be an aid to family history research, by indicating which living people you're related to. What it can't do – at present – is tell you exactly who you're descended from.

A number of single-ancestor, surname and group DNA projects are in progress around the world. You can find information on these and links to them at the website for Chris Pomery's book *DNA and Family History* (*www.dnaandfamilyhistory.com*). The site includes an overview of his own Pomeroy [*sic*] DNA Study.

DNA-testing companies

Around a dozen companies (mostly in the United States) offer DNA-testing services. Some of the tests are on the Y chromosome, some on mitochondrial DNA, and some on 'autosomal' DNA. This is the DNA in the non-sex chromosomes, from which you can get some indication of what major population groups your ancestors came from.

The UK-based Oxford Ancestors (*www.oxfordancestors.com*), founded by Professor Bryan Sykes, offers both a Y-chromosome test based on ten markers and an mtDNA test. If you have the Y-chromosome test done, you can have an additional test carried out to see whether your DNA matches what the company calls the 'Tribes of Britain'.

Professor Sykes says that 95 per cent of the Y-chromosome DNA of the male population of the British Isles today originates from the Celts, the Anglo-Saxons (and the Danish Vikings, whose DNA was too similar to be classified separately) and the Norwegian Vikings Oxford Ancestors also offers to check whether your Y-chromosome DNA signature shows you to be of what the company describes as 'probable direct descent' from Niall of the Nine Hostages, Somerled or Genghis Khan.

Both 23- and 43-marker Y-chromosome tests are provided by DNA Heritage (*www.dnaheritage.com*), which has offices in both the UK and the USA.

Family Tree DNA (*www.familytreedna.com*), based in the USA, carries out Y-chromosome tests, similar to those provided by Oxford Ancestors (the Y-chromosome test is based on twelve markers), as well as mtDNA tests. Family Tree DNA also provides Y-chromosome tests using thirty-seven and sixty-seven markers, however, as well as an mtDNA test on a full sequence of DNA.

Relative Genetics (*www.relativegenetics.com*) is a company in the American Sorenson group that specializes in genetic genealogy. It offers 18-, 26- and 43-marker Y-chromosome tests, as well as tests for one, two and three sequences of mtDNA. GeneTree (*www.genetree.com*) is another Sorenson company, whose speciality is paternity and legal DNA testing.

DNA Print Genomics (*www.ancestrybydna.com*) will test your autosomal DNA to determine whether you belong to the European, East Asian, Sub-Saharan African or Native American ancestry group. Trace Genetics (*www.tracegenetics.com*), which has a large Native American mtDNA database, is owned by DNA Print Genomics.

African Ancestry (*www.africanancestry.com*) matches your Y-chromosome or mtDNA test results against a database of over 11,000 paternal and over 13,000 maternal lineages from thirty countries and over 160 ethnic groups.

Family Tree DNA, Relative Genetics and Trace Genetics all offer Native American ancestry-validation services. Family Tree DNA's Y-chromosome test service allows you to check your results against known African and Cohanim (the hereditary Jewish priesthood of Biblical times) results.

Family Tree DNA hosts a discussion forum on its website, as does Oxford Ancestors. Both companies provide searchable databases of their mtDNA and Y-chromosome test results. The companies' customers are then able to contact other customers with matching results, if they wish.

Roots for Real (*www.rootsforreal.com*) carries out mtDNA, Y-chromosome and autosomal DNA tests, while GeoGene (*www.geogene.com*) carries out tests on mtDNA and an unspecified number of Y-chromosome markers. Both are UK-based testing companies.

Ethnoancestry (*www.ethnoancestry.com*) is a new British company that offers Y-chromosome and mtDNA tests, as well as a test of 'Pictishness'. The website has comprehensive information links to sources of information on genetic genealogy in general and various haplogroups (DNA patterns) in particular. Some of these sources are rather technical.

Molecular Genealogy Research Project

So far, most of the testing services that are publicly available have been confined to analysing the DNA in the Y chromosome and in the mitochondria. A more ambitious study – the Molecular Genealogy Research Project (MGRP) – is being carried out in the United States by the Sorenson Molecular Genealogy Foundation (SMGF) (*www. smgf.org*), which is also looking at the autosomal (non-sex) chromosomes.

The MGRP is collecting 100,000 DNA samples and genealogies from people over eighteen who can provide a complete pedigree chart for a minimum of four generations. The information collected so far has been made available on the SMGF website, where you can now search a database of over 15,000 individual Y-chromosome and more than 4,000 mtDNA samples and genealogies. The autosomal samples are not yet available online.

Wish-list for the coming years

More and more records containing information useful for tracing your ancestors are becoming available online, but there are still many that are not available. Here's my personal wish-list of records that I'd like to see digitized, indexed and online by 2020:

- England and Wales: Parish registers
- Wales: Wills and administrations
- England: Prerogative Court of York wills and administrations
- England: Diocesan wills and administrations
- Scotland: Old Parish Register burials
- Ireland: Civil registration
- Ireland: Church registers
- Ireland: Tithe applotment books
- Isle of Man/Channel Islands: Civil registration
- Isle of Man/Channel Islands: Parish registers
- Isle of Man/Channel Islands: Wills and administrations

- British Isles: Poor Law records, electoral registers, poll books, hospital records, prison records, court records, etc.

In addition, I'd like to see:

- all family history societies have a resource/research centre;
- a universal Y-chromosome DNA surname database;
- all counties have Online Parish Clerks;
- Scottish family history societies make their project information available at Family History Online (or a similar Scottish website);
- the publication of the Scottish National Burial Index CD.

The story of you: Judith Mooney

Before she started tracing her ancestors, Judith used to feel her family was almost 'meagre'. 'I had one sister and her three children, my mother and father, one aunt and uncle, one cousin, and one set of grandparents that I'd known,' she says.

As Judith started her research, her family just mushroomed, and now she says she feels like a thread in a large woven tapestry. 'I have roots extending outwards and downwards, going pretty wide and pretty deep. It has somehow anchored me in life, and I've learned so much along the way. I'm now fascinated with social history – the way people lived, the kind of jobs they had, the way they thought and behaved – connecting all this to the big events in the world. It's broadened my knowledge and understanding of life immensely.'

What may happen in the future

Governments and local authorities have seen the advantages of digitizing record collections that were previously available free of charge and making these accessible online on a pay-per-view basis. If enough record collections are digitized, then expensive-to-run archive buildings could be closed, as has already happened in London.

When the Family Records Centre (FRC) was opened in London in 1997 to combine the General Register Office's birth, marriage and death indexes for England and Wales with the census records of The National Archives, no one expected it to close after only eleven years in operation. However, the high rental cost of the FRC's central London premises, coupled with the easy availability online of digitized versions of its census records, has brought this about.

In the future, as more and more records are digitized by county record offices in England and Wales, we shall probably see those archives being combined with others in large regional record offices or in existing institutions such as The National Archives and the National Library of Wales. So, as some records become more readily available, others will be less accessible.

Another recent trend is for commercial companies to digitize records (often in partnership with record offices), with indexing being carried out in a short space of time by overseas subcontractors, usually in India. The availability of digitized census returns at the websites of Ancestry.co.uk, Find My Past (*www.findmypast.com*), British Origins (*www.britishorigins.com*) and others has hit sales of census indexes and transcriptions carried out by family history societies, as well as commercially produced census CDs.

Many free indexing projects were started by enthusiasts (such as the FreeBMD English and Welsh births, marriages and deaths index and the Irish 1901 census of Leitrim, Mayo, Roscommon and Sligo), because at that time there seemed to be no likelihood of an official index ever appearing. In these two cases, however, attitudes have changed, and official indexes and digitized records are now being created.

While enthusiasts' free transcriptions are likely to continue in demand when the alternative is a pay-per-view site, it remains to be seen how they'll fare in competition with free official websites (such as the National Archives of Ireland's census site, which will include free digital images of census returns). In some cases (such as the official ONS English and Welsh births, marriages and deaths index), although the official index may be accessible free of charge, it may lack some of the search facilities available at sites set up by family historians.

Another change taking place in the family history world is the replacement of paper newsletters and journals by much cheaper electronic publications. The FFHS has ceased publication of its half-yearly journal, replacing it with some articles on its website and an e-zine (e-mail newsletter). In the US, George Morgan of the Florida Genealogical Society (founded in 1958) reports that the society has switched from paper publication of its bi-monthly newsletter to a 'blog' (web log), while its half-yearly journal has been replaced by a more traditional-style website.

We don't know yet what the future may hold for family history. A hundred years ago, no one foresaw the arrival of computers, the Internet or DNA testing. In the next century, no doubt there will be advances that would seem just as amazing (or far-fetched) to us now, as today's advances would have to our great-grandparents. Perhaps in the future each of us will be walking around with an implant containing our known ancestry (or maybe that's what our DNA is). Maybe someone will even come up with a way to communicate with our deceased ancestors, apart from using séances. Who knows.

Good luck with your researches.

Appendices

A. Free online family history resources and information

The Internet now provides access to a good deal of family history information. Unfortunately, digitized versions of primary records (such as census returns, wills, and Scottish birth, marriage and death records) are available only through pay-per-view or subscription services, and the cost can soon mount up.

There are, however, many websites providing indexes to civil registration records, parish registers, census returns and wills, as well as transcriptions of census records, baptisms, marriages and burials, and a variety of other information. Some of these sites have been set up by public bodies, while others are 'labours of love'. The good news is that access to most of them is completely free of charge.

Indexes of births, marriages and deaths

Instead of using pay-per-view or subscription websites to search the national indexes of civil registration births, marriages and deaths in England and Wales, you can search without payment well over 100 million records that are already online at the volunteer FreeBMD Project (*http://freebmd.rootsweb.com*). FreeBMD is building an online database of the index references, mainly for the period 1837–1903.

FreeBMD has also made available free of charge online images of the General Register Office's printed indexes to the birth, marriage and death records, as has the commercial family history company Ancestry.co.uk (*www.ancestry.co.uk*).

Another volunteer indexing project is UKBMD (*www.ukbmd.org. uk*), which acts as a portal to several websites providing access to online versions of the birth, marriage and death indexes compiled in local registry offices in England and Wales. The scheme began in Cheshire in 2000, and has since grown to cover more than twenty counties, all but one of which provides access free of charge. (If you click on the 'census' button on the left-hand side of the UKBMD pages, you'll see a long list of websites – not all free – that provide access to census and similar records.)

Census returns, indexes and substitutes

Transcriptions of the 1881 census for England, Wales, the Isle of Man and the Channel Islands are accessible free of charge at the LDS Family Search website (*www.familysearch.org*), and also at the Federation of Family History Societies' Family History Online website at *www.familyhistoryonline.net*. You can search the index of the 1881 census free of charge at Ancestry.co.uk, or via The National Archives (TNA) website (*www.nationalarchives.gov.uk*), but you'll have to pay to see images of the actual records.

You can also carry out a free search of the index of what is now Genes Reunited's 1901 census website (*www.1901census.national archives.gov.uk*). Online access to the records of the 1841–1901 censuses is free of charge onsite at the Family Records Centre in central London and at TNA at Kew. (For Scotland, however, you'll have to pay even to search the indexes of the 1841–1901 censuses online at the Scotland's People website at *www.scotlandspeople.gov. uk* or at Ancestry.co.uk.

The aim of FreeCEN, the Free Census Project (*http://freecen. rootsweb.com*), is to make transcriptions of the 1841–1871 and 1891 censuses available online free of charge. So far, at least half the information is online for the following counties (those in italics are 100 per cent online):

- 1841: *Aberdeenshire, Angus, Argyll,* Ayrshire, *Banffshire, Bute, Caithness, Cornwall,* Dumfriesshire, *East Lothian,* Fife, Inverness-shire, Kincardineshire, *Kinross-shire,* Lanarkshire, *Midlothian, Moray, Nairnshire,* Renfrewshire, Ross and Cromarty, *Roxburghshire, Warwickshire, Wigtownshire* and West Lothian;

- **1851**: Aberdeenshire, Ayrshire, Banffshire, *Bute*, Caithness, Cornwall, *East Lothian, Moray, Nairnshire* and Roxburghshire;
- **1861**: *Bute*, Caithness, *Cornwall*, Devon, *East Lothian*, Nairnshire and Scottish shipping;
- **1871**: Cornwall, Denbighshire, Flintshire, Herefordshire and Nairnshire;
- **1891**: *Bedfordshire, Cornwall*, Denbighshire, *Devon*, Flintshire, Sussex and *Warwickshire*.

In addition, more than 700 transcriptions of censuses for parishes in the Cotswold Hills and surrounding areas (mainly in Gloucestershire) are accessible at *www.allthecotswolds.com*.

At the website of Dumfries and Galloway's Libraries, Information and Archives service (*www.dumgal.gov.uk/services/depts/comres/library/archives.asp*), you'll find several databases created in conjunction with the Friends of the Archives, including the 1851 census for the counties of Dumfriesshire, Kirkcudbrightshire and Wigtownshire.

An indexed transcription of the 1901 census for some Irish counties is available at the Leitrim-Roscommon Genealogy Website (*www.leitrim-roscommon.com*). Counties Leitrim, Mayo, Roscommon and Sligo are complete, with County Wexford still in progress. In addition, the 1901 census for County Clare has been indexed and transcribed by the Clare County Library (*www.clarelibrary.ie*).

As the earlier censuses for Ireland have all been destroyed (other than a few fragments), the land valuation of Ireland carried out under the direction of Richard Griffith between 1847 and 1864 serves as a census substitute, although it lists only heads of households. You can view a transcription of Griffith's Valuation for County Clare at the Clare County Library website, for County Waterford at the Waterford County Library site (*www.waterfordcountylibrary.ie/library/web*), while transcriptions of parts of the counties of Galway, Leitrim, Limerick, Mayo and Roscommon are accessible at the Leitrim-Roscommon site.

In addition, you can search Griffith's Valuation for the nine counties of Ulster (Antrim, Armagh, (London)Derry, Down, Fermanagh and Tyrone in Northern Ireland; and Cavan, Donegal and Monaghan in the Irish Republic) at the Ulster Ancestry website (*www.ulster ancestry.com/search.html*).

You can find more census transcriptions and other local population lists at the Census Finder website (*www.censusfinder.com/united_kingdom.htm*).

Parish register transcriptions and indexes

Rather than paying to search for English and Welsh baptisms and marriages (1538–1837) in the databases at the Family History Online website, or Scottish baptisms and marriages (1553–1854) at the Scotland's People website, you can find most of these events in the International Genealogical Index (IGI) at the LDS Family Search site. The site also allows you to search for the children of a couple by specifying the names of the parents, which can't be done at the other two sites.

You'll find free information at the websites of the Online Parish Clerks (OPC) scheme, under which volunteers collect, collate and transcribe parish registers, census returns, monumental inscriptions and local histories. The scheme is still in its infancy, but has now grown to cover nine counties. You can find the county websites via the Cornish site (*http://west-penwith.org.uk/opc.htm*) where the OPC scheme began.

FreeREG (*www.freereg.org.uk*) is a sister project to FreeBMD and FreeCEN, and is making parish register entries for England, Wales, Scotland and the Isle of Man available free of charge.

Various individual enthusiasts have put parish records online at their own websites, such as Michael Cheeseman's Parish Register Indexes at *www.rootsweb.com/~engdorse/English.html*, which contain many transcriptions of parish registers for Dorset and a few for Suffolk.

Malcolm Platt-Grigg's UK Transcriptions website (*http://uk transcriptions.accessgenealogy.com*) provides access to various parish registers and some census returns, plus links to about thirty similar sites.

At GENUKI (*www.genuki.org.uk*), the virtual genealogical reference library for the UK and the Republic of Ireland, you'll find links to all sorts of interesting family and local history websites, including those devoted to particular parishes. Not every local site is covered, however, so that it's worthwhile also running a general search for the parish name using Google or another search engine.

Newspaper indexes

Thanks to the Bath Record Office, you can search an index of information from the *Bath Chronicle* from 1770–1800 at *www.bathnes. gov.uk/BathNES/lifeandleisure/leisure/localarchives/georgian/default. htm.*

Swansea Libraries have indexed the *Cambrian*, the first English-language newspaper published in Wales. Nearly half a million index entries are accessible online, including births, marriages and deaths from 1804–1914 (including some from the *South Wales Daily Post*) and other entries up to 1876. You'll find the index at *www.swansea. gov.uk/index.cfm?articleid=5673.*

Some nineteenth-century abstracts and extracts from the *West Briton and Cornwall Advertiser* are online at *http://freepages. genealogy.rootsweb.com/~wbritonad/cornwall/intro.html.*

The 'Gaelic Village' website Am Baile contains an online newspaper index for:

- *Inverness Journal* (1807–49)
- *Inverness Advertiser* (1849–85)
- *Scottish Highlander* (1885–98)
- *Inverness Courier* (1879, 1898–1901)
- *John O'Groat Journal* (1836–87)

The index is searchable at *www.ambaile.org.uk/newspapers/ index.jsp.*

The British Library (*www.bl.uk*) is digitizing around 4 million pages of London, British national, English regional, Scottish, Welsh and Northern Irish newspapers. The first million pages were made available to users in UK Higher and Further Education colleges in 2007. All 4 million pages are scheduled for worldwide web access in 2008.

Tip: Access old copies of *The Times* free of charge through your public library's website

A number of public libraries are now subscribing to *The Times* Digital Archive, which provides access to digitized copies of *The Times* from 1785–1985. Many of the library services allow you to log on to the Digital Archive from your home computer by entering your library card number via the library's website.

You may think it unlikely that your ancestors would have been mentioned in *The Times*. In the nineteenth century, however, it was quite common for the newspaper to reprint items from local newspapers about unusual events. In addition, major disasters were reported in *The Times*, often with lists of the names of those involved.

Mailing lists and message boards

At GENUKI (*www.genuki.org.uk/indexes/MailingLists.html*), you can find a list of UK and Ireland family history mailing lists through which you can send messages to other list members asking for help with your research. The upside of belonging to a list is that you may receive invaluable help and perhaps make contact with some fourth or fifth cousins. The downside, however, is that you'll receive by e-mail all the messages sent by the other members.

Most of the mailing lists are run by RootsWeb (*http://lists.rootsweb. com*) or Yahoo (*http://groups.yahoo.com*). At RootsWeb, you can search in or browse through its many mailing list archives (and thus avoid receiving a vast number of e-mail messages), but Yahoo requires you to subscribe to a list to view its archive postings.

There are several web-based family history message board websites, on which you post queries or comments, and return to the website for any replies. These include:

- *Family Tree Magazine/Practical Family History (www.family-tree.co.uk/phpBB2/index.php)*;
- Genealogy Marketplace (*www.genealogymarketplace.co.uk/phpbb/index.php?c=3*);
- RootsChat (*www.rootschat.com*);
- Talking Scot (*www.talkingscot.com/forum*);
- UK Genealogy Forum (*www.uk-genealogy.org.uk/phpBB2/index.php*).

Archives and libraries

The major archives and libraries of the United Kingdom and the Irish Republic provide various free information sheets that you can view and print out at home. At the TNA website, via its 'Getting Started' pull-down menu, you'll find over 150 research guides on subjects ranging from 'British Army: useful sources for tracing soldiers' to 'Jack the Ripper: the Whitechapel Murders' and 'The *Titanic*'.

The National Archives of Scotland (*www.nas.gov.uk*) has over forty family history guides on topics such as 'Crime and criminals', 'Records of the poor' and 'Sasines' (a type of Scottish land record). At the National Library of Scotland's website, you'll find online maps and town plans of Scotland in its Digital Library (*www.nls.uk/digitallibrary/map/index.html*).

In the Family History pages of the website of the National Library of Wales (*www.llgc.org.uk*), you can search in online databases of Welsh marriage bonds (1661–1837) and gaol files (1730–1830).

The National Archives of Ireland's website at *www.nationalarchives.ie* has pages on genealogy (including useful Irish sources), while the National Library of Ireland (*www.nli.ie*) has a section on 'Family History Research in the National Library'.

The Public Record Office of Northern Ireland (*www.proni.gov.uk*) provides online information leaflets describing the various records that it holds as well as giving advice on how to use them. In addition, you can search the online databases of freeholders and signatories to the Ulster Covenant of 1912.

The Irish Republic's General Register Office website (*www.*

groireland.ie) contains sections on 150 years of civil registration in Ireland, and the modernization programme in the Republic. You can also find useful information on tracing your family tree at the websites of the General Register Offices for England and Wales (*www.gro. gov.uk*), Scotland (*www.gro-scotland.gov.uk*) and Northern Ireland (*www.groni.gov.uk*).

Family history software

Even family history software can be free of charge. Instead of *buying* a genealogy program, you can download Personal Ancestral File (PAF) from the Family Search website (*www.familysearch.org*) of the Church of Jesus Christ of Latter-day Saints (LDS). The software comes complete with a user manual.

PAF lets you enter the names of all your ancestors and other relatives, or import an existing family file in the standard GEDCOM format. The program is not as sophisticated as those that you pay for, but it does let you print out family group records, ancestry diagrams and pedigree charts. To print a family tree, however, you'll need an additional program, such as PAF Companion or GenoPro, available as shareware from *www.genopro.com*.

B. Pay-per-view/subscription charges for online databases, fees for certificates and charges for genetic tests

Find My Past www.findmypast.com

Pay-per-view charges:

- £6.95 for 60 units, which expire after 90 days;
- £14.95 for 150 units, which expire after 180 days;
- £24.95 for 280 units, which expire after 365 days;
- £49.95 for 670 units, which expire after 365 days;
- £99.95 for 2,000 units, which expire after 365 days.

One unit equals one image page. If you purchase a new price plan before the old one expires, the outstanding units are then carried forward to the new expiry date. Alternatively, you can buy vouchers at a cost of £5 for fifty units, which expire after ninety days, or pay through your telephone bill with BT's 'click&buy' scheme.

Alternatively, you can buy one of Find My Past's subscription packages:

- *Discovery* package: £65 for a year's unlimited access to:
  - GRO birth, marriage and death (BMD) indexes 1837–2004;
  - overseas BMD indexes (including war deaths) 1871–1994;
  - England and Wales censuses 1841–71 and 1891.
- *Voyager* package: £25 for thirty days' unlimited access to:
  - UK outbound passenger lists (BT27).
- *Explorer* package: £125 for a year's unlimited access to:
  - all databases included in *Discovery* and *Voyager* packages;
  - divorces and matrimonial causes;

- military collection (thirty-eight databases);
- migration records;
- occupations and directories;
- BMDs at sea;
- Death Duty registers.

1901 *Census for England and Wales (Genes Reunited)* *www.1901census.nationalarchives.gov.uk*

£5 for 500 credits valid for seven days. As part of the £5 charge, it costs fifty credits to view a transcription of an individual person's entry, fifty more to view a transcription of the rest of the people in the same household, or seventy-five to view the digital image of a page from the census returns. Alternatively, you can buy a voucher for £5, giving you 500 credits valid for six months, once the voucher is activated.

192.com www.192.com

- £9.95 (plus VAT) for 5 credits valid for six months;
- £34.95 (plus VAT) for 100 credits valid for six months;
- £84.95 (plus VAT) for 300 credits valid for six months;
- £149.95 (plus VAT) for 600 credits valid for six months.

One search on the electoral roll costs one credit.

Ancestry.co.uk www.ancestry.co.uk

- UK Deluxe membership: access to all UK and Ireland databases for £79.95 a year or £9.95 for one month;
- World Deluxe membership: access to all databases, including UK and Ireland and USA for £199.95 a year or £24.95 for one month.

Alternatively, you can buy twelve record views for £6.95 direct from Ancestry (or ten record views in the form of a pre-paid voucher from one of a number of resellers) valid for fourteen days.

Ayrshire Ancestors *www.ayrshireancestors.co.uk*

£10 for three months' unlimited access to databases.

BMD Index *www.bmdindex.co.uk*

- £5 for 50 viewing credits valid for 90 days, with unlimited searching credits;
- £14.95 for 200 viewing credits valid for a year, with unlimited searching credits.

See also (The) Genealogist below.

British Origins *www.britishorigins.com*

Subscriptions to British Origins alone cost:

- £6.50 for a 72-hour subscription;
- £8.95 for a monthly subscription.

Combined subscriptions to both British and Irish Origins cost:

- £7.50 for a 72-hour subscription;
- £10.50 for a monthly subscription;
- £47 for an annual subscription.

Burke's Peerage *www.burkes-peerage.net*

- £15.95 (+ VAT) for 24 hours' access to Burke's online database of Peerage and Landed Gentry (£9.95 + VAT to renew);
- £64.95 (+ VAT) for an annual subscription.

CenQuest *www.cenquest.co.uk*

£5 for 100 days' access.

Documents Online *www.nationalarchives.gov.uk/ documentsonline*

£3.50 to view an image.

Family History Online *www.familyhistoryonline.net*

Payments of £5, £10, £20 or £50 can be made online, or you can buy pre-paid vouchers for £5 or £10 from various suppliers. As part of one of these charges, you can view entries in the databases at charges, mainly between 3p and 10p per record. The image of a church costs 50p, while you pay £2 to view the image of a gravestone.

Family Relatives *www.familyrelatives.org*

- £6 buys 60 units valid for 90 days;
- £8 buys 100 units valid for 90 days;
- £12 buys 160 units valid for 90 days;
- £25 buys 340 units valid for 180 days;
- £50 buys 700 units valid for 180 days;
- £100 buys 1,500 units valid for 180 days.

It will cost you two units to view a page of search results (up to twenty names), and a further one unit to view the image of an index page. The site also contains many records that are free to view.

(The) Genealogist *www.thegenealogist.co.uk*

You can either subscribe to the site for:

- £14.95 for a quarter (minimum term twelve months), providing 75 credits;
- £24.95 for a quarter (minimum term three months), providing 175 credits;
- £55.95 for a year, providing 800 credits;
- £68.95 for a year, with unlimited credit;
- £149.95 for a year, with unlimited credit (for professional genealogists).

These subscriptions give you access to all birth, marriage and death indexes, census indexes and records, and Phillimore's marriage register transcriptions. Alternatively, you can buy pay-per-view subscriptions to individual census indexes, census transcripts, directories, parish register marriage transcripts and specialist indexes at varying prices.

General Register Office (England and Wales) Certificate Ordering Service www.gro.gov.uk/gro/content/certificates

It costs £7 to order a full certificate of birth, marriage or death through the GRO website, or £23 for priority (next day) service. These charges also apply if you order a certificate in person at the Family Records Centre.

If you supply the full GRO index reference, it costs £8.50 for a full certificate by post, phone or fax, and £24.50 for the priority service. Without the index reference, the charges are £11.50 and £27.50 respectively.

General Register Office (Northern Ireland) www.groni.gov.uk

There is a charge of £11 for a birth, marriage or death certificate, or £27 for priority (same day) service. You can apply online via the website, download an application form to apply by post or fax, or apply by phone or in person in Belfast. If you supply full details of the entry required, including register entry number and date of registration, the fee is reduced to £5.50, but this does not apply to online orders.

General Register Office (Republic of Ireland) www.groireland.ie/apply_for_a_cert.htm

There is no online ordering service, but a birth, marriage or death certificate costs €10 to order by post or fax. You can download an application form from the website.

If you carry out a search in person in Dublin, it will cost you €2 to search the indexes over a period of five years for a specific entry. Alternatively, you can pay €20 to search the indexes for up to seven hours.

General Register Office for Scotland (GROS) Certificate Ordering Service www.gro-scotland.gov. uk/famrec/index.htm

It costs £13 for a birth, marriage or death certificate, census return or parish register entry, if you order by post, phone or fax, and £11 if you order in person in Edinburgh. A priority order will cost you £10 more. You can download an application form from the website.

If you visit New Register House in Edinburgh, for £17 a day, you can have access to digitized images of the birth, marriage, death and census records right up to the present day, which you can then print out at a charge of 50p per copy.

See also Scotland's People below for the cost of online access to the records.

General Registry (Isle of Man) www.gov.im/registries/ general/civilregistry/welcome.xml

The charge for a birth, marriage or death certificate is £6, or £8 without the appropriate reference number. You can download an application form from the website.

Genes Reunited www.genesreunited.co.uk

A year's membership costs £9.95.

(The) Greffe (Guernsey) (no website)

A full birth, marriage or death certificate costs £5, with a search fee of a further £5. If you go to the Greffe in person, for £1 you can see the actual records, from which you can make notes.

Irish Ancestors http://scripts.ireland.com/ancestor/ index.cfm

You pay €50 for thirty units, which are used to pay for premium searches at charges between one and ten units. Alternatively, you can pay for detailed information on a pay-per-view basis at prices such as €7 and €25.

Irish Family Research *www.irishfamilyresearch.co.uk*

Full membership costs £35 for a year, providing access to all search-able databases.

Irish Genealogy Ltd *www.irishgenealogy.ie*

You can commission a search for a birth or baptism in the database of one of Ireland's Genealogical Research Centres at a charge of €45. A birth search can be carried out for any of Ireland's thirty-two counties, but a baptism search is possible for only thirteen counties. If the search is unsuccessful, €20 will be refunded.

Irish Origins *www.irishorigins.com*

- £4.50 for a 72-hour subscription;
- £8.95 for a monthly subscription.

See British Origins above for combined subscriptions to both websites.

Lost Cousins *www.lostcousins.com*

A single subscription for a year costs £10, while the price of a joint subscription is £12.50.

McKirdy Index *www.mckirdyindex.co.nz*

- 'Bronze' membership costs NZ $5.00 for three months, providing basic search results, and no location details;
- 'Silver' membership costs NZ $9.00 for three months, providing detailed search results, and allowing searching by location;
- 'Gold' membership costs NZ $15.00 for three months, or NZ $45.00 for twelve months, providing detailed search results, and allowing searching by location. This level also allows you to view all the details of a record, including everyone named in an entry.

Military Genealogy www.military-genealogy.com

£5 will buy you ten credits, while the cost of viewing a soldier's record is one credit, and that of a memorial scroll is five credits.

Naval Biographical Database www.navylist.org

Standard reports cost £5 for 1–10 search 'hits' (where each hit contains one to three dates, with the report stating the source of the information), £10 for 11–20 hits, and £15 for 21–30 hits.

Police and 'Black Sheep' indexes www.lightage.demon.co.uk

It costs £8 for major reports, and £4 for minor reports. Discounts on major reports: two for £14, three for £20, four for £26, five for £32, six for £38 and seven for £44.

Scotland's People www.scotlandspeople.gov.uk

You pay £6 for thirty 'page credits', valid for ninety days. When the session expires, credits are not lost, but added to those in the next session you purchase. Searching the statutory (civil registration), census and parish register indexes costs one credit for a page of up to twenty-five results, while viewing an image costs five credits. Searching the index of wills and inventories is free of charge, and the cost of viewing the image of a will is £5 (regardless of the number of pages). An official printed copy of a record will cost you £10.

Scots Origins Experts Research (Sighting Service) www.scotsorigins.com

It costs £8 for the transcription of a statutory (civil registration) record and £9 for an Old Parish Register entry, with a refund of £3 if the record can't be found.

(The) Scotsman Digital Archive http://archive. scotsman.com

- £7.95 buys 24 hours' access to the database;
- £12.95 buys 48 hours' access to the database;
- £19.95 buys one week's access to the database;
- £39.95 buys one month's access to the database;
- £159.95 buys one year's access to the database.

Statistical Account of Scotland http://edina.ac.uk/ statacc

There is a charge of £40 per year (plus VAT) for the subscription service for non-academic users (which provides extras such as the ability to 'cut and paste' from transcripts of the accounts), but the basic service is free of charge.

Stepping Stones www.stepping-stones.co.uk

- £5 for 10 online viewing credits valid for 14 days;
- £15 for 32 online viewing credits valid for 14 days;
- £20 for 50 online viewing credits valid for 14 days.

Superintendent Registrar (Jersey) (no website)

The cost of a birth, marriage or death certificate is £10, provided you can supply the relevant date, name and parish. Otherwise you pay a further £7 for a five-year search for a birth or death, or £14 for a marriage. In addition, there is a postal handling charge of £1 for overseas and 50 pence for Britain and Ireland.

If you visit the Superintendent Registrar in person, you are allowed limited access to the registers by appointment from Monday–Friday between 9 and 11 a.m.

Tracesmart www.tracesmart.co.uk

One month's unlimited access to databases, including electoral rolls, property sales, directory enquiries, and birth, marriage and death indexes, costs £14.95.

UKBMD *www.ukbmd.org.uk*

The charge for ordering a birth, marriage or death certificate from a local register office is £7. In most cases, you can download an application form, and in a few cases, you can place an order online.

Ulster Historical Foundation *www.ancestryireland.com*

- annual membership of the Ulster Genealogical and Historical Guild costs £30;
- annual membership of the Guild with publications sent by airmail costs £35;
- five-year membership of the Guild with publications sent by airmail costs £90;
- life membership of the Guild with publications sent by airmail costs £210.

Charges for Genetic Tests

African Ancestry *www.africanancestry.com*

- Y-chromosome (9 markers)   US $349
- mtDNA   US $349

DNA Heritage *www.dnaheritage.com*

- Y-chromosome (23 markers)   US $138
- Y-chromosome (43 markers)   US $199

DNA Print Genomics *www.dnaprint.com*

- Autosomal DNA (176 markers)   US $240

Family Tree DNA *www.familytreedna.com*

- Y-chromosome (12 markers)   US $149
- Y-chromosome (37 markers)   US $259
- Y-chromosome (67 markers)   US $349

- mtDNA   US $129
- mtDNA (high resolution)   US $189
- mtDNA (full sequence)   US $495

GeneTree www.genetree.com

- Y-chromosome   US $245
- mtDNA   US $245
- Autosomal DNA (175 markers)   US $240

GeoGene www.geogene.com

- Y-chromosome   US $180
- mtDNA   US $180

Oxford Ancestors www.oxfordancestors.com

- Y-chromosome (10 markers)   £180
- mtDNA   £180

Roots for Real www.rootsforreal.com

- Y-chromosome   US $270
- mtDNA   US $270

Most of these companies offer discounted prices for combinations of tests, and for group testing.

C. British and Irish
website addresses

Introduction

Census Finder *www.censusfinder.com*

Commonwealth War Graves Commission *www.cwgc.org*

Cyndi's List of Genealogy Sites on the Internet *www.cyndislist.com*

Documents Online (The National Archives) *www.nationalarchives. gov.uk/documentsonline*

Family History in India *members.ozemail.com.au/~clday*

Family Records *www.familyrecords.gov.uk*

Family Search (LDS Church website) *www.familysearch.org*

General Register Office (GRO) Certificate Ordering Service *www.gro.gov.uk/gro/content/certificates*

General Register Office (Northern Ireland) (GRONI) *www.groni. gov.uk*

Genes Reunited *www.genesreunited.co.uk*

GENUKI (Genealogy UK and Ireland) *www.genuki.org.uk*

Moving Here *www.movinghere.org.uk*

Scotland's People *www.scotlandspeople.gov.uk*

UK GenWeb *www.ukgenweb.com*

Chapter 2. Archives and libraries in Britain and Ireland

Access to Archives (A2A) *www.a2a.org.uk*

Archives Network Wales (ANW) *www.archivesnetworkwales.info*

Aylesbury Gaol database *www.buckscc.gov.uk/bucks_prisoners/ index.htm*

Bedfordshire Gaol register *http://apps.bedfordshire.gov.uk/grd*

Borthwick Institute for Archives (BIA) *www.york.ac.uk/inst/bihr*

Bristol Record Office index of wills *www.bristol-city.gov.uk/ccm/navigation/leisure-and-culture/libraries/archives*

British Library (BL) *www.bl.uk*

British Origins *www.britishorigins.com*

Cheshire Record Office catalogue and other databases *www.cheshire.gov.uk/Recordoffice/catalogues*

Court of Great Sessions of Wales *www.llgc.org.uk/sesiwn_fawr/index_s.htm*

Documents Online *www.nationalarchives.gov.uk/documentsonline*

Dorset History Centre *www.dorsetforyou.com/index.jsp?articleid=2203*

Dumfries and Galloway 1851 census returns *www.dumgal.gov.uk/dumgal/MiniWeb.aspx?id=86&menuid=921&openid=921*

Dundee City Archives databases *www.fdca.org.uk/databases.htm*

Durham County Record Office *www.durham.gov.uk/recordoffice*

Family Records Centre (FRC) *www.familyrecords.gov.uk/frc*

General Register Office (Northern Ireland) (GRONI) *www.groni.gov.uk*

General Register Office (Republic of Ireland) (GROI) *www.groireland.ie*

General Register Office for Scotland (GROS) *www.gro-scotland.gov.uk*

Glamorgan Record Office *www.glamro.gov.uk*

Gloucestershire Genealogical Database *www.gloucestershire.gov.uk/index.cfm?ArticleID=1335*

Irish Origins *www.irishorigins.com*

Isle of Wight databases *www.iwight.com/library/record%5Foffice/Databases*

Lancashire County Constabulary database *www.lancashire.gov.uk/education/record_office/records/police.asp*

Lincolnshire transportation database *www.lincolnshire.gov.uk/archives/section.asp?docId=29249&catId=6722*

Manorial Documents Register *www.nationalarchives.gov.uk/mdr*

NAI transportation database *www.nationalarchives.ie/topics/transportation/search01.html*

(The) National Archives (TNA) *www.nationalarchives.gov.uk*

National Archives of Ireland (NAI) *www.nationalarchives.ie*
National Archives of Scotland (NAS) *www.nas.gov.uk*
National Library of Ireland (NLI) *www.nli.ie*
National Library of Scotland (NLS) *www.nls.uk*
National Library of Wales (NLW) *www.llgc.org.uk*
NLS Digital Library *www.nls.uk/maps/index.html*
NLW marriage bonds *www.llgc.org.uk:81*
Powys Heritage Online *http://history.powys.org.uk*
Public Record Office of Northern Ireland (PRONI) *www.proni. gov.uk*
Representative Church Body Library (RCBL) *www.ireland. anglican.org/library*
SCAN Virtual Vault *www.scan.org.uk/researchrtools/virtualvault.htm*
Scotland's People *www.scotlandspeople.gov.uk*
Scottish Archive Network (SCAN) *www.scan.org.uk/aboutus/ indexonline.htm*
Scottish Documents *www.scottishdocuments.com*
Virtual Mitchell *www.mitchelllibrary.org/virtualmitchell*
Warwickshire prisoner database *www.warwickshire.gov.uk*
Wiltshire communities *www.wiltshire.gov.uk/community*
Wiltshire and Swindon Record Office *www.wiltshire.gov.uk/ archives.htm*
'(The) Word on the Street' *www.nls.uk/broadsides/index.html*

Chapter 5. Births, marriages and deaths (England and Wales)

Ancestry.co.uk *www.ancestry.co.uk*
BMD Index *www.bmdindex.co.uk*
Family Relatives *www.familyrelatives.org*
Find My Past *www.findmypast.com*
FreeBMD *http://freebmd.rootsweb.com*
General Register Office (GRO) *www.gro.gov.uk*
GRO Certificate Ordering Service *www.gro.gov.uk/gro/content/ certificates*
Office of National Statistics *www.statistics.gov.uk*
UKBMD *www.ukbmd.org.uk*

Chapter 6. Census returns (England and Wales)

1901 Census *www.1901census.nationalarchives.gov.uk*
Ancestry.co.uk *www.ancestry.co.uk*
British Origins *www.britishorigins.com*
Census Finder *www.censusfinder.com*
Census Online *www.census-online.com*
Family History Online *www.familyhistoryonline.net*
Family Search *www.familysearch.org*
Find My Past *www.findmypast.com*
FreeCEN *http://freecen.rootsweb.com*
(The) Genealogist *www.thegenealogist.co.uk*
Genes Reunited *www.genesreunited.co.uk*
Stepping Stones *www.stepping-stones.co.uk*
UKBMD *www.ukbmd.org.uk*

Chapter 7. Parish and other church registers (England and Wales)

Ancestry.co.uk *www.ancestry.co.uk*
Annotated Burials at Westbury on Severn 1889–1895 *www.rebus. demon.co.uk/wos_br.htm*
British Origins *www.britishorigins.com*
Census Finder *www.censusfinder.com*
Cornwall Online Parish Clerks *www.cornwall-opc.org*
Cyndi's List *www.cyndislist.com*
England GenWeb *www.rootsweb.com/~engwgw*
Family History Online *www.familyhistoryonline.net*
Family Relatives *www.familyrelatives.org*
Family Search *www.familysearch.org*
GENUKI *www.genuki.org.uk*
Hugh Wallis's Genealogical Websites *http://freepages.genealogy. rootsweb.com/~hughwallis*
National Burial Index coverage at the Federation of Family History Societies website *www.ffhs.org.uk/General/Projects/ NBIcounties.htm*
National Library of Wales marriage bonds *www.llgc.org.uk:81*

One-Place Studies Index *www.wirksworth.org.uk/A43-OPS.htm*
UK Genealogy Archives *www.uk-genealogy.org.uk/Registers/index.html*
UKBMD *www.ukbmd.org.uk*
Wales GenWeb *www.walesgenweb.com*

Chapter 8. Wills and administrations (England and Wales)

Bristol wills *www.bristol-city.gov.uk/ccm/navigation/leisure-and-culture/libraries/archives*
British Origins *www.britishorigins.com*
Cheshire wills *www.cheshire.gov/uk/Recordoffice/Wills*
Derbyshire wills *www.wirksworth.org.uk/WILLS.htm*
Documents Online *www.nationalarchives.gov.uk/documentsonline*
Family History Online *www.familyhistoryonline.net*
GENUKI *www.genuki.org.uk*
Gloucestershire Genealogical Database *www.gloucestershire.gov.uk/index.cfm?ArticleID=1335*
Kent wills *www.kentarchaeology.org.uk/Research/Libr/Wills/WillsIntro.htm*
London and Middlesex wills *www.cityoflondon.gov.uk/corporation/wills*
Wiltshire and Swindon Record Office *http://history.wiltshire.gov.uk/heritage*

Chapter 9. More sources for Welsh ancestry

Association of Family History Societies of Wales (AFHSW) *www.fhswales.info*
(The) Cambrian Index *www2.swansea.gov.uk/_info/cambrian*
Cardiff Mariners *www.cardiffmariners.org.uk*
Cardiganshire FHS *www.heaton.celtic.co.uk/cgnfhs*
Carmarthenshire FHS *www.carmarthenshirefhs.co.uk*
CenQuest *www.cenquest.co.uk/Home.htm*
Data Wales *www.data-wales.co.uk*
Documents Online *www.nationalarchives.gov.uk/documentsonline*

Family History Online *www.familyhistoryonline.net*

Family Search *www.familysearch.org*

Gathering the Jewels *www.gtj.org.uk*

GENUKI (Wales) *www.genuki.org.uk/big/wal*

Hugh Wallis's Genealogical Websites *http://freepages.genealogy.*
rootsweb.com/~hughwallis

Morgan Society *http://freepages.genealogy.rootsweb.*
com/~morgansociety/index.html

National Library of Wales (NLW) *www.llgc.org.uk*

NLW Cardiganshire Constabulary register of criminals *www.llgc.*
org.uk/drych/drych_s071.htm

NLW 'Crime and Punishment' *www.llgc.org.uk/sesiwn_fawr/*
index_s.htm

NLW marriage bonds *www.llgc.org.uk:81*

NLW St Asaph 'Notitiae' *www.llgc.org.uk/drych/Notitiae/nll_s001.*
htm

North Wales BMD Indexes *www.northwalesbmd.org.uk*

Online Genealogical Research Engine (OGRE) *www.cefnpennar.com*

Powys Heritage Online *history.powys.org.uk*

Relative Links: Research in Wales *homepages.rootsweb.com/~riggs/*
links/Wales.htm

Swansea Mariners *www.swanseamariners.org.uk*

Welsh Coal Mines *www.welshcoalmines.co.uk*

Welsh Family History Archive *www.jlb2005.plus.com/wales*

Welsh Mariners *www.welshmariners.org.uk*

Wrexham BMD Indexes *www.wrexham.gov.uk/english/community/*
genealogy/MarriageIndexSearchForm.cfm

Chapter 10. Example English county: Cornwall

Camborne parish *http://freepages.genealogy.rootsweb.*
com/~camborneopc

Cornish Ancestors *www.cornish-ancestors.co.uk/home.htm*

Cornish Cemeteries *http://members.tripod.com/chrisuphill/*
cemeteries.htm#Search

Cornish Census Search *http://freepages.genealogy.rootsweb.*
com/~wgeorge/census_search.html

Cornish Emigration *www.bbc.co.uk/legacies/immig_emig/england/ cornwall/index.shtml*

(The) Cornish in Latin America *www.projects.ex.ac.uk/ cornishlatin/index.php*

(The) Cornish in West Cork http://members.lycos.co.uk/troonexiles/ the_cornish_in_west_cork.htm

Cornish Mining *www.cornish-mining.org.uk*

Cornish Mining Index *www.cornwall-online.co.uk/genealogy.htm*

Cornish Parish Register Index *www.cornwalleng.com*

Cornish Surnames *http://freepages.history.rootsweb.com/~kernow/ index.htm*

Cornwall Centre *http://db.cornwall.gov.uk/librarydb/info/details. asp?Ibid=7*

Cornwall Inscriptions Project *www.cornwallinscriptions.co.uk/ index.html*

Cornwall Online Census Project (COCP) *http://freepages. genealogy.rootsweb.com/~kayhin/ukocp.html*

Cornwall online parish clerks *www.cornwall-opc.org*

Cornwall Record Office *www.cornwall.gov.uk/cro*

Historic Cornwall *www.cornwall.gov.uk/history/default.htm*

Victoria County History of Cornwall *www.cornwallpast.net*

Chapter 12. Births, marriages, deaths and census returns (Scotland)

North Perthshire Family History Group *www.npfhg.org*
Scotland's People *www.scotlandspeople.gov.uk*

Chapter 13. Parish and other church registers (Scotland)

Family Search *www.familysearch.org*
Scotland's People *www.scotlandspeople.gov.uk*
Scottish Documents *www.scottishdocuments.com*

Chapter 14. Wills and inventories (Scotland)

National Archives of Scotland (NAS) *www.nas.gov.uk*
Scotland's People *www.scotlandspeople.gov.uk*

Chapter 15. Records online (Scotland)

Ancestry.co.uk *www.ancestry.co.uk*

Ayrshire Ancestors *www.ayrshireancestors.co.uk*

Ayrshire Roots *http://fp.ayrshireroots.plus.com/Genealogy/Records/Census/1851/1851.htm*

Broadsides *www.nls.uk/broadsides*

Burke's Peerage and Gentry Scottish resources *www.burkes-peerage.net/sites/common/sitepages/lisco.asp*

Drew's Genealogy and Ancestor Search *http://members.aol.com/drewhss/drew.htm*

Dumfries and Galloway indexes *www.dumgal.gov.uk/dumgal/MiniWeb.aspx?id=86&menuid=921&openid=921*

Family Search *www.familysearch.org*

FreeCEN *http://freecen.rootsweb.com*

Friends of Dundee City Archives *www.fdca.org.uk/databases.htm*

Glasgow Southern Necropolis *www.southernnec.20m.com*

Highland Archives *www.internet-promotions.co.uk/archives/index.htm*

Inveraray Jail *www.inverarayjail.co.uk/Former_prisoners/index.asp*

McKirdy Index *www.mckirdyindex.co.nz*

Mull Genealogy *www.mullgenealogy.co.uk*

Orkney Genealogy *www.cursiter.com*

Roots Hebrides *www.rootshebrides.com*

Roxburghshire Lieutenancy Book *www.scan.org.uk/researchrtools/lieutenancy.htm*

Scotland's People *www.scotlandspeople.gov.uk*

Scots Origins *www.scotsorigins.com*

ScotsFind *www.scotsfind.org*

(The) Scotsman Digital Archive *http://archive.scotsman.com*

Scottish Strays Marriage Index *www.mlfhs.org.uk*

Statistical Accounts of Scotland *http://edina.ac.uk/statacc*

Chapter 17. Births, marriages, deaths and census returns (Ireland)

Census Finder *www.censusfinder.com/ireland.htm*

Clare County Library *www.clarelibrary.ie*

Family Search *www.familysearch.org*
General Register Office (Irish Republic) *www.groireland.ie*
General Register Office (Northern Ireland) (GRONI) *www.groni. gov.uk*
Irish Origins *www.irishorigins.com*
Leitrim-Roscommon Genealogy Website *www.leitrim-roscommon. com*
Public Record Office of Northern Ireland (PRONI) *www.proni. gov.uk*
Ulster Ancestry *www.ulsterancestry.com/search.html*
Ulster Historical Foundation *www.ancestryireland.co.uk*
Waterford County Library *www.waterfordcountylibrary.ie*

Chapter 18. Church registers and wills (Ireland)

Celtic Cousins *www.celticcousins.net/ireland*
CMC Record Project *www.cmcrp.net*
Eneclann *www.eneclann.ie*
Fianna Guide to Irish Genealogy *www.rootsweb.com/~fianna*
Galway IGP *www.rootsweb.com/~irlgal2/index.htm*
Ireland GenWeb *www.irelandgenweb.com*
Irish Ancestors *http://scripts.ireland.com/ancestor/index.cfm*
Irish Family History Foundation (IFHF) *www.irish-roots.net*
Irish Family History Research *www.irishfamilyresearch.co.uk*
Irish Genealogy Ltd *www.irishgenealogy.ie*
Irish Origins *www.irishorigins.com*
Irish World *www.irish-world.com*
National Archives of Ireland (NAI) probate lists *www.nation alarchives.ie/research/probate.htm*
Northern Ireland GenWeb *www.rootsweb.com/~nirwgw*
Ulster Historical Foundation *www.ancestryireland.co.uk*

Chapter 19. Manx and Channel Islands records

Alex Glendinning's Channel Islands *http://user.itl.net/~glen/CIintro. html*
Jersey Archive *www.jerseyheritagetrust.org/sites/archive/archive.html*

Manx National Heritage Library (MNHL) *www.gov.im/mnh*
Priaulx Library *www.priaulx.gov.gg*

Chapter 20. Immigration to Britain and Ireland

eUCLid (UCL Library online catalogue) *http://library.ucl.ac.uk/F*
French Protestant Hospital *www.frenchhospital.org.uk*
Huguenot Library *www.ucl.ac.uk/Library/huguenot.shtml*
Huguenot Society of Great Britain and Ireland *www.huguenot
   society.org.uk*
Jewish Communities and Records – United Kingdom (JCR-UK)
   www.jewishgen.org/jcr-uk
Jewish Genealogical Society of Great Britain *www.jgsgb.org.uk*
JewishGen UK Database *www.jewishgen.org/databases/UK*
London Metropolitan Archives *www.cityoflondon.gov.uk/Corpora-
   tion/leisure_heritage/libraries_archives_museums_galleries/lma/lma.
   htm*
Moving Here *www.movinghere.org.uk*
(The) National Archives (TNA) *www.nationalarchives.gov.uk*
Romany and Traveller Family History Society *www.rtfhs.org.uk*
Scottish Jewish Archives Centre *www.sjac.org.uk*
Yad Vashem Holocaust Memorial Museum *www.yadvashem.org*

Chapter 21. Emigration from Britain and Ireland to the United States, Canada, Australia, New Zealand and South Africa

General

Commonwealth War Graves Commission *www.cwgc.org*
Cyndi's List *www.cyndislist.com*
Find My Past *www.findmypast.com*
Immigrant Ships Transcribers Guild *www.immigrantships.net*
Lincolnshire transportation database *www.lincolnshire.gov.uk/
   section.asp?catId=6724*
Scottish Emigration Database *www.abdn.ac.uk/emigration/index.
   html*
(The) Ships List *www.theshipslist.com*

United States

Ancestry.com *www.ancestry.com*
Arizona births and deaths *http://genealogy.az.gov*
Castle Garden immigration centre *http://castlegarden.org/index.html*
Census Finder *www.censusfinder.com*
Ellis Island federal immigration centre *www.ellisisland.org*
Family Search *www.familysearch.org*
(Steve) Morse search forms *www.stevemorse.org*
National Association of Counties *www.naco.org/Template.cfm?Section=Find_a_County&Template=/cffiles/counties/usamap.cfm*
US GenWeb *www.usgenweb.org*
Vital records offices *www.vitalrec.com*

Canada

Ancestry.ca *www.ancestry.ca*
British Columbia vital event indexes *www.bcarchives.gov.bc.ca/textual/governmt/vstats/v_events.htm#indexes*
Canada Gen Web *www.rootsweb.com/~canwgw*
Canadian Genealogy and History Links *www.islandnet.com/~jveinot/cghl/cghl.html*
Canadian Genealogy Centre *www.collectionscanada.ca/genealogy/index-e.html*
- Canadian censuses online *www.collectionscanada.ca/genealogy/022-911-e.html*
- Church archives *www.collectionscanada.ca/genealogy/022-806-e.html*
- Early immigrant records and online databases *www.collectionscanada.ca/genealogy/022-908.002-e.html*
- Immigration records online database (1925–35) *www.collectionscanada.ca/archivianet/020118_e.html*
- Passenger lists (1865–1935) and various online databases *www.collectionscanada.ca/genealogy/022-908.003-e.html*
- Provincial and territorial archives *www.collectionscanada.ca/genealogy/022-802-e.html*

- Provincial and territorial governments *www.collectionscanada. ca/genealogy/022-907.003-e.html*
- Provincial archives and vital statistics agencies *www. collectionscanada.ca/genealogy/022-906.006-e.html*

Immigrants to Quebec and Ontario (1801–49) *www.ingeneas.com/ free/index.html*

Manitoba vital event indexes *http://web2.gov.mb.ca/cca/vital/ Query.php*

New Brunswick vital event indexes *http://archives.gnb.ca/APPS/ GovRecs/VISSE/?L=EN*

Newfoundland censuses online *http://ngb.chebucto.org/census. shtml*

Ontario Wesleyan Methodist baptisms *http://freepages.genealogy. rootsweb.com/%7Ewjmartin/wm-index.htm*

Quebec Roman Catholic baptisms, marriages and burials database *www.genealogie.umontreal.ca/en/acces.htm*

Saskatchewan vital event indexes *http://vsgs.health.gov.sk.ca/vsgs_ srch.aspx*

Australia

Ancestry.com.au *www.ancestry.com.au*

Australia GenWeb *www.australiagenweb.org*

Australian Family History Compendium *www.cohsoft.com.au/afhc*

(Scottish) Highlands and Islands Emigration Society database *www.scan.org.uk/researchrtools/emigration.htm*

Irish transportation database *www.nationalarchives.ie/genealogy/ transportation.html*

Links to transportation websites (in the UK and Australia) *www. lincolnshire.gov.uk/section.asp?catId=6724*

National Archives of Australia *www.naa.gov.au*

- Fact Sheet 2 (contact details for state archives) *www.naa.gov.au/ Publications/fact_sheets/fs02.html*
- Fact Sheet 89 (contact details for registrars of births, marriages and deaths) *www.naa.gov.au/publications/fact_sheets/fs89.html*
- Fact Sheet 227 (immigration and naturalization) *www.naa.gov. au/Publications/fact_sheets/fs227.html*

New South Wales church and civil registration online index *www.bdm.nsw.gov.au/familyHistory/searchHistoricalRecords.htm*

New South Wales State Records online indexes *www.records.nsw.gov.au/archives/indexes_online_3357.asp*

Queensland State Archives *www.archives.qld.gov.au*

- Immigration and other online indexes *www.archives.qld.gov.au/research/indexes.asp*
- Online index of wills *www.archives.qld.gov.au/research/index/wills.asp*

South Australia online certificate ordering *www.ocba.sa.gov.au/bdm/applying/online/applyonline.html*

Tasmania Archives Office *www.archives.tas.gov.au*

- Convict and other indexes *www.archives.tas.gov.au/nameindexes*
- Early census returns online index *http://portal.archives.tas.gov.au/menu.aspx?search=10*
- Online wills and administrations index *http://portal.archives.tas.gov.au/menu.aspx?search=9*

Victoria Births, Deaths and Marriages Online Shop (index and images) *http://online.justice.vic.gov.au/servlet/bdm_home*

Victoria Public Record Office online databases (including immigration and convicts) *www.access.prov.vic.gov.au/public/PROVguides/PROVguide023/PROVguide023.jsp*

Western Australia civil registration online index *www.justice.wa.gov.au/portal/server.pt/gateway/PTARGS_0_2_323_201_0_43/http%3B/justicecontent.extranet.justice.wa.gov.au/F/familyhistory.aspx?uid=7603-9553-6410-6954*

New Zealand

Archives New Zealand *www.archives.govt.nz*

Auckland City Libraries *www.aucklandcitylibraries.com*

- Electoral rolls (1881) *http://o-www.aucklandcity.govt.nz.www.elgar.govt.nz/dbtw-wpd/electoral/electoral.html*
- Passenger Arrivals (1838–86 and 1909–21) *http://o-www.aucklandcity.govt.nz.www.elgar.govt.nz/dbtw-wpd/passengers/passenger.html*

- Police Census (1842–6) *http://o-www.aucklandcity.govt.nz.www.
  elgar.govt.nz/dbtw-wpd/policecensus/census.html*

Central Registry of Births, Deaths and Marriages (with
downloadable forms) *www.bdm.govt.nz*

Links to immigration and other databases *www.nzhistory.net.nz/
handsonhistory/genealogy-links*

New Zealand Cemeteries Online *http://nzgenealogy.rootschat.net/
cemetery.html*

New Zealand GenWeb *www.rootsweb.com/~nzlwgw*

New Zealand Society of Genealogists online databases of sheep
owners, freeholders and 'First Families' *www.genealogy.org.nz*

Presbyterian marriages in Otago and Southland (1848–1920)
*http://archives.presbyterian.org.nz/marriageregisters/
otagosouthlandmarriages.htm*

South Africa

1820 Settlers *www.geocities.com/settlers1820*

Ancestry 24 *www.genealogy.co.za/Ancestry24.aspx?page=content/
home*

National Archives of South Africa's NAAIRS (National Automated Archival Information Retrieval System) *www.national.
archives.gov.za/index.htm*

Rhodes University (Cory Library) *http://campus.ru.ac.za/index.php
?action=category&category=2635*

South Africa's Stamouers (Founders) *www.stamouers.com*

South African Genealogy *http://home.global.co.za/~mercon*

- Addresses of Department of Home Affairs, NASA repositories
  and other bodies *http://home.global.co.za/~mercon/addres.htm*

South African Genealogy *www.sagenealogy.co.za*

South African Passenger Lists *http://sa-passenger-list.za.net/index.
php*

University of the Witwatersrand holdings *www.wits.ac.za/histp/
collections.htm*

Chapter 22. The East India Company

Access to Archives (A2A) *www.a2a.org.uk*
Families in British India Society (FIBIS) *www.fibis.org*
Family History in India *http://members.ozemail.com.au/~clday*
Genealogy in India *www.ans.com.au/~rampais/genelogy/india/
indexes/index.htm*
India Office Records: Family History Sources *www.bl.uk/
collections/oiocfamilyhistory/family.html*

Chapter 23. Records of the British Army, Royal Navy, Royal Marines and Royal Air Force

Household Cavalry Museum *www.householdcavalry.gvon.com/
museum.htm*
National Army Museum *www.national-army-museum.ac.uk*
Nelson Society *www.nelson-society.org.uk/html/family_life.htm*

Chapter 24. Military records and memorials on the Internet

British War Memorial Project *www.britishwargraves.org.uk*
Commonwealth War Graves Commission (CWGC) *www.cwgc.org*
Documents Online *www.nationalarchives.gov.uk/documentsonline*
Family Relatives *www.familyrelatives.org*
Find My Past *www.findmypast.com*
Lost Generation *www.channel4.com/history/microsites/L/lost
generation*
Maritime Memorials *www.nmm.ac.uk/memorials*
Military Genealogy *www.military-genealogy.com*
(The) National Archives (TNA) *www.nationalarchives.gov.uk*
Naval Biographical Database *www.navylist.org*
Nelson's captains *www.nelson-society.org.uk/html/trafalgar_
captains.htm*
Officers Died *members.tripod.com/~Glosters/memindex3.htm*
Official HMS *Victory* Website *www.hms-victory.com*
Roll of Honour *www.roll-of-honour.com*
Scots at War *www.fettes.com/scotsatwar/rollofhonour.htm*

Soldiers' Memorials *www.angelfire.com/mp/memorials/memindz1. htm*

TNA Catalogue *www.nationalarchives.gov.uk/catalogue*

TNA Trafalgar database *www.nationalarchives.gov.uk/trafalgar ancestors*

Trafalgar Roll *www.ageofnelson.org/TrafalgarRoll/index.html*

Trafalgar Roll *www.genuki.org.uk/big/eng/Trafalgar*

UK National Inventory of War Memorials *www.ukniwm.org.uk*

World War One Cemeteries *www.ww1cemeteries.com*

Chapter 25. Electoral rolls

192.com *www.192.com*

Northern Ireland freeholders' records *www.proni.gov.uk/free holders*

Tracesmart *www.tracesmart.co.uk*

Chapter 26. Background information

British History Online *www.british-history.ac.uk*

Census Finder *www.censusfinder.com*

Historical Directories *www.historicaldirectories.org*

Old Towns of England *www.oldtowns.co.uk*

Police, 'Black Sheep' and Other Indexes *www.lightage.demon. co.uk*

Proceedings of the Old Bailey *www.oldbaileyonline.org*

Statistical Accounts of Scotland *http://edina.ac.uk/statacc*

Victoria County History *www.victoriacountyhistory.ac.uk*

- Cornwall *www.cornwallpast.net*
- County Durham *www.durhampast.net*
- Derbyshire *www.derbyshirepast.net*
- Essex *www.essexpast.net*
- Gloucestershire *www.gloucestershirepast.net*
- Middlesex *www.middlesexpast.net*
- Northamptonshire *www.northamptonshirepast.net*
- Oxfordshire *www.oxfordshirepast.net*
- Somerset *www.somersetpast.net*
- Staffordshire *www.staffordshirepast.net*

- Sussex *www.vchsussex.net*
- Wiltshire *www.wiltshirepast.net*
- Yorkshire *www.yorkshirepast.net*

Workhouses *www.workhouses.org.uk*

Chapter 27. Online family history portals

Census Finder *www.censusfinder.com/united_kingdom.htm*
Cyndi's List *www.cyndislist.com*
Family Records *www.familyrecords.gov.uk*
GENUKI *www.genuki.org.uk*
Walsham-le-Willows *www.walsham-le-willows.org*
World GenWeb *www.worldgenweb.org*

- British Isles GenWeb *www.britishislesgenweb.org*
- England *www.rootsweb.com/~engwgw*
- Scotland *www.scotlandgenweb.org*
- Wales *www.walesgenweb.com*
- Ireland (Republic of) *www.irelandgenweb.com*
- Northern Ireland *www.rootsweb.com/~nirwgw*
- Isle of Man *www.britishislesgenweb.org/~iom*
- Gibraltar *www.britishislesgenweb.org/~gibraltar*
- Caribbean Islands *www.britishislesgenweb.org/carribbean.html*
- Falkland Islands *www.britishislesgenweb.org/~falklandislands*
- St Helena *website.lineone.net/~sthelena/familyhistory.htm*

Chapter 28. Making contact with your cousins online

British Genealogy forums *www.british-genealogy.com/forums*
Dick Eastman's Online Genealogy Newsletter blog *http://eogn. typepad.com/eastmans_online_genealogy*
Family Tree Magazine/Practical Family History forums *www. family-tree.co.uk/phpBB2/index.php*
Genealogy Marketplace forums *www.genealogymarketplace.co.uk/ phpbb/index.php?c=3*
Genes Reunited *www.genesreunited.co.uk*
GenForum *http://genforum.genealogy.com/regional/countries.*

GENUKI list of mailing lists *www.genuki.org.uk/indexes/ MailingLists.html*

Google Groups *http://groups.google.co.uk*

Lost Cousins *www.lostcousins.com*

RootsChat forums *www.rootschat.com*

RootsWeb *www.rootsweb.com*

Talking Scot forums *www.talkingscot.com/forum*

UK Genealogy Forum *www.uk-genealogy.org.uk/phpBB2/indexphp*

Yahoo! UK & Ireland Groups *http://uk.dir.groups.yahoo.com/dir/ Family__Home/Genealogy*

Chapter 29. Family history societies

Aberdeen and North East Scotland FHS monumental inscription index *www.abdnet.co.uk/mi-index*

Association of Family History Societies of Wales (AFHSW) *www. fhswales.info*

Bristol and Avon FHS South Gloucestershire burials index *www. bafhs.org.uk/burialindex/burials.htm*

Federation of Family History Societies (FFHS) *www.ffhs.org.uk*

Gloucestershire FHS catalogue *mysite.wanadoo-members.co.uk/ gfhs/LibCat/LibCat.htm*

Gloucestershire FHS resources list *mysite.wanadoo-members.co.uk/ gfhs/ResourceList.htm*

Guild of One-Name Studies *www.one-name.org*

Herefordshire FHS monumental inscription index *www.rootsweb. com/~ukhfhs/miindex.html*

(The) Irish Ancestral Research Association (TIARA) *www.tiara.ie*

Scottish Association of Family History Societies (SAFHS) *www. safhs.org.uk*

(City of) York FHS index of York Assizes prisoners *www.york familyhistory.org.uk/assizes.htm*

Conclusion: the past, present and future of family history

African Ancestry *www.africanancestry.com*

DNA and Family History (website for Chris Pomery's book) *www. dnaandfamilyhistory.com*

DNA Heritage *www.dnaheritage.com*

DNA Print Genomics *www.ancestrybydna.com*

Ethnoancestry *www.ethnoancestry.com*

Family Tree DNA *www.familytreedna.com*

GeneTree *www.genetree.com*

GeoGene *www.geogene.com*

Oxford Ancestors *www.oxfordancestors.com*

Relative Genetics *www.relativegenetics.com*

Roots for Real *www.rootsforreal.com*

Sorenson Molecular Genealogy Foundation (SMGF) *www.smgf. org*

Trace Genetics *www.tracegenetics.com*

D. Addresses of family history societies

1. England

The addresses listed are private homes, therefore no telephone numbers are given.

Barnsley FHS
Gail Woodhead, 4 Cranford Gardens, Royston, Barnsley S71 4SP
E-mail: secretary@barnsleyfhs.co.uk
Website: *www.barnsleyfhs.co.uk*

Bedfordshire FHS
Anne Simmonds, PO Box 214, Bedford MK42 9RX
E-mail: bfhs@bfhs.org.uk
Website: *www.bfhs.org.uk*

Berkshire FHS
The Secretary, Berkshire FHS, Yeomanry House, 131 Castle Hill, Reading RG1 7TJ
E-mail: secretary@berksfhs.org.uk
Website: *www.berksfhs.org.uk*

Birmingham and Midland SGH
Mrs Jackie Cotterill, 5 Sanderling Court, Kidderminster DY10 4TS
E-mail: gensec@bmsgh.org
Website: *www.bmsgh.org*

Bradford FHS
Carol Duckworth, 5 Leaventhorpe Avenue, Fairweather Green,
Bradford, BD8 0ED
E-mail: secretary@bradfordfhs.org.uk
Website: *www.bradfordfhs.org.uk*

Bristol and Avon FHS
Margaret Smith, 7 Henleaze Park Drive, Bristol BS9 4LH
E-mail: secretary@bafhs.org.uk
Website: *www.bafhs.org.uk*

Buckinghamshire FHS
The Secretary, c/o PO Box 403, Aylesbury HP21 7GU
E-mail: society@bucksfhs.org.uk
Website: *www.bucksfhs.org.uk*

Buckinghamshire Genealogical Society
Eve McLaughlin, Varneys, Rudds Lane, Haddenham,
Buckinghamshire HP17 8JP
E-mail: kevin.quick@bucksgs.org.uk
Website: *www.bucksgs.org.uk*

Burntwood FH Group
Jennifer Lee, 8 Peakes Road, Rugeley, Staffordshire, WS15 2LY
E-mail: jennifer.lee@care4free.net
Website: *www.geocities.com/bfhg1986*

Calderdale FHS (incorporating Halifax & District)
Anne Whitaker, 13 Far View, Illingworth, Halifax HX2 9EW
E-mail: secretary@cfhsweb.co.uk
Website: *www.cfhsweb.co.uk*

Cambridgeshire FHS
David Wratten, 43 Eachard Road, Cambridge CB3 0HZ
E-mail: secretary@cfhs.org.uk
Website: *www.cfhs.org.uk*

Cambridge University Heraldry & Genealogy Society
c/o Crossfield House, Dale Road, Stanton, Bury St Edmunds,
Suffolk IP31 2DY
E-mail: mlm39@hermes.cam.ac.uk
Website: *www.cam.ac.uk/societies/cuhags*

Cheshire, The FHS of
Mike Craig, 10 Dunns Lane, Ashton, Chester CH3 8BU
E-mail: info@fhsc.org.uk
Website: *www.fhsc.org.uk*

Cheshire FHS, North
Rhoda Clarke, 2 Denham Drive, Bramhall, Stockport SK7 2AT
E-mail: r.demercado@ntlworld.com
Website: *www.ncfhs.org.uk*

Chesterfield and District FHS
D. Rogers, Correspondence Secretary, 2 Highlow Close,
Loundsley Green, Chesterfield, Derbyshire S40 4PG
E-mail: mail@cadfhs.org.uk
Website: *www.cadfhs.org.uk*

Cleveland FHS
A. Sampson, 1 Oxgang Close, Redcar, Cleveland TS10 4ND
E-mail: cleveland.fhs@ntlworld.com
Website: *www.clevelandfhs.org.uk*

Cornwall FHS
The Administrator, 5 Victoria Square, Truro, Cornwall TR1 2RS
E-mail: secretary@cornwallfhs.com
Website: *www.cornwallfhs.com*

Coventry FHS
Angela Crabtree, Barton Fields Cottage, 1 Barton Fields, Ecton,
Northamptonshire NN6 0BF
E-mail: gen-sec@covfhs.org
Website: *www.covfhs.org*

Cumbria FHS
Mrs M. Russell, 32 Granada Road, Denton, Manchester M34 2IJ
No e-mail address
Website: *www.cumbriafhs.com*

Derbyshire FHS
Dave Bull, Bridge Chapel House, St Mary's Bridge, Sowter Road,
Derby DE1 3AT
No e-mail address
Website: *www.dfhs.org.uk*

Devon FHS
The Secretary, Devon FHS, PO Box 9, Exeter, Devon EX2 6YP
E-mail: secretary@devonfhs.org.uk
Website: *www.devonfhs.org.uk*

Doncaster and District FHS
Mrs M. Staniforth, 5 Breydon Avenue, Cusworth, Doncaster
DN5 8JZ
E-mail: secretary@doncasterfhs.co.uk
Website: *www.doncasterfhs.co.uk*

Dorset FHS
Treetops Research Centre, Suite 5 Stanley House, 3 Fleets Lane,
Poole, Dorset BH15 3AJ
E-mail: contact@dorsetfhs.org.uk
Website: *www.dorsetfhs.org.uk*

Eastbourne and District FHS (Family Roots)
John Crane, 8 Park Lane, Hampden Park, Eastbourne BN21 2UT
E-mail: johnandval.crane@tiscali.co.uk
Website: *www.eastbournefhs.org.uk*

Essex Society for Family History
Mrs A. Church, Windyridge, 32 Parsons Heath, Colchester,
Essex CO4 3HX
E-mail: secretary@esfh.org.uk
Website: *www.esfh.org.uk*

Felixstowe FHS
Mrs J. S. Campbell, 7 Victoria Road, Felixstowe, Suffolk
IP11 7PT
E-mail: fxfhs@hotmail.com
Website: *www.btinternet.com/~woodsbj/ffhs*

Fenland FHS
Judy Green, Rose Hall, Walpole Bank, Walpole St Andrew,
Wisbech PE14 7JD
E-mail: judy.green@farming.me.uk
Website: *www.fenlandfhs.org.uk*

Folkestone and District FHS
Janet Powell, Kingsmill Down, Hastingleigh, Ashford, Kent
TN25 5JJ
E-mail: secretary@folkfhs.org.uk
Website: *www.folkfhs.org.uk*

Furness FHS
Miss J Fairbairn, 64 Cowlarns Road, Barrow-in-Furness
LA14 4HJ
E-mail: julia.fairbairn@virgin.net
Website: *www.furnessfhs.co.uk*

Gloucestershire FHS
Alex Wood, 37 Barrington Drive, Hucclecote, Gloucestershire
GL3 3BT
E-mail: gfhs@blueyonder.co.uk
Website: *www.gfhs.org.uk*

Hampshire Genealogical Society
Sheila Brine, 3 Elaine Gardens, Lovedean, Waterlooville,
Hampshire PO8 9QS
E-mail: secretary@hgs-online.org.uk
Website: *www.hgs-online.org.uk*

Harrogate and District FHS
Wendy Symington, 18 Aspin Drive, Knaresborough, North Yorks
HG5 8HH
No e-mail address
No website

Hastings and Rother FHS
Linda Smith, 355 Bexhill Road, St Leonards-on-Sea, East Sussex
TN38 8AJ
E-mail: enquiries@hrfhs.org.uk
Website: *www.hrfhs.org.uk*

Herefordshire FHS
Brian Prosser, 6 Birch Meadow, Gosmore Road, Clehonger,
Herefordshire HR2 9RH
E-mail: prosser_brian@hotmail.com
Website: *www.rootsweb.com/~ukhfhs*

Hertfordshire FHS
Amelia Cheek, 38 Roselands Avenue, Hoddesdon,
Hertfordshire EN11 9BB
E-mail: secretary@hertsfhs.org.uk
Website: *www.hertsfhs.org.uk*

Hillingdon FHS
Mrs G. May, 20 Moreland Drive, Gerrards Cross,
Buckinghamshire SL9 8BB
E-mail: Gillmay@dial.pipex.com
Website: *www.hfhs.co.uk*

Huddersfield and District FHS
Alan Stewart-Kaye, 63 Dunbottle Lane, Mirfield, West Yorkshire
WF14 9JJ
E-mail: secretary@hdfhs.org.uk
Website: *www.hdfhs.org.uk*

Huntingdonshire FHS
Mrs C. Kesseler, 42 Crowhill, Godmanchester, Cambridgeshire,
PE29 2NR
E-mail: secretary@huntsfhs.org.uk
Website: *www.huntsfhs.org.uk*

Isle of Axholme FHS
Norma Neill (Secretary), 'Colywell', 43 Commonside,
Westwoodside, Doncaster DN9 2AR
E-mail: secretary@axholme-fhs.org.uk
Website: *www.axholme-fhs.org.uk*

Isle of Wight FHS
Brenda Dodgson, 9 Forest Dell, Winford, Sandown, Isle of Wight
P36 OLG
E-mail: brendave@dodgson9.freeserve.co.uk
Website: *www.isle-of-wight-fhs.co.uk*

Keighley and District FHS
Mrs S. Daynes, 2 The Hallowes, Shann Park, Keighley, West
Yorkshire BD20 6HY
No e-mail address (use online form)
Website: *www.keighleyfamilyhistory.org.uk*

Kent FHS
Kristin Slater, Bullockstone Farm, Bullockstone Road, Herne,
Kent CT6 7NL
E-mail: secretary@kfhs.org.uk
Website: *www.kfhs.org.uk*

Kent FHS, North West
Vera Bailey, 58 Clarendon Gardens, Stone, Dartford, Kent
DA2 6EZ
E-mail: secretary@nwkfhs.org.uk
Website: *www.nwkfhs.org.uk*

Lancashire FH and Heraldry Society
Joyce Monks, 21 Baytree Road, Clayton-le-Woods, Lancashire
PR6 7JW
E-mail: secretary@lfhhs.org.uk
Website: *www.lfhhs.org.uk*

Lancashire Parish Register Society
Alan Kenwright, 19 Churton Grove, Shevington Moor, Wigan,
Lancashire WN6 0SZ
E-mail: akenwright@yahoo.com
Website: *www.lprs.org.uk*

Lancaster FH Group
Mrs P. Harrison, 116 Bowerham Road, Lancaster LA1 4HL
E-mail: secretary@lfhg.org
Website: *www.lfhg.org*

Leicestershire & Rutland FHS
Joan Rowbottom, 37 Cyril Street, Leicester LE3 2FF
E-mail: secretary@lrfhs.org.uk
Website: *www.lrfhs.org.uk*

Letchworth and District FH Group
Helen Fitzgibbons, 2 Cross Street, Letchworth Garden City,
Hertfordshire SG6 4UD
E-mail: hfitz45@ntlworld.com
Website: *www.letchworthgardencity.net/LDFHG/Index.html*

Lincolnshire FHS
Brenda Coulson, 57 Lupin Road, Lincoln LN2 4GB
E-mail: secretary@lincolnshirefhs.org.uk
Website: *www.lincolnshirefhs.org.uk*

Liverpool and SW Lancashire FHS
David Guiver, 11 Bushbys Lane, Formby, Liverpool L37 2DX
E-mail: DavidGuiver@aol.com
Website: *www.liverpool-genealogy.org.uk*

London FHS, East of
Ian Whaley, 46 Brights Avenue, Rainham, Essex RM13 9NW
E-mail: eolfhs@btopenworld.com
Website: *www.eolfhs.org.uk*

London, Westminster and Middlesex FHS
Mr and Mrs Pyemont, 57 Belvedere Way, Kenton, Harrow,
Middlesex HA3 9XQ
E-mail: william.pyemont@virgin.net
Website: *www.lnmfhs.dircon.co.uk*

Malvern FHS
Betty Firth, Apartment 5, Severn Grange, Northwick Road,
Bevere, Worcester WR3 7RE
E-mail: betty.firth@virgin.net
Website: *www.mfhs.org.uk*

Manchester and Lancashire FHS
Clayton House, 59 Piccadilly, Manchester M1 2AQ
Tel: +44 (0) 161 236 9750
E-mail: office@mlfhs.org.uk
Website: *www.mlfhs.org.uk*

Mansfield and District FHS
Miss B. E. Flintham, 15 Cranmer Grove, Mansfield,
Nottinghamshire NG19 7JR
No e-mail address
No website

Middlesex FHS, West
Tony Simpson, 32 The Avenue, Bedford Park, Chiswick,
London W4 1HT
E-mail: secretary@west-middlesex-fhs.org.uk
Website: *www.west-middlesex-fhs.org.uk*

Morley and District FH Group
Carol Sklinar, 1 New Lane, East Ardsley, Wakefield WF3 2DP
E-mail: carol@morleyfhg.co.uk
Website: *www.morleyfhg.co.uk*

Norfolk FHS
Edmund G. Perry, Kirby Hall, 70 St Giles Street,
Norwich NR2 1LS
E-mail: nfhs@paston.co.uk
Website: *www.norfolkfhs.org.uk*

Norfolk FHS, Mid
Kate Easdown, Secretary MNFHS, 47 Greengate, Swanton
Morley, Dereham, Norfolk NR20 4LX
E-mail: keasdown@aol.com
Website: *www.mnfhs.freeuk.com*

Northamptonshire FHS
Keith Steggles, 22 Godwin Walk, Ryehill,
Northampton NN5 7RW
E-mail: secretary@northants-fhs.org
Website: *www.northants-fhs.org*

North Meols FHS
Jane Scarisbrick, 6 Millars Place, Marshside, Southport,
Lancashire PR9 9FU
E-mail: jane.scarisbrick@virgin.net
Website: *www.nmfhssouthport.co.uk*

Northumberland and Durham FHS
Frances Norman, 23 Monkton Avenue, Simonside, South Shields
NE34 9RX
E-mail: frances@fnorman.fsnet.co.uk
Website: *www.ndfhs.org.uk*

Nottinghamshire FHS
Stuart Mason, 26 Acorn Bank, West Bridgford, Nottingham
NG2 7DU
E-mail: secretary@nottsfhs.org.uk
Website: *www.nottsfhs.org.uk*

Nuneaton and North Warwickshire FHS
Peter Lee, PO Box 2282, Nuneaton, Warwickshire CV11 9ZT
E-mail: Nuneatonian2000@aol.com
Website: *www.nnwfhs.org.uk*

Ormskirk and District FHS
PO Box 213 Aughton, Ormskirk, Lancashire L39 5WT
E-mail: secretary@odfhs.org.uk
Website: *www.odfhs.org.uk*

Oxfordshire FHS
Mrs J. Kennedy, 19 Mavor Close, Woodstock, Oxford OX20 1YL
E-mail: secretary@ofhs.org.uk
Website: *www.ofhs.org.uk*

Peterborough and District FHS

Margaret Brewster, 111 New Road, Woodston, Peterborough
PE2 9HE
E-mail: meandmygarden@hotmail.com
Website: *www.peterborofhs.org.uk*

Pontefract and District FHS

Glynis Tate, Eadon House, Main Street, Hensall, Goole
DN14 0QZ
E-mail: secretary@pontefractfhs.org.uk
Website: *www.pontefractfhs.org.uk*

Ripon Historical Society & FHG

Mary Moseley, 42 Knox Avenue, Harrogate, North Yorkshire
HG1 3JB
E-mail: RHSinfo@aol.com (membership queries)
Website: *www.yorksgen.co.uk/rh/rh1.htm*

Rotherham FHS

Brian Allott, Secretary, 36 Warren Hill, Rotherham S61 3SX
E-mail: secretary@rotherhamfhs.co.uk
Website: *www.rotherhamfhs.co.uk*

Royston and District FHS

Kay Curtis, 'Baltana', London Road, Barkway, Nr Royston,
Hertfordshire SG8 8EY
E-mail: kay.tails@virgin.net
Website: *www.roystonfhs.org*

Rugby FH Group

John A. Chard, Springfields, Rocheberie Way, Rugby CV22 6EG
E-mail: j.chard@ntlworld.com
Website: *www.rugbyfhg.co.uk*

Selby FHS
Marilyn Newall, Keswick House, Kelfield Road, Riccall, York
YO19 6PG
E-mail: m_newall@hotmail.com
Website: *www.geocities.com/selbyfamilyhistory*

Sheffield and District FHS
Diane Maskell, 5 Old Houses, Piccadilly Road, Chesterfield
S61 OEH
E-mail: secretary@sheffieldfhs.org.uk
Website: *www.sheffieldfhs.org.uk*

Shropshire FHS
Mrs D. Hills, Redhillside, Ludlow Road, Church Stretton,
Shropshire SY6 6AD
E-mail: secretary@sfhs.org.uk
Website: *www.sfhs.org.uk*

Somerset and Dorset FHS
Secretary, PO Box 4502 Sherborne DT9 6YL
E-mail: society@sdfhs.org
Website: *www.sdfhs.org*

Suffolk FHS
Mrs P. Marshall, 2 Flash Corner, Theberton, Leiston, Suffolk
IP16 4RW
E-mail: admin@suffolkfhs.org.uk
Website: *www.suffolkfhs.org.uk*

Surrey FHS, East
119 Keevil Drive, London SW19 6TF
E-mail: secretary@eastsurreyfhs.org.uk
Website: *www.eastsurreyfhs.org.uk*

Surrey FHS, West
Ann Sargeant, 21 Sheppard Road, Basingstoke, Hampshire
RG21 3HT
E-mail: secretary@wsfhs.org
Website: *www.wsfhs.org*

Sussex FHG
Val Orr, 54 Heron Way, Horsham, Sussex RH13 6DL
E-mail: secretary@sfhg.org.uk
Website: *www.sfhg.org.uk*

Tunbridge Wells FHS
Roy Thompson, 5 College Drive, Tunbridge Wells, Kent TN2 3PN
E-mail: roythompson@mailsnare.net
Website: *www.tunwells-fhs.co.uk*

Wakefield and District FHS
Kathy Wattie, Secretary, 12 Malting Rise, Robin Hood,
Wakefield, West Yorkshire WF3 3AY
E-mail: secretary@wdfhs.co.uk
Website: *www.wdfhs.co.uk*

Waltham Forest FHS
Mr B. F. Burton, 49 Sky Peals Road, Woodford Green, Essex
IG8 9NE
No e-mail address
No website

Warwickshire FHS
Chairman, 44 Abbotts Lane, Coventry CV1 4AZ
E-mail: chairman@wfhs.org.uk
Website: *www.wfhs.org.uk*

Weston-super-Mare FHS
Brian Airey, 125 Totterdown Road, Weston-super-Mare BS23 4LW
E-mail: secretary@wsmfhs.org.uk
Website: *www.wsmfhs.org.uk*

Wharfedale FHG
Mrs Susan Hartley, 1 West View Court, Yeadon, Leeds LS19 7HX
E-mail: hon.secretary@wfhg.org.uk
Website: *www.yorksgen.co.uk/wfhg/wfhg.htm*

Wigan F and LHS
John Wogan, 678 Warrington Road, Goose Green, Wigan,
Lancashire WN3 6XN
E-mail: johnwogan@blueyonder.co.uk
Website: *www.ffhs.org.uk/members/wigan.htm*

Wiltshire FHS
Diana Grout, 42 Stokehill, Hilperton, Trowbridge, Wiltshire
BA14 7TJ
E-mail: secretary@wiltshirefhs.co.uk
Website: *www.wiltshirefhs.co.uk*

Woolwich and District FHS
Edna Reynolds, 54 Parkhill Road, Bexley, Kent DA5 1HY
E-mail: FrEdnaFHS@aol.com
No website

York and District FHS, City of
Mary Varley, Ascot House, Cherry Tree Avenue, Newton-on-Ouse,
York YO30 2BN
E-mail: secretary@yorkfamilyhistory.org.uk
Website: *www.yorkfamilyhistory.org.uk*

Yorkshire Archaeological Society FH Section
Mrs J. Butler, Secretary, c/o YAS, Claremont, 23 Clarendon Road,
Leeds LS2 9NZ
E-mail: secretary@yorkshireroots.org.uk
Website: *www.yorkshireroots.org.uk*

Yorkshire FHS, East
Mrs M. Oliver, 12 Carlton Drive, Aldbrough, East Yorkshire
HU11 4SF
E-mail: secretary@eyfhs.org.uk
Website: *www.eyfhs.org.uk*

Yorkshire FHSs, London Group of
Ian Taylor, 1 Waverley Way, Carshalton Beeches, Surrey SM5 3LQ
E-mail: ian-taylor@blueyonder.co.uk
Website: *www.genuki.org.uk/big/eng/YKS/Misc/FHS*

2. Scotland

Aberdeen and North East Scotland FHS
(covering the historic counties of Aberdeen, Banff, Kincardine
and Moray)
Family History Shop, 164 King Street, Aberdeen AB24 5BD
Tel: +44 (0) 1224 646323
E-mail: enquiries@anesfhs.org.uk
Website: *www.anesfhs.org.uk*

Alloway and Southern Ayrshire FHS
Alloway Parish Church Hall, Auld Nick's View, Alloway, Ayr
KA7 4PQ
No e-mail address (use online form)
Website: *www.asafhs.co.uk*

Anglo-Scottish FHS
Clayton House, 59 Piccadilly, Manchester M1 2AQ
Tel: +44 (0) 161 236 9750
E-mail: office@mlfhs.org.uk
Website: *www.mlfhs.org.uk*

Borders FHS
(covering the historic counties of Berwick, Peebles, Roxburgh and Selkirk)
Ronald Morrison, Buchan Cottage, Duns Castle, Duns TD11 3NW
No e-mail address (use online form)
Website: *www.bordersfhs.org.uk*

Caithness FHS
Sandy Gunn, 9 Provost Cormack Drive, Thurso KW14 7ES
E-mail: sandy.gunn@btinternet.com
Website: *www.caithnessfhs.org.uk*

Central Scotland FHS
(covering the historic counties of Clackmannan and Stirling, as well as the western part of Perthshire and the parishes of Bo'ness and Carriden in West Lothian)
11 Springbank Gardens, Dunblane FK15 9JX
No e-mail address (use online form)
Website: *www.csfhs.org.uk*

Dumfries and Galloway FHS
(covering the historic counties of Dumfries, Kirkcudbright and Wigtown)
Family History Centre, 9 Glasgow Street, Dumfries DG2 9AF
Tel: +44 (0) 1387 248093
E-mail: secretary@dgfhs.org.uk
Website: *www.dgfhs.org.uk*

East Ayrshire FHS
c/o The Dick Institute, Elmbank Avenue, Kilmarnock KA1 3BU
E-mail: enquiries@eastayrshirefhs.org.uk
Website: *www.eastayrshirefhs.org.uk*

Fife FHS
Glenmoriston, Durie Street, Leven, Fife KY8 4HF
E-mail: webadmin@fifefhs.org
Website: *www.fifefhs.org*

Glasgow and West of Scotland FHS
(covering the historic counties of Argyll, Ayr, Bute, Dunbarton,
Lanark and Renfrew, as well as part of Stirlingshire)
Unit 13, 32 Mansfield Street, Glasgow G11 5QP
Tel: +44 (0) 141 339 8303
No e-mail addresses (use online form)
Website: *www.gwsfhs.org.uk*

Highland FHS
(covering the historic counties of Caithness, Inverness, Nairn, Ross and
Cromarty, and Sutherland, as well as the northern parishes of Argyll)
c/o Reference Room, Public Library, Farraline Park,
Inverness IV1 1NH
E-mail: jdurham@highlandfhs.org.uk
Website: *www.highlandfhs.org.uk*

Lanarkshire FHS
26A Motherwell Business Centre, Coursington Road, Motherwell,
Lanarkshire ML1 1PW
E-mail: infoLFHS@aol.com
Website: *www.lanarkshirefhs.org.uk*

Largs and North Ayrshire FHS
c/o Largs Library, 18 Allanpark Street, Largs KA30 9AG
E-mail: webmaster@largsnafhs.org.uk (general enquiries)
Website: *www.largsnafhs.org.uk/home.htm*

Lothian FHS
c/o Lasswade High School Centre, Eskdale Drive, Bonnyrigg,
Midlothian EH19 2LA
E-mail: lothiansfhs@hotmail.com
Website: *www.lothiansfhs.org.uk*

Orkney FHS
Orkney Library and Archive, 44 Junction Road, Kirkwall
KW15 1HG
E-mail: olaf.mooney@virgin.net
Website: *www.genuki.org.uk/big/sct/OKI/ofhs.html*

Renfrewshire FHS
PO Box 9239, Kilmacolm PA13 4WZ
No e-mail address (use online form)
Website: *www.renfrewshirefhs.co.uk*

SCOTSLOT
Elizabeth van Lottum, 16 Bloomfield Road, Harpenden,
Hertfordshire AL5 4DB
E-mail: lizvanlottum@waitrose.com
No website

Scottish Genealogy Society
Library and Family History Centre, 15 Victoria Terrace,
Edinburgh EH1 2JL
Tel: +44 (0) 131 220 3677
E-mail: sales@scotsgenealogy.com
Website: *www.scotsgenealogy.com*

Shetland FHS
6 Hillhead, Lerwick, Shetland ZE1 0EJ
E-mail: secretary@shetland-fhs.org.uk
Website: *www.shetland-fhs.org.uk*

Tay Valley FHS
(covering the historic counties of Angus, Fife, Kinross and Perth)
Research Centre, 179–181 Princes Street, Dundee DD4 6DQ
Tel: +44 (0) 1382 461845
E-mail: tvfhs@tayvalleyfhs.org.uk
Website: *www.tayvalleyfhs.org.uk*

Troon @ Ayrshire FHS
c/o M.E.R.C. Troon Public Library, South Beach, Troon,
Ayrshire KA10 6EF
E-mail: info@troonayrshirefhs.org.uk
Website: *www.troonayrshirefhs.org.uk*

West Lothian FHS
23 Templar Rise, Livingstone EH54 6PJ
E-mail: honsec@wlfhs.org.uk
Website: *www.wlfhs.org.uk*

3. Wales

Cardiganshire FHS
Menna H. Evans, Adran Casgliadau, c/o National Library of
Wales, Aberystwyth, Ceredigion SY23 3BU
E-mail: sec@cgnfhs.org.uk
Website: *www.cgnfhs.org.uk*

Clwyd FHS
Mrs A. Anderson, The Laurels, Dolydd Road, Cefn Mawr,
Wrexham LL14 3NH
No e-mail address (use online form)
Website: *www.clwydfhs.org.uk*

Dyfed FHS
Beti Williams, 12 Elder Grove, Llamgunnor, Carmarthen
SA31 2LQ
E-mail: secretary@dyfedfhs.org.uk
Website: *www.dyfedfhs.org.uk*

Glamorgan FHS
Mrs R. Williams, 93 Pwllygath Street, Bridgend CF36 6ET
E-mail: secretary@glamfhs.org
Website: *www.glamfhs.org*

Gwent FHS
Secretary, 11 Rosser Street Wainfelin, Pontypool NP4 6EA
E-mail: secretary@gwentfhs.info
Website: *www.gwentfhs.info*

Gwynedd FHS
J. Bryan Jones, 7 Victoria Road, Old Colwyn, Conwy LL29 9SN
E-mail: bryan.jones8@btinternet.com
Website: *www.gwynedd.fsbusiness.co.uk*

Montgomeryshire Genealogical Society
Sue Harrison-Stone, Cambrian House, Brimmon Lane, Newtown,
Powys SY16 1BY
E-mail: sue_powys@hotmail.com
Website: *home.freeuk.net/montgensoc*

Powys FHS
Roger Pearson, Waterloo Cottage, Llandeilo Graban, Builth Wells,
Powys LD2 3SJ
E-mail: rspearson@breathemail.com
Website: *www.rootsweb.com/~wlspfhs*

4. Northern Ireland

North of Ireland FHS
G. M. Siberry, c/o Graduate School of Education, The Queen's
University of Belfast, 69 University Street, Belfast BT7 1HL
E-mail: enquiries@nifhs.org
Website: *www.nifhs.org*

Ulster Genealogical and Historical Guild
12 College Square East, Belfast BT1 6DD
Tel: +44 (0) 28 90 332288
E-mail: enquiry@uhf.org.uk
Website: *www.ancestryireland.com*

5. Republic of Ireland

Genealogical Society of Ireland
Michael Merrigan, 11 Desmond Avenue, Dun Laoghaire,
County Dublin
E-mail: eolas@familyhistory.ie
Website: *www.familyhistory.ie*

Irish FHS
Secretary, PO Box 36, Naas, County Kildare
E-mail: ifhs@eircom.net
Website: *http://homepage.eircom.net/~ifhs*

6. Isle of Man

Isle of Man FHS
Priscilla Lewthwaite, Pear Tree Cottage, Lhergy Cripperty, Union
Mills IM4 4NF
E-mail: iomfhs@manx.net
Website: *www.isle-of-man.com/interests/genealogy/fhs*

7. Jersey

Channel Islands FHS
Mrs P. A. Neale, Secretary, PO Box 507, St Helier JE4 5TN
E-mail: picus@jerseymail.co.uk
Website: *www.channelislandshistory.com*

8. Guernsey

La Société Guernesiaise (FH Section)
Family History Section, PO Box 314, St Peter Port GY1 3TG
No e-mail address (use online form)
Website: *www.societe.org.gg/sections/familyhistorysec.htm*

9. Other societies in the UK

Anglo-German FHS
Peter Towey, 20 Skylark Rise, Woolwell, Plymouth PL6 7SN
E-mail: GwendolineDavis@aol.com
Website: *www.art-science.com/agfhs*

Anglo-Italian FHS
Elaine Collins (Chairman), 3 Calais Street, London SE5 9LP
E-mail: chairman@anglo-italianfhs.org.uk
Website: *www.anglo-italianfhs.org.uk*

Catholic FHS
Margaret Bowery, 9 Snows Green Road, Shotley Bridge, Consett, County Durham DH8 0HD
E-mail: catholicfhs@ntlworld.com
Website: *www.catholic-history.org.uk/cfhs/index.htm*

Families in British India Society
Peter Bailey, Sentosa, Godolphin Road, Weybridge, Surrey KT13 0PT
E-mail: fibis-chairman@fibis.org
Website: *www.fibis.org*

Irish Genealogical Research Society
Peter Manning, 18 Stratford Avenue, Rainham, Gillingham, Kent ME8 0EP
E-mail: info@igrsoc.org
Website: *www.igrsoc.org*

Jewish Genealogical Society of Great Britain
Mr A. Winner, PO Box 13288, London N3 3WD
E-mail: enquiries@jgsgb.org.uk
Website: *www.jgsgb.org.uk*

Quaker FHS
Liz Butler, 3 Sheridan Place, Hampton, Middlesex TW12 2SB
E-mail: info@qfhs.co.uk
Website: *www.qfhs.co.uk*

Railway Ancestors FHS
Jeremy Engert, Lundy, King Edward Street, Barmouth,
Gwynedd LL42 1NY
No e-mail address (use online form)
Website: *www.railwayancestors.fsnet.co.uk*

Romany and Traveller FHS
Mrs J. Keet-Black, 6 St James Walk, South Chailey, East Sussex
BN8 4BU
No e-mail address (use online form)
Website: *www.rtfhs.org.uk*

Society of Genealogists
14 Charterhouse Buildings, Goswell Road, London ECIM 7BA
E-mail: genealogy@sog.org.uk
Website: *www.sog.org.uk*

10. Some overseas family history societies

10a. United States of America

British Isles FHS – USA
Secretary, 2531 Sawtelle Boulevard, PMB#134, Los Angeles, CA
90064–3124
E-mail: Cardi2@aol.com
Website: *www.rootsweb.com/~bifhsusa*

Federation of Genealogical Societies
PO Box 200940, Austin, TX 78720-0940
E-mail: fgs-office@fgs.org
Website: *www.fgs.org* (contains link to search facility for US and
Canadian societies)

International Society for British Genealogy and Family History
PO Box 350459, Westminster, CO 80035-0459
E-mail: isbgfh@yahoo.com
Website: *www.isbgfh.org*

10b. Canada

British Isles FHS of Greater Ottawa
Box 38026, Ottawa, Ontario K2C 3Y7
E-mail: queries@bifhsgo.ca
Website: *www.bifhsgo.ca* (contains links to other Canadian societies)

10c. Australia

Australasian Federation of Family History Organisations Inc.
PO Box 3012, Weston Creek, ACT 2611
E-mail: secretary@affho.org
Website: *www.affho.org* (contains links to member societies)

Society of Australian Genealogists
Richmond Villa, 120 Kent Street, Observatory Hill, Sydney, New South Wales 2000
E-mail: info@sag.org.au
Website: *www.sag.org.au*

10d. New Zealand

New Zealand Society of Genealogists Inc.
PO Box 8795, Symonds Street, Auckland 1035
E-mail: nzsg-contact@genealogy.org.nz
Website: *www.genealogy.org.nz*

10e. South Africa

Genealogical Society of South Africa
Suite 143, Postnet X2600, Houghton 2041
E-mail: secretary@ggsa.info
Website: *www.ggsa.info*

E. Addresses of major archives and libraries in Britain and Ireland

1. England

1a. National and regional archives

Borthwick Institute for Archives (BIA)
University of York, Heslington, York YO10 5DD
Tel: +44 (0) 1904 321166 (search room enquiries and document orders)
or +44 (0) 1904 321160 (other enquiries)
E-mail: bihr500@york.ac.uk
Website: *www.york.ac.uk/inst/bihr*

British Library (BL)
96 Euston Road, London NW1 2DB
Tel: +44 (0) 870 444 1500
No general e-mail address
Website: *www.bl.uk*

Family Records Centre (FRC)
Myddelton Street, Islington, London EC1R 1UW
Tel: 0845 603 7788 (BMD certificates)
or +44 (0) 20 8392 5300 (other enquiries)
E-mail: certificate.services@ons.gsi.gov.uk (certificate enquiries) or frc@nationalarchives.gov.uk (other enquiries)
Website: *www.familyrecords.gov.uk/frc*

The National Archives (TNA)
Kew, Richmond, Surrey TW9 4DU
Tel: +44 (0) 20 8876 3444
No general e-mail address
Website: *www.nationalarchives.gov.uk*

1b. County and other area record offices

Barnsley Archive and Local Studies Department
Central Library, Shambles Street, Barnsley S70 2JF
Tel: +44 (0) 1226 773950
E-mail: Archives@barnsley.gov.uk
Website: *www.barnsley.gov.uk/service/libraries/archives.asp*

Bath and North East Somerset Record Office
Guildhall, Bath BA1 5AW
Tel: +44 (0) 1225 477421
E-mail: archives@bathnes.gov.uk
Website: *www.batharchives.co.uk*

Bedfordshire and Luton Archives and Records Service
County Hall, Cauldwell Street, Bedford MK42 9AP
Tel: +44 (0) 1234 228833/22
E-mail: archive@bedscc.gov.uk
Website: *www.bedfordshire.gov.uk/archive*

Berkshire Record Office
9 Coley Avenue, Reading RG1 6AF
Tel: +44 (0) 118 901 5132
E-mail: ARCH@Reading.gov.uk
Website: *www.berkshirerecordoffice.org.uk*

Berwick-upon-Tweed Record Office
Borough Council House, Wallace Green, Berwick-upon-Tweed
TD15 1ED
Tel: +44 (0) 1289 301865
E-mail: lb@berwick-upon-tweed.gov.uk
Website: *www.swinhope.myby.co.uk/NRO/index.html*

Birmingham City Archives
Central Library, Chamberlain Square, Birmingham B3 3HQ
Tel: +44 (0) 121 303 4217
E-mail: archives@birmingham.gov.uk
Website: *www.birmingham.gov.uk/archives*

Bolton Archive and Local Studies Service
Central Library, Civic Centre, Le Mans Crescent, Bolton BL1 1SE
Tel: +44 (0) 1204 332185
E-mail: archives.library@bolton.gov.uk
Website: *www.bolton.gov.uk/portal/page?_pageid=59,37953&_dad=portal92&_schema=PORTAL92*

Bristol Record Office
'B' Bond Warehouse, Smeaton Road, Bristol BS1 6XN
Tel: +44 (0) 117 922 4224
E-mail: bro@bristol-city.gov.uk
Website: *www.bristol-city.gov.uk/recordoffice*

Buckinghamshire Studies, Centre for
County Hall, Walton Street, Aylesbury HP20 1UU
Tel: +44 (0) 1296 382587
E-mail: archives@buckscc.gov.uk
Website: *www.buckscc.gov.uk/archives*

Bury Archives Service
Moss Street, Bury BL9 0DG
Tel: +44 (0) 161 253 6782
E-mail: archives@bury.gov.uk
Website: *www.bury.gov.uk/archives*

Cambridgeshire County Record Office, Cambridge
Shire Hall, Castle Hill, Cambridge CB3 0AP
Tel: +44 (0) 1223 717281
E-mail: county.records.cambridge@cambridgeshire.gov.uk
Website: *www.cambridgeshire.gov.uk/archives*

Cambridgeshire County Record Office, Huntingdon
Grammar School Walk, Huntingdon PE29 3LF
Tel: +44 (0) 1480 375842
E-mail: county.records.hunts@cambridgeshire.gov.uk
Website: *www.cambridgeshire.gov.uk/archives*

Cheshire and Chester Archives and Local Studies
Duke Street, Chester CH1 1RL
Tel: +44 (0) 1244 602574
E-mail: recordoffice@cheshire.gov.uk
Website: *www.cheshire.gov.uk/recoff/home.htm*

Cornwall Record Office
Old County Hall, Truro TR1 3AY
Tel: +44 (0) 1872 323127
E-mail: CRO@cornwall.gov.uk
Website: *www.cornwall.gov.uk/index.cfm?articleid=307*

Coventry Archives
John Sinclair House, Canal Basin, Coventry CV1 4LY
Tel: +44 (0) 24 7678 5164
E-mail: archives@coventry.gov.uk
Website: *www.coventry.gov.uk/ccm/content/city-development
directorate/culture-%26-leisure/history-heritage/archives-and-
local-history.en*

Cumbria Record Office, Carlisle Headquarters
The Castle, Carlisle CA3 8UR
Tel: +44 (0) 1228 607285
E-mail: carlisle.record.office@cumbriacc.gov.uk
Website: *www.cumbria.gov.uk/archives*

Cumbria Record Office and Local Studies Library, Barrow
140 Duke Street, Barrow-in-Furness LA14 1XW
Tel: +44 (0) 1229 894363
E-mail: barrow.record.office@cumbriacc.gov.uk
Website: *www.cumbria.gov.uk/archives*

Cumbria Record Office, Kendal
County Offices, Kendal LA9 4RQ
Tel: +44 (0) 1539 773540
E-mail: kendal.record.office@cumbriacc.gov.uk
Website: *www.cumbria.gov.uk/archives*

Cumbria Record Office and Local Studies Library, Whitehaven
Scotch Street, Whitehaven CA28 7NL
Tel: +44 (0) 1946 852920
E-mail: whitehaven.record.office@cumbriacc.gov.uk
Website: *www.cumbria.gov.uk/archives*

Derbyshire Record Office
New Street, Matlock DE4 3AG
(Postal address) County Hall, Matlock DE4 3AG
Tel: +44 (0) 1629 580000
E-mail: record.office@derbyshire.gov.uk
Website: *www.derbyshire.gov.uk/recordoffice*

Devon Record Office
Great Moor House, Bittern Road, Sowton, Exeter EX2 7NL
Tel: +44 (0) 1392 384253
E-mail: devrec@devon.gov.uk
Website: *www.devon.gov.uk/record_office.htm*

Doncaster Archives Department
King Edward Road, Balby, Doncaster DN4 0NA
Tel: +44 (0) 1302 859811
E-mail: doncaster.archives@doncaster.gov.uk
Website: *www.doncaster.gov.uk*

Dorset History Centre
Bridport Road, Dorchester DT1 1RP
Tel: +44 (0) 1305 250550
E-mail: archives@dorsetcc.gov.uk
Website: *www.dorsetforyou.com/archives*

Dudley Archives and Local History Service
Mount Pleasant Street, Coseley, Dudley WV14 9JR
Tel: +44 (0) 1384 812770
E-mail: archives.centre@dudley.gov.uk
Website: *www.dudley.gov.uk/index.asp?pgid=9144*

Durham County Record Office
County Hall, Durham DH1 5UL
Tel: +44 (0) 191 383 3253/3
E-mail: record.office@durham.gov.uk
Website: *www.durham.gov.uk/recordoffice*

East Riding of Yorkshire Archives Service
The Chapel, Lord Roberts Road, Beverley
(Postal address) County Hall, Beverley, North Humberside
HU17 9BA
Tel: +44 (0) 1482 392790
E-mail: archives.service@eastriding.gov.uk
Website: *www.eastriding.gov.uk/libraries/archives/archives.html*

East Sussex Record Office
The Maltings, Castle Precincts, Lewes, East Sussex BN7 1YT
Tel: +44 (0) 1273 482349
E-mail: archives@eastsussex.gov.uk
Website: *www.eastsussex.gov.uk/useourarchives*

Essex Record Office
Wharf Road, Chelmsford CM2 6YT
Tel: +44 (0) 1245 244644
E-mail: ero.enquiry@essexcc.gov.uk
Website: *www.essexcc.gov.uk/ero*

Essex Record Office, Colchester and North-East Essex Branch
Stanwell House, Stanwell Street, Colchester CO2 7DL
Tel: +44 (0) 1206 572099
E-mail: ero.enquiry@essexcc.gov.uk
Website: *www.essexcc.gov.uk/ero*

Gloucestershire Archives
Clarence Row, Alvin Street, Gloucester GL1 3DW
Tel: +44 (0) 1452 425295
E-mail: archives@gloucestershire.gov.uk
Website: *www.gloucestershire.gov.uk/archives*

Greater Manchester County Record Office
56 Marshall Street, New Cross, Manchester M4 5FU
Tel: +44 (0) 161 832 5284
E-mail: archives@gmcro.co.uk
Website: *www.gmcro.co.uk*

Guildhall Library
Aldermanbury, London EC2P 2EJ
Tel: +44 (0) 20 7332 1862 and 1863
E-mail: manuscripts.guildhall@cityoflondon.gov.uk
Website: *www.cityoflondon.gov.uk/Corporation/leisure_heritage/
libraries_archives_museums_galleries/city_london_libraries/
guildhall_lib.htm*

Hampshire Record Office
Sussex Street, Winchester SO23 8TH
Tel: +44 (0) 1962 846154
E-mail: enquiries.archives@hants.gov.uk
Website: *www.hants.gov.uk/record-office/index.html*

Herefordshire Record Office
The Old Barracks, Harold Street, Hereford HR1 2QX
Tel: +44 (0) 1432 260750
E-mail: archives@herefordshire.gov.uk
Website: *www.herefordshire.gov.uk/archives*

Hertfordshire Archives and Local Studies
County Hall, Hertford SG13 8EJ
Tel: +44 (0) 1438 737333
E-mail: hertsdirect@hertscc.gov.uk
Website: *www.hertsdirect.org/heritage*

Hull City Archives
79 Lowgate, Hull HU1 1HN
Tel: +44 (0) 1482 615102
E-mail: City.Archives@hullcc.gov.uk
Website: *www.hullcc.gov.uk*

Isle of Wight Record Office
26 Hillside, Newport PO30 2EB
Tel: +44 (0) 1983 823820/1
E-mail: record.office@iow.gov.uk
Website: *www.iwight.com/library/record_office/default.asp*

Kentish Studies, Centre for
County Hall, Maidstone ME14 1XQ
Tel: +44 (0) 1622 694363
E-mail: archives@kent.gov.uk
Website: *www.kent.gov.uk/leisure-and-culture/archives-and-local-history/archive-centres/centre-for-kentish-studies.htm*

Lancashire Record Office
Bow Lane, Preston PR1 2RE
Tel: +44 (0) 1772 533039
E-mail: record.office@ed.lancscc.gov.uk
Website: *www.archives.lancashire.gov.uk*

Leicestershire, Leicester and Rutland, Record Office for
Long Street, Wigston Magna, Leicester LE18 2AH
Tel: +44 (0) 116 257 1080
E-mail: recordoffice@leics.gov.uk
Website: *www.leics.gov.uk/index/community/museums/record_office.htm*

Lincolnshire Archives
St Rumbold Street, Lincoln LN2 5AB
Tel: +44 (0) 1522 526204 or 01522 782040
E-mail: lincolnshire_archive@lincolnshire.gov.uk
Website: *www.lincolnshire.gov.uk/archives*

London Metropolitan Archives
Address: 40 Northampton Road, London ECIR OHB
Tel: +44 (0) 20 7332 3820
E-mail: ask.lma@cityoflondon.gov.uk
Website: *www.cityoflondon.gov.uk/Corporation/leisure_heritage/
libraries_archives_museums_galleries/lma*

Manchester Archives and Local Studies
Central Library, St Peter's Square, Manchester M2 5PD
Tel: +44 (0) 161 234 1980
E-mail: archiveslocalstudies@manchester.gov.uk
Website: *www.manchester.gov.uk/libraries/arls/index.htm*

Merseyside Record Office
Central Library, William Brown Street, Liverpool L3 8EW
Tel: +44 (0) 151 233 5817
E-mail: recoffice.central.library@liverpool.gov.uk
Website: *www.liverpool.gov.uk*

Norfolk Record Office
The Archive Centre, Martineau Lane, Norwich NRI 2DQ
Tel: +44 (0) 1603 222599
E-mail: norfrec@norfolk.gov.uk
Website: *http://archives.norfolk.gov.uk*

North Devon Library and Record Office
Tuly Street, Barnstaple EX31 1EL
Tel: +44 (0) 1271 388607
E-mail: ndevrec@devon.gov.uk
Website: *www.devon.gov.uk/index/democracycommunities/
neighbourhoods-villages/record_office/north_record_office.htm*

North East Lincolnshire Archives
Town Hall, Town Hall Square, Grimsby DN31 1HX
Tel: +44 (0) 1472 323585
E-mail: John.Wilson@nelincs.gov.uk
Website: *www.nelincs.gov.uk/Leisure/Archives*

North Yorkshire County Record Office
Malpas Road, Northallerton DL7 8TB
Tel: +44 (0) 1609 777585
E-mail: archives@northyorks.gov.uk
Website: *www.northyorks.gov.uk/archives*

Northamptonshire Record Office
Wootton Hall Park, Northampton NN4 8BQ
Tel: +44 (0) 1604 762129
E-mail: archivist@northamptonshire.gov.uk
Website: *www.northamptonshire.gov.uk/Community/record/about_us.htm*

Northumberland Record Office
Melton Park, North Gosforth, Newcastle-upon-Tyne NE3 5QX
Tel: +44 (0) 191 236 2680
E-mail: libraries@northumberland.gov.uk
Website: *http://pscm.northumberland.gov.uk/portal/page?_pageid=106,54411&_dad=portal92&_schema=PORTAL92&pid=448*

Northumberland Record Office, Morpeth
The Kylins, Loansdean, Morpeth NE61 2EQ
Tel: +44 (0) 1670 504084
E-mail: libraries@northumberland.gov.uk
Website: *http://pscm.northumberland.gov.uk/portal/page?_pageid=106,54411&_dad=portal92&_schema=PORTAL92&pid=448*

Nottinghamshire Archives
County House, Castle Meadow Road, Nottingham NG2 1AG
Tel: +44 (0) 115 958 1634
Email: archives@nottscc.gov.uk
Website: *www.nottinghamshire.gov.uk/archives*

Oldham Local Studies and Archives
84 Union Street, Oldham OL1 1DN
Tel: +44 (0) 161 911 4654
E-mail: archives@oldham.gov.uk
Website: *www.oldham.gov.uk/community/local_studies/index.shtml*

Oxfordshire Record Office
St Luke's Church, Temple Road, Cowley, Oxford OX4 2HT
Tel: +44 (0) 1865 398200
E-mail: archives@oxfordshire.gov.uk
Website: *www.oxfordshire.gov.uk/records*

Plymouth and West Devon Record Office
Unit 3, Clare Place, Plymouth PL4 0JW
Tel: +44 (0) 1752 305940
E-mail: pwdro@plymouth.gov.uk
Website: *www.plymouth.gov.uk/archives*

Rotherham Archives and Local Studies
Central Library, Walker Place, Rotherham S65 1JH
Tel: +44 (0) 1709 823 616
E-mail: archives@rotherham.gov.uk
Website: *www.rotherham.gov.uk*

St Helens Local History and Archives Library
Central Library, Gamble Institute, Victoria Square, St Helens
WA10 1DY
Tel: +44 (0) 1744 456952
E-mail: localhistory@sthelens.gov.uk
Website: *www.sthelens.gov.uk*

Sheffield Archives
52 Shoreham Street, Sheffield S1 4SP
Tel: +44 (0) 114 203 9395
E-mail: archives@sheffield.gov.uk
Website: *www.sheffield.gov.uk/in-your-area/libraries/find/archives/sheffield-archives*

Shropshire Archives
Castle Gates, Shrewsbury SY1 2AQ
Tel: +44 (0) 1743 255350
E-mail: archives@shropshire-cc.gov.uk
Website: *www.shropshirearchives.co.uk*

Somerset Archive and Record Service
Obridge Road, Taunton TA2 7PU
Tel: +44 (0) 1823 337600
E-mail: Archives@somerset.gov.uk
Website: *www.somerset.gov.uk/archives*

Staffordshire and Stoke-on-Trent Archive Service: Staffordshire County Record Office
Eastgate Street, Stafford ST16 2LZ
Tel: +44 (0) 1785 278379
E-mail: staffordshire.record.office@staffordshire.gov.uk
Website: *www.staffordshire.gov.uk/archives*

Staffordshire and Stoke-on-Trent Archive Service: Lichfield Record Office
Lichfield Library, The Friary, Lichfield WS13 6QG
Tel: +44 (0) 1543 510720
E-mail: lichfield.record.office@staffordshire.gov.uk
Website: *www.staffordshire.gov.uk/archives*

Stockport Archive Service
Central Library, Wellington Road South, Stockport SK1 3RS
Tel: +44 (0) 161 474 4530
E-mail: localheritagelibrary@stockport.gov.uk
Website: *www.stockport.gov.uk/content/leisureculture/libraries/localheritagelibrary*

Suffolk Record Office, Bury St Edmunds Branch
Raingate Street, Bury St Edmunds IP33 2AR
Tel: +44 (0) 1284 352352
E-mail: bury.ro@libher.suffolkcc.gov.uk
Website: *www.suffolkcc.gov.uk/sro*

Suffolk Record Office, Ipswich Branch
Gatacre Road, Ipswich IP1 2LQ
Tel: +44 (0) 1473 584541
E-mail: ipswich.ro@libher.suffolkcc.gov.uk
Website: *www.suffolkcc.gov.uk/sro*

Suffolk Record Office, Lowestoft Branch
Central Library, Clapham Road, Lowestoft NR32 1DR
Tel: +44 (0) 1502 405357
E-mail: lowestoft.ro@libher.suffolkcc.gov.uk
Website: *www.suffolkcc.gov.uk/sro*

Surrey History Centre
130 Goldsworth Road, Woking GU21 6ND
Tel: +44 (0) 1483 518 737
E-mail: shs@surreycc.gov.uk
Website: *www.surreycc.gov.uk/surreyhistoryservice*

Teesside Archives
Exchange House, 6 Marton Road, Middlesborough, Cleveland
TS1 1DB
Tel: +44 (0) 1642 248321
E-mail: teessidearchives@middlesbrough.gov.uk
Website: *www.middlesbrough.gov.uk/ccm/navigation/leisure-and-culture/libraries/archives*

Tyne and Wear Archives Service
Blandford House, Blandford Square, Newcastle-upon-Tyne
NE1 4JA
Tel: +44 (0) 191 232 6789
E-mail: twas@gateshead.gov.uk
Website: *www.tyneandweararchives.org.uk*

Walsall Local History Centre
Essex Street, Walsall WS2 7AS
Tel: +44 (0) 1922 721305/6
E-mail: localhistorycentre@walsall.gov.uk
Website: *www.walsall.gov.uk/localhistorycentre*

Warwickshire County Record Office
Priory Park, Cape Road, Warwick CV34 4JS
Tel: +44 (0) 1926 738959
E-mail: recordoffice@warwickshire.gov.uk
Website: *www.warwickshire.gov.uk/countyrecordoffice*

West Sussex Record Office
Sherburne House, 3 Orchard Street, Chichester
(Postal address) County Hall, Chichester PO19 1RN
Tel: +44 (0) 1243 753600
E-mail: records.office@westsussex.gov.uk
Website: *www.westsussex.gov.uk/ccm/navigation/libraries-and-archives*

West Yorkshire Archive Service, Wakefield Headquarters
Newstead Road, Wakefield WF1 2DE
Tel: +44 (0) 1924 305980
E-mail: wakefield@wyjs.org.uk
Website: *www.archives.wyjs.org.uk*

West Yorkshire Archive Service, Bradford
15 Canal Road, Bradford BD14AT
Tel: +44 (0) 1274 731931
E-mail: bradford@wyjs.org.uk
Website: *www.archives.wyjs.org.uk*

West Yorkshire Archive Service, Calderdale
Central Library, Northgate House, Northgate, Halifax HX1 1UN
Tel: +44 (0) 1422 392636
E-mail: calderdale@wyjs.org.uk
Website: *www.archives.wyjs.org.uk*

West Yorkshire Archive Service, Kirklees
Huddersfield Central Library, Princess Alexandra Walk,
Huddersfield HD1 2SU
Tel: +44 (0) 1484 221966
E-mail: kirklees@wyjs.org.uk
Website: *www.archives.wyjs.org.uk*

West Yorkshire Archive Service, Leeds
Chapeltown Road, Sheepscar, Leeds LS7 3AP
Tel: +44 (0) 113 214 5814
E-mail: leeds@wyjs.org.uk
Website: *www.archives.wyjs.org.uk*

Wigan Archives Service
Town Hall, Market Square, Leigh WN7 2DY
Tel: +44 (0) 1942 404431
E-mail: heritage@wlct.gov.uk
Website: *www.wlct.org/Culture/Heritage/archives.htm*

Wiltshire and Swindon Record Office
Libraries and Heritage HQ, Wiltshire County Council, Bythesea
Road, Trowbridge BA14 8BS
Tel: +44 (0) 1225 713709
E-mail: wsro@wiltshire.gov.uk
Website: *www.wiltshire.gov.uk/leisure-and-culture/access-to-records/
wiltshire-and-swindon-record-office.htm*

Wirral Archives
Wirral Museum, Town Hall, Hamilton Street,
Birkenhead CH41 5BR
Tel: +44 (0) 151 666 3903
E-mail: archives@wirral-libraries.net
Website: *www.wirral-libraries.net/archives*

Wolverhampton Archives and Local Studies
42–50 Snow Hill, Wolverhampton WV2 4AG
Tel: +44 (0) 1902 552480
E-mail: wolverhamptonarchives@dial.pipex.com
Website: *www.wolverhampton.gov.uk/archives*

Worcestershire Record Office, City Centre Branch
Worcestershire Library and History Centre, Trinity Street,
Worcester WR1 2PW
Tel: +44 (0) 1905 765922
E-mail: WLHC@worcestershire.gov.uk
Website: *www.worcestershire.gov.uk/records*

Worcestershire Record Office, County Hall Branch
County Hall, Spetchley Road, Worcester WR5 2NP
Tel: +44 (0) 1905 766351
E-mail: RecordOffice@worcestershire.gov.uk
Website: *www.worcestershire.gov.uk/records*

York City Archives Department
Art Gallery Building, Exhibition Square, York YO1 7EW
Tel: +44 (0) 1904 551878/9
E-mail: archives@york.gov.uk
Website: *www.york.gov.uk/libraries/archives/index.html*

2. Scotland

2a. *National record offices*

General Register Office for Scotland (GROS)
New Register House, 3 West Register Street, Edinburgh EH1 3YT
Tel: +44 (0) 131 334 0380
No general e-mail address
Website: *www.gro-scotland.gov.uk*

National Archives of Scotland (NAS)
HM General Register House, 2 Princes Street, Edinburgh
EH1 3YY
Tel: +44 (0) 131 535 1314
E-mail: enquiries@nas.gov.uk
Website: *www.nas.gov.uk*

National Library of Scotland (NLS)
George IV Bridge, Edinburgh EH1 1EW
Tel: +44 (0) 131 623 3700
E-mail: enquiries@nls.uk (for pre-order enquiries)
Website: *www.nls.uk*

2b. *Local archives*

Aberdeen City Archives
Old Aberdeen House, Dunbar Street, Aberdeen AB24 3UY
Tel: +44 (0) 1224 522513
E-mail: archives@aberdeencity.gov.uk
Website: *www.aberdeencity.gov.uk/archives*

Dumfries and Galloway Archives
Archive Centre, 33 Burns Street, Dumfries DG1 2PS
Tel: +44 (0) 1387 269254
E-mail: Libs&I@dumgal.gov.uk
Website: *http://www.dumgal.gov.uk/lia*

Dundee City Archives
1 Shore Terrace, Dundee DD1 3AH
Postal address: Support Services Department, 21 City Square,
Dundee DD1 3BY
Tel: +44 (0) 1382 434494
E-mail: archives@dundeecity.gov.uk
Website: *www.dundeecity.gov.uk/archives*

Edinburgh City Archives
Department of Corporate Services, City of Edinburgh
Council, City Chambers, High Street, Edinburgh EH1 1YJ
Tel: +44 (0) 131 529 4616
No e-mail address (use online form)
Website: *www.edinburgh.gov.uk/CEC/Corporate_Services/
Corporate_Communications/archivist/Edinburgh_City_
Archives.html*

Glasgow City Archives
Mitchell Library, 210 North Street, Glasgow G3 7DN
Tel: +44 (0) 141 287 2910
E-mail: archives@cls.glasgow.gov.uk
Website: *www.glasgowlibraries.org*

Highland Council Archives
Inverness Library, Farraline Park, Inverness IV1 1NH
Tel: +44 (0) 1463 220330
E-mail: archives@highland.gov.uk
Website: *www.highland.gov.uk/leisure/archives*

Orkney Library and Archive
44 Junction Road, Kirkwall KW15 1AG
Tel: +44 (0) 1856 873166
E-mail: archives@orkneylibrary.org.uk
Website: *www.orkneylibrary.org.uk/html/archive.htm*

Perth and Kinross Council Archive
AK Bell Library, 2–8 York Place, Perth PH2 8EP
Tel: +44 (0) 1738 477012
E-mail: archives@pkc.gov.uk
Website: *www.pkc.gov.uk/archives*

Scottish Borders Archive and Local History Centre
Heritage Hub, Hawick TD9 0AE
Tel: +44 (0) 1450 360 699
E-mail: archives@scotborders.gov.uk
No website

Shetland Archives
44 King Harald Street, Lerwick ZE1 0EQ
Tel: +44 (0) 1595 696247
E-mail: brian.smith@sic.shetland.gov.uk
Website: *www.shetland.gov.uk/archives*

3. Wales

3a. National record office

National Library of Wales (NLW)
Aberystwyth, Ceredigion SY23 3BU
Tel: +44 (0) 1970 632 800
E-mail: holi@llgc.org.uk (Head of Reader Services)
Website: *www.llgc.org.uk*

3b. County record offices

Anglesey County Record Office
Shire Hall, Glanhwfa Road, Llangefni, Gwynedd LL77 7TW
Tel: +44 (0) 1248 752080
E-mail: archives@anglesey.gov.uk
Website: *www.anglesey.gov.uk/doc.asp?cat=2667*

Carmarthenshire Archive Service
Parc Myrddin, Richmond Terrace, Carmarthen SA31 1DS
Tel: +44 (0) 1267 228232
E-mail: archives@carmarthenshire.gov.uk
Website: *www.carmarthenshire.gov.uk*

Ceredigion Archives
Swyddfa'r Sir, Marine Terrace, Aberystwyth SY23 2DE
Tel: +44 (0) 1970 633697/8
E-mail: archives@ceredigion.gov.uk
Website: *http://ceredigion-archives.org.uk*

Conwy Archive Service
Old Board School, Lloyd Street, Llandudno LL30 2YG
Tel: +44 (0) 1492 860882
E-mail: archifau.archives@conwy.gov.uk
Website: *www.conwy.gov.uk/archives*

Denbighshire Record Office
46 Clwyd Street, Ruthin, Clwyd LL15 1HP
Tel: +44 (0) 1824 708250
E-mail: archives@denbighshire.gov.uk
Website: *www.denbighshire.gov.uk*

Flintshire Record Office
The Old Rectory, Hawarden, Deeside CH5 3NR
Tel: +44 (0) 1244 532364
E-mail: archives@flintshire.gov.uk
Website: *www.flintshire.gov.uk/archives*

Glamorgan Record Office
Glamorgan Building, King Edward VII Avenue, Cathays Park,
Cardiff CF10 3NE
Tel: +44 (0) 29 2078 0282
E-mail: glamro@cardiff.ac.uk
Website: *www.glamro.gov.uk*

Gwent Record Office
County Hall, Cwmbran NP44 2XH
Tel: +44 (0) 1633 644886
E-mail: gwent.records@torfaen.gov.uk
Website: *www.llgc.org.uk/cac/cac0004.htm*

Gwynedd Archives, Caernarfon Record Office
Victoria Dock, Caernarfon LL55 1SH
Postal address: County Offices, Shirehall Street, Caernarfon,
Gwynedd LL55 1SH
Tel: +44 (0) 1286 679095
E-mail: archives@gwynedd.gov.uk
Website: *www.gwynedd.gov.uk/archives*

Gwynedd Archives, Meirionnydd Record Office
Ffordd y Bala, Dolgellau, Gwynedd LL40 2YF
Tel: +44 (0) 1341 424682
E-mail: archives.dolgellau@gwynedd.gov.uk
Website: *www.gwynedd.gov.uk/archives*

Pembrokeshire Record Office
The Castle, Haverfordwest SA61 2EF
Tel: +44 (0) 1437 763707
E-mail: Claire.Orr@Pembrokeshire.gov.uk
Website: *www.llgc.org.uk/cac/cac0002.htm*

Powys County Archives Office
County Hall, Llandrindod Wells LD1 5LG
Tel: +44 (0) 1597 826088
E-mail: archives@powys.gov.uk
Website: *http://archives.powys.gov.uk*

West Glamorgan Archive Service
County Hall, Oystermouth Road, Swansea SA1 3SN
Tel: +44 (0) 1792 636589
E-mail: westglam.archives@swansea.gov.uk
Website: *http://www.swansea.gov.uk/westglamorganarchives*

Wrexham Archives and Local Studies Service
A. N. Palmer Centre, County Buildings, Regent Street,
Wrexham LL11 1RB
Tel: +44 (0) 1978 317973
E-mail: archives@wrexham.gov.uk
Website: *http://www.wrexham.gov.uk/archives*

4. Northern Ireland

General Register Office (Northern Ireland) (GRONI)
Oxford House, 49–55 Chichester Street, Belfast BT1 4HL
Tel: +44 (0) 28 9025 2000
E-mail: gro.nisra@dfpni.gov.uk
Wesbite: *www.groni.gov.uk*

Public Record Office of Northern Ireland (PRONI)
66 Balmoral Avenue, Belfast BT9 6NY
Tel: +44 (0) 28 9025 5905
E-mail: proni@dcalni.gov.uk
Website: *www.proni.gov.uk*

5. Republic of Ireland

General Register Office (Ireland) (GROI)
Government Offices, Convent Road, Roscommon (headquarters)
and Joyce House, 8–11 Lombard Street East, Dublin (research
room)
Tel: +353 (0) 90 663 2900
No e-mail address (use online form)
Website: *www.groireland.ie*

National Archives of Ireland (NAI)
Bishop Street, Dublin 8
Tel: +353 (0) 1 407 2303
E-mail: mail@nationalarchives.ie
Website: *www.nationalarchives.ie*

National Library of Ireland (NLI)
Kildare Street, Dublin 2
Tel: +353 (0) 1 603 0200
E-mail: info@nli.ie
Website: *www.nli.ie*

Representative Church Body Library (RCBL)
Braemor Park, Churchtown, Dublin 14
Tel: +353 (0) 1 492 3979
E-mail: library@ireland.anglican.org
Website: *www.ireland.anglican.org*

Valuation Office (VO)
Irish Life Centre, Abbey Street Lower, Dublin 1
Tel: +353 (0) 1 817 1000
E-mail: info@valoff.ie
Website: *www.valoff.ie*

6. Isle of Man

General Registry
The Registries Building, Deemster's Walk, Bucks Road, Douglas
IM1 3AR
Tel: +44 (0) 1624 687039
E-mail: civil@registry.gov.im
Website: *www.gov.im/registries*

Manx National Heritage Library
Douglas IM1 3LY
Tel: +44 (0) 1624 648000
E-mail: enquiries@mnh.gov.im
Website: *www.gov.im/mnh*

7. Jersey

Jersey Archive
Clarence Road, St Helier JE2 4JY
Tel: +44 (0) 1534 833300
E-mail: archives@jerseyheritagetrust.org
Website: *www.jerseyheritagetrust.org/sites/archive/archive.html*

Office of the Superintendent Registrar
10 Royal Square, St Helier JE2 4WA
Tel: +44 (0) 1534 441335
No e-mail address (use online form)
Website: *www.gov.je/HomeAffairs/Registrar*

Société Jersiaise
7 Pier Road, St Helier JE2 4XW
Tel: +44 (0) 1534 758314
E-mail: societe@societe-jersiaise.org
Website: *www.societe-jersiaise.org*

8. Guernsey

The Greffe
Royal Court House, St Peter Port GY1 2PB
Tel: +44 (0) 1481 725277
E-mail: hm_greffier@court1.guernsey.gov.uk
No website

Priaulx Library
Candie Road, St Peter Port GY1 1UG
Tel: +44 (0) 1481 721998
E-mail: priaulx.library@gov.gg
Website: *www.priaulx.gov.gg*

F. Addresses of LDS Family History Centres in Britain and Ireland

The LDS Church stresses that because of their limited numbers, its Family History Centre staff are unable to deal with postal enquiries, therefore postcodes are not given for the addresses. Because the centres are not open all day or every day, you need to phone to check their opening hours.

1. England

Aldershot
St Georges Road, Aldershot, Hampshire
Tel: +44 (0) 1252 321460

Ashton
Patterdale Road, Crowhill Estate, Ashton-under-Lyne, Lancashire
Tel: +44 (0) 161 330 3453

Barrow
Abbey Road, Barrow-in-Furness, Cumbria
Tel: +44 (0) 1229 820050

Billingham
The Linkway, Billingham, Stockton-on-Tees
Tel: +44 (0) 1642 563162

Blackpool
Warren Drive, Cleveleys, Blackpool, Lancashire
Tel: +44 (0) 1253 858218

Boston
Woodthorpe Avenue, Fishtoft, Boston, Lincolnshire
Tel: +44 (0) 1522 680117

Bristol
721 Wells Road, Whitchurch, Bristol
Tel: +44 (0) 1275 838326

Cambridge
670 Cherry Hinton Road, Cambridge
Tel: +44 (0) 1223 247010

Canterbury
Forty Acres Road, Canterbury, Kent
Tel: +44 (0) 1227 765431

Carlisle
Langrigg Road, Morton Park, Carlisle, Cumbria
Tel: +44 (0) 1228 526767

Cheltenham
Thirlestaine Road, Cheltenham, Gloucestershire
Tel: +44 (0) 1242 523433

Chester
St David's Park, Ewloe, Flintshire
Tel: +44 (0) 1244 530710

Coventry
Riverside Close, Whitley, Coventry
Tel: +44 (0) 24 7630 3316

Crawley
Old Horsham Road, Crawley, West Sussex
Tel: +44 (0) 1293 516151

Dereham
Yaxham Road, East Dereham, Norfolk
Tel: +44 (0) 1362 851500

Exeter
Wonford Road, Off Barrack Road, Exeter, Devon
Tel: +44 (0) 1392 250723

Forest of Dean
Wynols Hill, Queensway, Coleford, Gloucestershire
Tel: +44 (0) 1594 832904

Gillingham
2 Twydall Lane, Gillingham, Kent
Tel: +44 (0) 1634 388900

Grimsby
Linwood Avenue, Waltham Road, Grimsby, Lincolnshire
Tel: +44 (0) 1472 828876

Harborne
38–42 Lordswood Road, Harborne, Birmingham
Tel: +44 (0) 121 427 6858

Hastings
2 Ledsham Avenue, St Leonards-on-Sea, East Sussex
Tel: +44 (0) 1424 754563

Helston
Clodgey Lane, Helston, Cornwall
Tel: +44 (0) 1326 564503

High Wycombe
743 London Road, High Wycombe, Buckinghamshire
Tel: +44 (0) 1494 459979

Huddersfield
12 Halifax Road, Birchencliffe, Huddersfield, Kirklees
Tel: +44 (0) 1484 454573

Hull
727 Holderness Road, Kingston-upon-Hull
Tel: +44 (0) 1482 701439

Ipswich
42 Sidegate Lane West, Ipswich, Suffolk
Tel: +44 (0) 1473 723182

King's Lynn
Reffley Lane, King's Lynn, Norfolk
Tel: +44 (0) 1553 670000

Lancaster
Overangle Road, Lancaster, Lancashire
Tel: +44 (0) 1524 33571

Leeds
Vesper Road, Hacksworth, Leeds
Tel: +44 (0) 113 258 5297

Leicester
Wakerley Road, Leicester
Tel: +44 (0) 116 249 0099

Lichfield
Purcell Avenue, Lichfield, Staffordshire
Tel: +44 (0) 1543 414843

Lincoln
Skellingthorpe Road, Lincoln
Tel: +44 (0) 1522 680117

Liverpool
4 Mill Bank, West Derby, Liverpool
Tel: +44 (0) 151 252 0614

London (Hyde Park)
64–68 Exhibition Road, London
Tel: +44 (0) 20 7589 8561

London (Wandsworth)
149 Nightingale Lane, Balham, London
Tel: +44 (0) 20 8675 4811

Lowestoft
165 Yarmouth Road, Lowestoft, Suffolk
Tel: +44 (0) 1502 573851

Macclesfield
Victoria Road, Macclesfield, Cheshire
Tel: +44 (0) 1625 427236

Maidstone
76B London Road, Maidstone, Kent
Tel: +44 (0) 1622 757811

Manchester
Altrincham Road, Wythenshawe, Manchester
Tel: +44 (0) 161 902 9279

Mansfield
Southridge Drive, Mansfield, Nottinghamshire
Tel: +44 (0) 1623 662333

Newcastle-under-Lyme
The Brampton, Newcastle-under-Lyme, Staffordshire
Tel: +44 (0) 1782 630178

Newport (Isle of Wight)
Chestnut Close, Shide Road, Newport
Tel: +44 (0) 1983 532833

Northampton
137 Harlestone Road, Northampton
Tel: +44 (0) 160 458 7630

Norwich
19 Greenways, Norwich, Norfolk
Tel: +44 (0) 1603 452440

Nottingham
Stanhome Square, West Bridgford, Nottingham
Tel: +44 (0) 115 923 3856

Orpington
Station Approach, Orpington, Kent
Tel: +44 (0) 1689 837342

Peterborough
Cottesmore Close, off Atherstone Avenue, Netherton Estate,
Peterborough
Tel: +44 (0) 1733 263374

Plymouth
Mannamead Road, Hartley, Plymouth, Devon
Tel: +44 (0) 1752 668666

Pontefract
Park Villas Drive, Pontefract, Wakefield
Tel: +44 (0) 1977 600308

Poole
8 Mount Road, Parkstone, Poole, Dorset
Tel: +44 (0) 1202 730646

Portsmouth
Kingston Crescent, Portsmouth, Hampshire
Tel: +44 (0) 23 9269 6243

Preston
Temple Way, Hartwood Green, Chorley, Lancashire
Tel: +44 (0) 1257 226145

Rawtenstall
Haslingden New Road, Rawtenstall, Lancashire
Tel: +44 (0) 1282 412748

Reading
280 The Meadway, Tilehurst, Reading, Berkshire
Tel: +44 (0) 118 941 0211

Redditch
321 Evesham Road, Crabbs Cross, Redditch, Worcestershire
Tel: +44 (0) 1527 401543

Romford (Hornchurch)
64 Butts Green Road, Hornchurch, Essex
Tel: +44 (0) 1708 620727

Scarborough
Stepney Road, Scarborough, North Yorkshire
Tel: +44 (0) 1723 507239

Sheffield
Wheel Lane, Grenoside, Sheffield
Tel: +44 (0) 114 245 3124

St Albans (Luton)
Cutenhoe Road, Luton, Bedfordshire
Tel: +44 (0) 1582 482234

St Austell
Kingfisher Drive, St Austell, Cornwall
Tel: +44 (0) 1726 69912

Staines
41 Kingston Road, Staines, Surrey
Tel: +44 (0) 1784 462627

Stevenage
Buckthorne Avenue, Stevenage, Hertfordshire
Tel: +44 (0) 1438 351553

Sunderland
Queen Alexandra Road, Sunderland
Tel: +44 (0) 191 528 5787

Sutton Coldfield
187 Penns Lane, Sutton Coldfield, Birmingham
Tel: +44 (0) 121 386 4902

Telford
72 Glebe Street, Wellington, Shropshire
Tel: +44 (0) 1952 257443

Thetford
Station Road, Thetford, Norfolk
Tel: +44 (0) 1842 755472

Trowbridge
Brook Road, Trowbridge, Wiltshire
Tel: +44 (0) 1225 777097

Watford
Hempstead Road, Watford, Hertfordshire
Tel: +44 (0) 1923 251471

Wednesfield
Linthouse Lane, Wednesfield, Wolverhampton
Tel: +44 (o) 1902 724097

Weymouth
396 Chickerell Road, Weymouth, Dorset
No telephone number

Worcester
Canada Way, Lower Wick, Worcester
Tel: +44 (o) 1905 420341

Worthing
Goring Street, Worthing, West Sussex
Tel: +44 (o) 1903 241829

Yate
Wellington Road, Yate, South Gloucestershire
Tel: +44 (o) 1454 323004

Yeovil
Lysander Road, Forest Hill, Somerset
Tel: +44 (o) 1935 426817

York
West Bank, Acomb, York
Tel: +44 (o) 1904 786784

2. Scotland

Aberdeen
North Anderson Drive, Aberdeen
Tel: +44 (o) 1224 692206

Alloa
Grange Road, Westend Park, Alloa, Clackmannanshire
Tel: +44 (o) 1259 211148

Ayr
Corner of Orchard Avenue and Mossgiel Road, Ayr
No telephone number

Dumfries
36 Edinburgh Road, Albanybank, Dumfries
Tel: +44 (0) 1387 254865

Dundee
Bingham Terrace, Dundee
Tel: +44 (0) 1382 451247

Edinburgh
30A Colinton Road, Edinburgh
Tel: +44 (0) 131 313 2762

Elgin
Pansport Road, Elgin, Moray
Tel: +44 (0) 1343 546429

Glasgow
35 Julian Avenue, Kelvinside, Glasgow
Tel: +44 (0) 141 357 1024

Invergordon
Kilmonivaig Seafield, Portmahomack, Highland
Tel: +44 (0) 1862 871631

Inverness
13 Ness Walk, Inverness, Highland
Tel: +44 (0) 1463 231220

Kirkcaldy
Winifred Crescent, Forth Park, Kirkcaldy, Fife
Tel: +44 (0) 1592 640041

Lerwick
44 Prince Alfred Street, Lerwick, Shetland
Tel: +44 (0) 1595 695732

Montrose
Coronation Way, Montrose, Angus
Tel: +44 (0) 1674 675 753

Paisley
Glenburn Road, Paisley, Renfrewshire
Tel: +44 (0) 141 884 2780

Stornoway
Newton Street, Stornoway, Isle of Lewis, Western Isles
Tel: +44 (0) 1851 870972

3. Wales

Cardiff
Heol-Y-Deri, Cardiff
Tel: +44 (0) 2920 625342

Cwmbran
The Highway, Croesceiliog, Cwmbran, Torfaen
Tel: +44 (0) 1633 483 856

Gaerwen
Holyhead Road, Gaerwen, Anglesey
Tel: +44 (0) 1248 421 894

Merthyr Tydfil
Nantygwenith Street, Merthyr Tydfil
Tel: +44 (0) 1685 722455

Newcastle Emlyn
Cardigan Road, Newcastle Emlyn, Ceredigion
Tel: +44 (0) 1239 711472

Rhyl
171 Vale Road, Rhyl, Denbighshire
Tel: +44 (0) 1745 331172

Swansea
Cockett Road, Cockett, Swansea
Tel: +44 (0) 1792 585792

4. Northern Ireland

Belfast
403 Holywood Road, Belfast
Tel: +44 (0) 28 9076 9839

Coleraine
8 Sandelfields, Knocklynn Road, Coleraine, County Londonderry
Tel: +44 (0) 28 7032 1214

Londonderry
Racecourse Road, Belmont Estate, Londonderry
Tel: +44 (0) 28 7135 0179

5. Republic of Ireland

Cork
Sarsfield Road, Wilton, Cork
Tel: +44 (0) 21 4897050

Dublin
Finglas Road, Glasnevin, Dublin
No telephone number

Limerick
Doradoyle Road, Limerick
Tel: +44 (0) 61 309 443

6. Isle of Man

Douglas
Woodside, Woodburn Road, Douglas
Tel: +44 (0) 1624 675834

G. Addresses of Irish Genealogical Research Centres

Antrim and **Down**
Balmoral Building, 12 College Square East, Belfast BT1 6DD, Northern Ireland
Tel: +44 (0) 28 9033 2288
E-mail: enquiry@uhf.org.uk
Website: *www.ancestryireland.com*

Armagh
Armagh Ancestry, 38A English Street, Armagh BT61 7BA, Northern Ireland
Tel: +44 (0) 28 3752 1802
E-mail: ancestry@armagh.gov.uk
Website: *www.visitarmagh.com*

Carlow
No centre

Cavan
Cavan Genealogy, 1st Floor, Johnston Central Library, Farnham Street, Cavan, Republic of Ireland
Tel: +353 (0) 49 4361094
E-mail: cavangenealogy@eircom.net
No website

Clare

Clare Heritage Centre, Genealogical Centre, Church Street,
Corofin, County Clare, Republic of Ireland
Tel: + 353 (0) 65 6837955
E-mail: clareheritage@eircom.net
Website: *www.clare.irish-roots.net*

Cork City

No centre

Cork North

Mallow Heritage Centre, 27–28 Bank Place, Mallow, County
Cork, Republic of Ireland
Tel: +353 (0) 22 50302
Contact: Martina Aherne
E-mail: mallowhc@eircom.net
No website

Derry/Londonderry

The Genealogy Centre, 10 Craft Village, Shipquay Street, Derry
BT48 6AR, Northern Ireland
Tel: +44 (0) 28 7126 9792
No e-mail (use online form)
Website: *www.irishgenealogy.ie/csi/derry/services/research_report/
research_report.cfm*

Donegal

Donegal Ancestry, The Quay, Ramelton, County Donegal,
Republic of Ireland
Tel: +353 (0) 74 9151266
Contact: Joan Patton
E-mail: info@donegalancestry.com
Website: *www.donegalancestry.com*

Down

See Antrim

Dublin North
Swords Historical Society Company, Carnegie Library,
North Street, Swords, County Dublin, Republic of Ireland
Tel: +353 (0) 1 8400080
Contact: Bernadette Marks
E-mail: swordsheritage@eircom.net
No website

Dublin South
Dun Laoghaire Heritage Society, Moran Park House, Dun
Laoghaire, County Dublin, Republic of Ireland
Tel: +353 (0) 1 2047264
Contact: Catherine Moran
E-mail: heritage@dlrcoco.ie
No website

Fermanagh and **Tyrone**
Irish World Family History Services, Family History Suite,
51 Dungannon Road, Coalisland BT71 4HP, County Tyrone,
Northern Ireland
Tel: +44 (0) 28 8774 6065
Contact: Willie O'Kane
E-mail: info@irish-world.com
Website: *www.irish-world.com*

Galway East
East Galway Family History Society, Woodford Heritage Centre,
Woodford, Loughrea, County Galway, Republic of Ireland
Tel: +353 (0) 90 9749309
Contact: Angela Canning
E-mail: galwayroots@eircom.net
Website: *www.galwayroots.com*

Galway West
Galway Family History Society West Ltd, St Joseph's Community
Centre, Shantalla, County Galway, Republic of Ireland
Tel: +353 (0) 91 860464
Contact: Mary Murray
E-mail: galwayfhswest@eircom.net
No website

Kerry
No centre

Kildare
Kildare History and Family Research Centre, Riverbank,
Main Street, Newbridge, County Kildare, Republic of Ireland
Tel: +353 (0) 45 433602
Contact: Karel Kiely
E-mail: kildaregenealogy@iol.ie
Website: *www.kildare.ie/genealogy* and *www.kildare.ie/heritage*

Kilkenny
Kilkenny Archaeological Society, Rothe House, Parliament Street,
Kilkenny, Republic of Ireland
Tel: +353 (0) 56 7722893
Contact: Mary Flood
E-mail: rothehouse@eircom.net
Website: *www.kilkennyarchaeologicalsociety.ie*

Laois (formerly **Queen's County**) and **Offaly** (formerly **King's
County**)
Laois and Offaly Family History Research Centre, Bury Quay,
Tullamore, County Offaly, Republic of Ireland
Tel: +353 (0) 506 21421
E-mail: ohas@iol.ie
Website: *www.irishmidlandsancestry.com*

Leitrim

Leitrim Genealogy Centre, Ballinamore, County Leitrim, Republic of Ireland
Tel: +353 (0) 71 9644012
Contact: Brid Sullivan
E-mail: leitrimgenealogy@eircom.net
Website: *http://homepage.eircom.net/~leitrimgenealogy*

Limerick

Limerick Genealogy, c/o Limerick County Library HQ, 58 O'Connell Street, Limerick, Republic of Ireland
Tel: +353 (0) 61 496542
E-mail: research@limerickgenealogy.com
Website: *www.limerickgenealogy.com*

Longford

Longford Genealogy, 1 Church Street, Longford, Republic of Ireland
Tel: +353 (0) 43 41235
E-mail: longroot@iol.ie
No website

Louth

Louth Co. Library, Roden Place, Dundalk, County Louth, Republic of Ireland
Tel: +353 (0) 42 9335457
E-mail: referencelibrary@louthcoco.ie
Website: *www.louthcoco.ie*

Mayo North

Mayo North Family History Research Centre, Enniscoe, Castlehill, Ballina, County Mayo, Republic of Ireland
Tel: +353 (0) 96 31809
Contact: Bridie Greavy
E-mail: normayo@iol.ie
Website: *www.irish-roots.net/mayo/Mayo.htm*

Mayo South
South Mayo Family Research, Main Street, Ballinrobe, County
Mayo, Republic of Ireland
Tel: +353 (0) 94 9541214
Contact: Gerard Delaney
E-mail: soumayo@iol.ie
Website: *www.irish-roots.net/mayo/Mayo.htm*

Meath
Meath Heritage and Genealogy Centre, Town Hall, Castle Street,
Trim, County Meath, Republic of Ireland
Tel: +353 (0) 46 9436633
Contact: Noel French
E-mail: meathhc@iol.ie
Website: *www.meathroots.com*

Monaghan
No centre

Offaly
See Laois

Roscommon
Roscommon Heritage and Genealogical Centre, Church Street,
Strokestown, County Roscommon, Republic of Ireland
Tel: +353 (0) 71 9633380
Contact: Mary Skelly
E-mail: info@roscommonroots.com
Website: *www.roscommonroots.com*

Sligo
County Sligo Heritage and Genealogy Society, Aras Reddan,
Temple Street, Sligo, Republic of Ireland
Tel: +353 (0) 71 9143728
Contact: Theresa Finnegan
E-mail: heritagesligo@tinet.ie
Website: *www.sligoroots.com*

Tipperary North
North Tipperary Genealogy and Heritage Services, The Governor's
House, Kickham Street, Nenagh, County Tipperary, Republic of
Ireland
Tel: +353 (0) 67 33850
Contact: Nora O'Meara
E-mail: tipperarynorthgenealogy@eircom.net
Website: *www.tipperarynorth.ie/genealogy*

Tipperary South
Bru Boru Heritage Centre, Rock of Cashel, Cashel, County
Tipperary, Republic of Ireland
Tel: +353 (0) 62 61122
Contact: Deirdre Walsh
E-mail: bruboru@comhaltas.com
Website: *www.comhaltas.com*

Tyrone
See Fermanagh

Waterford
Waterford Heritage Services, St Patrick's Church, Jenkin's Lane,
Waterford, Republic of Ireland
Tel: +353 (0) 51 876123
E-mail: mnoc@iol.ie
Website: *www.waterford-heritage.ie*

Westmeath
Dún na Sí Heritage Centre, Knockdomney, Moate, County
Westmeath, Republic of Ireland
Tel: +353 (0) 90 6481183
Contact: Teresa Finnerty
E-mail: dunnasimoate@eircom.net
No website

Wexford
Co. Wexford Heritage and Genealogy Society, Yola Farmstead,
Folk Park, Tagoat, Rosslare, County Wexford, Republic of Ireland
Tel: +353 (0) 53 32611
Contact: Pat Stafford
E-mail: wexgen@eircom.net
Website: *http://homepage.eircom.net/~yolawexford/genealogy.htm*

Wicklow
Wicklow Family History Centre, Wicklow's Historic Gaol,
Kilmantin Hill, Wicklow Town, Republic of Ireland
Tel: +353 (0) 404 20126
Contact: Catherine Wright
E-mail: wfh@eircom.net
Website: *www.wicklow.ie*

Select bibliography

British Family History

Adolph, Anthony, *Tracing Your Family History* (2nd edition, 2005), London: Collins.

Barratt, Nick, *The Family Detective* (2006), London: Ebury Press.

Blatchford, Robert (ed.), *The Family and Local History Handbook* (10th edition, 2006), York: Robert Blatchford Publishing.

Chapman, Colin R., *Pre-1841 Censuses & Population Listings in the British Isles* (5th edition, 1998), Dursley: Lochin.

Chater, Kathy, *How to Trace Your Family Tree in England, Ireland, Scotland and Wales* (2003), London: Hermes House.

Christian, Peter, *The Genealogist's Internet* (3rd edition, 2005), Richmond: The National Archives.

Currer-Briggs, Noel, *Worldwide Family History* (1982), London: Routledge & Kegan Paul.

Gibson, Jeremy and Mervyn Medlycott, *Local Census Listings 1522–1930: Holdings in the British Isles* (3rd edition with amendments, 2001), Bury: Federation of Family History Societies.

Hamilton-Edwards, Gerald, *In Search of Ancestry* (3rd edition, 1974), Chichester: Phillimore.

Herber, Mark, *Ancestral Trails* (2nd edition, 2004), Stroud: Sutton.

Hey, David, *Journeys in Family History* (2004), Richmond: The National Archives.

Humphery-Smith, Cecil (ed.), *The Phillimore Atlas & Index of Parish Registers* (3rd edition, 2003), Chichester: Phillimore.

Peacock, Caroline, *The Good Web Guide: Genealogy* (3rd edition, 2003), London: The Good Web Guide.

Steel, Don, *Discovering Your Family History* (2nd edition, 1986), London: British Broadcasting Corporation.

Thomas, Jenny (with Matthew L. Helm and April Leigh Helm), *Genealogy Online for Dummies* (2006), Chichester: John Wiley and Sons.

Scottish Family History

The Parishes, Registers and Registrars of Scotland (1993), Edinburgh: Scottish Association of Family History Societies.

Bigwood, Rosemary, *Tracing Scottish Ancestors* (2001), Glasgow: HarperCollins.

Cory, Kathleen B., *Tracing Your Scottish Ancestry* (3rd edition, 2004), Edinburgh: Polygon.

Holton, Graham S. and Jack Winch, *Discover Your Scottish Family History: Internet and Traditional Resources* (2003), Edinburgh: Edinburgh University Press.

Irvine, Sherry, *Scottish Ancestry* (2003), North Provo: MyFamily.com.

James, Alwyn, *Scottish Roots* (3rd edition, 2002), Edinburgh: Luath Press.

Jonas, Linda and Paul Milner, *A Genealogist's Guide to Discovering Your Scottish Ancestors* (2002), Cincinnati: Betterway Books.

Sinclair, Cecil, *Tracing Your Scottish Ancestors* (2003), Edinburgh: Mercat Press.

Steel, D. J., *Sources for Scottish Genealogy and Family History* (1970), London: Society of Genealogists (National Index of Parish Registers Volume XII).

Stewart, Alan, *Gathering the Clans: Tracing Scottish Ancestry on the Internet* (2004), Chichester: Phillimore.

Welsh Family History

Ifans, Dafydd, *Nonconformist Registers of Wales* (1994), Aberystwyth: National Library of Wales.

Rowlands, John and Sheila (eds.), *Welsh Family History: A Guide to Research* (2nd edition, 1998), Bury: Federation of Family History Societies.

Williams, C. J. and J. Watts-Williams (compilers), *Parish Registers of Wales* (2nd edition, 2000), Aberystwyth: National Library of Wales.

Irish Family History

Begley, Donal F., *The Ancestral Trail in Ireland: A Companion Guide* (1982), Dublin: Heraldic Artists.

— (ed.), *Irish Genealogy: A Record Finder* (1981), Dublin: Heraldic Artists.

Davis, Bill, *Irish Ancestry: A Beginner's Guide* (2001), Bury: Federation of Family History Societies.

Grenham, John, *Tracing Your Irish Ancestors* (3rd edition, 2006), Dublin: Gill & Macmillan.

Surnames

Adam, Frank, *The Clans, Septs and Regiments of the Scottish Highlands* (8th edition, 1970), Stirling: Johnston and Bacon.

Black, George F., *The Surnames of Scotland* (1996), Edinburgh: Birlinn.

Hanks, Patrick and Flavia Hodges, *A Dictionary of Surnames* (1988), Oxford: Oxford University Press.

Hey, David, *Family Names and Family History* (2000), London: Hambledon & London.

Innes of Learney, Sir Thomas, *The Tartans of the Clans and Families of Scotland* (7th edition, 1964), Edinburgh: Johnston and Bacon.

MacLysaght, Edward, *The Surnames of Ireland* (6th edition, 1985), Dublin: Irish Academic Press.

Martine, Roddy, *Scottish Clan & Family Names* (1992), Edinburgh: Mainstream.

McKinley, Richard, *A History of British Surnames* (1990), London: Longman.

Reaney, P. H. and R. M. Wilson, *A Dictionary of English Surnames* (1995), Oxford: Oxford University Press.

Rowlands, John and Sheila, *The Surnames of Wales* (1996), Bury: Federation of Family History Societies.

Whyte, Donald, *Scottish Surnames* (2000), Edinburgh: Birlinn.

DNA

Cavalli-Sforza, Luigi Luca, *Genes, Peoples and Languages* (2001), London: Penguin.

Oppenheimer, Stephen, *Out of Eden* (revised edition, 2004), London: Robinson.

—, *The Origins of the British* (2006), London: Constable.

Pomery, Chris, *DNA and Family History* (2004), Richmond: The National Archives.

Savin, Alan, *DNA for Family Historians* (2000), Maidenhead: Alan Savin.

Sykes, Bryan, *The Seven Daughters of Eve* (2002), London: Corgi.
—, *Adam's Curse* (2003), London: Bantam.
—, *Blood of the Isles* (2006), London: Bantam.
Watson, James, *DNA: The Secret of Life* (2003), New York: Knopf.

Index

Note: Page numbers in *italic* refer to illustrations